INTRODUCTION to TRANSPORTATION SYSTEMS

Lonnie E. Haefner
Washington University

HOLT, RINEHART AND WINSTON
New York   Chicago   San Francisco   Philadelphia
Montreal   Toronto   London   Sydney   Tokyo
Mexico City   Rio de Janeiro   Madrid

Copyright © 1986 by CBS College Publishing
All rights reserved.
Address correspondence to:
383 Madison Avenue, New York, NY 10017

Library of Congress Cataloging-in-Publication Data

Haefner, Lonnie E.
  Introduction to transportation systems.

  Bibliography: p. **473**
  Includes index.
  1. Transportation.   I. Title.
HE151.H23   1986   380.5   86-3078
ISBN 0-03-063937-9

Printed in the United States of America
Published simultaneously in Canada
6 7 8 9   038   9 8 7 6 5 4 3 2 1

CBS College Publishing
Holt, Rinehart & Winston
The Dryden Press
Saunders College Publishing

Contents

iii

Preface

This book is intended as a basic undergraduate text in transportation engineering in the civil engineering curriculi. Its breadth of coverage of professional topics makes it an important reference for the practicing engineer and transportation professional. It is based on over fifteen years of teaching transportation fundamentals at two major universities, and several years of professional practice as a transportation research engineer and consultant. It is grounded in my utmost conviction that the modern transportation professional must be eclectic, and integrate knowledge of sound transportation engineering fundamentals with understanding of regulatory processes and their implications, and a sense of how things are executed in the legislative, political, and policy processes that ultimately shape the transportation engineer's resources to deal with today's challenges.

It is within the above philosophical framework that the content and progression of material in the book is set. After a minimal introduction and history of transportation, the student is led to examine *all* aspects (planning, design, and regulation and operation) of *each* mode separately, beginning with the easiest one to understand, that is, the highway system, and progressing to the most difficult ones to digest, air and water transportation. After providing a thorough background in all the separate modes, the transportation planning mechanisms and a discussion of federal and state agency administration structures are introduced. A chapter on recent emerging energy problems follows, and the text closes with a chapter on financing mechanisms across all modes, related congressional and White House activities, and a synthesis of national transportation policy issues.

The advantage of this approach is that the student becomes well versed in the engineering and regulation fundamentals of each mode first, and subsequently studies their merger in the multimodel format, and finally sees the societal-administrative-policy aspects of transportation engineering operations, components, and decisions in the last chapters. Thus, this text covers the entire gamut from fundamentals to policy.

In any major intellectual effort of the magnitude of producing a book, the author stands in great indebtedness to a large number of obvious and subtle contributors. It is no different with this effort, and sincere acknowledgement is due to several individuals and professional groups who submitted photographic and tabular material; to Olin Library of Washington University; to the Transportation Center Library of Northwestern University, and Mary Roy, who ably directs their vast collection of resources without which this effort would have been next to impossible; to my secretarial and research staff at the University and Doug Laird and Greg Moore, who assisted in the instructor's manual; to the resources of the Civil Engineering Department at Washington University and Phil Gould, the Chairman, who intimately understands the commitment necessary to produce a quality book; to John J. Beck of Holt, Rinehart and Winston, Tom Farrell and Rachel Hockett of Cobb-Dunlop Publishers Services, all of whom ably guided the voyage of production; and to several professional reviewers, R. L. Carstens, Iowa State University, Kenneth N. Derucher, Stevens Institute of Technology, G. Scott Rutherford, Director of the Transportation Center, and Ronald L. Terrel, both of the University of Washington, James I. Taylor, Associate Dean of Engineering, University of Notre Dame, Richard P. Guenthner, Marquette University, and Everett C. Carter, University of Maryland, whose incisive comments made it a better text. I wish to express my gratitude to Professors Berry, Morlok, Stopher, Rath, Hurter, Garrison, Taafe, and Baerwald, whose input to my graduate education had a lasting impact on my professional life; to my wife and children who tolerated the time, effort, and disruption required to get this text done, particularly to my wife Jean, who typed, cut and pasted, and organized the final, completed work; and finally to my parents, who made sure that I received a quality education.

L. E. H.
Kirkwood, Missouri

1 Introduction: The Basis of Transportation Engineering

Since early times the concept of a transportation system, even in its primitive form, has been necessary to bind together the daily activities of the human population. As society grew more complex, so did transportation technology, engineering design, construction, and policy. Virtually no individual is unaffected by the need for transportation.

The objective of this book is, after brief introductory and historical chapters, to present an instructional state-of-the-art text on transportation engineering, suitable for undergraduate course instruction at the baccalaureate civil engineering level.

The text proceeds by having the student examine *all* aspects (planning, design, cost, regulation, and operation) of *each* mode separately, beginning with the most familiar, the highway system, and progressing to the most difficult to digest, air and water transportation. Subsequently, after providing a thorough background in all of the modes, the mechanisms of transportation planning and a discussion of federal and state agency administration structures are introduced. This is followed by a chapter on emerging energy problems and a closing chapter on national transportation financing and policy, treating Congressional and White House administrative activities, and a synthesis of national transportation policy issues.

The advantage of this procedure is that, after becoming well versed in the engineering and regulatory fundamentals of each mode, the student is led to their merger in the multimodal format, and ultimately presented with the societal administrative-policy aspects of transportation engineering operations, components, and decisions. The result is a text that covers the entire transportation spectrum, from engineering fundamentals to policy.

Spatial Significance of U.S. Transportation Resources

The U.S. transportation system is a massive investment in roads, railways and rail yards, waterways, pipelines, docks, piers, locks, and air fields. The extent of government-provided facilities is shown in Figures 1–1 through 1–4, which

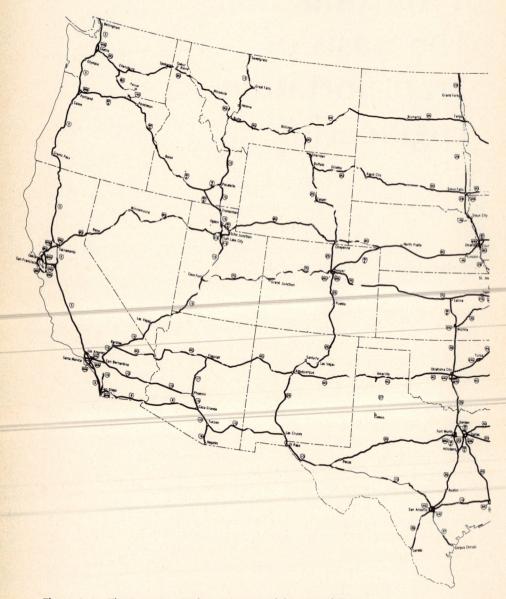

Figure 1–1   The Interstate Highway System of the United States
(*Source:* Courtesy Federal Highway Administration, U.S. Department of Transportation, Washington, D.C.)

present maps of the interstate highway system, class I and II rail operations, major port resources, and major airport hubs. These facilities exist to implement the nation's capability to operate—socially, economically, culturally, and for purposes of national defense.

National economic impacts exist as shown in Figure 1–5, which illustrates 1979

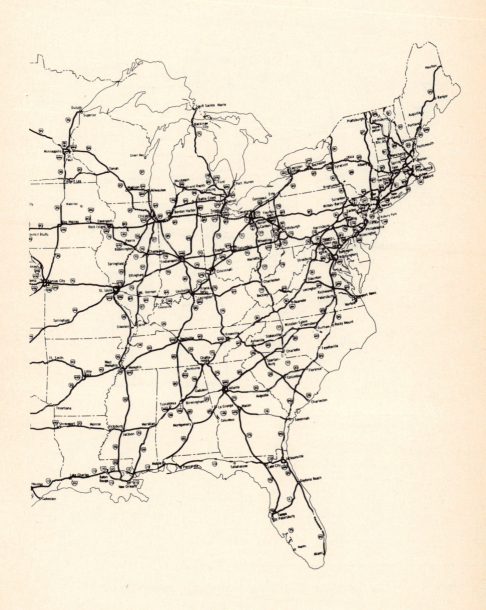

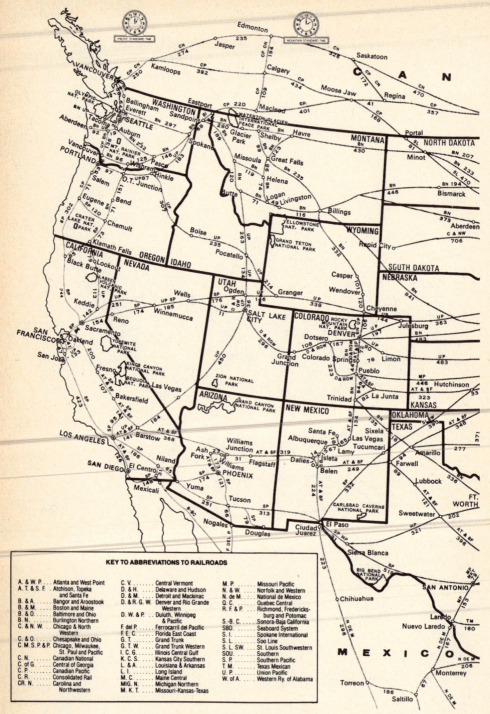

Figure 1–2 Class I and Class II Rail Operations in the United States

(*Source:* Courtesy Association of American Railroads, Washington, D.C.)

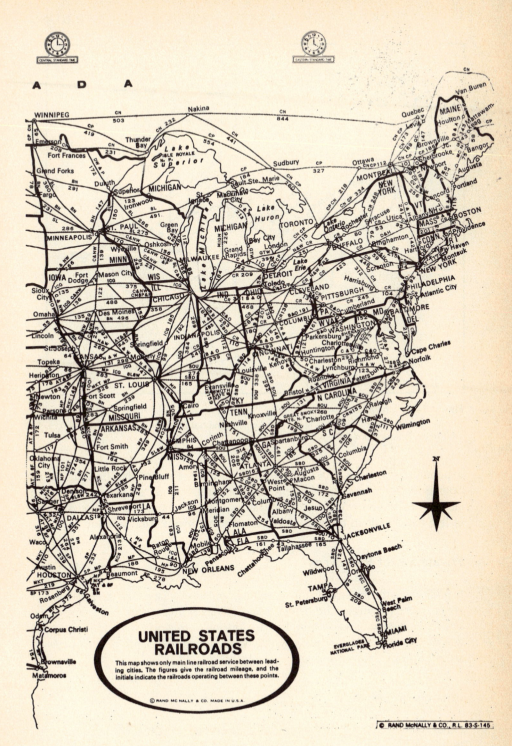

UNITED STATES RAILROADS

This map shows only main line railroad service between leading cities. The figures give the railroad mileage, and the initials indicate the railroads operating between these points.

© RAND MC NALLY & CO. MADE IN U.S.A.

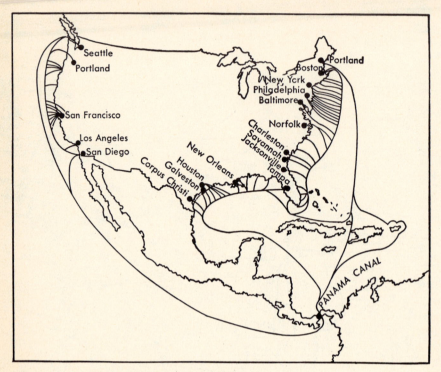

Figure 1–3   United States Deep-Water Ports
(*Source:* National Resources Planning Board, Transportation and National Policy, Washington, D.C., U.S. Government Printing Office, 1942.)

expenditures and revenues in billions of dollars that involve production or operation of transportation system components. A significant percentage of the labor force has some relationship to transportation in its daily work. Roughly one in five individuals in the work force is associated with transportation.

Private Sector Resources

In addition to the impacts on the working population at large and the provision of government resources, the private sector, as its primary user, has tremendous assets involved with the system. Further, during both world wars, transportation was *the* key factor in assembling and moving equipment and troops to coastal areas for deployment overseas.

Impacts on Life-style

Other than the raw statistics, a subjective appreciation of the impact of transportation on society, life-style, and well-being cannot be overestimated. Basically, good

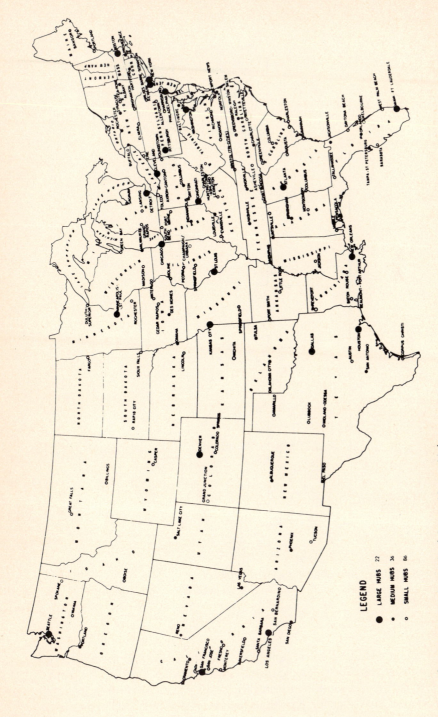

Figure 1–4 Major United States Airport Hubs

(*Source:* Office of Management Services, Federal Aviation Authority, Washington, D.C.)

7

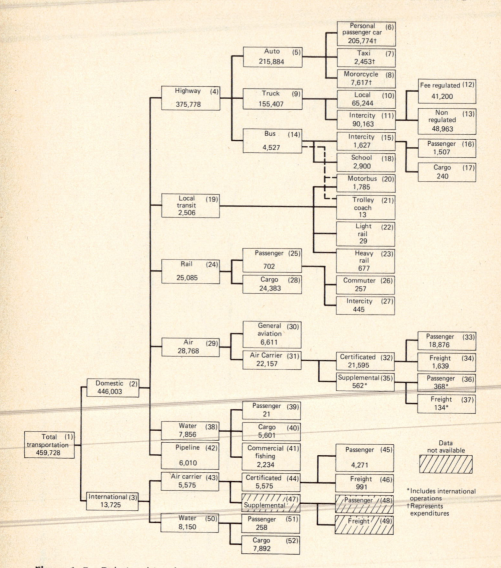

Figure 1–5 Relationship of GNP to Transportation
(*Source: National Transportation Statistics,* Annual Report, Washington, D.C., U.S. Government Printing Office, September 1981.)

transportation, whether local, regional, or national, makes locations more accessible. As a result, travel between the various areas increases, thus attracting investment in local resources and, in turn, inspiring exploration of new ones. In this way transportation is a lever for growth, opening up new industrial. commercial,

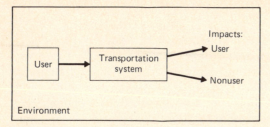

Figure 1–6   Transportation–Environment
Conceptual Relationships

residential, cultural, and social opportunities. Developed countries or regions typically have excellent transportation systems, whereas lesser developed countries have poor systems. As improved transportation lowers the costs of moving people and goods, the country tends to operate more efficiently, and to maximize its profits, assets, and net worth.

Components of the System

It should be obvious that provision of such a system calls for the utmost in planning, engineering, construction, and managerial resources. A major feature of this book will be to instruct the student in the basics of these, on a mode-by-mode basis, and then to close with a synthesis of all modes, resulting in a global approach to understanding current transportation systems. As a crude beginning to such understanding, and as a rudimentary basis for involving ourselves with the system, consider Figure 1–6.

We can think of the transportation system as existing as a resource supply that users employ. In so doing they create impacts on, or changes in, the milieu, or environment, in which the system is situated. These impacts are of two generic types: *user*—where travel time, safety, comfort, and convenience of the modal user are changed for better or worse; and *nonuser,* where those people, entities, and things not using the system are affected by its use—noise levels, air quality, property values, land-use plan cohesiveness, tax base, levels of employment, level of commercial development, gross national product, and economic value added. Thus both user and nonuser alterations may indicate the need for changes in the system, through design, regulation, planning, or enforcement.

The contents of this book may be viewed as the study of all the attributes in Figure 1–6 worthy of knowledge to allow appropriate components to be manipulated to achieve effective and efficient transportation. After a brief chapter on history, we begin with a major component of transportation, the highway and motor carriage system.

References

Haefner, L. E., E. J. Carter, and J. W. Hall. *An Informational Report on Techniques for Evaluating Factors Relevant to Decision Making on Highway Locations.* Washington, D.C.: U.S. Department of Transportation, Federal Highway Administration, December 1972.

Haefner, L. E., E. J. Carter, and J. W. Hall. *Literature References on Techniques for the Evaluation of Factors Relevant to Decision Making on Highway Locations.* Washington, D.C.: U.S. Department of Transportation, Federal Highway Administration, January 1972.

Hille, Stanley J., and Richard F. Poist, Jr., Editors. *Transportation: Principles and Perspectives.* Danville, Ill.: Interstate Printers and Publishers, 1974.

Hudson, Charles L., Evelyn S. Putnam, and Roy Hildestad. *Vehicle Characterization for the TAPCUT Project: Materials, Energy, and Residuals of Manufacture for Vehicles, Fuels, and Rights-of-Way.* Argonne, Ill.: Argonne National Laboratory, 1981.

Mitchell, Edward J., Editor. *Oil Pipelines and Public Policy.* Washington, D.C.: American Enterprise Institute for Public Policy Research, 1979.

National Transportation Statistics, Annual Report. Washington, D.C.: U.S. Government Printing Office, 1981.

Sources of Information in Transportation, 2d ed. Evanston, Ill.: Northwestern University Press, 1981.

2 History of Transportation

Prior to beginning substantive study of the fundamentals of transportation engineering, it is appropriate to assess the vital role transportation has played in the history of civilized development, particularly that of the United States. Economic, cultural, and political developments have followed paths parallel to that of major transportation technology and route breakthroughs. Each major historical transportation change or event has had repercussions on urbanization, cultural patterns, mass movement and behavior, and the status of preexisting modes.

Pre-Nineteenth-Century Transportation

Some important achievements associated with the early history of civilization have had significant relevance to the development of transportation. Two are particularly notable for their influence: early water transportation and the era of Roman roads.

Early Water Transport—Circa 3000 B.C.

Among the ancient nations, the Egyptians and Phoenicians can be credited with first realizing the relationship of massive transport capabilities to cultural growth and economic dominance. They are credited with the first provision of transportation technology for significant economic and political use. About 3000 B.C. their development of ships with combined sail and oar power, side-paddle rudder systems, and ramming bow allowed them to ply trade routes and mount a strong defense against their enemies. This led to the early development of sea trade routes in the Mediterranean, which were augmented by the Greeks about 700 B.C. The Norse began to use larger rowing galleys in 1200–700 B.C., bringing trading activities to the northern parts of the Atlantic.

The Spanish and Portuguese modernized the functional concepts of seaborne transportation in the fifteenth century, utilizing three- and four-masted sailing ships, known as galleons and caravelles; these were square-rigged sailing vessels, capable of housing crew, ammunition, and cargo. Vessels such as these were used by Columbus on his voyages to the New World. As colonization developed worldwide in the sixteenth and seventeenth centuries, the French and English built four-masted transoceanic sailing ships to carry grain, minerals, and manufactured products between the nations of Europe, Asia, South America, and North America and their colonies. The significance of ocean transportation in transportation history is that it allowed the opening up of various parts of the world, formerly unknown to the early civilized nations of Europe. With this came new areas to be exploited for their natural resources, often through colonization and colonial dominance. In turn a significant volume of trade began to emerge, resulting in the establishment of recognized sea routes and opportunities for cultural interchange among world populations. Thus evolved the concept of regional specialization and the resultant greater diversity of products available at local markets, gathered through the trading process.

Roman Roads —312 B.C.

Similar to the international "civilization" of various areas of the world resulting from ocean transportation, the need for internal civilization became evident. The most prominent historical example of this was the development of the Roman road system. During 312 B.C. the Roman Empire planned and began execution of an expansive system of highways that radiated from Rome to distant parts of the empire, with the primary goal of providing economic and military access to its settlements. A major segment of the system was the Via Appia (Appian Way) from Rome to Brendice, a distance of 366 miles, used for the movement of troops to Greece. A second link, from Rome to Naples, was used for the ultimate movement of troops to Africa. These early roads met surprisingly high design and paving standards, even by modern criteria. A major subgrade was constructed and compacted by a lime mortar, upon which a wearing surface of thin stone was placed, resulting in a pavement 3 to 4 feet thick. Drainage principles were applied to the cross section, which was 14–16 feet wide, with graveled shoulder, resulting in a right-of-way dimension of approximately 40 feet. Heavy cuts, massive arch bridges, and steep (20 percent) grades were employed.

The Romans are credited with being the only truly competent road engineers in early history, synthesizing economic, political, geographical, and construction factors in a planning, design, and construction procedural approach. For their subgrades and surfaces, they utilized a cement mix, the origin of which was lost with the fall of the Roman Empire—a fall attributed in great part to the fact that the empire's enemies were able to gain control of the Roman roadway system. Virtually all other roads in early civilized Europe were poorly designed and constructed of dirt.

Following the Roman period, little technological improvement was noted until the late 1870s in Europe, when McAdam of Scotland developed a low-labor-intensive technique to offset the loss of forced road labor gangs. The depth of composite was reduced to 10 inches. It consisted of small stones mixed with large ones, which interlocked because of the stones' angularity, and utilized waterproof coverings and bituminous types of materials. This was the forerunner of asphalt pavements as we know them today. Improved drainage, level cross sections, and lesser grades and curves allowed these roads to be built cheaply, to be usable in all weather, and to be relatively maintenance-free. The roads resulted in the stimulation of intra-European trade, travel, and economic growth, and to the clustering of people into villages and the formation of large cities. The technology was ultimately transferred to North and South American road development.

History of U.S. Transportation

Following these early developments in transportation, the United States made historical strides in development across all transportation modes from the nation's beginnings, through colonialization, independence, and westward expansion.

Transportation in the Nineteenth Century

The most meaningful early thrust in the United States was the push inland and westward, using the natural river system of the continent. During 1817–1840, known as the "early river" period, steamboats had been invented and plied the major eastern rivers, as well as the Mississippi and Ohio rivers, at 6 miles per hour (mph) upstream and 12 mph downstream. Trade developed between trappers, Indians, and early frontier settlers and speculators and the major cities, resulting in small settlements along river banks. The cities of St. Louis and New Orleans became major centers of culture, merchandising, trade, and river-related finance. This continued until 1860, when the steamboats began to feel major effects of overland competition with the development of the railroad.

The Canal System

A major parallel system in the eastern United States appeared with the development of a canal system, localizing internal trade on the eastern seaboard. The Erie

Canal, connecting Albany to Buffalo, New York, on the banks of Lake Erie, was the first important canal. These canals were roughly 15 to 30 feet wide, allowing a towboat to be pulled by mules or horses on a developed path on the shoreline, called a towpath. They were used for hauling produce and pelts to settlements and finished products to the rural hinterlands. Other major canals developed in the East until about 1840, including the Chesapeake and Ohio Canal along the Potomac River, the Delaware and Hudson Canal, and others, as shown in Figure 2–1. Many of the early canals shown here were used to connect the soft coal fields of Pennsylvania with deep-water ports. The Erie Canal and associated canal network offered an east–west diversion of traffic formerly going up the Mississippi and radiating eastward and westward from its banks. Thus the canal system served to strengthen the eastern bloc of early U.S. cities, particularly New York, with

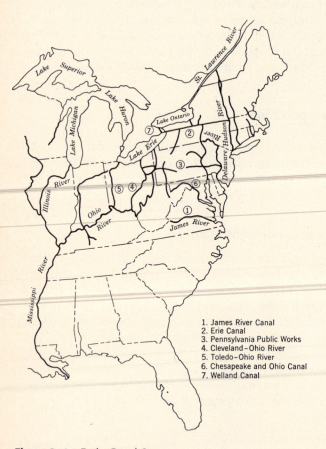

1. James River Canal
2. Erie Canal
3. Pennsylvania Public Works
4. Cleveland–Ohio River
5. Toledo–Ohio River
6. Chesapeake and Ohio Canal
7. Welland Canal

Figure 2–1 Early Canal Systems

(*Source:* William W. Hay, *An Introduction to Transportation Engineering*, 2d. ed., New York, John Wiley, 1961, 1977. Used by permission.)

Philadelphia and Baltimore becoming lesser dominant East Coast trade and financial centers. The Erie Canal was a colossal financial success, paying off its entire capital cost in the first seven years of operation.

As a result of this early and obvious success, other states and private companies began a boom of canal building, resulting in many unsound financial facilities and a surfeit of canal capacity; most of the systems fell into financial ruin by 1837, signaling an end to the canal era.

Early Turnpikes

An appropriate adjunct to water-borne transportation was the provision of facilities where the natural waterways and the canals did not go. Early surface transportation of inland and cross-country freight was accomplished by pack-horse franchise businesses, which cut trails out of the wilderness for this purpose. These trails eventually were widened and wagon usage ultimately produced recognizable, though primitive, roadways.

As demand increased, by 1800 private companies had banded together to build good roads, termed "turnpikes," or toll roads, where one paid a toll to travel on an improved right-of-way. One of the most important of these was the Philadelphia and Lancaster Turnpike. In 1818 the federal government built the Cumberland Road from Cumberland, Maryland, to Vandalia, Illinois, now the route of Interstate 70. As in the canal era, there was massive overbuilding, often by marginal operators, and this and the advent of the railroads in the mid-1800s served to diminish the importance of turnpike operations and to curb new development.

Modern Transportation in the United States

The Rail Era

The invention of the steam locomotive in Liverpool, England, in 1829 and its subsequent use in the United States ultimately led to the building of trackage inland in America. Further construction resulted in the development of a modern rail network, which was completed in the 1950s. However, the major period of expansion was that from 1830 to 1890. This was the Golden Era of rail development in the United States, which saw the linking of the nation's coasts and the opening up of settlements and mining and agricultural interests across all the habitable parts of the country. Examples of this expansion are shown in Figures 2–2 through 2–4.

Very early in the system development, to spur activity, the railroads were given the power of eminent domain, and this, coupled with infusion of U.S. and European capital, permitted them to grow quite rapidly. In addition, local governments often granted lands or gave generous capital loans, in their desire to have rail access to their communities and the resulting economic opportunities.

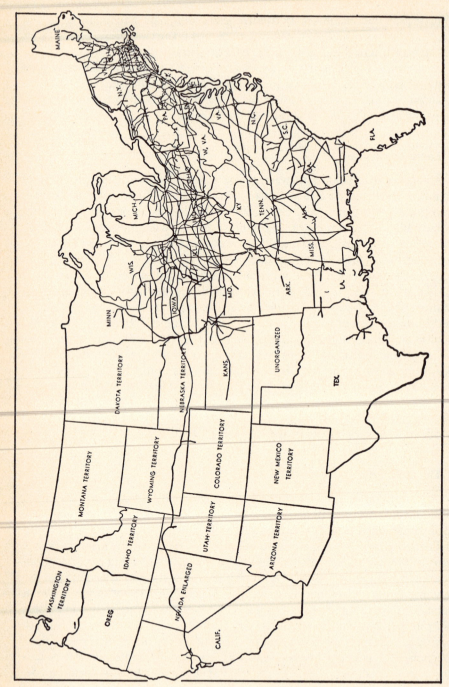

Figure 2-2 Railroads in the United States in 1870

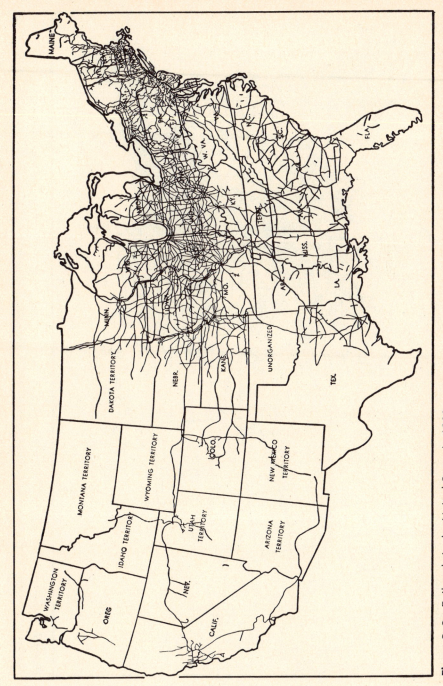

Figure 2–3 Railroads in the United States in 1880

(*Source*: Carlton J. Corliss, *Development of Railroad Transportation in the U.S.*, Washington, D.C., Association of American Railroads, 1945.)

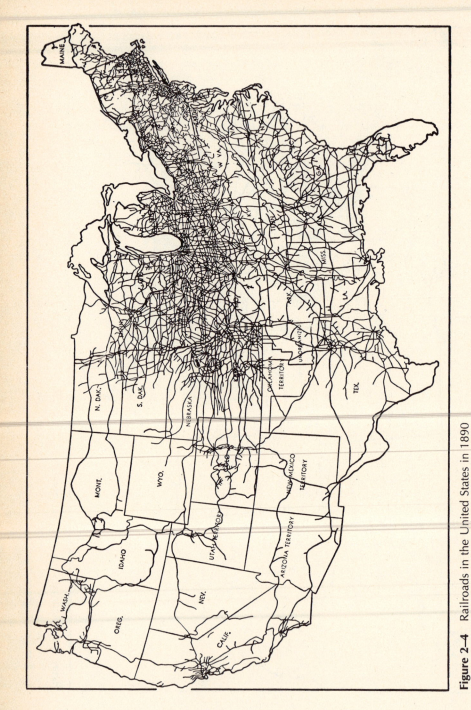

Figure 2–4 Railroads in the United States in 1890

(*Source*: Carlton J. Corliss, *Development of Railroad Transportation in the U.S.*, Washington, D.C., Association of American Railroads, 1945.)

Monopoly and special banking privileges were granted to railroads by states, as was tax exemption. Surveying assistance was offered by the federal government, but the most significant aid was in the form of the federal "Land Grant" package. This granted a free right-of-way 20 feet wide for active railroad construction, thus increasing the economic value of lands around such rail connections and towns in their path. In exchange for this, the railroads carried government troops, mail, and federal cargo at reduced rates. The result was that the railroads by the late 1800s had acquired awesome power through the control of economic, industrial, and financial decisions in these regions.

In addition to the planning and historical consequences, many technological breakthroughs have been witnessed since 1860. Most significant were the advent of diesel-electric locomotives, supplanting steam in 1934; standardized track with gages; intermodal, piggyback, and containerized service in the 1950s; and the concept of unit trains in 1980.

The Highway Era

The emergence of the U.S. highway system from that of reasonably low-level turnpike and local road systems did not really occur until 1921. The federal government, seeing the wisdom of supplementing a national rail system with a national road system, passed the *Federal Highway Act of 1921,* which allowed 7 percent of the total dirt road mileage of the country to be improved with federal funds, matched by state funds and maintained by the state.

Continuing this planning process further, the 1944 Federal Aid Highway Act added another tier to the system, termed the secondary system, largely composed of farm-to-market roads. This was the era of desire to improve the local distribution and market system, often referred to as "getting the farmer out of the mud." A major milestone in the 1944 act was the selection of a system to be known as the "National System of Interstate and Defense Highways," covering 40,000 miles and connecting the principal metropolitan areas, thus forming the backbone of the U.S. road system. The system was extended in 1956 to 41,000 miles and provided for 90 percent federal and 10 percent state financing. This ushered in the modern era of intercity highway travel and major usage of interstate commercial trucking as a viable freight system and a major competitor to the railroads. Other highway acts have been passed subsequent to 1956, and are the appropriate subjects of the chapter on national policy. Figure 2–5 illustrates the national interstate system per 1956.

Waterway Era

In a like manner, certain cultural, growth, and technological changes had to occur to restimulate water transportation, to bring it from its canal and frontier steamboat era to modern times. Prior to 1914 intercoastal shipping, whether by sail or steam, was around Cape Horn, a treacherous passage with highly un-

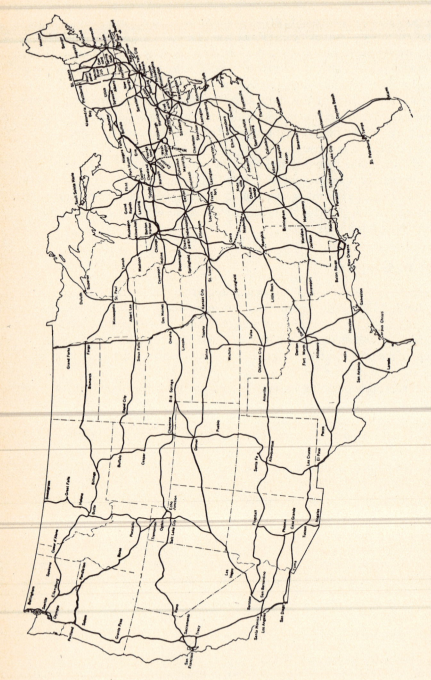

Figure 2–5 The Interstate Highway System of 1956
(Courtesy of the Bureau of Public Roads, Washington, D.C.)

predictable wind and weather patterns. With the completion of the Panama Canal in 1914, safe, reasonably direct passage of ocean freighters was made possible, thus increasing ocean-borne traffic significantly. However, World War II and the specter of attack on the high seas eventually stopped all U.S. ocean trade.

As the result of weak attempts to restore private activity after the war, the government formed the War Shipping Board in 1945. Its function was to operate coastwide and oceanic shipping as a government entity until the private sector had restabilized. In 1945 this board was reorganized as the United States Maritime Commission. By 1945 private operations had been revitalized and this function of the Commission ceased. Parallel to this, the inland waterway system was also undergoing structural and regulatory changes. In 1901 the First National Rivers and Harbors Congress met in Baltimore, largely to attempt to pick up the pieces of the industry in decline after the prerail era up through 1860. The commission reported a blue-ribbon set of findings that urged the Congress to declare the Inland Waterway System a national resource, and to make improvements in the national system on a scale commensurate with the needs of the people. As a result, President Theodore Roosevelt formed the Inland Waterway Commission, a federal entity, to prepare a national waterways plan. This commission was succeeded by the National Waterways Commission of 1909, which made specific recommendations to the Congress and suggested means for better rail–water cooperation.

A major federal effort was made to demonstrate commitment to the system through the formation of the governmentally owned Federal Barge Line in 1920. Its formation was designed to show efficiency of barge operations on the major tributaries. Such operations were ultimately deemed successful, and in 1953 the line was sold to a public corporation. Many private sector interests operate in a modern format of barge transportation, making use of the modern inland river system, as illustrated in Figure 2–6.

The Air Transportation Era

Perhaps the most exotic part of the history of transportation technology is contained in the development of the air mode. It began in 1903, when the Wright brothers carried out the first successful flight, at Kitty Hawk, North Carolina. Development continued and received a boost by World War I, when aircraft became a significant aspect of attack-force technology. Following the war, civilian aircraft use was further stimulated by mail contracts and routes in 1918, with the first transcontinental commercial flights in 1919. World War II saw the advent of improved design, navigation, and power and vastly increased production of aircraft, both defense and civilian, to carry personnel and cargo during the conflict.

The post–World War II period witnessed major technological and planning advances in the air mode. Development of the turbojet engine in 1959 led to dramatic performance changes in aircraft and their related design, size, and passenger-carrying capabilities. During the 1960s the uniformity and designation

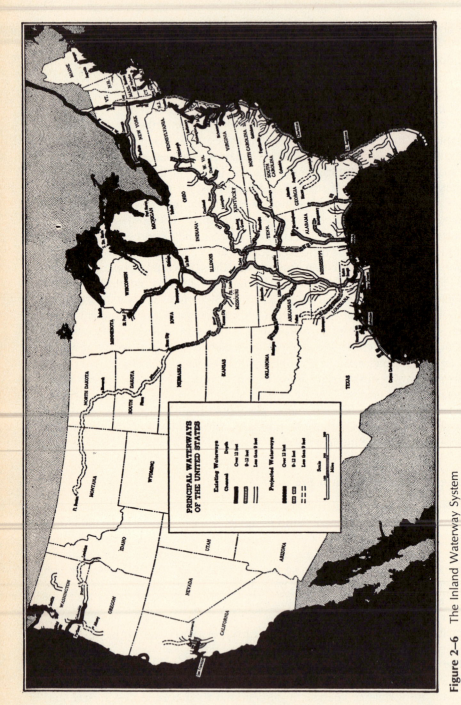

Figure 2–6 The Inland Waterway System

(From President's Water Resources Policy Committee, A Water Policy for the American People (Washington, D.C.: U.S. Government Printing Office, 1950), Vol. I, pp. 206–7.)

of a national and international set of freight and commuter routes and major and secondary hub airports were established. These were concurrently aided by the development of radar, air controller systems, and a set of "skyways" navigationally and electronically connected across the United States. The first major comprehensive National Airport Plan addressing future United States' needs was undertaken in 1959. Shortly thereafter wide-bodied oversized "jumbo jets" capable of very large capacities (300-person payload) and international travel were designed. These were in operation by 1972, internationalizing flight technology and economies of scale in world travel.

Thus this chapter has seen the evolution of a truly remarkable spectrum of technological, operational, legislative, and regulatory growth in transportation historical events from 3000 B.C. through the 1970s. This evolution has yielded the modern design, planning, and policy processes to be covered in forthcoming chapters.

References

Hille, Stanley J., and Richard F. Poist, Jr., Editors. *Transportation: Principles and Perspectives*. Danville, Ill.: Interstate Printers and Publishers, 1974.

Locklin, D. Philip. *Economics of Transportation,* 5th ed. Homewood, Ill.: Richard D. Irwin, 1960.

Locklin, D. Philip. Economics of Transportation, 7th ed. Homewood, Ill.: Richard D. Irwin, 1972.

Mitchell, Edward J., Editor. *Oil Pipelines and Public Policy*. Washington, D.C.: American Enterprise Institute for Public Policy Research, 1979.

Sources of Information in Transportation, 2d ed. Evanston, Ill.: Northwestern University Press, 1981.

Westmayer, Russell E. *Economics of Transportation*. Englewood Cliffs, N.J.: Prentice-Hall, 1952.

3 Basic Types of Highway Studies

Prior to beginning formal study of transportation engineering, it is appropriate to become acquainted with the various fundamental types of studies used in the discipline. Although many of the study mechanics described in this chapter will be elaborated on throughout the text, they are initially presented to give the student an overview of the basic nature of information to be collected on any system that will require transportation engineering analysis.

Inventories

Perhaps the most basic type of study made is an inventory of the system in its present form, essentially a description and measurement of the system "as is." Although this can be done for any of the modes, the fundamental system that illustrates needed data for further engineering work is the highway system. A typical highway inventory will involve riding each mile of the system and noting the following information, by mile marker, on the established roadway mileage system.

1. The type and condition of structures.
2. Abutting land uses.
3. Percent grade.
4. Degree of curvature.

   5. Sight distance.
   6. Railroad crossing conditions and protective devices.
   7. Exact distance of segment under study.
   8. Right-of-way.
   9. Number of lanes.
   10. Width of lanes.
   11. Type of shoulder.
   12. Width of shoulder.
   13. Pavement type on moving lanes.
   14. Shoulder pavement treatment.
   15. Special safety features (guardrail, barrier, etc.).
   16. Traffic signal types.
   17. Marking and signing.
   18. Traffic volumes.
   19. Condition of pavement.

Essentially these data are necessary to provide basic physical, design, and construction engineering information about the system. Where possible they are recorded in conjunction with a photo-logging operation, which yields a visual record of the items collected. Normally the items collected are taken from the field sheets, coded, and adapted for computer storage on disk or tape to allow printout information or screen call-up for checking or modification of each item as appropriate. The items typically are rechecked every five years, depending on funding sources, or whenever significant traffic, construction, design, or environmental changes occur.

Traffic Volume Surveys

The inventory may be conceived as a review of the presence and condition of the supply of the system. The traffic volume surveys may be viewed as a review of demand for and use of the system.

   Again, using the highway system as a typical example, the following types of volume information are collected.

   Average daily traffic (ADT). The average twenty-four-hour volume to be expected on a facility.

   Peak-hour volumes. The highest four consecutive fifteen-minute volumes counted during a twenty-four-hour period. Typically thought of as the "rush hour," these volumes may in fact occur any time during the twenty-four-hour period at the facility. They typically equal 10 percent of the average daily traffic.

   The foregoing volumes are counted by using the following techniques.

1. *Continuous key counting stations*—A twenty-four-hour count is developed by a permanently maintained station, usually a recorder set permanently in the pavement, with count impulses being relayed to a centralized recording computer by use of leased telephone or power lines. This will typically be used on major freeways or truck routes through a state to yield accurate volume histories on selected highway facilities considered vital to the state and nation.

2. *Coverage counts*—These may be manual or automatic. The automatic process makes use of a counter with pneumatic hoses stretched across the pavement to show impulse counts by number of axles. The count is usually scheduled for two to fourteen days at a site. Appropriate historical factors are then employed to relate the sample counting period volume to ADT, to arrive at a realistically reasonable estimate of ADT and related peak-hour volumes.

In a like manner, *manual counts* are used for intersections and their turning movements. They employ a manual count board and diagram as shown in Figure 3–1. Counts are usually taken by a two- or three-person observation team at the intersection for periods of two, four, six, or twelve hours and are appropriately factored to yield ADT and peak-hour volumes.

The foregoing are often presented as shown in Figure 3–2, with scaled bandwidths showing relative ADT or peak-hour volumes. Volumes can also be illustrated with a fraction, such as 2,300/23,000, where the counts for roadway links are vehicles per day (ADT) in the denominator and vehicles per hour (VPH-peak hour) in the numerator. At intersections these units become vehicles per day (ADT) and vehicles per hour of green time (VPHG) for the peak-hour movement respectively. There typically exists a historically stable increase per year in volumes on a county- or statewide basis in the range of 2–10 percent. This can be used, in a simplistic sense, to extrapolate future volumes on the network by use of:

$$V_{t+n} = (V_t)(K)(n)$$

where

$$t = \text{current year}$$
$$V_{t+n} = \text{future volume at } n \text{ years from current year}$$
$$K = \text{annual traffic growth rate, percent}$$

Origin–Destination Surveys

A more generalized and comprehensive study analysis is that of an origin–destination survey. Using field investigation and graphic techniques, the study attempts to answer several questions: Where are people traveling? Where did they

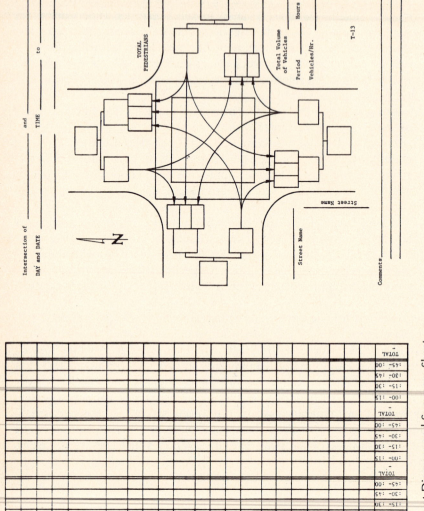

Figure 3–1 Manual Count Diagram and Summary Sheet

(*Source:* Donald E. Cleveland, Editor, *Manual of Traffic Engineering Studies*, 3d ed., Washington, D.C., Institute of Transportation Engineers, 1964.)

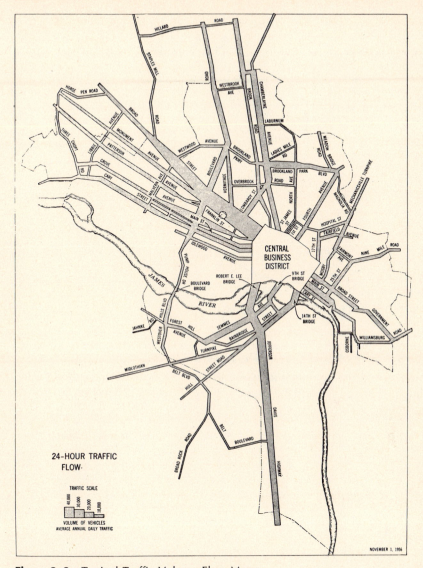

Figure 3–2 Typical Traffic Volume Flow Maps
(*Source:* Donald E. Cleveland, Editor, *Manual of Traffic Engineering Studies,* 3d ed., Washington, D.C., Institute of Transportation Engineers, 1964.)

start from? What is their destination? This information allows insight as to relative need and appropriate location of various types of transportation facilities.

Origin–destination studies are of two general types. A *cordon* study, wherein a critical study area is bounded and movement in and out of the area is monitored, is shown in Figure 3–3. Alternatively a *screen-line* study may be used, which is the

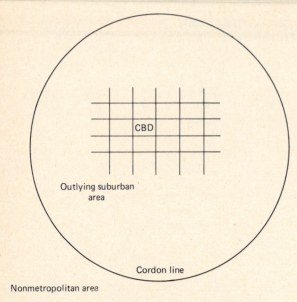

Figure 3–3   Origin-Destination Cordon Study

monitoring of movement across a boundary or barrier, such as a river or a county or state line, as illustrated in Figure 3–4.

In both cases the study area is divided into square zones of homogeneous land use, and these are designated the coded points of origin or destination, as shown in Figure 3–5.

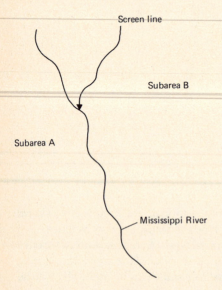

Figure 3–4   Origin-Destination Screen-Line Study

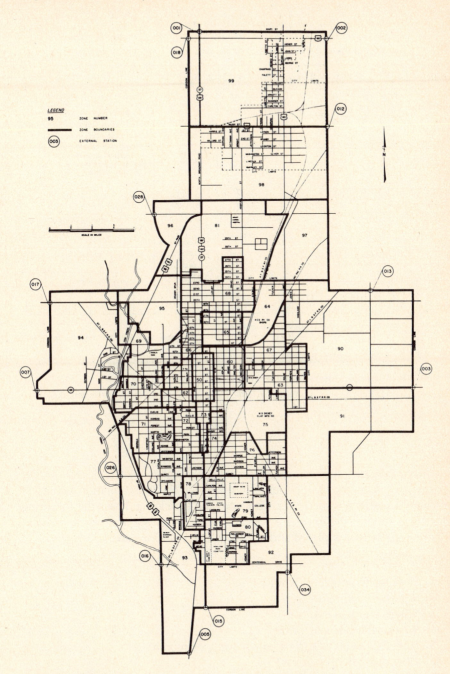

Figure 3–5   Sample Zoning System for a Hypothetical City
(*Source: Traffic Assignment Manual*, U.S. Department of Commerce, Washington, D.C., June 1964.)

```
            DAN RYAN EXPRESSWAY ORIGIN AND DESTINATION STUDY
       This Study is sponsored by the City of Chicago, County of Cook and State of Illinois
       PLEASE ANSWER QUESTIONS AND DROP IN MAIL BOX - - NO STAMP REQUIRED

CARD NO. 3 5 9   STATION 8 4   DATE 5 2 3 3   HOUR [ ][ ]   VEHICLE TYPE [ ]

Where Did This Trip Begin?        What Time Did    What Is The      Please Check The Expressway
                                  You Leave        Purpose Of       Used (if any) On This Trip.
--------------------------------  Starting Point?  This Trip?       If None, Please Check None.
Street Address
                                                                    Lake Shore Drive        [ ]
                                                   To Work    [ ]   Dan Ryan Expressway     [ ]
--------------------------------  ---------------  To Shop    [ ]   Congress Expressway     [ ]
City                                               To Home    [ ]   Northwest Expressway    [ ]
                                                   To Others  [ ]   Calumet Expressway      [ ]
                                                                    Chicago Skyway          [ ]
                                                                    None                    [ ]

Where Will This Trip End?         What Time Did    How Often        What Streets Will You Use For
                                  You Arrive At    Do You Make      The Longest Part Of Your Trip?
--------------------------------  Final Desti-     This Trip
Street Address                    nation?          Each Week?
                                                   5 Times    [ ]   East-West Street
                                                     Or More
--------------------------------  ---------------  3 Times    [ ]
City                                               1 Time     [ ]
                                                   Seldom     [ ]   North-South Street

    Where Will You Leave the Expressway on This Trip?
                                                    Thank You Very Much For Your Cooperation.
                  ----------------------
                       Name of Street
```

Figure 3–6   Sample Origin-Destination Postcard Questionnaire
(*Source:* Donald E. Cleveland, Editor, *Manual of Traffic Engineering Studies,* 3d ed., Washington, D.C., Institute of Transportation Engineers, 1964.)

A 10 percent sample, or other statistically valid number of all traffic crossing the cordon or screen-line boundaries, is interviewed. The most common technique involves a roadside interviewer who stops the traveler and asks the following questions, or gives the traveler a postcard with such questions on it, as shown in Figure 3–6, to be completed and returned. The questions are:

1. How many people in family?
2. Where did you start trip?
3. Where will you end trip?
4. What is the purpose of trip?
5. How frequently is trip taken per week or month?
6. How many people in car?
7. What type of vehicle is it?

A different, more expensive approach may be to pick a 2 percent random sample of all households in the region, interview them in their homes, and ask detailed questions concerning the relationship of their socioeconomic life-style to their daily travel patterns. This is much more expensive, but allows a comprehensive profile of travel behavior for the region to be developed.

An alternative field technique is a license plate survey. This is often utilized in small cordon areas where details of the use of the street pattern are desired. At each entering and exiting street of the cordon boundary, monitors using two-way radios record the license plate numbers of vehicles entering and leaving the street. These are then computer matched, showing points of entry and exit in the small cordon area and thus allowing a detailed review of traffic patterns within the cordon. This technique is *limited* to *practical small enclosures* (eight square blocks, preferably less) and requires *very coordinated* field work.

The descriptive graphics depicting the origin–destinations resulting from any of the techniques are termed desire lines, and are displayed as shown in Figure 3–7. The incidence of origin and destination among the gridded zones is readily

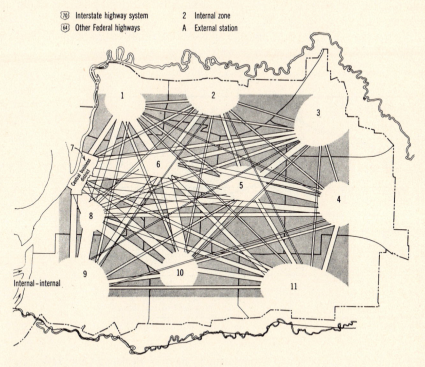

Figure 3–7   Traffic Desire Lines, Ottumwa, Iowa

apparent, showing locations of high incidence of travel and trip terminations, such as the central business district, airports, industrial parks, and shopping centers.

Parking Studies

Parking studies are a related set of pertinent analyses. These employ field techniques similar to both volume and origin–destination data-collection methods. One may categorize parking studies as requiring three components: demand, supply, and turnover.

A *demand* study is an analysis of the need for parking. It may be obtained by a simple counting procedure, which counts the public and private spaces in use hourly, daily, weekly, or monthly—or, like the origin–destination study, it may make use of questionnaires distributed at each lot, which ask questions about parking frequency, duration, and specific lot choice. In either case the hourly, daily, and/or weekly vehicle demand for parking is assessed by these methods.

A *supply* study is the totaling of all spaces available, public and private, with their relevant regulations, thus completely inventorying the parking resources of the study area.

A parking *turnover* study is the attempt to assess the relationship of supply and

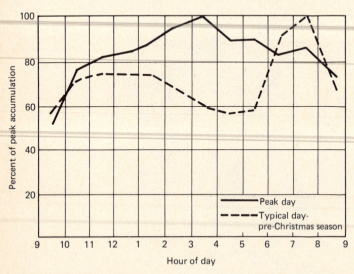

Figure 3–8 Parking Turnover and Accumulation Pattern on Peak and Other Days at a Typical Shopping Center.

(*Source:* A. M. Voorhees and C. E. Crow, "Shopping Center Parking Requirements," Shopping Centers and Parking, Highway Research Board No. 130, Washington, D.C., 1966, p. 22.)

demand by monitoring the frequency of change of usage of parking space by vehicles. Each space in the system, or component random spaces in the system, may be monitored every ten, thirty, or sixty minutes, of two, four, eight, or twenty-four hours to assess whether the space has changed parkers or is vacant. Comparing this information with the supply analysis allows the turnover curve of Figure 3–8 to be generated, and permits one to see whether the present number of spaces in the system is adequate, given the mean duration and turnover rate of parkers.

Accident Studies

Another important basic class of studies is that of auto accident studies. Accident report forms, such as that shown in Figure 3–9, are filed upon occurrence of the incident. The most fundamental accident study is a statistical tabulation of accident type and severity at a site, cross-classified as shown in Table 3–1. This table illustrates accidents at an intersection, where the parameters are measured in accidents per million vehicles (ACC/MV). At a nonintersection location, they are measured in accidents per million vehicle-miles (ACC/MVM).

Means and variances of the categories in Table 3–1, appropriate combinations of categories, and the grand sample are developed for the site, and compared with quality-control statistical indicators to discern whether or not the site should be termed hazardous. This is often accompanied by a "spot map" of the location of accidents, with color codes to show the location of property damage, personal injury, and fatalities.

Another study, expanding on these concepts, is the before-and-after study. A site, typically termed hazardous, has remedial construction, design, or traffic control work done on it. Then the statistics for a three-year period after the improvement are compared with statistics for three years prior to improvement to

Table 3–1   Accident Rate and Classification, ACC/MV

	Property Damage Only	Personal Injury	Fatality
Rear end	3.4	1.6	0.008
Right angle	2.1	1.1	0.006
Sideswipe	0.5	0.1	0.001
Head-on	0.5	0.8	0.028
Backing	0.75	0.6	0.003
Left turn	4.1	2.2	0.016
Right turn	4.2	2.1	0.018
Pedestrian involvement	0.0	3.7	0.16

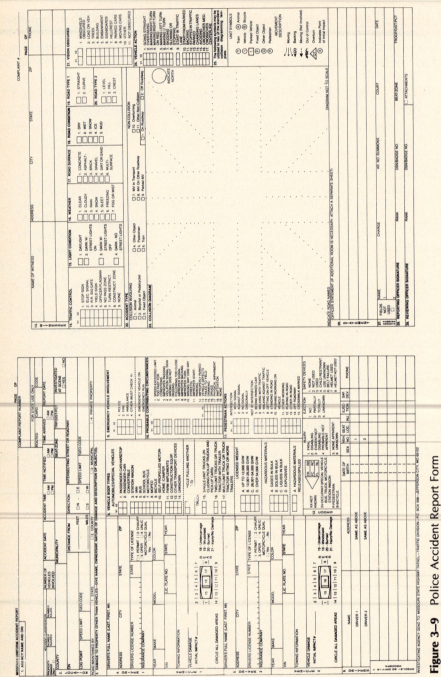

Figure 3–9 Police Accident Report Form

(*Source:* National Safety Council, City of Webster Groves, Mo. Police Department, 1985.)

see if a statistically significant improvement in accident rates has resulted from the modification at the site.

A third type of study, quite involved, is typically used only in fatal and complex accidents or accidents warranting investigation because of court judgment and insurance claims. In these the accident is reconstructed in the laboratory, using models of the vehicles, in an attempt to simulate the travel paths and impacts from the collision. In such accidents fatality investigation teams, usually composed of automotive and/or mechanical engineers, a medical doctor, a traffic engineer, and police officers, are called to the scene of an accident before vehicles are moved. They record pavement and skid conditions, the condition of the occupants, and the impact position of the vehicle, along with pictures of these. The attempt in this study approach is to learn more about the source, cause, and consequences of severe accidents, in an effort to improve current preventative measures.

Conclusion

The studies covered in this chapter are an overview of the most fundamental of data systems required to design, construct, maintain, and operate a highway transportation system. They form a threshold of knowledge prior to study of the actual planning and engineering of each of the other modal subsystems. These basic study designs will be expanded and combined with other refined techniques relevant to each chapter throughout the book.

References

Cleveland, Donald E., Editor. *Manual of Traffic Engineering Studies,* 3d ed. Washington, D.C.: Institute of Traffic Engineers, 1964.

Haefner, L. E., E. J. Carter, and J. W. Hall. *An Informational Report on Techniques for Evaluating Factors Relevant to Decision Making on Highway Locations.* Washington, D.C.: U.S. Department of Transportation, Federal Highway Administration, December 1972.

Haefner, L. E., E. J. Carter, and J. W. Hall. *Literature References on Techniques for the Evaluation of Factors Relevant to Decision Making on Highway Locations.* Washington, D.C.: U.S. Department of Transportation, Federal Highway Administration, January 1972.

Meyburg, Arnim H., and Peter R. Stopher. *Urban Transportation Modeling and Planning.* Lexington, Mass.: Lexington Books, 1975.

Transportation and Traffic Engineering Handbook. Englewood Cliffs, N.J.: Prentice-Hall (Institute of Traffic Engineers), 1976.

4 Highway Transportation

The highway system is the most universally understood and visible part of the U.S. transportation inventory. Virtually all of us drive or have been transported via an automobile at sometime. It is a fundamental mode of public use, offering a staggering investment in construction and maintenance. This chapter illustrates the basic design, operational, and regulatory aspects of highway transportation systems.

Geometric Design

Geometric design is the fundamental engineering effort in designing a highway system. It may be defined as that phase of highway design dealing with the profile and alignment from the pavement up. Therefore, soils and pavement design are excluded from this definition. Geometric design encompasses development of roadway designs that may accommodate general types of vehicle dimensions currently in use in the United States, as illustrated in Table 4–1.

Elements of Geometric Design

There are several "elements" or components of geometric design involved in synthesizing a roadway, as illustrated and discussed in the following sections.

39

Table 4–1 Design Vehicles

Design Vehicle Type	Symbol	Dimension (ft)									
		Overall			Overhang						
		Height	Width	Length	Front	Rear	WB_1	WB_2	S	T	WB_3
Passenger car	P	4.25	7	19	3	5	11				
Single unit truck	SU	13.5	8.5	30	4	6	20				
Single unit bus	BUS	13.5	8.5	40	7	8	25				
Articulated bus	A-BUS	10.5	8.5	60	8.5	9.5	18		4[a]	20[a]	
Combination trucks											
Intermediate semitrailer	WB-40	13.5	8.5	50	4	6	13	27			
Large semitrailer	WB-50	13.5	8.5	55	3	2	20	30			
"Double bottom" semitrailer—full trailer	WB-60	13.5	8.5	65	2	3	9.7	20	4[b]	5.4[b]	20.9
Recreation vehicles											
Motor home	MH		8	30	4	6	20		18		
Car and camper trailer	P/T		8	49	3	10	11	5	18		
Car and boat trailer	P/B		8	42	3	8	11	5	15		

[a] = Combined dimension 24, split is estimated.
[b] = Combined dimension 9, 4, split is estimated.
WB_1, WB_2, WB_3, are effective vehicle wheelbases.
S is the distance from the rear effective axel to the hitch point.
T is the distance from the hitch point to the lead effective axel of the following unit.
(*Source: A Policy on Geometric Design of Highways and Streets*, Washington, D.C., American Association of State Highway and Transportation Officials, 1984. Used by permission.)

40

Sight Distance

Sight distance is defined as the length of highway ahead that is visible to the driver. This length is composed of two components in seconds, as follows:

1. *Brake reaction distance,* which is the distance traversed between the instant the driver perceives a hazard and the instant the brakes are applied. The period of time safely allowed in design for this component, called *brake reaction time,* is 2.5 seconds.
2. *Braking distance* = *d* = distance and time for the vehicle to stop, given that brakes have been applied:

$$d = \frac{V^2}{30f}$$

where

d = braking distance, feet
V = initial speed, mph
f = coefficient of friction between tires and pavement

Typical level stopping sight distances for worst-case wet-pavement conditions are as shown in Table 4–2.

The effect of grades, up to down, will be noticeable on stopping sight distance, as shown in the following adjustable formula for *d.*

$$d = \frac{V^2}{30(f \pm g)}$$

where g = percent of grade divided by 100.

Passing Sight Distance   The other major entity of sight distance is that of passing sight distance, which is the distance required for a vehicle to pass another safely on a two-lane undivided roadway. The distance components are governed by the assumptions shown in Table 4–3, and are as follows:

1. Assumptions
   a. The overtaken vehicle travels at uniform speed.
   b. The passing vehicle has reduced speed and trails the overtaken vehicle as it enters a passing section.
   c. When the passing section is reached, the driver requires a short period of time to perceive the clear passing section and to react to start a maneuver.
   d. Passing is accomplished under what may be termed a delayed start and a hurried return in the face of opposing traffic. The passing vehicle acceler-

Table 4–2 Stopping Sight Distance (Wet Pavements)

Design Speed (mph)	Assumed Speed for Condition (mph)	Brake Reaction		Coefficient of Friction f	Braking Distance on Level[a] (feet)	Stopping Sight Distance	
		Time (seconds)	Distance (feet)			Computed[a] (feet)	Rounded for Design (feet)
20	20–20	2.5	73.3– 73.3	0.40	33.3– 33.3	106.7–106.7	125–125
25	24–25	2.5	88.0– 91.7	0.38	50.5– 54.8	138.5–146.5	150–150
30	28–30	2.5	102.7–110.0	0.35	74.7– 85.7	177.3–195.7	200–200
35	32–35	2.5	117.3–128.3	0.34	100.4–120.1	217.7–248.4	225–250
40	36–40	2.5	132.0–146.7	0.32	135.0–166.7	267.0–313.3	275–325
45	40–45	2.5	146.7–165.0	0.31	172.0–217.7	318.7–382.7	325–400
50	44–50	2.5	161.3–183.3	0.30	215.1–277.8	376.4–461.1	400–475
55	48–55	2.5	176.0–201.7	0.30	256.0–336.1	432.0–537.8	450–550
60	52–60	2.5	190.7–220.0	0.29	310.8–413.8	501.5–633.8	525–650
65	55–65	2.5	201.7–238.3	0.29	347.7–485.6	549.4–724.0	550–725
70	58–70	2.5	212.7–256.7	0.28	400.5–583.3	613.1–840.0	625–850

[a]Different values for the same speed result from using unequal coefficients of friction.
(Source: A Policy on Geometric Design of Highways and Streets, Washington, D.C., American Association of State Highway and Transportation Officials, 1984. Used by permission.)

Table 4–3 Elements of Safe Passing Sight Distance—Two-Lane Highways

Speed Group (mph)	30–40	40–50	50–60	60–70
Average Passing Speed (mph)	34.9	43.8	52.6	62.0
Initial maneuver:				
a = average acceleration (mph/sec)[a]	1.40	1.43	1.47	1.50
t_1 = time (sec)[a]	3.6	4.0	4.3	4.5
d_d = distance traveled (ft)	145	215	290	370
Occupation of left lane:				
t_2 = time (sec)[a]	9.3	10.0	10.7	11.3
d_2 = distance traveled (ft)	475	640	825	1,030
Clearance length:				
d_3 = distance traveled (ft)[a]	100	180	250	300
Opposing vehicle:				
d_4 = distance traveled (ft)	315	425	550	680
Total distance, $d_1 + d_2 + d_3 + d_4$ (ft)	1,035	1,460	1,915	2,380

[a]For consistent speed relation, observed values adjusted slightly.
(*Source: A Policy on Geometric Design of Highways and Streets,* Washington, D.C., American Association of State Highway and Transportation Officials, 1984. Used by permission.)

ates during the maneuver and its average speed during the occupancy of the left lane is 10 mph higher than that of the overtaken vehicle.
  e. When the passing vehicle returns to its lane, there is a suitable clearance length between it and the oncoming vehicle in the other lane.
2. Basic distance components, as illustrated in Figure 4–1:
  d_1 = distance traversed during perception and reaction time and during the initial acceleration to the point of encroachment on the left lane.
  d_2 = distance traveled while the passing vehicle occupies the left lane.
  d_3 = distance between the passing vehicle at the end of its maneuver and the opposing vehicle.
  d_4 = distance traversed by an opposing vehicle for two thirds of the time the passing vehicle occupies the left lane, or two thirds of d_2.

In the foregoing:

$$d_1 = 1.47t_1 \left(v - m + \frac{at_1}{2} \right)$$

where

t_1 = time of initial maneuver, seconds
a = average acceleration, mphps
v = average speed of passing vehicle, mph
m = difference in speed of passed vehicle and passing vehicle, mph

and

$$d_2 = 1.47 v t_2$$

where

t_2 = time vehicle occupies the left lane, seconds
v = average speed of passing vehicle, mph

and

$$d_3 = 110 - 300 \text{ feet}$$

and

$$d_4 = \frac{2d_2}{3}$$

These distance components operate consecutively as shown in Figure 4–1, and combine to form the graphic relationship shown in Figure 4–2. The ultimate

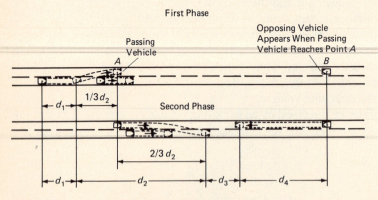

Figure 4–1 Passing Sight Distance Components

(*Source: A Policy on Geometric Design of Highways and Streets,* Washington, D.C., American Association of Highway and Traffic Officials, 1984. Used by permission.)

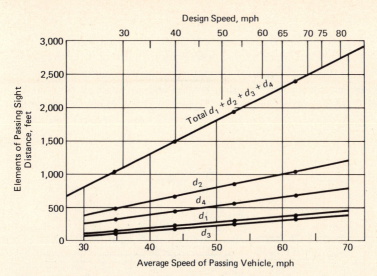

Figure 4–2   Elements of and Total Passing Sight Distance—Two-Lane Highways

(*Source: A Policy on Geometric Design of Highways and Streets,* Washington, D.C., American Association of Highway and Traffic Officials, 1984. Used by permission.)

result is a set of design standards, shown in Table 4–4, which illustrates the combined elements of safe passing sight distance on two-lane highways and the related minimum safe passing sight distances.

Table 4–4   Minimum Passing Sight Distance for Design of Two-Lane Highways

Design Speed (mph)	Assumed Speeds		Minimum Passing Sight Distance (ft)	
	Passed Vehicle (mph)	Passing Vehicle (mph)	Computed	Rounded
20	20	30	810	800
30	26	36	1,090	1,100
40	34	44	1,480	1,500
50	41	51	1,840	1,800
60	47	57	2,140	2,100
65	50	60	2,310	2,300
70	54	64	2,490	2,500

(*Source: A Policy on Geometric Design of Highways and Streets,* Washington, D.C., American Association of State Highway and Transportation Officials, 1984. Used by permission.)

Horizontal Alignment

Horizontal alignment is the horizontal curvature that establishes the directionality of the road. It is composed of superelevation, radius of curvature, and length of curvature. Sections without curvature—that is, straight road—are known as *tangent* sections. Superelevation is the bank, or angle of transverse pitch for the road cross section, which may be arrayed for a variety of rotation types, as shown in Figure 4–3. The formula is related to vehicle speed *V,* and side

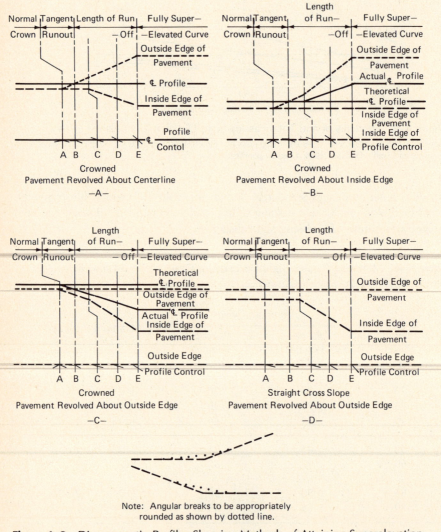

Figure 4–3 Diagrammatic Profiles Showing Methods of Attaining Superelevation

(*Source: A Policy of Geometric Design of Highways and Streets,* Washington, D.C., American Association of Highway and Traffic Officials, 1984. Used by permission.)

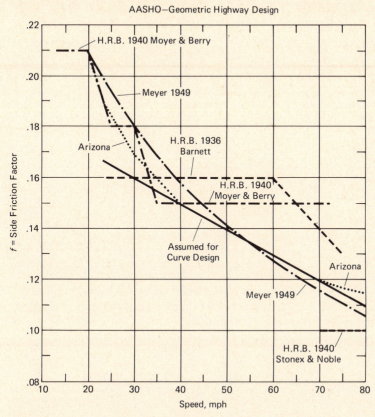

Figure 4–4 Side Friction Factors for Rural Highways and High-Speed Urban Streets
(*Source: A Policy on Geometric Design of Highways and Streets,* Washington, D.C., American Association of Highway and Traffic Officials, 1984. Used by permission.)

friction factor for a variety of pavement types, as shown in Figure 4–4. The formula, incorporating curve design parameters, is:

$$e + f = \frac{0.067V^2}{R} = \frac{V^2}{15R}$$

where

$e =$ rate of roadway superelevation, foot/foot
$f =$ side friction factor
$V =$ vehicle speed, mph
$R =$ radius of curve, feet

Using conversions, the rest of appropriate horizontal curve layout parameters can be determined as follows:

Using the arc definition:

1. For radius

$$R_{min} = \frac{V^2}{15(e + f)}$$

2. For degree

$$D_{max} = \frac{5,729.6}{R}$$

3. By substitution

$$D_{max} = \frac{85,660\ (e + f)}{V^2}$$

The graphical and tabular relations of the above are shown in Table 4–5, yielding a look-up table of appropriate combinations of these design component, which yield compatible horizontal curves for driver negotiation. The following numerical example illustrates their computation.

Assume a design speed of 50 mph, with an e of 0.05 and f of 0.14, find R_{min} and D_{max}:

$$R_{min} = \frac{V^2}{15(e + f)} = \frac{(50)^2}{15(0.05 + .14)} = \frac{2,500}{15(0.19)} = \frac{2,500}{2.85}$$

$$R_{min} = 877.19 \text{ ft}$$

$$D_{max} = \frac{5,729.6}{R} = \frac{5,729.6}{877.19} = 6.5°$$

or by substitution

$$D_{max} = \frac{85,660(e + f)}{V^2} = \frac{85,660(0.19)}{2,500} = \frac{16,275.4}{2,500}$$

$$D = 6.5°$$

Types of Curves

The foregoing formula can be used in a variety of curve types, including a simple single-arc circular curve, a three-centered curve, and a three-centered compound curve, all illustrated in Figure 4–5.

Also related is the concept of a spiral curve, which is a curve of varying curvature

Table 4–5 Maximum Degree of Curve and Minimum Radius Determined for Limiting Values of *e* and *f*, Rural Highways and High-Speed Urban Streets

Design Speed (mph)	Maximum e	Maximum f	Total (e + f)	Maximum Degree of Curve	Rounded Maximum Degree of Curve	Minimum Radius (feet)
20	0.04	0.17	0.21	44.97	45.0	127
30	0.04	0.16	0.20	19.04	19.0	302
40	0.04	0.15	0.19	10.17	10.0	573
50	0.04	0.14	0.18	6.17	6.0	955
60	0.04	0.12	0.16	3.81	3.75	1,528
20	0.06	0.17	0.23	49.25	49.25	116
30	0.06	0.16	0.22	20.94	21.0	273
40	0.06	0.15	0.21	11.24	11.25	509
50	0.06	0.14	0.20	6.85	6.75	849
60	0.06	0.12	0.18	4.28	4.25	1,348
65	0.06	0.11	0.17	3.45	3.5	1,637
70	0.06	0.10	0.16	2.80	2.75	2,083
20	0.08	0.17	0.25	53.54	53.5	107
30	0.08	0.16	0.24	22.84	22.75	252
40	0.08	0.15	0.23	12.31	12.25	468
50	0.08	0.14	0.22	7.54	7.5	764
60	0.08	0.12	0.20	4.76	4.75	1,206
65	0.08	0.11	0.19	3.85	3.75	1,528
70	0.08	0.10	0.18	3.15	3.0	1,910
20	0.10	0.17	0.27	57.82	58.0	99
30	0.10	0.16	0.26	24.75	24.75	231
40	0.10	0.15	0.25	13.38	13.25	432
50	0.10	0.14	0.24	8.22	8.25	694
60	0.10	0.12	0.22	5.23	5.25	1,091
65	0.10	0.11	0.21	4.26	4.25	1,348
70	0.10	0.10	0.20	3.50	3.5	1,637

NOTE: In recognition of safety considerations, use of e_{max} = 0.04 should be limited to urban conditions.
(*Source: A Policy on Geometric Design of Highways and Streets,* Washington, D.C., American Association of State Highway and Transportation Officials, 1984. Used by permission.)

throughout its length. Spirals are often used to provide transition from straight tangent sections to a horizontal circular curve, or from one curve to another. There are several advantages of spirals.[1]

[1]From *A Policy on Geometric Highway Design of Rural Highways,* Washington, D.C., American Association of State Highway Officials, 1965; and *A Policy on Geometric Design of Highways and Streets,* Washington, D.C., American Association of State Highway and Transportation Officials, 1984.

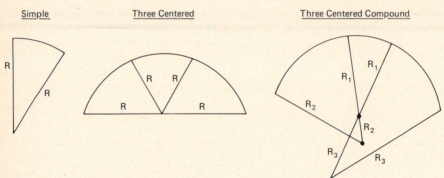

Figure 4–5   Types of Circular Curve

1. Properly designed transition curves provide a natural easy-to-follow path for drivers, such that the centrifugal force increases and decreases gradually as a vehicle enters and leaves a circular curve. This minimuzes encroachment upon adjoining traffic lanes, tends to promote uniformity in speed, and results in increased safety.

2. The transition curve length provides a convenient desirable arrangement for superelevation runoff. The transition between the normal cross-slope and the fully superelevated section on the curve can be effected along the length of transition curve in a manner closely fitting the speed–radius relation for the vehicle transversing it. Where superelevation runoff is effected without a transition curve, usually partly on tangent, the driver approaching a curve may have to steer opposite to the direction of the curve ahead when on the superelevated tangent portion in order to keep the vehicle on tangent. This is an unnatural manuever and explains in part why many vehicles drift to the inside on curves.

3. Where the pavement section is to be widened around a circular curve, the spiral facilitates the transition in width. Use of spirals not only permits simplification of design procedure, but also provides flexibility, in that widening on sharp curves can be applied, in part, on the outside of pavement without a reverse-edge alignment.

4. The appearance of the highway is enhanced by the application of spirals. Their use avoids the noticeable breaks at the beginning and ending of circular curves, which may be distorted further by superelevation runoff. Spirals are an essential part of the natural flowing alignment that appears pleasing and fitting to the conditions.

Length of Spiral

A spiral curve's length can be calculated as follows:

$$L = \frac{3.15V^3}{RC}$$

where

> L = minimum length of spiral curve, feet
> V = speed, mph
> R = curve radius, feet
> C = 1–3

The following example illustrates the above computations

Assume

> V = 55 mph
> R = 900 feet
> C = 2

$$L = \frac{3.15V^3}{RC} = \frac{3.15(55)^3}{900(2)} = \frac{3.15(166,375)}{1,800}$$

$$L = \frac{524,081.25}{1,800}$$

$$L = 291.16 \text{ feet}$$

The superelevation, or bank, on a curvature is attained by a gradual change over a fixed distance. This fixed distance is called the *superelevation runoff,* and exists in relation to the rate *e,* for various desired *design speeds* of the highway, as illustrated in Table 4–6.

Vertical Curvature

Vertical curvature is the other component of design, the hills and valleys of the roadway, recomposing new grades from the original topography by virtue of earthwork construction that incorporates appropriate vertical curve formulas. These formulas are developed with respect to maximum grades as related to various speed levels, and the capability of large trucks to negotiate the grade in snow and ice. Figure 4–6 shows the relationship of critical lengths, grade percent combinations, and resulting speed reduction on such grades by major trucks. Two types of vertical curves exist: *crests* or upgrades, and *sags* or downgrades. They may be circular or parabolic as shown in Figure 4–7. Their formulas, as shown in the following, are a function of whether they are crest or sag, and do or do not incorporate passing sight distance in the curve design.

1. Basic formulas—crest vertical curves, stopping sight distance, assuming the height of eye is 3.50 feet, and the height of object is 6 inches:
   a. Definitions,

   > S = stopping sight distance
   > L = length, feet

Table 4–6   Length Required for Superelevation Runoff—Two-Lane Pavements

Superelevation Rate, e	L—Length of Runoff (feet) for Design Speed (mph) of:						
	20	30	40	50	60	65	70
	12-foot lanes						
0.02	30	35	40	50	55	60	60
0.04	60	70	85	95	110	115	120
0.06	95	110	125	145	160	170	180
0.08	125	145	170	190	215	230	240
0.10	160	180	210	240	270	290	300
	10-foot lanes						
0.02	25	30	35	40	45	50	50
0.04	50	60	70	80	90	95	100
0.06	80	90	105	120	135	145	150
0.08	105	120	140	160	180	190	200
0.10	130	150	175	200	225	240	250
Design minimun length regardless of superelevation	50	100	125	150	175	190	200

(*Source: A Policy on Geometric Design of Highways and Streets,* American Association of State Highway and Transportation Officials, 1984. Used by permission.)

b. If $S < L$, then

$$L = \frac{AS^2}{1,329}$$

c. If $S > L$, then

$$L = 2S - \frac{1,329}{A}$$

where

A = algebraic difference in grades, percent

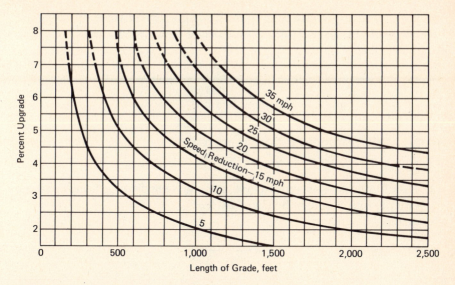

Figure 4–6 Critical Lengths of Grade for Design; Assumed Typical Heavy Truck of 400 Pounds Per Horsepower

(*Source: Special Report 87, Highway Capacity Manual,* Washington, D.C., Highway Research Board, 1965.)

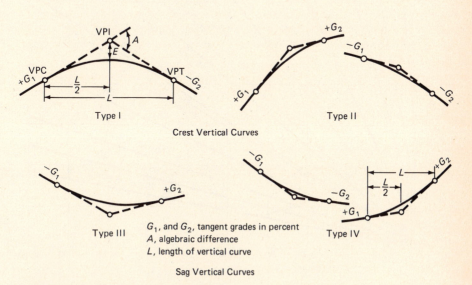

Figure 4–7 Types of Vertical Curves

(*Source: A Policy on Geometric Design of Highways and Streets,* Washington, D.C., American Association of Highway and Traffic Officials, 1984. Used by permission.)

2. Basic formulas—crest vertical curves, passing sight distance, assuming the height of object s 4.25 feet and the height of eye is 3.50 feet:
   a. If $S < L$,

$$L = \frac{AS^2}{3{,}093}$$

   b. If $S > L$,

$$L = 2S - \frac{3{,}093}{A}$$

3. Basic formulas—sag vertical curve, stopping sight distance, using headlight criteria, with headlight height of 2.0 feet:
   a. If $S < L$,

$$L = \frac{AS^2}{400 + 3.5S}$$

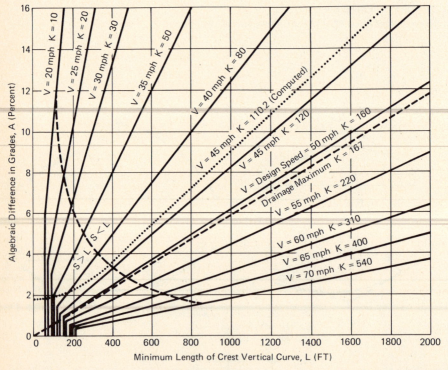

Figure 4–8   Design Controls for Crest Vertical Curves, for Stopping Sight Distance and Open Road Conditions

(*Source: A Policy on Geometric Design of Highways and Streets,* Washington, D.C., American Association of Highway and Traffic Officials, 1984. Used by permission.)

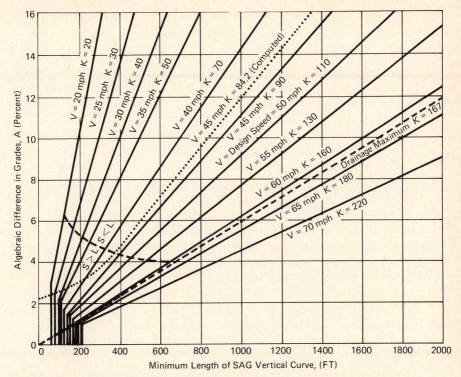

Figure 4–9 Design Controls for Sag Vertical Curves, Open Road Conditions

(*Source: A Policy on Geometric Design of Highways and Streets,* Washington, D.C., American Association of Highway and Traffic Officials, 1984. Used by permission.)

b. If $S > L$,

$$L = 2S - \frac{400 + 3.5S}{A}$$

where L and A are as before and S = headlight beam distance in feet.

These are incorporated into a design control as shown in the graphs of Figures 4–8 and 4–9 for crest and sag curves, using the formula:

$$K = \frac{L}{A}$$

where

L = length of vertical curve
A = algebraic difference in grades

It is most important to synthesize the design controls of horizontal and vertical curves.[2]

1. Curvature and grades should be in proper balance. Tangent alignment or flat curvature at the expense of steep or long grades, and excessive curvature with flat grades, are both poor design. A logical design is a compromise between the two, which offers the most safety, capacity, ease and uniformity of operation, and pleasing appearance within the practical limits of terrain and area traversed.

2. Vertical curvature superimposed upon horizontal curvature, or vice versa, generally results in a more pleasing facility, but it should be analyzed for effect upon traffic. Successive changes in profile not in combination with horizontal curvature may result in a hazardous condition. The use of horizontal and vertical alignments in combination, however, may also result in certain hazardous arrangements, as discussed in the following.

3. Sharp horizontal curvature should not be introduced at or near the top of a pronounced crest vertical curve. This condition is hazardous in that the driver cannot perceive the horizontal changes in alignment, especially at night when the headlight beams go straight ahead into space. The hazard of this arrangement is avoided if the horizontal curvature leads the vertical curvature, that is, the horizontal curve is made longer than the vertical curve. Also, suitable design can be achieved by using design values well above the minimum for the design speed.

4. Somewhat allied to the foregoing, sharp horizontal curvature should not be introduced at or near the low point of a pronounced sag vertical curve. Because the road ahead is foreshortened, any but flat horizontal curvature assumes an undesirable distorted appearance. Further, vehicular speeds, particularly of trucks, often are high at the bottom of grades and erratic operation may result, especially at night.

5. On two-lane highways, the need for safe passing sections at frequent intervals and for an appreciable percentage of the length of the highway often supersedes the general desirability for combination of horizontal and vertical alignment. In these cases it is necessary to work toward long tangent sections to secure sufficient passing sight distance in design.

6. Horizontal curvature and profile should be made as flat as feasible at highway intersections where sight distance along both highways is important and vehicles may have to slow down or stop.

7. On divided highways variation in the width of median and the use of separate profiles and horizontal alignments should be considered to derive design and operational advantages of one-way roadways. Where traffic justifies provision of four lanes, a superior design without additional cost generally results from the concept and logical design basis of one-way roadways.

[2]From *A Policy on Geometric Highway Design of Highways and Streets,* Washington, D.C., American Association of State Highway and Transportation Officials, 1984.

Table 4−7 Normal Pavement Cross-Slope

Surface Type	Range in Cross-Slope Rate (percent)
High	1.5–2
Intermediate	1.5–3
Low	2–6

(*Source: A Policy on Geometric Design of Highways and Streets*, Washington, D.C., American Association of State Highway and Transportation Officials, 1984. Used by permission.)

Cross-Section Elements

The design across the pavement and right-of-way boundaries is known as the cross section. It is comprised of three types of pavement:

High—Portland cement concrete pavement (PCCP) or high-type asphalt
Intermediate—bituminous, related seal coating
Low—gravel, loose rock

Each of these will have varying cross-slopes to handle the drainage and vehicle control. The ranges are shown in Table 4–7.

In addition the lane widths will also vary, with the high type being 12 feet wide, the intermediate 11–12 feet wide, and the low 9–10 feet in width. Shoulders for the high type will be 10–12 feet and paved; intermediate will be 8 feet in width, and low 4 feet in width, both untreated. Side-slope design corresponds to the designation of regions as shown in Figure 4–10, and is dimensioned according to the height of cut or fill of the roadway, as shown in Table 4–8.

Table 4−8 Guide for earth slopes design

Height of Cut or Fill (feet)	Earth Slope, Horizontal to Vertical, for Type of Terrain		
	Flat or Rolling	Moderately Steep	Steep
0–4	6:1	4:1	4:1
4–10	4:1	4:1	2:1[a]
10–15	4:1	2.50:1	1.75:1[a]
15–20	2:1[a]	2:1[a]	1.75:1[a]
Over 20	2:1[a]	2:1[a]	1.75:1[a]

[a]Slopes 2:1 or steeper should be subject to a soil stability analysis and should be reviewed for safety.
(*Source: A Policy on Geometric Design of Highways and Streets*, Washington, D.C., American Association of State Highway and Transportation Officials, 1984. Used by permission.)

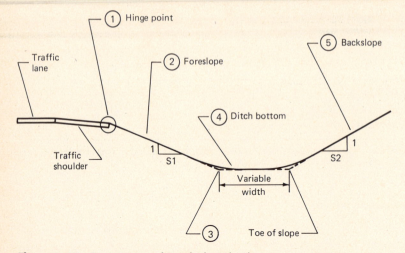

Figure 4–10 Designation of Roadside Side-Slope Design Regions

(*Source: A Policy on Geometric Design of Highways and Streets,* American Association of State Highway and Transportation Officials, 1984. Used by permission.)

Medians will be raised or depressed 4 to 30 feet in width, either sodded or with fill. Typical cross sections and their right-of-way dimensions are shown in Figure 4–11. The ultimate objective in good cross-section design is to achieve *balance,* where nothing is eccentric in its dimensions as compared with the rest of the components.

Intersection Design

A major component of geometric design is the design of intersections. Several types of design exist, as illustrated in Figure 4–12. A general typology of intersections and their operation is as shown in Figure 4–13.

The design of an intersection is typically an interactive process, combining design with the forthcoming capacity computations. General principals of design are:

1. Minimize skew.
2. Minimize points of conflict between vehicles.
3. Minimize abrupt and unfamiliar operations.
4. Minimize dead space, that is, excessive space in the intersection.
5. Provide obvious and easily negotiable vehicle paths.

Closely related to these is the concept of using channelization to help facilitate intersection design. Channelization is the referencing of nontraversible areas of

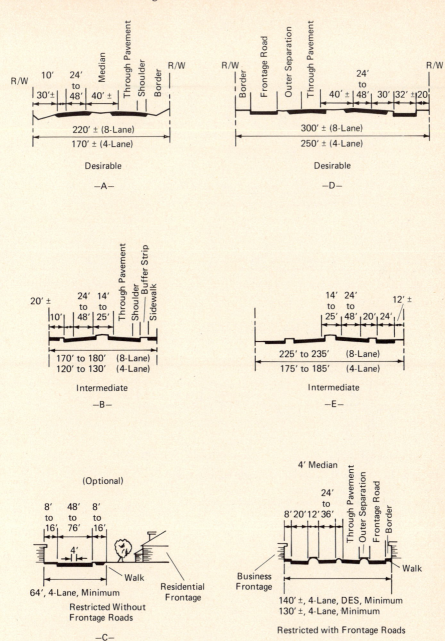

Figure 4–11 Cross Sections of Arterial Streets with and Without Frontage Roads

(*Source: A Policy on Geometric Design of Highways and Streets,* Washington, D.C., American Association of Highway and Traffic Officials, 1984. Used by permission.)

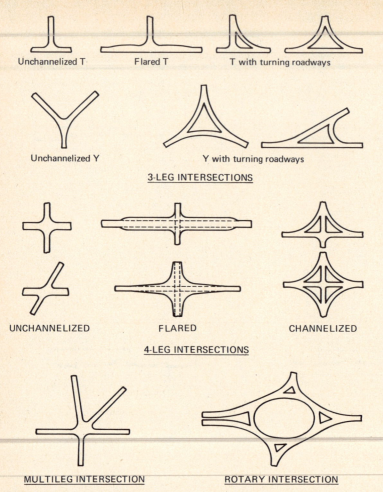

Unchannelized T   Flared T   T with turning roadways

Unchannelized Y   Y with turning roadways

3-LEG INTERSECTIONS

UNCHANNELIZED   FLARED   CHANNELIZED

4-LEG INTERSECTIONS

MULTILEG INTERSECTION   ROTARY INTERSECTION

Figure 4–12   General Types of At-Grade Intersections

(*Source: A Policy on Geometric Design of Rural Highways,* Washington, D.C., American Association of State Highway and Transportation Officials, 1966. Used by permission.)

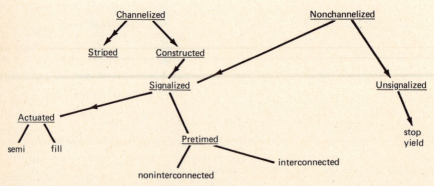

Channelized   Nonchannelized

Striped   Constructed

Signalized   Unsignalized

Actuated

semi   fill   Pretimed   stop
                                              yield
                          interconnected

              noninterconnected

Figure 4–13   General Typology of Intersections

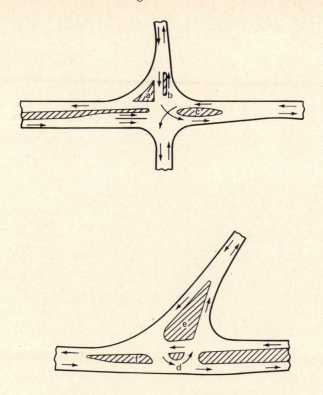

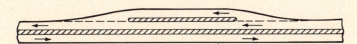

Figure 4–14   General Types and Shapes of Islands

(*Source: A Policy on Geometric Design of Highways and Streets,* Washington, D.C., American Association of Highway and Traffic Officials, 1984. Used by permission.)

the intersection, by striping and marking or constructing solid masses fitting the channelized dimensions. The purpose of channelization are:

1. To reduce dead space.
2. To separate conflict.
3. To guide traffic.

As illustrated in Figure 4–14, several types of channelization exist, each employing islands and suited to achieve the foregoing purposes in a variety of different intersection configurations. The common types of islands are:

1. Triangular
2. Elongated
3. Bulb type
4. Bulletnose

The approach to intersection design procedures is as follows:

1. Determine present and projected volumes for both ADT and peak hour.
2. Determine percentage turning movements at each intersection approach.
3. Review the type of intersecting streets, and the present intersection design on site.
4. Analyze accident rates and severity.
5. Review pedestrian–vehicle interaction.
6. Look closely at amount of dead space present in the current intersection.

Intersection design is largely a cut-and-try procedure, making use of the traffic, accident, cost, topographical, and current site-design information available. The specific design steps are as follows:

1. Develop a line diagram of traffic and movements.
2. Review collision diagrams associated with accident analyses.
3. Review condition diagrams associated with accident analyses.
4. Review basic topography.
5. Lay out movements—by control option and signal phasing.
6. Develop vehicular lane movements required.
7. Rough out intersection.
8. Refine design with appropriate trade-offs: cost versus right-of-way versus signal control versus capacity versus accident rates.

Interchanges

In a like manner, more complex intersecting points of high-volume activity require grade separation to handle traffic effectively. Such grade separations are known as *interchanges.* Examples of interchanges are illustrated in Figure 4–15, and offer the following advantages and disadvantages in their use.[3]

Advantages

1. The capacity of the through traveled ways within the interchange can be made to approach or equal that outside the interchange.
2. Increased safety is provided for through and left-turning traffic. Right-

[3]From *A Policy on Geometric Design of Rural Highways,* Washington, D.C., American Association of State Highway and Transportation Officials, 1965.

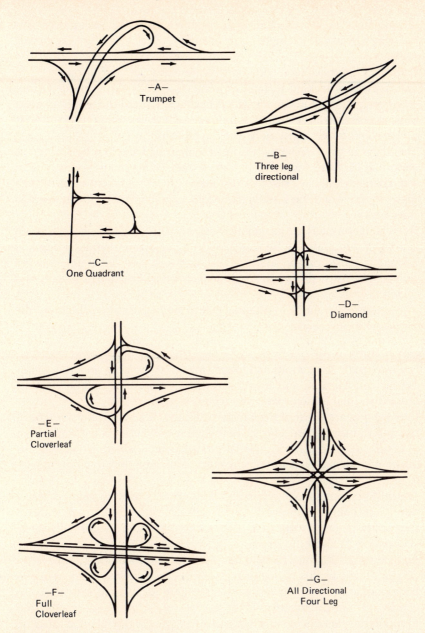

Figure 4–15 Interchange Types

(*Source: A Policy on Geometric Design of Highways and Streets,* Washington, D.C., American Association of Highway and Traffic Officials, 1984. Used by permission.)

turning movements make the same maneuver as on at-grade intersections but generally in a much higher type of facility, which also results in greater safety.

3. Stops and appreciable speed changes are eliminated for through movements. Drivers making turning movements usually slow down, but not excessively, on adequately designed facilities. Overall the ability to keep moving results in large savings in time and vehicle operating costs and adds to the comfort and convenience of the motorist.

4. The highway grade separation is flexible in design and may be adapted to almost all likely angles and positions of intersecting roads. Sometimes an interchange eliminates steep or distorted vertical alignment on a through highway that would be unduly hazardous in conjunction with an at-grade intersection.

5. Interchanges usually are adaptable to stage construction. The structure with one or more ramps can be made to form a complete operating unit and additional ramps can be added at later stages. At directional interchanges one or more structures and some roadways may be omitted initially and added later as required.

6. The grade separation is an essential part of the highest type of highway, the expressway or freeway.

Disadvantages

1. Highway grade separations and interchanges are costly. Engineering, right-of-way, construction, and maintenance, with some few exceptions, cost more than their counterparts in a typical at-grade design.

2. Interchanges are not foolproof with regard to traffic operation. The layout may be confusing (particularly where there is not a complete complement of ramps) to some drivers, especially those unfamiliar with it. However, as driver experience with interchanges has increased, better usage has resulted.

3. The undercrossing grade separation does not lend itself to stage construction. Accordingly it is always desirable initially to span the ultimate width of the facility below. In the case of an undercrossing, it is normally more economical to build the structure full width.

4. A grade separation may make it necessary to introduce undesirable crests and sags in the profile of one or both intersecting highways, particularly in flat topography. The long approaches required in flat areas may be costly, usually are not as attractive as those constructed in rolling terrain, and introduce an element of hazard due to lessened sight distance and travel on elevated roadways.

5. A simple interchange is not readily adaptable to a multileg intersection with five or more approaches. In such cases it may be necessary to join some of the roads outside the interchange area proper, or to provide a multi-structure interchange type.

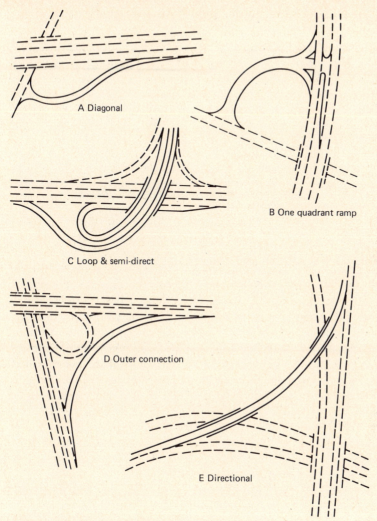

A Diagonal

B One quadrant ramp

C Loop & semi-direct

D Outer connection

E Directional

Figure 4–16   General Types of Ramps

(*Source: A Policy on Geometric Design of Highways and Streets,* Washington, D.C., American Association of Highway and Traffic Officials, 1984. Used by permission.)

Integral parts of interchanges are connected by ramps and collector-distributor roads of varying capacity and design, as illustrated in Figure 4–16. These designs are correlated with the appropriate design speed of the freeway and their ramp radii of curvature, as appropriate, as illustrated in Table 4–9.

Specific geometric design details of ramps are as follows:

Grade: 4–6 percent; 5 percent maximum in snow and ice environments. *Never* use a high speed and a high grade in combination.

Table 4–9 Guide Values for Ramp Design Speed as Related to Highway Design Speed

Highway design speed (mph)	30	40	50	60	65	70
Ramp design speed (mph)						
Upper range (85%)	25	35	45	50	55	60
Middle range (70%)	20	30	35	45	45	50
Lower range (50%)	15	20	25	30	30	35
Corresponding minimum radius (feet)			See Table 4–5			

(*Source: A Policy on Geometric Design of Highways and Streets,* Washington, D.C., American Association of State Highway and Transportation Officials, 1984. Used by permission.)

Access-Controlled Facilities and Interchanges

It is appropriate to conclude this section with comments on access-controlled facilities and their relationship to various interchange types. By definition a *full-access*-controlled facility is one where all intersecting roadways exist with grade separations, making use of interchanges and ramps to achieve turning movements. *Partial-access*-controlled facilities are those which have some intersections at grade and some grade separations. Typically full-access-controlled facilities are freeways or expressways, as typified by the interstate highway system, and represent the highest type of geometric design. Their design characteristics are:

1. High-type pavements—PCCP.
2. Twelve-foot lane widths.
3. Ten–twelve-foot improved shoulders.
4. Minimum of two moving lanes in each direction, separated by appropriate median width or median barrier.
5. Flowing alignments: grades = 3 percent maximum; curves = three–four-degree maximum
6. A 200–300-foot right-of-way.
7. The use of frontage roads in conjunction with interchanges, to collect and distribute local traffic accessing the freeway.

With these facilities the following interchange types are appropriate for use under the conditions specified:

Cloverleaf Cloverleaves are used for relatively large traffic loads where right-of-way is not a problem.

Diamonds Diamonds are appropriate where right-of-way is constrained, as in urban areas, and in areas of retaining walls, adjacent to tunnels, and in deep urban cuts. They are generally capable of less capacity and storage than other interchanges. This is often mitigated by signalization in high-volume urban areas.

Semidirectionals and Directionals   Semidirectionals are used for *very* large amounts of traffic, where only some turning movements are high at the interchange. However a full directional interchange is employed where *all* turning movements are exceptionally high, such as the merger of two freeways, each carrying 100,000 ADT. The capacity of semidirectionals and directionals is high, but travel time on the connecting ramps may be lengthy, and confusion may result for the unitiated driver. Good directional signing is very necessary for the effective operation of these facilities.

All these interchange types may be signalized to increase capacity. Freeway and interchange construction is expensive, however, and cloverleaf and semidirectional and directional interchanges are *extremely* expensive owing to structural complexity, amount of linear feet of pavement needed for ramps, signing, and right-of-way land requirements.

Examples of these complex interchanges are shown in Figures 4–17 through 4–19.

Highway Capacity

The second major entity of importance in this chapter is highway capacity. The fundamentals of capacity terminology, roadway capacity, and intersection capacity are presented.

Basic Capacity Definitions

Several basic definitions are in order prior to developing capacity computations. They are:

1. *Capacity*   The maximum rate of flow at which vehicles can pass a point or segment of roadway in one direction under prevailing traffic and roadway conditions.
2. *Operating speed*   The highest overall speed at which a driver can travel on a given highway under favorable weather conditions and under prevailing traffic conditions without at any time exceeding the safe speed as determined by the design speed on a section-by-section basis.
3. *Density*   The number of vehicles occupying a unit length of the through traffic lanes of a roadway at any given instant, expressed in vehicles per mile, or passenger cars per lane (pcpl).
4. *Peak-hour factor (PHF)*   A ratio of the volume occurring during the peak hour to the maximum rate of flow during a given time period within the peak hour. It is a measure of peaking characteristics, whose maximum attainable value is one. The term must be qualified by a specified short

Figure 4–17   Freeway with a Diamond Interchange

(*Source: A Policy on Geometric Design of Highways and Streets,* Washington, D.C., American Association of Highway and Traffic Officials, 1984. Used by permission.)

period within the hour; this is usually five or six minutes for freeway operation and fifteen minutes for intersections and multilane and arterial facilities. For example, a typical quotation for freeways might be "a peak-hour factor of 0.80 based on a five-minute rate of flow."

5. *Ideal conditions*   A set of traffic and roadway conditions considered to be the best possible; includes uninterrupted flow, a minimum of two lanes for the exclusive use of traffic in each direction, 12-foot lane width, no lateral obstructions closer than six feet to the traveled way, and 70 mph design

Figure 4–18   Semidirectional Interchange with Loops
(*Source:* A Policy on Geometric Design of Highways and Streets, Washington, D.C., American Association of Highway and Traffic Officials, 1984. Used by permission.)

speed, with the exact specifications of ideal conditions varying with the type of facility.

6. *Level of service*   A letter designation (from A to F) that generally characterizes the quality of traffic service experienced by motorists in any given situation; intended to reflect such characteristics as travel time, freedom to maneuver, comfort and convenience, safety and others. The short-form notation for this definition is LOS in computational usage.

7. *Maximum service flow rate*   The highest rate of flow that can be

Figure 4–19   Four-Level Directional Interchange
(*Source: A Policy on Geometric Design of Highways and Streets,* Washington, D.C., American Association of Highway and Traffic Officials, 1984. Used by permission.)

accommodated on a highway facility under ideal conditions, while maintaining operating characteristics for a stated level of service; a value of maximum service flow rate is specific to a given level of service.

8. *Headway*   Time or distance converted to seconds between the rear bumper of one vehicle and the front bumper of another.

9. *ADT*   Average twenty-four-hour daily traffic volume passing a point on a facility.

10. *Peak-hour volume*   The highest consecutive sixty minute volume on a facility. Often known to the lay person as the "rush hour," however, it can occur any time during a twenty-four-hour period.
11. *Interrupted flow*   Traffic flow that is required to stop at some point in the stream to allow crossing traffic to move. A street with an intersection has interrupted flow.
12. *Uninterrupted flow*   Through-street flow; no requirements to stop, such as a country road with no driveways, or miles of freeway.
13. *Platoon*   A closely grouped elemental component of traffic, composed of several vehicles, moving or standing ready to move over a roadway, with clear speaces ahead and behind.
14. *Progression*   Traffic operation within a signal system in which the successive signal faces controlling a given street give "go" indications in accordance with a time schedule to permit, as nearly as possible, continuous operation of groups of vehicles along the street at a planned rate of speed, which may vary in different part of the system.
15. *Street and facility classifications*
    a. *Arterial highway*   A highway primarily for through traffic, usually on a continuous route.
    b. *Expressway*   A divided arterial highway for through traffic with full or partial access control.
    c. *Freeway*   An expressway with full control of access.

Basic Speed-Flow and Volume Relationships

The fundamental relationships that form the basis for analysis of flow are illustrated in Figure 4–20. Figure 4–21 illustrates the relationship between volume and density. Note that in Figure 4–20, as volume goes up, speed goes down until total congestion is reached at point D and volume no longer increases, due to total jam conditions. This is the equivalent of being on point S on the q - k curve at Figure 4–21, as density simultaneously goes up with volume. This point D is termed *saturated flow,* or critical density.

Basic Components of Capacity Calculations

Various types of functional classes of roadways have specific capacity values for ideal conditions, as shown in Table 4–10.

The ideal baseline volumes shown in the table are modified to reflect operating conditions, resulting in a capacity for a particular level of service, or quality of traffic flow. As defined previously, several tangible and intangible things make up "level of service" for the driver. Only a few of these can be truly measured. Thus for operational level of service criteria, we use the following.

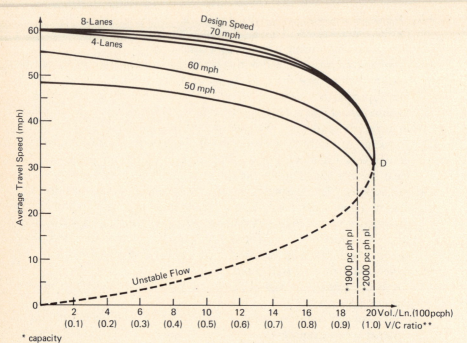

Figure 4–20 Speed–Flow Relationships Under Ideal Conditions

(*Source:* Highway Capacity Manual 1985, Special Report 209, Washington, D.C.: Transportation Research Board, National Research Council.)

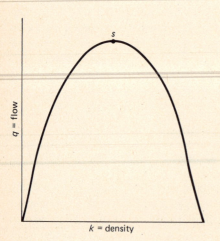

Figure 4–21 Relationship Between Flow and Density

Table 4–10   Type of Roadway Versus Capacity

Type	Capacity, pcphpl*
Freeway	2,000
Multilane	2,000
Two-lane two-way—50/50 directional split	2,800 total of both directions

*Passenger cars per hour per lane.
(*Source:* Highway Capacity Manual 1985, Special Report 209. Washington D.C.: Transportation Research Board, National Research Council.)

1. The *V/C* ratio or volume/capacity ratio, which is the actual demand volume desiring to use the facility divided by the computed capacity of the facility.
2. Operating speed.
3. Density.

This concept is developed graphically in Figure 4–22. A visual example of various levels of service is illustrated in Figure 4–23. Note that we move from free

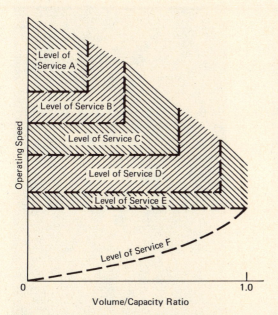

Figure 4–22   General Concept of Relationship of Levels of Service to Operating Speed and Volume/Capacity Ratio (Not to scale).

(*Source: Special Report 87, Highway Capacity Manual,* Washington, D.C., Highway Research Board, 1965.)

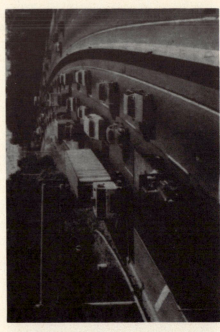

Level-of-service D.

Level-of-service E.

Level-of-service A.

Level-of-service B.

Level-of-service F.

Level-of-service C.

Figure 4–23 Visual Illustration of Levels of Service

flow, defined as level of service A, through continually more congested levels of service to level of service E, and finally to total jam and congested conditions at level of service F, with $V/C > 1.00$. For purposes of design, level of service C is considered the adequate capacity design goal to be achieved.

Factors Affecting Uninterrupted-Flow Capacity

Several factors affect uninterrupted-flow capacity. They are:

1. Lane width.
2. Lateral clearance, which is the distance from the edge of the pavement to obstructions, such as guardrail, walls, and poles.
3. Grades.
4. Percent of heavy-duty, light-duty, and recreational vehicles in the traffic stream.
5. Characteristics of driving population—whether weekday commuter or weekend recreational.

Uninterrupted-Flow-Capacity Computations

The uninterrupted-flow computations will be illustrated for a freeway, a multi-lane highway, and a two-lane, two-way undivided roadway. In each case the process is essentially the same, where the base capacity is modified by particular combinations of the foregoing factors that account for lessening of capacity.

Freeways   The basic freeway computational formats are as follows:

$$MSF_i = C_j \times V/C$$

where

MSF_i = the maximum service flow rate per lane for LOS_i under ideal conditions, pcph

$(V/C)_i$ = the maximum volume to capacity ratio associated with LOS

C_j = capacity under ideal conditions for a freeway element of design speed j; assumed to be as follows: 2,000 pcphpl (passenger cars per hour per lane) for 60-mph and 70-mph segments; 1,900 pcphpl for 50-mph segments

and

$$SF_i = MSF_i \times N \times f_w \times f_{hv} \times f_p$$

Table 4–11 Levels of Service for Basic Freeway Sections

LOS	Density (PC/MI/LN)	70 mph Design Speed			60 mph Design Speed			50 mph Design Speed		
		Speed[b] (mph)	v/c	MSF[a] (pcphpl)	Speed[b] (mph)	v/c	MSF[a] (pcphpl)	Speed[b] (mph)	v/c	MSF[a] (pcphpl)
A	≤ 12	≥ 60	0.35	700	—	—	—	—	—	—
B	≤ 20	≥ 57	0.54	1,100	≥ 50	0.49	1,000	—	—	—
C	≤ 30	≥ 54	0.77	1,550	≥ 47	0.69	1,400	≥ 43	0.67	1,300
D	≤ 42	≥ 46	0.93	1,850	≥ 42	0.84	1,700	≥ 40	0.83	1,600
E	≤ 67	≥ 30	1.00	2,000	≥ 30	1.00	2,000	≥ 28	1.00	1,900
F	> 67	< 30	c	c	< 30	c	c	< 28	c	c

[a]Maximum service flow rate per lane under ideal conditions.
[b]Average travel speed.
[c]Highly variable, unstable.
NOTE: All values of MSF Rounded to the nearest 50 vph.
(*Source:* Highway Capacity Manual 1985, Special Report 209. Washington D.C.: Transportation Research Board, National Research Council.)

Table 4–12 Adjustment Factor for Restricted Lane Width and Lateral Clearance

	Adjustment Factor, f_w							
	Obstructions on One Side of the Roadway				Obstructions on Both Sides of the Roadway			
	Lane Width (feet)				Lane Width (feet)			
Distance From Traveled Pavement[a] (feet)	12	11	10	9	12	11	10	9
	Four-Lane Freeway (Two Lanes Each Direction)							
≥ 6	1.00	0.97	0.91	0.81	1.00	0.97	0.91	0.81
5	0.99	0.96	0.90	0.80	0.99	0.96	0.90	0.80
4	0.99	0.96	0.90	0.80	0.98	0.95	0.89	0.79
3	0.98	0.95	0.89	0.79	0.96	0.93	0.87	0.77
2	0.97	0.94	0.88	0.79	0.94	0.91	0.86	0.76
1	0.93	0.90	0.85	0.76	0.87	0.85	0.80	0.71
0	0.90	0.87	0.82	0.73	0.81	0.79	0.74	0.66
	Six- or Eight-Lane Freeway (Three or Four Lanes Each Direction)							
≥ 6	1.00	0.96	0.89	0.78	1.00	0.96	0.89	0.78
5	0.99	0.95	0.88	0.77	0.99	0.95	0.88	0.77
4	0.99	0.95	0.88	0.77	0.98	0.94	0.87	0.77
3	0.98	0.94	0.87	0.76	0.97	0.93	0.86	0.76
2	0.97	0.93	0.87	0.76	0.96	0.92	0.85	0.75
1	0.95	0.92	0.86	0.75	0.93	0.89	0.83	0.72
0	0.94	0.91	0.85	0.74	0.91	0.87	0.81	0.70

[a]Certain types of obstructions, high-type median barriers in particular, do not cause any deleterious effect on traffic flow. Judgment should be exercised in applying these factors.

(*Source:* Highway Capacity Manual 1985, Special Report 209. Washington D.C.: Transportation Research Board, National Research Council.)

where

SF = the service flow rate for LOS_i under prevailing roadway and traffic conditions for N lanes in one direction in vph (vehicles per hour)

N = the number of lanes in one direction of the freeway

f_w = factor to adjust for the effects of restricted lane width and/or lateral clearances

f_{hv} = factor to adjust for the effect of heavy vehicles (trucks, buses, and recreational vehicles) in the traffic stream

f_p = factor to adjust for the effect of driver population

These two equations can obviously be combined as follows:

$$SF_i = C_j \times (V/C)_i \times N \times f_w \times f_{hv} \times f_p$$

Data relating to the foregoing factors are given in Tables 4–11 through 4–20. One of the factors, f_{hv}, requires additional elaboration. This factor is found in multiple steps:

1. The *passenger car equivalent* (pce) is found from Tables 4–13 through 4–18 for each truck, bus, and/or recretional vehicle for the traffic and roadway conditions under study. These values, known as E_T, E_B, and E_R for trucks, buses, and recreational vehicles, respectively, represent the number of passenger cars that would consume the same percentage of the freeway's capacity as one truck, bus, or recreational vehicle under the prevailing roadway and traffic conditions. The operation can be performed for either *extended general freeway segments* illustrated in Table 4–13, containing several variable grades in level, rolling, or mountainous terrain or *specific grades* of *specific lengths,* as illustrated in Tables 4–14 through 4–18.

Table 4–13   Passenger-Car Equivalents on Extended General Freeway Segments

Factor	Type of Terrain		
	Level	Rolling	Mountainous
E_T for trucks	1.7	4.0	8.0
E_B for buses	1.5	3.0	5.0
E_R for RVs	1.6	3.0	4.0

(*Source:* Highway Capacity Manual 1985, Special Report 209. Washington D.C.: Transportation Research Board, National Research Council.)

Table 4–14 Passenger-Car Equivalents for Typical Trucks (200 LB/HP)

Grade (%)	Length (miles)	Passenger-Car Equivalent, E_T															
		Four-Lane Freeways								Six–Eight-Lane Freeways							
	Percent Trucks	2	4	5	6	8	10	15	20	2	4	5	6	8	10	15	20
<1	All	2	2	2	2	2	2	2	2	2	2	2	2	2	2	2	2
1	0–½	2	2	2	2	2	2	2	2	2	2	2	2	2	2	2	2
	½–1	3	3	3	3	3	3	3	3	3	3	3	3	3	3	3	3
	≥ 1	4	3	3	3	3	3	3	3	4	3	3	3	3	3	3	3
2	0–¼	4	4	4	3	3	3	3	3	4	4	4	3	3	3	3	3
	¼–½	5	4	4	3	3	3	3	3	5	4	4	3	3	3	3	3
	½–¾	6	5	5	4	4	4	4	4	6	5	5	4	4	4	4	4
	¾–1½	7	6	6	5	4	4	4	4	7	5	5	5	4	4	4	4
	≥ 1½	8	6	6	6	5	5	4	4	8	6	6	5	4	4	4	4
3	0–¼	6	5	5	5	4	4	4	3	6	5	5	5	4	4	4	3
	¼–½	8	6	6	6	5	5	5	4	7	6	6	6	5	5	5	4
	½–1	9	7	7	6	5	5	5	5	9	7	7	6	5	5	5	5
	1–1½	9	7	7	7	6	6	5	5	9	7	7	6	5	5	5	5
	≥ 1½	10	7	7	7	6	6	5	5	10	7	7	6	5	5	5	5

Grade	Length																
4	0–¼	4	4	4	4	5	6	6	7	7	6	6	5	4	4	4	4
	¼–½	5	5	5	5	7	7	7	10	10	7	7	6	5	5	5	5
	½–1	5	5	6	6	8	8	8	12	12	8	8	6	6	6	5	5
	≥ 1	6	6	7	8	9	9	9	13	13	9	9	8	8	7	6	6
5	0–¼	5	5	5	5	6	6	6	8	8	6	6	5	5	5	5	5
	¼–½	5	5	5	6	7	7	8	10	10	8	7	6	6	5	5	5
	½–1	7	7	7	8	10	11	11	12	12	11	10	8	8	7	7	7
	≥ 1	7	7	7	8	10	11	11	14	14	11	10	8	8	7	7	7
6	0–¼	5	5	5	5	6	7	7	9	9	7	7	6	6	6	6	6
	¼–½	6	6	6	6	8	8	9	13	13	9	8	7	7	7	6	6
	½–¾	6	6	6	7	8	9	9	13	13	9	9	8	7	7	7	7
	≥ ¾	8	8	8	9	11	10	12	17	17	13	11	10	9	9	8	8

NOTE: If a length of grade falls on a boundary condition, the equivalent for the longer grade category is used. For any grade steeper than the percentage shown, use the next higher grade category.

(*Source:* Highway Capacity Manual 1985, Special Report 209. Washington D.C.: Transportation Research Board, National Research Council.)

Table 4–15 Passenger-Car Equivalents for Light Trucks (100 LB/HP)

Grade (%)	Length (miles)	Passenger-Car Equivalent, E_T Four-Lane Freeways								Six–Eight-Lane Freeways							
	Percent Trucks	2	4	5	6	8	10	15	20	2	4	5	6	8	10	15	20
≤2	All	2	2	2	2	2	2	2	2	2	2	2	2	2	2	2	2
3	0–¼	3	3	3	3	3	3	3	3	3	3	3	3	3	3	3	3
	¼–½	4	4	4	3	3	3	3	3	4	4	4	3	3	3	3	3
	½–¾	4	4	4	4	3	3	3	3	4	4	4	3	3	3	3	3
	¾–1	5	4	4	4	3	3	3	3	5	4	4	4	3	3	3	3
	>1	6	5	5	5	4	4	4	3	6	5	5	4	4	4	3	3
4	0–¼	4	4	4	3	3	3	3	3	5	4	4	4	3	3	3	3
	¼–½	5	5	5	4	4	4	4	4	5	4	4	4	4	4	4	4
	½–1	6	5	5	5	4	4	4	4	6	5	5	4	4	4	4	4
	>1	7	6	6	5	4	4	4	4	7	5	5	5	4	4	4	4
5	0–¼	6	5	5	5	4	4	4	3	6	5	5	5	4	4	4	3
	¼–1	8	7	7	6	5	5	5	5	8	7	7	6	5	5	5	5
	>1	9	7	7	6	5	5	5	5	8	7	7	6	5	5	5	5
6	0–¼	7	5	5	5	4	4	4	4	7	5	5	5	4	4	3	3
	¼–1	9	7	7	6	5	5	5	5	8	7	7	6	5	5	5	5
	>1	9	7	7	6	6	5	5	5	9	7	7	6	5	5	5	5

NOTE: If a length of grade falls on a boundary condition, the equivalent from the longer grade category is used. For any grade steeper than the percentage shown, use the next higher grade category.
(*Source:* Highway Capacity Manual 1985, Special Report 209. Washington D.C.: Transportation Research Board, National Research Council.)

2. Compute the heavy-vehicle adjustment factor f_{hv} using the values of E_T, E_B, and E_R and the proportion of each type of vehicle in the traffic stream (P_T, P_B, P_R).

The computational formula is:

$$f_{hv} = \frac{1}{1 + P_T(E_T - 1) + P_R(E_R - 1) + P_B(E_B - 1)}$$

where

$$
\begin{aligned}
f_{hv} &= \text{the adjustment factor for the combined effect by trucks,} \\
&\quad \text{recreational vehicles, and buses in the traffic stream} \\
E_T, E_R, E_B &= \text{the passenger car equivalents for trucks, recreational vehi-} \\
&\quad \text{cles, and buses respectively} \\
P_T, P_R, P_B &= \text{the proportion of trucks, recreational vehicles, and buses,} \\
&\quad \text{respectively, in the traffic stream}
\end{aligned}
$$

The results of these calculations are illustrated in Table 4–19.

Example Computation   An older four-lane urban freeway with a 60-mph design speed serves a directional peak-hour volume of 1,900 vph with 6 percent trucks and a peak-hour factor (PHF) of 0.95. The freeway has 11-foot lanes, with *no* lateral clearance at both the pavement edge and the median, and is located in generally rolling terrain. Develop the level of service on the facility. Compute how much additional weekday traffic volume could be accommodated before saturation. Average travel speed during the peak fifteen minutes has been determined to be 35 mph.

Solution:

$$V/C = SF/[C_J \times N \times f_w \times f_{hv} \times f_p]$$

and

$$
\begin{aligned}
C_J &= 2{,}000 \text{ pcphpl} \\
N &= 2 \\
E_T &= 4 \text{ (from Table 4–13)} \\
f_{hv} &= 0.85 \ (0.06 \text{ truck, } E_T = 4) \text{ (from Table 4–19)} \\
f_w &= 0.79\text{---11-foot lanes, obstructions both sides at 0 feet clearance (from} \\
&\quad \text{Table 4–12)} \\
f_p &= 1.00\text{---weekday (from Table 4–20)} \\
SF &= 1{,}900/0.95 = 2{,}000
\end{aligned}
$$

Table 4–16 Passenger-Car Equivalents for Heavy Trucks (300 LB/HP)

Grade (%)	Length (miles)	Passenger-Car Equivalent, E_T															
		Four-Lane Freeways								Six–Eight-Lane Freeways							
	Percent Trucks	2	4	5	6	8	10	15	20	2	4	5	6	8	10	15	20
< 1	All	2	2	2	2	2	2	2	2	2	2	2	2	2	2	2	2
1	0–¼	2	2	2	2	2	2	2	2	2	2	2	2	2	2	2	2
	¼–½	3	3	3	3	3	3	3	3	3	3	3	3	3	3	3	3
	½–¾	4	4	4	4	3	3	3	3	4	4	4	3	3	3	3	3
	¾–1	5	4	4	4	3	3	3	3	5	4	4	3	3	3	3	3
	1–1½	6	5	5	5	4	4	4	3	6	5	5	4	4	4	3	3
	> 1½	7	5	5	5	4	4	4	3	7	5	5	5	4	4	3	3
2	0–¼	4	4	4	3	3	3	3	3	4	4	4	3	3	3	3	3
	¼–½	7	6	6	5	4	4	4	4	7	5	5	5	4	4	4	4
	½–¾	8	6	6	5	5	4	4	4	8	6	6	6	5	5	4	4
	¾–1	8	6	6	6	5	5	5	5	8	6	6	6	5	5	5	5
	1–1½	9	7	7	7	6	6	5	5	9	7	7	6	5	5	5	5
	> 1½	10	7	7	7	6	6	5	5	10	7	7	6	5	5	5	5

Grade (%)	Length (mi)	A1	A2	A3	A4	A5	A6	A7	A8	B1	B2	B3	B4	B5	B6	B7	B8
3	0–¼	3	4	4	4	5	5	5	6	3	4	4	4	5	5	5	6
	¼–½	5	5	5	5	6	7	7	8	5	5	5	6	6	7	7	9
	½–¾	5	5	5	5	6	7	8	10	6	6	7	7	8	8	8	12
	¾–1	6	6	6	6	7	8	8	11	7	7	7	8	9	9	9	13
	>1	7	7	7	7	8	9	9	12	7	8	8	8	9	10	10	14
4	0–¼	4	4	4	4	5	5	5	7	3	4	4	4	5	5	5	7
	¼–½	6	6	6	6	7	8	8	10	5	6	6	6	7	8	8	12
	½–¾	6	7	7	7	8	9	9	11	6	7	7	7	8	9	9	13
	¾–1	7	8	8	8	9	10	10	12	7	8	8	8	9	10	10	15
	>1	8	8	9	9	9	10	10	13	8	9	9	9	10	12	12	17
5	0–¼	5	5	5	5	6	6	6	8	5	5	5	5	6	6	7	8
	¼–½	6	6	7	7	8	8	9	11	7	7	7	8	9	9	9	13
	½–¾	9	9	9	10	11	11	14	20	8	11	11	11	14	15	15	20
	>¾	11	11	11	12	13	14	16	17	11	13	13	13	16	17	17	22
6	0–¼	5	5	5	5	6	7	7	9	5	5	5	5	6	7	7	9
	¼–½	8	8	8	9	10	10	10	13	8	8	8	9	10	12	12	17
	>½	14	14	14	15	17	17	17	20	14	14	14	15	16	18	18	28

NOTE: If a length of grade falls on a boundary condition, the equivalent from the longer grade category is used. For any grade steeper than the precent shown, use the next higher grade category.

(Source: Highway Capacity Manual 1985, Special Report 209. Washington D.C.: Transportation Research Board, National Research Council.)

Table 4–17 Passenger-Car Equivalents for Recreational Vehicles

Passenger-Car Equivalent, E_R

Grade (%)	Length (miles)	Four-Lane Freeways								Six–Eight-Lane Freeways							
Percent RVs		2	4	5	6	8	10	15	20	2	4	5	6	8	10	15	20
< 2	All	2	2	2	2	2	2	2	2	2	2	2	2	2	2	2	2
3	0–½	3	2	2	2	2	2	2	2	2	2	2	2	2	2	2	2
	≥ ½	4	3	3	3	3	3	3	3	4	3	3	3	3	3	3	3
4	0–¼	3	2	2	2	2	2	2	2	3	2	2	2	2	2	2	2
	¼–¾	4	3	3	3	3	3	3	3	4	3	3	3	3	3	3	3
	≥ ¾	5	4	4	4	3	3	3	3	4	4	4	4	3	3	3	3
5	0–¼	4	3	3	3	3	3	3	3	4	3	3	3	2	2	2	2
	¼–¾	5	4	4	4	4	4	4	4	5	4	4	4	4	4	4	4
	≥ ¾	6	5	4	4	4	4	4	4	5	5	4	4	4	4	4	4
6	0–¼	5	4	4	4	3	3	3	3	5	4	4	3	3	3	3	3
	¼–¾	6	5	5	4	4	4	4	4	6	4	4	4	4	4	4	4
	≥ ¾	7	6	6	6	5	5	5	5	6	5	5	5	4	4	4	4

NOTE: If a length of grade falls on a boundary condition, the equivalent from the longer grade category is used. For any grade steeper than the percent shown, use the next higher grade category.

(Source: Highway Capacity Manual 1985, Special Report 209. Washington D.C.: Transportation Research Board, National Research Council.)

Table 4–18   Passenger-Car Equivalents for Buses

Grade (%)	Passenger-Car Equivalent, E_B
0–3	1.6
4[a]	1.6
5[a]	3.0
6[a]	5.5

[a]Use generally restricted to grades more than ¼ mile long.
(*Source:* Highway Capacity Manual 1985, Special Report 209. Washington D.C.: Transportation Research Board, National Research Council.)

and now

$$V/C = \frac{2,000}{2,000 \times 2 \times 0.79 \times 0.85 \times 1.00}$$

$$= \frac{2,000}{2,686} = 0.74; \text{ therefore, the level of service is } D$$

and

$$C = SF_E = C_j \times N \times (V/C) \times f_w \times f_{hv} \times f_p$$

where

V/C at capacity $(LOS_E) = 1.00$

so that:

$$C = 2,000 \times 2 \times 1.0 \times 0.79 \times 0.85 \times 1.00 = 2,686 \text{ vph}$$

Thus:

2,686 vph = capacity, as above
− 1,900 vph = actual flow rate
786 vehicles additionally capable of being accommodated during the peak fifteen minutes

which is the equivalent of

786 × 0.95 = 747 additional vph over the entire peak hour before capacity is reached

Table 4–19 Adjustment Factor for the Effect of Trucks, Buses, or Recreational Vehicles in the Traffic Stream

PCE E_T E_R or E_B	Adjustment Factor, f_{hv}														
	Proportion of Trucks, P_T; RVs, P_R; or Buses, P_B														
	0.01	0.02	0.03	0.04	0.05	0.06	0.07	0.08	0.09	0.10	0.12	0.14	0.16	0.18	0.20
2	0.99	0.98	0.97	0.96	0.95	0.94	0.93	0.93	0.92	0.91	0.89	0.88	0.86	0.85	0.83
3	0.98	0.96	0.94	0.93	0.91	0.89	0.88	0.86	0.85	0.83	0.81	0.78	0.76	0.74	0.71
4	0.97	0.94	0.92	0.89	0.87	0.85	0.83	0.81	0.79	0.77	0.74	0.70	0.68	0.65	0.63
5	0.96	0.93	0.89	0.86	0.83	0.81	0.78	0.76	0.74	0.71	0.68	0.64	0.61	0.58	0.56
6	0.95	0.91	0.87	0.83	0.80	0.77	0.74	0.71	0.69	0.67	0.63	0.59	0.56	0.53	0.50
7	0.94	0.89	0.85	0.81	0.77	0.74	0.70	0.68	0.65	0.63	0.58	0.54	0.51	0.48	0.45
8	0.93	0.88	0.83	0.78	0.74	0.70	0.67	0.64	0.61	0.59	0.54	0.51	0.47	0.44	0.42
9	0.93	0.86	0.81	0.76	0.71	0.68	0.64	0.61	0.58	0.56	0.51	0.47	0.44	0.41	0.38
10	0.92	0.85	0.79	0.74	0.69	0.65	0.61	0.58	0.55	0.53	0.48	0.44	0.41	0.38	0.36
11	0.91	0.83	0.77	0.71	0.67	0.63	0.59	0.56	0.53	0.50	0.45	0.42	0.38	0.36	0.33
12	0.90	0.82	0.75	0.69	0.65	0.60	0.57	0.53	0.50	0.48	0.43	0.39	0.36	0.34	0.31
13	0.89	0.81	0.74	0.68	0.63	0.58	0.54	0.51	0.48	0.45	0.41	0.37	0.34	0.32	0.29
14	0.88	0.79	0.72	0.66	0.61	0.56	0.52	0.49	0.46	0.43	0.39	0.35	0.32	0.30	0.28
15	0.88	0.78	0.70	0.64	0.59	0.54	0.51	0.47	0.44	0.42	0.37	0.34	0.31	0.28	0.26
16	0.87	0.77	0.69	0.63	0.57	0.53	0.49	0.45	0.43	0.40	0.36	0.32	0.29	0.27	0.25
17	0.86	0.76	0.68	0.61	0.56	0.51	0.47	0.44	0.41	0.38	0.34	0.31	0.28	0.26	0.24
18	0.85	0.75	0.66	0.60	0.54	0.49	0.46	0.42	0.40	0.37	0.33	0.30	0.27	0.25	0.23
19	0.85	0.74	0.65	0.58	0.53	0.48	0.44	0.41	0.38	0.36	0.32	0.28	0.26	0.24	0.22
20	0.84	0.72	0.64	0.57	0.51	0.47	0.42	0.40	0.37	0.34	0.30	0.27	0.25	0.23	0.21
21	0.83	0.71	0.63	0.56	0.50	0.45	0.41	0.38	0.36	0.33	0.29	0.26	0.24	0.22	0.20
22	0.83	0.70	0.61	0.54	0.49	0.44	0.40	0.37	0.35	0.32	0.28	0.25	0.23	0.21	0.19
23	0.82	0.69	0.60	0.53	0.48	0.43	0.39	0.36	0.34	0.31	0.27	0.25	0.22	0.20	0.19
24	0.81	0.68	0.59	0.52	0.47	0.42	0.38	0.35	0.33	0.30	0.27	0.24	0.21	0.19	0.18
25	0.80	0.67	0.58	0.51	0.46	0.41	0.37	0.34	0.32	0.29	0.26	0.23	0.20	0.18	0.17

NOTE: This table should not be used when the combined percentage of buses and RVs in the traffic stream is more than one-fifth the percentage of trucks.
(Source: Highway Capacity Manual 1985, Special Report 209. Washington D.C.: Transportation Research Board, National Research Council.)

Table 4–20   Adjustment Factor for the Character of the Traffic Stream

Traffic Stream Type	Factors, f_p
Weekday or commuter	1.0
Other	0.75–0.90[a]

[a]Engineering judgment must be exercised in selecting an exact value.
(*Source:* Highway Capacity Manual 1985, Special Report 209. Washington D.C.: Transportation Research Board, National Research Council.)

Multilane Highways   The procedure for two-way multilane highways is very similar to that for freeways, with one-factor modification as shown in the following. The relationships are:

$$SF = \frac{V}{PHF}$$

$$SF_i = MSF_i \times N \times f_w \times f_{hv} \times f_E \times f_p$$

$$MSF_i = C_J \times \left(\frac{V}{C}\right)_i$$

and

$$SF_i = C_J \times \left(\frac{V}{C}\right) \times N \times f_w \times f_{hv} \times f_E \times f_p$$

Tables 4–21 through 4–31 contain appropriate geometric and roadway information to process computations for multilane facilities. All relationship definitions are as before, with the addition of a new factor f_E, illustrated in Table 4–30, which is a factor for the highway and development environment. It is an attempt to stratify, by rural or urban, the amount of delay influence on capacity due to the presence of turning movements at the roadside margin. Some judgment should be used in the use of this new factor in capacity computation, as precise quantification is not yet available.

Example Calculation: Given an undivided suburban multilane (four lanes) highway segment with telephone poles 2 feet from the pavement edge, the facility exists in a level terrain, has 11-foot lanes, and its design speed is 60 mph, with a driving population consisting of commuters. The roadway carries an 1,800 peak-hour demand, with 15 percent trucks and a PHF of 0.90. What is the level of service on this facility?

Solution:

$$SF = \frac{V}{PHF} = \frac{1,800}{0.90} = 2,000 \text{ vph}$$

$$V/C = \frac{SF}{[C_J \times N \times f_w \times f_{hv} \times f_E \times f_p]}$$

where

SF = 2,000 vph from above
C_J = 2,000 pcphpl
N = 2
f_w = 0.92 (from Table 4–22)
E_T = 1.7 (level terrain) (from Table 4–23)

and using the F_{hv} calculation format discussed earlier:

$$F_{hv} = \frac{1}{[1 + P_T(E_T - 1)]} = \frac{1}{[1.0 + 0.15(1.7 - 1)]} = 0.90$$

f_E = 0.80 (from Table 4–30)

f_p = 1.00 (from Table 4–31)

Therefore:

$$V/C = \frac{2,000}{(2,000 \times 2 \times 0.92 \times 0.90 \times 0.80 \times 1.0)} = \frac{2,000}{2,649.6}$$

= 0.75, which is level of service C (from Table 4–21)

Two-Lane, Two-Way Facilities   Two-lane, two-way facilities are developed in a computational manner similar to that for other uninterrupted flow facilities. However, allowance is made for the presence of opposing traffic, the passing maneuver, and the impact of reduced speeds and/or sight distance on the upgrades.

Ideal Conditions   The statement of ideal conditions is modified in light of the foregoing. It consists of:

1. Design speed greater than or equal to 60 mph.
2. Lane widths greater than or equal to 12 feet.
3. Clear shoulders wider than or equal to 6 feet.
4. No "no passing zones" on the highway.
5. All passenger cars in traffic stream.
6. A 50/50 directional traffic split.
7. No impediments to through traffic due to traffic control or turning vehicles.
8. Level terrain.

Table 4–21 Level-of-Service Criteria for Multilane Highways

Level of Service	Density (pc/mi/ln)	70 mph Design Speed			60 mph Design Speed			50 mph Design Speed		
		Speed[a] (mph)	v/c	MSF[b] (pcphpl)	Speed[a] (mph)	v/c	MSF[b] (pcphpl)	Speed[a] (mph)	v/c	MSF[b] (pcphpl)
A	≤ 12	≥ 57	0.36	700	≥ 50	0.33	650	—	—	—
B	≤ 20	≥ 53	0.54	1,100	≥ 48	0.50	1,000	≥ 42	0.45	850
C	≤ 30	≥ 50	0.71	1,400	≥ 44	0.65	1,300	≥ 39	0.60	1,150
D	≤ 42	≥ 40	0.87	1,750	≥ 40	0.80	1,600	≥ 35	0.76	1,450
E	≤ 67	≥ 30	1.00	2,000	≥ 28	1.00	2,000	≥ 30	1.00	1,900
F	> 67	< 30	c	c	< 28	c	c	< 30	c	c

[a]Average travel speed.
[b]Maximum rate of flow per lane under ideal conditions, rounded to the nearest 50 pcphpl.
[c]Highly variable.
(*Source:* Highway Capacity Manual 1985, Special Report 209. Washington D.C.: Transportation Research Board, National Research Council.)

Table 4–22 Adjustment Factor for Restricted Lane Width and Lateral Clearance

Distance from Edge of Traveled Way to Obstruction[a] (feet)	Adjustment Factor, f_w							
	Obstruction on One Side of Roadway[b]				Obstruction on Both Sides of Roadway[c]			
	Lane Width (feet)				Lane Width (feet)			
	12	11	10	9	12	11	10	9
Four-Lane Divided Multilane Highways (Two Lanes Each Direction)								
≥ 6	1.00	0.97	0.91	0.81	1.00	0.97	0.91	0.81
4	0.99	0.96	0.90	0.80	0.98	0.95	0.89	0.79
2	0.97	0.94	0.88	0.79	0.94	0.91	0.86	0.76
0	0.90	0.87	0.82	0.73	0.81	0.79	0.74	0.66
Six-Lane Divided Multilane Highways (Three Lanes Each Direction)								
≥ 6	1.00	0.96	0.89	0.78	1.00	0.96	0.89	0.78
4	0.99	0.95	0.88	0.77	0.98	0.94	0.87	0.77
2	0.97	0.93	0.87	0.76	0.96	0.92	0.85	0.75
0	0.94	0.91	0.85	0.74	0.91	0.87	0.81	0.70
Four-Lane Undivided Multilane Highways (Two Lanes Each Direction)								
≥ 6	1.00	0.95	0.89	0.77	NA	NA	NA	NA
4	0.98	0.94	0.88	0.76	NA	NA	NA	NA
2	0.95	0.92	0.86	0.75	0.94	0.91	0.86	NA
0	0.88	0.85	0.80	0.70	0.81	0.79	0.74	0.66

Six-Lane Undivided Multilane Highways (Three Lanes Each Direction)

≥ 6	1.00	0.95	0.89	0.77	NA	NA	NA
4	0.99	0.94	0.88	0.76	NA	NA	NA
2	0.97	0.93	0.86	0.75	0.96	0.92	0.85
0	0.94	0.90	0.83	0.72	0.91	0.87	0.81

[a] Use the average distance to obstruction on "both sides" where the distance to obstructions on the left and right differs.
[b] Factors for one-sided obstruction allow for the effect of opposing flow.
[c] Two-sided obstructions include one roadside and one median obstruction. Median obstruction may exist in the median of a divided multilane highway or in the center of an undivided highway which periodically divides to go around bridge abutments or other center objects.
NA = Not applicable; use factor for one-sided obstruction.
(Source: Highway Capacity Manual 1985, Special Report 209. Washington D.C.: Transportation Research Board, National Research Council.)

Table 4–23 Passenger-Car Equivalents on Extended General Multilane Highway Segments

Factor	Type of Terrain		
	Level	Rolling	Mountainous
E_T for Trucks	1.7	4.0	8.0
E_B for Buses	1.5	3.0	5.0
E_R for RVs	1.6	3.0	4.0

(*Source:* Highway Capacity Manual 1985, Special Report 209. Washington D.C.: Transportation Research Board, National Research Council.)

Table 4–24 Passenger-Car Equivalents for Typical Trucks (200 LB/HP)

Grade (%)	Length (miles)	Passenger-Car Equivalent, E_T Four-Lane Highways								Six-Lane Highways							
Percent Trucks		2	4	5	6	8	10	15	20	2	4	5	6	8	10	15	20
<1	All	2	2	2	2	2	2	2	2	2	2	2	2	2	2	2	2
1	0–½	2	2	2	2	2	2	2	2	2	2	2	2	2	2	2	2
	½–1	3	3	3	3	3	3	3	3	3	3	3	3	3	3	3	3
	≥ 1	4	3	3	3	3	3	3	3	4	3	3	3	3	3	3	3
2	0–¼	4	4	4	3	3	3	3	3	4	4	4	3	3	3	3	3
	¼–½	5	4	4	3	3	3	3	3	5	4	4	3	3	3	3	3
	½–¾	6	5	5	4	4	4	4	4	6	5	5	4	4	4	4	4
	¾–1½	7	6	6	5	4	4	4	4	7	5	5	5	4	4	4	4
	≥ 1½	8	6	6	6	5	5	4	4	8	6	6	5	4	4	4	4
3	0–¼	6	5	5	5	4	4	4	3	6	5	5	5	4	4	4	3
	¼–½	8	6	6	6	5	5	5	4	7	6	6	6	5	5	5	4
	½–1	9	7	7	6	5	5	5	5	9	7	7	6	5	5	5	5
	1–1½	9	7	7	7	6	6	5	5	9	7	7	6	5	5	5	5
	≥ 1½	10	7	7	7	6	6	5	5	10	7	7	6	5	5	5	5

Grade	Length of grade (mi)																
4	0–¼	4	4	4	4	5	6	6	7	4	4	4	4	5	6	6	7
	¼–½	5	5	5	5	6	7	7	9	5	5	5	5	6	7	7	10
	½–1	5	5	5	5	6	7	8	10	5	6	6	6	7	8	8	12
	≥1	6	6	6	7	8	9	9	11	6	7	8	8	9	9	9	13
5	0–¼	5	5	5	5	6	6	6	8	5	5	5	5	6	6	6	8
	¼–½	5	5	5	5	6	7	7	8	6	6	6	6	7	8	8	10
	½–1	7	7	7	7	8	9	10	12	8	8	8	8	10	11	11	12
	≥1	7	7	7	7	8	9	10	12	8	8	8	8	10	11	11	14
6	0–¼	5	5	5	5	6	7	7	9	6	6	6	6	7	7	7	9
	¼–½	6	6	6	6	7	8	8	11	7	7	7	7	8	9	9	13
	½–¾	6	6	7	7	8	9	9	11	7	7	7	7	8	9	9	13
	≥¾	8	8	8	8	9	10	10	13	9	9	9	9	11	12	12	17

NOTE: If a length of grade falls on boundary value, use the equivalent for the longer grade class. Any grade steeper than the percent stated must use the next higher grade category.

(*Source*: Highway Capacity Manual 1985, Special Report 209. Washington D.C.: Transportation Research Board, National Research Council.)

Table 4–25 Passenger-Car Equivalents for Heavy Trucks (300 LB/HP)

Grade (%)	Length (miles)	Passenger-Car Equivalent, E_T															
		Four-Lane Highways								Six-Lane Highways							
	Percent Trucks	2	4	5	6	8	10	15	20	2	4	5	6	8	10	15	20
<1	All	2	2	2	2	2	2	2	2	2	2	2	2	2	2	2	2
1	0–1/4	2	2	2	2	2	2	2	2	2	2	2	2	2	2	2	2
	1/4–1/2	3	3	3	3	3	3	3	3	3	3	3	3	3	3	3	3
	1/2–3/4	4	4	4	4	3	3	3	3	4	4	4	3	3	3	3	3
	3/4–1	5	4	4	4	3	3	3	3	5	4	4	4	3	3	3	3
	1–1½	6	5	5	5	4	4	4	3	6	5	5	4	4	4	3	3
	> 1½	7	5	5	5	4	4	4	3	7	5	5	5	4	4	3	3
2	0–1/4	4	4	4	3	3	3	3	3	4	4	4	3	3	3	3	3
	1/4–1/2	7	6	6	5	4	4	4	4	7	5	5	5	4	4	4	4
	1/2–3/4	8	6	6	5	5	4	4	4	8	6	6	6	5	5	4	4
	3/4–1	8	6	6	6	5	5	5	5	8	6	6	6	5	5	5	5
	1–1½	9	7	7	7	6	6	5	5	9	7	7	6	5	5	5	5
	> 1½	10	7	7	7	6	6	5	5	10	7	7	6	5	5	5	5

Grade (%)	Length of grade (mi)	2	4	5	6	8	10	15	20		2	4	5	6	8	10	15	20
3	0–¼	6	5	5	5	4	4	4	3		6	5	5	5	4	4	4	3
	¼–½	9	7	7	6	5	5	5	5		8	7	7	6	5	5	5	5
	½–¾	12	8	8	7	6	6	6	5		10	8	7	6	5	5	5	5
	¾–1	13	9	9	8	7	7	7	6		11	8	8	7	6	6	6	6
	>1	14	10	10	8	8	8	8	7		12	9	9	8	7	7	7	7
4	0–¼	7	5	5	5	4	4	4	3		7	5	5	4	4	4	4	3
	¼–½	12	8	8	8	6	6	6	5		10	8	8	7	6	6	6	5
	½–¾	13	9	9	9	7	7	7	6		11	9	9	8	7	7	7	6
	¾–1	15	10	10	10	8	8	8	7		12	10	9	8	8	8	8	7
	>1	17	12	12	10	9	9	9	8		13	10	10	9	9	9	8	8
5	0–¼	8	6	6	6	5	5	5	5		8	6	6	6	5	5	5	5
	¼–½	13	9	9	9	7	7	7	7		11	8	8	8	7	7	6	6
	½–¾	20	15	15	14	11	11	11	11		14	11	11	11	11	11	9	9
	>¾	22	17	17	16	13	13	13	11		17	14	14	13	13	13	12	11
6	0–¼	9	7	7	7	6	6	6	6		9	7	6	6	5	5	5	5
	¼–½	17	12	12	12	9	9	9	9		13	10	9	8	8	8	8	8
	>½	28	22	22	21	18	18	18	18		20	17	16	15	14	14	14	14

NOTE: If a length of grade falls on a boundary value, the equivalent corresponding to the longer grade category is used. Any grade steeper than the percent shown must use the next higher grade category.

(*Source:* Highway Capacity Manual 1985, Special Report 209. Washington D.C.: Transportation Research Board, National Research Council.)

Table 4–26 Passenger-Car Equivalents for Light Trucks (100 LB/HP)

| Grade (%) | Length (miles) | Passenger-Car Equivalent, E_T | | | | | | | | | | | | | | | |
| | | Four-Lane Highways | | | | | | | | Six-Lane Highways | | | | | | | |
	Percent Trucks	2	4	5	6	8	10	15	20	2	4	5	6	8	10	15	20
≤2	All	2	2	2	2	2	2	2	2	2	2	2	2	2	2	2	2
3	0–1/4	3	3	3	3	3	3	3	3	3	3	3	3	3	3	3	3
	1/4–1/2	4	4	4	3	3	3	3	3	4	4	4	3	3	3	3	3
	1/2–3/4	4	4	4	4	3	3	3	3	4	4	4	3	3	3	3	3
	3/4–1	5	4	4	4	4	3	3	3	5	4	4	4	3	3	3	3
	>1	6	5	5	5	4	4	4	3	6	5	5	4	4	4	3	3
4	0–1/4	4	4	4	3	3	3	3	3	5	4	4	4	3	3	3	3
	1/4–1/2	5	5	5	4	4	4	4	4	5	4	4	4	4	4	4	4
	1/2–1	6	5	5	5	4	4	4	4	6	5	5	4	4	4	4	4
	>1	7	6	6	5	4	4	4	4	7	5	5	5	4	4	4	4
5	0–1/4	6	5	5	5	4	4	4	3	6	5	5	5	4	4	4	3
	1/4–1	8	7	7	6	5	5	5	5	8	7	7	6	5	5	5	5
	>1	9	7	7	6	5	5	5	5	8	7	7	6	5	5	5	5
6	0–1/4	7	5	5	5	4	4	3	3	7	5	5	5	4	4	3	3
	1/4–1	9	7	7	6	5	5	5	5	8	7	7	6	5	5	5	5
	>1	9	7	7	7	6	6	5	5	9	7	7	6	5	5	5	5

NOTE: If a length of grade falls on a boundary value, use the equivalent for the longer grade category. Any grade steeper than the percent shown must use the next higher grade category.

(*Source:* Highway Capacity Manual 1985, Special Report 209. Washington D.C.: Transportation Research Board, National Research Council.)

Table 4–27 Passenger-Car Equivalents for Recreational Vehicles

Grade (%)	Length (miles)	Four-Lane Highways								Six-Lane Highways							
Percent RVs		2	4	5	6	8	10	15	20	2	4	5	6	8	10	15	20
< 2	All	2	2	2	2	2	2	2	2	2	2	2	2	2	2	2	2
3	0–½	3	2	2	2	2	2	2	2	2	2	2	2	2	2	2	2
	≥ ½	4	3	3	3	3	3	3	3	4	3	3	3	3	3	3	3
4	0–¼	3	2	2	2	2	2	2	2	3	2	2	2	2	2	2	2
	¼–¾	4	3	3	3	3	3	3	3	4	3	3	3	3	3	3	3
	≥ ¾	5	4	4	4	3	3	3	3	4	4	4	4	3	3	3	3
5	0–¼	4	3	3	3	3	3	3	3	4	3	3	3	2	2	2	2
	¼–¾	5	4	4	4	4	4	4	4	5	4	4	4	4	4	4	4
	≥ ¾	6	5	4	4	4	4	4	4	5	5	4	4	4	4	4	4
6	0–¼	5	4	4	4	3	3	3	3	5	4	4	3	3	3	3	3
	¼–¾	6	5	5	4	4	4	4	4	6	4	4	4	4	4	4	4
	≥ ¾	7	6	6	6	5	5	5	5	6	5	5	5	4	4	4	4

The E_R column group heading spans the Four-Lane and Six-Lane Highways sections.

NOTE: If a length of grade falls on a boundary condition, the equivalent from the longer grade class is used. Any grade steeper than the percent shown must use the next higher grade category.

(*Source:* Highway Capacity Manual 1985, Special Report 209. Washington D.C.: Transportation Research Board, National Research Council.)

Table 4–28 Passenger-Car Equivalents for Buses

Grade	E_B
0–3	1.6
4[a]	1.6
5[a]	3.0
6[a]	5.5

[a]Use generally restricted to grades more than ¼ mile long.

The highest ideal volume under these *above* conditions is 2,800 pcph, total in both directions. Directional splits influence capacity as shown in Table 4–32.

Tables 4–33 through 4–42 supply appropriate data to perform all two-lane, two-way capacity calculations. The computational relationships are as follows:

$$V_c = \frac{V}{PHF}$$

where V is peak fifteen-minute volumes, both directions, and PHF is appropriately chosen from Table 4–35

$$SF_i = 2{,}800 \times (v/c) \times f_d \times f_w \times f_q \times f_{hv}$$

where SF is for total of both directions, and

f_d = factor for directional distribution
f_w = lane wifth and lateral clearance adjustment
f_q = a new factor for the operational effect of grades on traffic flow

$$f_q = \frac{1}{[1 + P_p I_p]}$$

where

P_p = proportion of passenger cars in the traffic stream, expressed as a decimal
I_p = impedance factor for passenger cars, expressed as $I_p = 0.02\,(E - E_o)$

where, in turn,

E = base passenger-car equivalent for a given percent grade, length of grade, and speed, selected from Table 4–41
E_o = base passenger car equivalent for 0 percent grade and a given speed, also selected from Table 4–41.

Table 4–29 Adjustment Factor for the Effect of Trucks, Buses, or Recreational Vehicles in the Traffic Stream

PCE E_T E_R E_B	Adjustment Factor, f_{hv} Percentage of Trucks, P_T; RVs, P_R; or Buses, P_B														
	1	2	3	4	5	6	7	8	9	10	12	14	16	18	20
2	0.99	0.98	0.97	0.96	0.95	0.94	0.93	0.93	0.92	0.91	0.89	0.88	0.86	0.85	0.83
3	0.98	0.96	0.94	0.93	0.91	0.89	0.88	0.86	0.85	0.83	0.81	0.78	0.76	0.74	0.71
4	0.97	0.94	0.92	0.89	0.87	0.85	0.83	0.81	0.79	0.77	0.74	0.70	0.68	0.65	0.63
5	0.96	0.93	0.89	0.86	0.83	0.81	0.78	0.76	0.74	0.71	0.68	0.64	0.61	0.58	0.56
6	0.95	0.91	0.87	0.83	0.80	0.77	0.74	0.71	0.69	0.67	0.63	0.59	0.56	0.53	0.50
7	0.94	0.89	0.85	0.81	0.77	0.74	0.70	0.68	0.65	0.63	0.58	0.54	0.51	0.48	0.45
8	0.93	0.88	0.83	0.78	0.74	0.70	0.67	0.64	0.61	0.59	0.54	0.51	0.47	0.44	0.42
9	0.93	0.86	0.81	0.76	0.71	0.68	0.64	0.61	0.58	0.56	0.51	0.47	0.44	0.41	0.38
10	0.92	0.85	0.79	0.74	0.69	0.65	0.61	0.58	0.55	0.53	0.48	0.44	0.41	0.38	0.36
11	0.91	0.83	0.77	0.71	0.67	0.63	0.59	0.56	0.53	0.50	0.45	0.42	0.38	0.36	0.33
12	0.90	0.82	0.75	0.69	0.65	0.60	0.57	0.53	0.50	0.48	0.43	0.39	0.36	0.34	0.31
13	0.89	0.81	0.74	0.68	0.63	0.58	0.54	0.51	0.48	0.45	0.41	0.37	0.34	0.32	0.29
14	0.88	0.79	0.72	0.66	0.61	0.56	0.52	0.49	0.46	0.43	0.39	0.35	0.32	0.30	0.28
15	0.88	0.78	0.70	0.64	0.59	0.54	0.51	0.47	0.44	0.42	0.37	0.34	0.31	0.28	0.26
16	0.87	0.77	0.69	0.63	0.57	0.53	0.49	0.45	0.43	0.40	0.36	0.32	0.29	0.27	0.25
17	0.86	0.76	0.68	0.61	0.56	0.51	0.47	0.44	0.41	0.38	0.34	0.31	0.28	0.26	0.24
18	0.85	0.75	0.66	0.60	0.54	0.49	0.46	0.42	0.40	0.37	0.33	0.30	0.27	0.25	0.23
19	0.85	0.74	0.65	0.58	0.53	0.48	0.44	0.41	0.38	0.36	0.32	0.28	0.26	0.24	0.22
20	0.84	0.72	0.64	0.57	0.51	0.47	0.42	0.40	0.37	0.34	0.30	0.27	0.25	0.23	0.21
21	0.83	0.71	0.63	0.56	0.50	0.45	0.41	0.38	0.36	0.33	0.29	0.26	0.24	0.22	0.20
22	0.83	0.70	0.61	0.54	0.49	0.44	0.40	0.37	0.35	0.32	0.28	0.25	0.23	0.21	0.19
23	0.82	0.69	0.60	0.53	0.48	0.43	0.39	0.36	0.34	0.31	0.27	0.25	0.22	0.20	0.19
24	0.81	0.68	0.59	0.52	0.47	0.42	0.38	0.35	0.33	0.30	0.27	0.24	0.21	0.19	0.18
25	0.80	0.67	0.58	0.51	0.46	0.41	0.37	0.34	0.32	0.29	0.26	0.23	0.20	0.18	0.17

(*Source:* Highway Capacity Manual 1985, Special Report 209. Washington D.C.: Transportation Research Board, National Research Council.)

Table 4–30 Adjustment Factor for Type of Multilane Highway and Development Environment, f_E

Type	Divided	Undivided
Rural	1.00	0.95
Suburban	0.90	0.80

(*Source:* Highway Capacity Manual 1985, Special Report 209. Washington D.C.: Transportation Research Board, National Research Council.)

Table 4–31 Adjustment Factor for Driver Population

Driver Population	Factor, f_p
Commuter, or other regular users	1.00
Recreational, or other nonregular uses	0.75–0.90

(*Source:* Highway Capacity Manual 1985, Special Report 209. Washington D.C.: Transportation Research Board, National Research Council.)

Table 4–32 Influence of Directional Splits on Capacity

Directional Split	Total Capacity, pcph	Ratio of Capacity to Ideal Capacity
50/50	2,800	1.00
60/40	2,650	0.94
70/30	2,500	0.89
80/20	2,300	0.83
90/10	2,100	0.75
100/0	2,000	0.71

(*Source:* Highway Capacity Manual 1985, Special Report 209. Washington D.C.: Transportation Research Board, National Research Council.)

Table 4–33 Level-of-Service Criteria for General Two-Lane Highway Segments

			v/c Ratio[a]					
			Level Terrain					
				Percent No-Passing Zones				
LOS	Percent Time Delay	Avg[b] Speed	0	20	40	60	80	100
A	≤ 30	≥ 58	0.15	0.12	0.09	0.07	0.05	0.04
B	≤ 45	≥ 55	0.27	0.24	0.21	0.19	0.17	0.16
C	≤ 60	≥ 52	0.43	0.39	0.36	0.34	0.33	0.32
D	≤ 75	≥ 50	0.64	0.62	0.60	0.59	0.58	0.57
E	> 75	≥ 45	1.00	1.00	1.00	1.00	1.00	1.00
F	100	45	—	—	—	—	—	—
			Rolling Terrain					
				Percent No-Passing Zones				
LOS	Percent Time Delay	Avg[b] Speed	0	20	40	60	80	100
A	≤ 30	≥ 57	0.15	0.10	0.07	0.05	0.04	0.03
B	≤ 45	≥ 54	0.26	0.23	0.19	0.17	0.15	0.13
C	≤ 60	≥ 51	0.42	0.39	0.35	0.32	0.30	0.28
D	≤ 75	≥ 49	0.62	0.57	0.52	0.48	0.46	0.43
E	> 75	≥ 40	0.97	0.94	0.92	0.91	0.90	0.90
F	100	< 40	—	—	—	—	—	—
			Mountainous Terrain					
				Percent No-Passing Zones				
LOS	Percent Time Delay	Avg[b] Speed	0	20	40	60	80	100
A	≤ 30	≥ 56	0.14	0.09	0.07	0.04	0.02	0.01
B	≤ 45	≥ 54	0.25	0.20	0.16	0.13	0.12	0.10
C	≤ 60	≥ 49	0.39	0.33	0.28	0.23	0.20	0.16
D	≤ 75	≥ 45	0.58	0.50	0.45	0.40	0.37	0.33
E	> 75	≥ 35	0.91	0.87	0.84	0.82	0.80	0.78
F	100	< 35	—	—	—	—	—	—

[a]Ratio of flow rate to an ideal capacity of 2,800 pcph in both directions.
[b]Average travel speed of all vehicles (in mph) for highways with design speed ≥ 60 mph; for highways with lower design speeds, reduce speed by 4 mph for each 10-mph reduction in design speed below 60 mph; assumes that speed is not restricted to lower values by regulation.
(*Source:* Highway Capacity Manual 1985, Special Report 209. Washington D.C.: Transportation Research Board, National Research Council.)

Table 4–34 Level-of-Service Criteria for Specific Grades

Level of Service	Average Upgrade Speed (mph)
A	≥ 55
B	≥ 50
C	≥ 45
D	≥ 40
E	≥ 25–40[a]
F	< 25–40[a]

[a]The exact speed at which capacity occurs varies with the percentage and length of grade, traffic composition, and volume; computational procedures are provided to find this value.
(*Source:* Highway Capacity Manual 1985, Special Report 209. Washington D.C.: Transportation Research Board, National Research Council.)

Table 4–35 Peak-Hour Factors for Two-Lane Highways Based on Random Flow

A. Level-of-Service Determinations

Total Two-Way Hourly Volume (VPH)	Peak-Hour Factor (PHF)	Total Two-way Hourly Volume (VPH)	Peak-Hour Factor (PHF)
100	0.83	1,000	0.93
200	0.87	1,100	0.94
300	0.90	1,200	0.94
400	0.91	1,300	0.94
500	0.91	1,400	0.94
600	0.92	1,500	0.95
700	0.92	1,600	0.95
800	0.93	1,700	0.95
900	0.93	1,800	0.95
		≥ 1,900	0.96

B. Service Flow-Rate Determinations

Level of service	A	B	C	D	E
Peak-hour factor	0.91	0.92	0.94	0.95	1.00

(*Source:* Highway Capacity Manual 1985, Special Report 209. Washington D.C.: Transportation Research Board, National Research Council.)

Table 4–36 Adjustment Factors for Directional Distribution on General Terrain Sections

Directional distribution	100/0	90/10	80/20	70/30	60/40	50/50
Adjustment factor, f_d	0.71	0.75	0.83	0.89	0.94	1.00

(*Source:* Highway Capacity Manual 1985, Special Report 209. Washington D.C.: Transportation Research Board, National Research Council.)

Table 4–37 Adjustment Factors for the Combined Effect of Narrow Lanes and Restricted Shoulder Width, f_w

Usable[a] Shoulder Width (Feet)	12-foot Lanes		11-foot Lanes		10-foot Lanes		9-foot Lanes	
	LOS A–D	LOS[b] E	LOS A–D	LOS[b] E	LOS A–D	LOS[b] E	LOS A–D	LOS[b] E
0	0.70	0.88	0.65	0.82	0.58	0.75	0.49	0.66
2	0.81	0.93	0.75	0.88	0.68	0.81	0.57	0.70
4	0.92	0.97	0.85	0.92	0.77	0.85	0.65	0.74
≥ 6	1.00	1.00	0.93	0.94	0.84	0.87	0.70	0.76

[a]Where shoulder width is different on each side of the roadway, use the average shoulder width.
[b]Factor applies for all speeds less than 45 mph.
(*Source:* Highway Capacity Manual 1985, Special Report 209. Washington D.C.: Transportation Research Board, National Research Council.)

Table 4-38 Average Passenger-Car Equivalents for Trucks, RVs, and Buses on Two-Lane Highways Over General Terrain Segments

Vehicle Type	Level of Service	Type of Terrain		
		Level	Rolling	Mountainous
Trucks, E_T	A	2.0	4.0	7.0
	B and C	2.2	5.0	10.0
	D and E	2.0	5.0	12.0
RVs, E_R	A	2.2	3.2	5.0
	B and C	2.5	3.9	5.2
	D and E	1.6	3.3	5.2
Buses, E_B	A	1.8	3.0	5.7
	B and C	2.0	3.4	6.0
	D and E	1.6	2.9	6.5

(*Source:* Highway Capacity Manual 1985, Special Report 209. Washington D.C.: Transportation Research Board, National Research Council.)

The heavy-vehicle factor is f_{HV}, computed as follows:

$$f_{HV} = 1/[1 + P_{HV}(E_{HV} - 1)]$$

where

f_{HV} = adjustment factor for the presence of heavy vehicles in the upgrade traffic stream

P_{HV} = total proportion of heavy vehicles (trucks + RVs + buses) in the upgrade traffic stream

E_{HV} = passenger-car equivalent for specific mix of heavy vehicles present in the upgrade traffic stream, computed as:

$$E_{HV} = 1 + (0.25 + P_{T/HV})(E - 1)$$

where

$P_{T/HV}$ = proportion of trucks among heavy vehicles; that is, the proportion of trucks in the traffic stream divided by the total proportion of heavy vehicles in the traffic stream

E = base passenger-car equivalent for a given percent grade, length of grade, and speed, selected from Table 4-41

Table 4–39 Values of v/c Ratio[a] vs. Speed, Percent Grade, and Percent No Passing Zones for Specific Grades

Percent Grade	Average Upgrade Speed (MPH)	Percent No-Passing Zones					
		0	20	40	60	80	100
3	55	0.27	0.23	0.19	0.17	0.14	0.12
	52.5	0.42	0.38	0.33	0.31	0.29	0.27
	50	0.64	0.59	0.55	0.52	0.49	0.47
	45	1.00	0.95	0.91	0.88	0.86	0.84
	42.5	1.00	0.98	0.97	0.96	0.95	0.94
	40	1.00	1.00	1.00	1.00	1.00	1.00
4	55	0.25	0.21	0.18	0.16	0.13	0.11
	52.5	0.40	0.36	0.31	0.29	0.27	0.25
	50	0.61	0.56	0.52	0.49	0.47	0.45
	45	0.97	0.92	0.88	0.85	0.83	0.81
	42.5	0.98	0.96	0.95	0.94	0.93	0.92
	40	1.00	1.00	1.00	1.00	1.00	1.00
5	55	0.25	0.21	0.16	0.12	0.08	0.04
	52.5	0.40	0.34	0.27	0.22	0.18	0.13
	50	0.61	0.51	0.42	0.34	0.28	0.22
	45	0.97	0.84	0.71	0.60	0.52	0.46
	42.5	0.98	0.87	0.78	0.70	0.63	0.56
	40	0.99	0.89	0.81	0.74	0.69	0.63
	35	1.00	0.92	0.87	0.82	0.79	0.76
	30	1.00	0.95	0.92	0.90	0.88	0.86
6	55	0.12	0.09	0.07	0.05	0.04	0.02
	52.5	0.27	0.22	0.17	0.14	0.12	0.08
	50	0.49	0.39	0.32	0.26	0.22	0.17
	45	0.89	0.75	0.63	0.53	0.46	0.41
	42.5	0.93	0.81	0.73	0.65	0.59	0.52
	40	0.97	0.86	0.79	0.72	0.67	0.61
	35	1.00	0.92	0.87	0.82	0.79	0.76
	30	1.00	0.95	0.92	0.90	0.88	0.86
7	55	0.00	0.00	0.00	0.00	0.00	0.00
	52.5	0.13	0.10	0.08	0.07	0.05	0.04
	50	0.34	0.27	0.22	0.18	0.15	0.12
	45	0.77	0.65	0.55	0.46	0.40	0.35
	42.5	0.86	0.75	0.67	0.60	0.54	0.48
	40	0.93	0.83	0.75	0.69	0.64	0.59
	35	1.00	0.92	0.87	0.82	0.79	0.76
	30	1.00	0.95	0.92	0.90	0.88	0.86

[a]Ratio of flow rate to ideal capacity of 2,800 pcph, assuming passenger-car operation is unaffected by grade.
NOTE: Interpolate for intermediate values of "Percent No Passing Zone"; round "Percent Grade" to the next higher integer value.
(*Source:* Highway Capacity Manual 1985, Special Report 209. Washington D.C.: Transportation Research Board, National Research Council.)

Table 4–40   Adjustment Factor for Directional Distribution of Specific Grades, f_d

Directional[a] Distribution	Adjustment Factor	Directional[a] Distribution	Adjustment Factor
100/0	0.58	40/60	1.20
90/10	0.64	30/70	1.50
80/20	0.70	20/80	1.93
70/30	0.78	10/90	2.51
60/40	0.87	0/100	3.32
50/50	1.00		

[a]Upgrade/downgrade
(*Source:* Highway Capacity Manual 1985, Special Report 209. Washington D.C.: Transportation Research Board, National Research Council.)

Table 4–41   Passenger-Car Equivalents for Specific Grades on Two-Lane Rural Highways, E and E_o

Grade (%)	Length of Grade (miles)	Average Upgrade Speed (mph)					
		55.0	52.5	50.0	45.0	40.0	30.0
0	All	2.1	1.8	1.6	1.4	1.3	1.3
3	¼	2.9	2.3	2.0	1.7	1.6	1.5
	½	3.7	2.9	2.4	2.0	1.8	1.7
	¾	4.8	3.6	2.9	2.3	2.0	1.9
	1	6.5	4.6	3.5	2.6	2.3	2.1
	1½	11.2	6.6	5.1	3.4	2.9	2.5
	2	19.8	9.3	6.7	4.6	3.7	2.9
	3	71.0	21.0	10.8	7.3	5.6	3.8
	4	a	48.0	20.5	11.3	7.7	4.9
4	¼	3.2	2.5	2.2	1.8	1.7	1.6
	½	4.4	3.4	2.8	2.2	2.0	1.9
	¾	6.3	4.4	3.5	2.7	2.3	2.1
	1	9.6	6.3	4.5	3.2	2.7	2.4
	1½	19.5	10.3	7.4	4.7	3.8	3.1
	2	43.0	16.1	10.8	6.9	5.3	3.8
	3	a	48.0	20.0	12.5	9.0	5.5
	4	a	a	51.0	22.8	13.8	7.4

Table 4—41   (continued)

Grade (%)	Length of Grade (miles)	Average Upgrade Speed (mph)					
		55.0	52.5	50.0	45.0	40.0	30.0
5	¼	3.6	2.8	2.3	2.0	1.8	1.7
	½	5.4	3.9	3.2	2.5	2.2	2.0
	¾	8.3	5.7	4.3	3.1	2.7	2.4
	1	14.1	8.4	5.9	4.0	3.3	2.8
	1½	34.0	16.0	10.8	6.3	4.9	3.8
	2	91.0	28.3	17.4	10.2	7.5	4.8
	3	a	a	37.0	22.0	14.6	7.8
	4	a	a	a	55.0	25.0	11.5
6	¼	4.0	3.1	2.5	2.1	1.9	1.8
	½	6.5	4.8	3.7	2.8	2.4	2.2
	¾	11.0	7.2	5.2	3.7	3.1	2.7
	1	20.4	11.7	7.8	4.9	4.0	3.3
	1½	60.0	25.2	16.0	8.5	6.4	4.7
	2	a	50.0	28.2	15.3	10.7	6.3
	3	a	a	70.0	38.0	23.9	11.3
	4	a	a	a	90.0	45.0	18.1
7	¼	4.5	3.4	2.7	2.2	2.0	1.9
	½	7.9	5.7	4.2	3.2	2.7	2.4
	¾	14.5	9.1	6.3	4.3	3.6	3.0
	1	31.4	16.0	10.0	6.1	4.8	3.8
	1½	a	39.5	23.5	11.5	8.4	5.8
	2	a	88.0	46.0	22.8	15.4	8.2
	3	a	a	a	66.0	38.5	16.1
	4	a	a	a	a	a	28.0

[a]Speed not attainable on grade specified.
NOTE: Round "Percent Grade" to next higher integer value.
(*Source:* Highway Capacity Manual 1985, Special Report 209. Washington D.C.: Transportation Research Board, National Research Council.)

Table 4–42 Maximum AADT's* vs. Level of Service and Type of Terrain for Two-Lane Rural Highways

	Level of Service				
K-Factor	A	B	C	D	E
	Level Terrain				
0.10	2,400	4,800	7,900	13.500	22,900
0.11	2,200	4,400	7,200	12,200	20,800
0.12	2,000	4,000	6,600	11,200	19,000
0.13	1,900	3,700	6,100	10,400	17,600
0.14	1,700	3.400	5,700	9,600	16,300
0.15	1,600	3,200	5,300	9,000	15,200
	Rolling Terrain				
0.10	1,100	2,800	5,200	8,000	14,800
0.11	1,000	2,500	4,700	7,200	13,500
0.12	900	2,300	4,400	6,600	12,300
0.13	900	2,100	4,000	6,100	11,400
0.14	800	2,000	3,700	5,700	10,600
0.15	700	1,800	3,500	5,300	9,900
	Mountainous Terrain				
0.10	500	1,300	2,400	3,700	8,100
0.11	400	1,200	2,200	3,400	7,300
0.12	400	1,100	2,000	3,100	6,700
0.13	400	1,000	1,800	2,900	6,200
0.14	300	900	1,700	2,700	5,800
0.15	300	900	1,600	2,500	5,400

*AADT is the Average Annual Daily Traffic, which is the total yearly volume divided by the number of days in the year.
NOTE: All values rounded to the nearest 100 vpd. Assumed conditions include 60/40 directional split, 14 percent trucks, 4 percent RV's, no buses, and appropriate PHF values from Table 8–3. For level terrain, 20 percent no passing zones were assumed; for rolling terrain, 40 percent no passing zones; for mountainous terrain, 60 percent no passing zones.
(*Source:* Highway Capacity Manual 1985, Special Report 209. Washington D.C.: Transportation Research Board, National Research Council.)

Procedures As before the general approach will be to compute service flow rates for each level of service and compare these values with the existing flow rate on the facility. This is done by using the following equation.

$$SF_i = 2,800 \times (V/C)_i \times f_d \times f_w \times f_{HV}$$

where all terms are as previously defined. The following computational steps are used.

1. Summarize all input data on traffic and roadway conditions, including:
   a. Existing or forecast peak hour volume, in vph.
   b. Peak hour factor, PHF.
   c. Traffic composition (percent trucks, percent RVs, percent buses).
   d. Directional distribution of traffic.
   e. Terrain type.
   f. Lane and usable shoulder widths, in feet.
   g. Design speed, in miles per hour.
2. Select appropriate values of the following factors for each LOS from the Tables 4–33 through 4–42:
   a. The V/C ratio.
   b. The directional distribution factor, f_d.
   c. Passenger-car equivalents, E_T, E_R, and E_B, for trucks, RVs, and buses.
3. Compute the heavy-vehicle factor, f_{HV}, for each LOS from:

$$f_{HV} = 1/[1 + P_T(E_T - 1) + P_R(E_R - 1) + P_B(E_B - 1)]$$

4. Compute the service flow rate, SF, for each LOS from:

$$SF_i = 2,800 \times (V/C)_i \times f_d \times f_w \times f_{HV}$$

5. Convert the existing or forecast volume to an equivalent flow rate, as follows:

$$v = V/PHF$$

6. Compare the actual flow rate of step 5 with the service flow rate of step 4 to determine the level of service.

Analysis of Sections with Specific Grades

The operational analysis of specific grades is somewhat similar to the procedure for general terrain segments. The level of service for the upgrade direction is required, and is found by comparing an actual two-way flow rate with the service flow rates for the various levels of service. The procedure is as follows:

1. Summarize all required input data on traffic and roadway conditions, including:
   a. Existing or forecast peak hour volume, in vph.
   b. Peak-hour factor, PHF.
   c. Traffic composition (percent trucks, percent RVs, percent buses, percent passenger cars).

    d. Directional distribution of traffic.

    e. Percent grade.

    f. Percent no-passing zones.

    g. Length of grade, in miles.

    h. Lane and usable shoulder width, in feet.

    i. Design speed, in miles per hour.

2. Select values of the following factors from the indicated Tables 4–33 through 4–42 for the following average speeds: 55 mph (LOS *A*), 52.5 mph, 50 mph (LOS *B*), 45 mph (LOS *C*), 40 mph (LOS *D*), and 30 mph. This range of speeds will allow the plotting of a service flow rate versus speed curve to find capacity and the speed at capacity.

    a. The *V/C* ratio.

    b. The directional distribution factor, f_d.

    c. The lane and shoulder width factor, f_w.

    d. The passenger-car equivalent, *E*, for the percent and length of grade, from Table 4–41.

3. Compute the grade factor, f_g, as follows:

$$f_g = 1/[1 + P_p I_p]$$

$$I_p = 0.02(E - E_o)$$

where all values are as previously defined.

4. Compute the heavy-vehicle factor, f_{HV}, for each of the speeds noted in step 2 as follows:

$$f_{HV} = 1/[1 + P_{HV}(E_{HV} - 1)]$$

$$E_{HV} = 1 + (0.25 + P_{T/HV})(E - 1)$$

$$P_{T/HV} = P_T/[P_T + P_R + P_B]$$

where all values are as previously defined.

5. Compute the service flow rate, SF, for each of the speeds noted in step 2 as follows:

$$SF_i = 2,800 \times (V/C)_i \times f_d \times f_w \times f_g \times f_{HV}$$

6. Plot each of the service flow rates versus speeds resulting from the computations of steps 2 through 5 on the grid included in Figure 4–24. The curve for speed at capacity versus flow rate at capacity already exists on this grid.

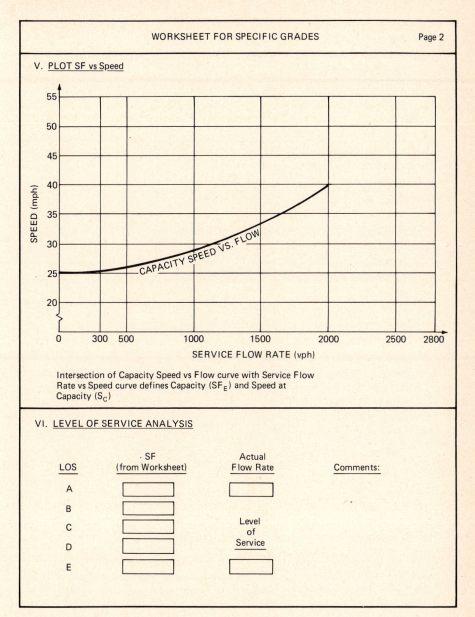

Figure 4–24 Worksheet for Operational Analysis of Specific Grades on Two-Lane Highways

(*Source:* Highway Capacity Manual 1985, Special Report 209. Washington D.C.: Transportation Research Board, National Research Council.)

7. Find the speed at capacity and the service flow rate at capacity from the intersection of the two curves on the plot of step 6.
8. Summarize the service flow rates for each level of service in the level of service analysis section.
9. Convert the actual or forecast volume to a flow rate, as follows:

$$v = V/PHF$$

10. Compare the actual flow rate of step 9 with the service flow rates of step 8 to determine the level of service.

Example

1. Description. A segment of rural two-lane highway has the following characteristics:
   a. Roadway characteristics—70-mph design speed; 12-foot lanes; 4-foot paved shoulders; level terrain; 0 percent no-passing zones; length = 5 miles.
   b. Traffic characteristics—60/40 directional split; 10 percent trucks; 5 percent recreational vehicles; 1 percent buses; 84 percent passenger cars.
   What is the capacity of the section? What is the maximum flow rate that can be accommodated at level of service *C*?
2. Solution. The solution to this problem is found by computing the service flow rates for levels of service *C* and *E* (capacity), using the following equation:

$$SF_i = 2,800 \times (V/C)_i \times f_d \times f_w \times f_{HV}$$

where

$$f_{HV} = 1/[1 + P_T(E_T - 1) + P_R(E_R - 1) + P_B(E_B - 1)]$$

The following values are used in the computations.

$(V/C)_c$ = 0.43 (Table 4–33, level terrain 0 percent no-passing zones, LOS *C*)
$(V/C)_E$ = 1.00 (Table 4–33, level terrain, 0 percent no-passing zones, LOS *E*)
f_d = 0.94 (Table 4–36, 70/30 split)
f_w = 0.92 (Table 4–37, 12-foot lanes, > 6-foot shoulders)
E_T = 2.2 for LOS *C*, 2.0 for LOS *E* (Table 4–38, level terrain)
E_R = 2.5 for LOS *C*, 1.6 for LOS *E* (Table 4–38, level terrain)
E_B = 2.0 for LOS *C*, 1.6 for LOS *E* (Table 4–38, level terrain)
P_T = 0.10
P_R = 0.05
P_B = 0.01

Therefore:

$$f_{HV}(\text{LOS } C) = 1/[1 + 0.10(2.2 - 1) + 0.05(2.5 - 1) + 0.01(2.0 - 1)]$$
$$= 0.83$$
$$f_{HV}(\text{LOS } E) = 1/[1 + 0.10(2.0 - 1) + 0.05(1.6 - 1) + 0.01(2.0 - 1)]$$
$$= 0.88$$

and

$$SF_C = 2,800 \times 0.43 \times 0.94 \times 0.92 \times 0.83 = 864 \text{ vph}$$
$$SF_E = 2,800 \times 1.00 \times 0.94 \times 0.92 \times 0.88 = 2,130 \text{ vph}$$

The above resulting computations indicate the highway will have an expected capacity of 2,130 vph, total in both directions, and can accommodate a flow rate of up to 864 vph at level of service *C*.

Interrupted-Flow Capacity and Level of Service

Level of service and capacity are also heavily involved in the analysis of intersections. This section will confine itself to the analysis of signalized intersections, and illustrate the newer capacity analysis and computational techniques forthcoming in the *1985 Highway Capacity Manual.*[4]

It is important to note that in the analysis of signalized intersections, both the capacity and the level of service must be analyzed separately and evaluated to yield the required knowledge about an intersection's operating characteristics.

Capacity analysis of intersection requires computation of *V/C* ratios for the intersection as a whole, and for individual movements within the intersection. The *V/C* ratio is the actual or projected rate of flow on an approach or designated group of lanes during a peak fifteen-minute interval divided by the capacity of the approach or designated group of lanes. Level of service is based upon the average stopped delay per vehicle for various movements within the intersection. While *V/C* affects delay, there are other parameters that more strongly affect it, such as the quality of progression and additional characteristics associated with traffic signal operations. To form a basis for analysis, the following briefly discusses traffic signal types and operating parameters.

Traffic Signals

Traffic signals allocate time in a variety of ways. The basic terminology of traffic signals is described here with a brief discussion of their impact on capacity.

---

[4]The tables and computational techniques in the following discussion of signalized intersection capacity were taken from the final draft copy of Chapter 9 of the forthcoming *1985 Highway Capacity Manual,* to be published as *Transportation Research Board Special Report 209.* Some of the discussion pertaining to intersection capacity was taken verbatim from Chapter 9 to preserve accuracy and appropriate emphasis on components of the revised intersection capacity calculation procedures. The author is indebted to the Transportation Research Board for permission to use this information.

The following terms are commonly used in traffic signal operation.

Cycle—any complete sequence of signal indications.

Cycle length—the total time for the signal to complete one cycle, stated in seconds, and given the symbol C.

Phase—the part of a cycle allocated to any combination of traffic movements receiving the right-of-way simultaneously during one or more intervals. Examples of two, three and four phase signal operations are shown in Figure 4–25.

Interval—a period of time during which all signal indications remain constant.

Change interval—the "yellow" plus "all red" intervals that occur between phases to provide for clearance of the intersection before conflicting movements are released; stated in seconds, and given the symbol Y.

Green time—the time within a given phase during which the "green" indication is shown; stated in seconds, and given the symbol G_i (for phase i).

Lost time—time during which the intersection is not effectively used by any movement; these times occur during the change interval (when the intersection is cleared), and at the beginning of each phase as the first few cars in a standing queue experience start-up delays.

Effective green time—the time during a given phase that is effectively available to the permitted movements; this is generally taken to be the green time plus the change interval minus the lost time for the designated phase; stated in seconds, and given the symbol g_i (for phase i).

Green ratio—the ratio of effective green time to the cycle length; given the symbol g_i/C (for phase i).

Effective red—the time during which a given movement or set of movements is effectively not permitted to move; stated in seconds, it is the cycle length minus the effective green time for a specified phase; given the symbol r_i.

Traffic signals may operate in three basic modes, depending upon the type of control equipment used.

1. *Pretimed operation.* Here the cycle length, phases, green times, and change intervals are all preset. The signal continually rotates through this defined cycle. Each cycle is the same, with the cycle length and phases constant. Depending on the equipment available, several preset timing patterns may be used, each being implemented automatically at fixed times of the day.

2. *Semi actuated operation.* In semiactuated operation, the designated main street has a "green" indication at all times until detectors on the side street determine that a vehicle or vehicles have arrived on one or both of the minor approaches. The signal then provides a "green" phase for the side street, after an appropriate change interval, which is retained until all vehicles are served, or until a preset maximum side-street green is reached. In this type of operation, the cycle length and green times may vary from

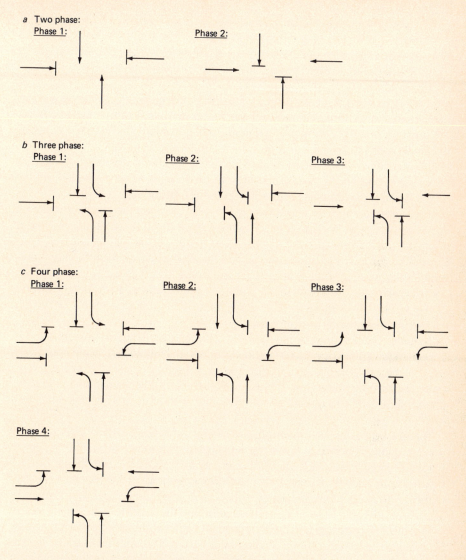

Figure 4–25 Examples of Intersection Phasing

cycle to cycle in response to demand. Because the green is always on the main street unless needed by side-street vehicles, side-street green times are virtually fully utilized, while all "excess" green time is allocated to the main street.

3. *Fully actuated operation.* In fully actuated operation, all signal phases are controlled by detector actuations. In general minimum and maximum

green times are specified for each phase, as is the phase sequence. In this form of control, cycle lengths and green times may vary considerably in response to demand. Certain phases in the cycle may be optional, and could be skipped entirely if no demand were sensed by detectors.

Many signal systems are currently controlled by computers. In such systems, the individual intersections generally operate under pretimed control, with the phasing plan and signal coordination being selected and controlled by the computer. Here, the computer serves as a master or supervisory controller.

The manner in which turns are accomodated also has a significant impact on intersection operations. Signal phasing can provide for either *protected* or *permitted* turning movements, defined as in the following.

A *permitted* turning movement is made through a conflicting pedestrian or opposing vehicle flow. Thus a left-turn movement made at the same time as the opposing through movement is considered to be "permitted," as is a right-turn movement made at the same time as pedestrian crossing in a conflicting crosswalk.

Protected turns are those made without these conflicts, such as turns made during an exclusive left-turn phase or a right-turn phase during which conflicting pedestrian movements are prohibited.

Permitted turns experience the friction of selecting and passing through gaps in a conflicting vehicle or pedestrian flow. A single permitted turn often consumes more of the available green time than a single protected turn. Either permitted or protected turning phases may be more "efficient" in a given situation, depending upon the turning and opposing volumes, intersection geometry, and other factors.

The preceding discussion emphasizes the fact that the capacity of an intersection is highly dependent upon the signalization present. Given the range of potential signal control schemes, this capacity is far more variable than for other types of facilities, where capacity is mainly dependent upon the geometric design of the roadway. In effect signalization that can be changed frequently and quickly allows considerable latitude in the management of the capacity of the intersection.

The capacity of designated lanes or groups of lanes within an approach may also be evaluated and determined as discussed herein. This may be done to isolate lanes serving a particular movement or movements, such as an exclusive right- or left-turn lane. Lanes designated for separate analysis are referred to as "lane groups." The procedure herein contains guidelines for when and how separate lane groups should be designated in an approach.

The capacity of a signalized intersection is based on the concept of saturation flow and saturation flow rates. *Saturation flow rate* is defined as the maximum rate of flow that can pass through a given intersection approach or lane group under prevailing traffic and roadway conditions—assuming that the approach or lane group had 100 percent of real time available as effective green time. Saturation flow rate is given the symbol s, and is expressed in units of vehicles per hour of effective green time (vphg).

The *flow ratio* for a given approach or lane group is defined as the ratio of the actual flow rate for the approach or lane group *(v)* to the saturation flow rate. The flow ratio is given the symbol $(v/s)_i$, for approach or lane group *i*).

The *capacity* of a given lane group or approach may be stated as:

$$c_i = s_i \times (g/C)_i$$

where

c_i = capacity of lane group or approach *i*, vph
s_i = saturation flow rate for lane group or approach *i*, vphg
$(g/C)_i$ = green ratio for lane group or approach *i*

The ratio of flow rate to capacity (*V/C*) is given the symbol *X* in intersection analysis. This new symbol is introduced to emphasize the strong relationship of capacity to signalization conditions, and for consistency with the literature, which also refers to this value as the "degree of saturation."

For a given lane group or approach *i*:

$$X_i = (V/C)_i = v_i/[s_i \times (g/C)_i]$$
$$X_i = v_i C/s_i g_i$$

where

X_i = *V/C* ratio for lane group or approach *i*
v_i = actual flow rate for lane group or approach *i*, vph
s_i = saturation flow rate for lane group or approach *i*, vphg
g_i = effective green time for lane group *i* or approach *i*, seconds

Values of X_i range from 1.00 when the flow rate equals capacity to 0.00 when the flow rate is zero.

The capacity of a full intersection is not a significant concept and is not specifically defined. Rarely do all movements at an intersection become saturated at the same time of day. It is the ability of individual movements to move through the intersection with efficiency that is the major concern.

Another capacity concept in the analysis of signalized intersections is, however, the *critical V/C ratio, X_c*. This is a *V/C* ratio for the intersection as a whole, that considering *only* the lane groups or approaches that have the highest flow ratio (*V/s*) for a given signal phase.

For example, in a two-phase signal, opposing approaches move during the same green time. Typically, one of these two approaches will require more green time than the other (it will have a higher flow ratio). This would be the critical approach for the subject signal phase. Each signal phase will have a critical lane group or approach that determines the green time requirements for the phase. Where signal phases overlap, the identification of these critical lane groups or approaches is somewhat complex.

The critical *V/C* ratio for the intersection is defined in terms of critical lane groups or approaches:

$$X_c = \sum_i (v/s)_{ci} \times (C/C - L)$$

where

X_c = critical *V/C* ratio for the intersection

$\sum_i (v/s)_{ci}$ = summation of flow ratios for all critical lane groups or approaches, *i*

C = cycle length, seconds

L = total lost time per cycle; computed as the sum of change interval and "start-up" lost time minus the portion of the change interval used by vehicles for each critical signal phase

This equation is helpful in evaluating the overall intersection with respect to geometrics and total cycle length provided, and also in estimating signal timings where they are not known or specified by local policies or procedures. It develops the *V/C* ratio for all critical movements, assuming green time has been appropriately or proportionally allocated. It is therefore possible to have a critical *V/C* ratio of less than 1.00, and still have individual movements oversaturated within the signal cycle. A critical *V/C* ratio less than 1.00, however, does indicate that all movements in the intersection can be accommodated within the defined cycle length and phase sequence by proportionally allocating green time. That is, the total available green time in the phase sequence is adequate to handle all movements if properly allocated.

Level of Service for Signalized Intersections

Level of service for signalized intersections is defined in terms of *delay*. Delay is a measure of driver discomfort, frustration, fuel consumption, and lost travel time. Specifically, level-of-service criteria are stated in terms of the average stopped delay per vehicle for a fifteen-minute analysis period. The criteria are given in Table 4–43.

Delay may be measured in the field, or be estimated with appropriate procedures. Delay is a complex measure, and is dependent upon several variables, including the quality of progression, cycle length, the green ratio, and the *V/C* ratio for the lane group or approach in question.

Level of service A describes operations with very low delay, that is, less than 5.0 seconds per vehicle. This occurs when progression is extremely favorable, and most vehicles arrive during the green phase. Most vehicles do not stop at all. Short cycle lengths may also contribute to low delay.

Level of service B describes operations with delay in the range of 5.1 to 15.0 seconds per vehicle. This generally occurs with good progression and/or short

Table 4—43 Level-of-Service Criteria for Signalized Intersections

Level of Service	Stopped Delay per Vehicle, seconds
A	≤ 5.0
B	5.1–15.0
C	15.1–25.0
D	25.1–40.0
E	40.1–60.0
F	> 60.0

(*Source:* Highway Capacity Manual 1985, Special Report 209. Washington D.C.: Transportation Research Board, National Research Council.)

cycle lengths. More vehicles stop than for LOS *A,* causing higher levels of average delay.

Level of service C describes operations with delay in the range of 15.1 to 25.0 seconds per vehicles. These higher delays may result from fair progression and/or longer cycle lengths. Individual cycle failures may begin to appear in this level. The number of vehicles stopping is significant at this level, though many still pass through the intersection without stopping.

Level of service D describes operations with delay in the range of 25.1 to 40.0 seconds per vehicles. At level *D* the influence of congestion becomes more noticeable. Longer delays may result from some combination of unfavorable progression, long cycle lengths, or high *V/C* ratios. Many vehicles stop, and the proportion of vehicles not stopping declines. Individual cycle failures are noticeable.

Level of service E describes operations with delay in the range of 40.1 to 60.0 seconds per vehicle. This is considered to be the limit of acceptable delay. These high delay values generally indicate poor progression, high cycle lengths, and high *V/C* ratios. Individual cycle failures are frequent occurrences.

Level of service F describes operations with delay in excess of 60.0 seconds per vehicle. This is considered to be unacceptable to most drivers. This condition often occurs with oversaturation, when arrival flow rates exceed the capacity of the intersection. It may also occur at high *V/C* ratios below 1.00 with many individual cycle failures. Poor progression and long cycle lengths may also be major contributing causes to such delay levels.

Relating Capacity and Level of Service

Because delay is complex its relationship to capacity is also complex. The levels of service of Table 4—43 have been established based upon the acceptability of various delays to drivers. It is important to note that this concept is not related to capacity in a simple relationship.

Previously, the lower bound of LOS *E* has always been defined to be capacity, that is, the *V/C* ratio is, by definition, 1.00. This *is not the case* for the procedures herein. It is possible, for example, to have delays in the range of LOS *F* (unacceptable) while the *V/C* ratio is below 1.00, perhaps as low as 0.75–0.85. Very high delays can occur at such *V/C* ratios when some combination of the following conditions exist: (1) the cycle length is long, (2) the lane group in question is disadvantaged (has a long red time) by the signal timing, and/or (3) the signal progression for the subject movements is poor.

The opposite can also occur. A saturated approach or lane group with *V/C* ratio of 1.00 may have low delays if: (1) the cycle length is short and/or (2) the signal progression is favorable for the subject movement. Therefore, the designation of LOS *F does not* automatically imply that the intersection, approach, or lane group is overloaded, nor does a level of service in the *A–E* range automatically imply that there is unused capacity available.

Thus it is worthwhile to repeat that the analysis of both capacity and level of service conditions is required fully to evaluate the operation of a signalized intersection.

Methodology and Techniques of Analysis

Appropriate operational analysis should result in the determination of capacity and level of service for each lane group or approach, as well as the level of service for the intersection as a whole. It requires detailed information be provided concerning geometric, traffic, and signalization conditions at the intersection. Such information may be known for existing cases, or projected for future situations.

The operational analysis of signalized intersections is divided into five distinct modules, as follows:

1. *Input module.* This analysis module focuses on the definition of all required information upon which subsequent computations are based. It includes all necessary data on intersection geometry, traffic volumes and conditions, and signalization. It is used to provide a summary for the remainder of the analysis.
2. *Volume-adjustment module.* Demand volumes are stated in terms of vehicles per hour for a peak hour. The volume-adjustment module converts these to flow rates for a peak fifteen-minute analysis period, and accounts for the effects of lane distribution. The definition of lane groups for analysis is also performed in this module.
3. *Saturation flow-rate module.* This module computes the saturation flow rate for each of the lane groups established for analysis. It is based upon the adjustment of an "ideal" saturation flow rate to reflect a variety of prevailing conditions.

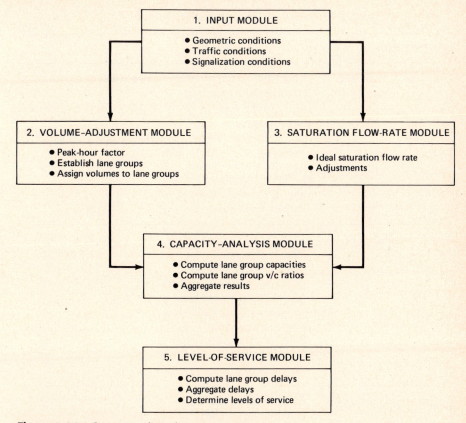

Figure 4–26   Operational Analysis Approach

(*Source:* Highway Capacity Manual 1985, Special Report 209. Washington D.C.: Transportation Research Board, National Research Council.)

4. *Capacity-analysis module.* Here, volumes and saturation flow rates are manipulated to compute the capacity and *V/C* ratios for each lane group, and the critical *V/C* ratio for the intersection as a whole.
5. *Level-of-service module.* In this module, delay is estimated for each lane group established for analysis. Delay measures are aggregated for approaches, and for the intersection as a whole, and levels of service are determined.

Figure 4–26 provides an illustration of the modules and the analysis procedure. Each of these modules is discussed in detail below.

Input Module

Table 4–44 provides a summary of the input information required to conduct analysis. The data needed fall into three main categories:

Table 4–44 Input Data Needs for Each Analysis Lane Group

Type of condition	Parameter	Symbol
Geometric conditions	Area type	CBD or other
	Number of lanes	N
	Lane widths, feet	W
	Grades, percent	+ (upgrade)
		– (downgrade)
	Existence of exclusive left-turn or right-turn lanes	
	Length of storage bay, left-turn or right-turn lanes	L_s
	Parking conditions	Y or N
Traffic conditions	Volumes by movement, vph	V_i
	Peak-hour factor	PHF
	Percent heavy vehicles	%HV
	Conflicting pedestrian flow rate, pedestrians per hour	PEDS
	Number of local buses stopping in intersection	N_B
	Parking activity, parking movements per hour	N_m
	Arrival type	
Signalization conditions	Cycle length, seconds	C
	Green time, seconds	G_i
	Actuated versus pretimed operation	A or P
	Pedestrian push button?	Y or N
	Minimum pedestrian green	G_p
	Phase plan	

(*Source:* Highway Capacity Manual 1985, Special Report 209. Washington D.C.: Transportation Research Board, National Research Council.)

Geometric Conditions Intersection geometry is generally presented in diagrammatic form, and must include all information on approach grades, the number and width of lanes, and parking conditions. The existence of exclusive left- or right-turn lanes should be noted, along with the storage lengths of such lanes.

Traffic Conditions Traffic volumes for the intersection are specified for each movement on each approach. Vehicle distribution is quantified as the percent of heavy vehicles (%HV) in each movement, where all vehicles with more than four wheels touching the pavement are considered to be heavy vehicles. The number of local buses on each approach are also identified. Only those buses making stops to pick up or discharge passengers at the intersection on either its approach or departure side are included in this number. Buses not making stops are considered heavy vehicles.

Data on pedestrian flows are required to analyze interference with permitted right-turn and left-turn movements. The pedestrian flow for a given vehicular approach is defined as the flow in the crosswalk interfering with right turns from the approach. Thus for a westbound approach, the pedestrian flow in the north crosswalk would be used. For an eastbound approach, the south crosswalk flow is used; for a northbound approach, the east crosswalk flow is used; and for a southbound approach, the west crosswalk flow is used.

A critical traffic characteristics required for analysis is the designation of arrival type on each approach. This is a general categorization that attempts to approximate the quality of progression on the approach. Five arrival types are defined for the dominant arrival flow as follows:

1. *Type 1.* This condition is defined as a dense platoon which arrives at the intersection at the beginning of the red phase. This is the worst platoon condition.
2. *Type 2.* This condition may be either a dense platoon arriving during the middle of the red phase, or a dispersed platoon arriving throughout the red phase. While better than type 1, this is still an unfavorable platoon condition.
3. *Type 3.* This condition represents totally random arrivals. This occurs when arrivals are widely dispersed throughout the red and green phases, and/or where the approach is totally uncoordinated with other signals—because it is at an isolated location or because nearby signals operate on different cycle lengths. This is an average condition.
4. *Type 4.* This condition is defined as a dense platoon that arrives during the middle of the green phase, or either a dispersed platoon arriving throughout the green phase. This is a moderately favorable platoon condition.
5. *Type 5.* This condition is defined as a dense platoon that arrives at the beginning of the green phase. It is the most favorable platoon condition.

The arrival type is best observed in the field. It should be determined as accurately as possible, as it has a significant impact on delay estimates and level of service determination. While there are no definitive parameters to quantify arrival type precisely, the following ratio is a useful value:

$$R_p = PVG/PTG$$

Table 4–45   Relationship Between Arrival Type and Platoon Ratio

Arrival Type	Range of Platoon Ratio, R_p
1	0.00–0.50
2	0.51–0.85
3	0.86–1.15
4	1.16–1.50
5	≥1.51

(*Source:* Highway Capacity Manual 1985, Special Report 209. Washington D.C.: Transportation Research Board, National Research Council.)

where

R_p = platoon ratio
PVG = percentage of all vehicles in the movement arriving during the green phase
PTG = percentage of the cycle that is green; $PTG = (G/C) \times 100$.

PVG must be observed in the field, but PTG is computed from the signal timing. Table 4–45 exhibits approximate ranges of R_p related to arrival type.

An additional condition of interest is the activity in parking lanes adjacent to analysis lane groups. Parking activity is measured in terms of the number of parking movements per hour within 250 feet of the intersection (N_m). Each vehicle that enters or leaves a parking place is considered a parking movement.

Signalization Conditions   Comprehensive information regarding signalization is required. This includes a phase diagram illustrating the phasing, cycle length, green times, and change intervals. Actuated phases should be identified, including the existence of push-button pedestrian-actuated phases. Where such pedestrian push buttons do not exist, the minimum green time for the phase should be indicated and must be provided for in the signal timing. The minimum green time for a phase may be estimated as:

$$G_p = 7.0 + (W/4.0) - Y$$

where

G_p = minimum green time, in seconds
W = distance from the curb to the center of the farthest travel lane on the street being crossed, in feet
Y = change interval (yellow + all-red time), seconds

When signal phases are actuated, the cycle length and green times are varying from cycle to cycle in response to demand. The operation of the signal should be observed in the field during the same period as volumes are observed. Average values of cycle length and green times may then be used in the analysis.

Default Values Occasionally some of the required field data will not be available. Where critical variables are missing, default values may be used for some of the variables without seriously affecting computations. Caution should be used in the application of such values, and it should be recognized that results become more approximate as more default values are used.

Table 4–46 summarizes default values for use where field data are not available.

This input module summarizes information that forms the basis for selecting computational values and procedures in the remaining modules.

Volume-Adjustment Module

Three major analytic steps are next performed in the volume-adjustment module: (1) movement volumes are adjusted to flow rates for a peak fifteen-minute period of analysis, (2) lane groups for analysis are established, and (3) lane group flows are adjusted to account for unbalanced lane utilization.

Adjustment of Movement Volumes to Reflect Peak-Flow Rates The initial computational process converts demands stated as hourly volumes to flow rates for the peak fifteen-minute period within the hour. This is done by dividing the movement volumes by an appropriate peak-hour factor (PHF), which may be defined for the intersection as a whole, for each approach, or for each movement.

Table 4–46 Default Values for Use in Operational Analysis

Parameter	Default Value
Conflicting pedestrian flow rate (PEDS)	Low pedestrian flow-50 pedestrians/hour
	Moderate pedestrian flow-200 pedestrians/hour
	High pedestrian flow-400 pedestrians/hour
Percent heavy vehicles (%HV)	2%
Peak-hour factor (PHF)	0.90
Grade	0%
Number of buses (N_B)	0 buses/hour
Number of parking movements (N_m)	20 movements/hour (where parking exists)
Arrival type	3

(*Source:* Highway Capacity Manual 1985, Special Report 209. Washington D.C.: Transportation Research Board, National Research Council.)

Thus:

$$v_p = V/PHF$$

where

v_p = flow rate during peak fifteen-minute period, vph
V = hourly volume, vph
PHF = peak-hour factor

Since all intersection movements may not peak at the same time, it is wise to observe fifteen-minute flows, and select critical periods for analysis. The conversion of hourly volumes to peak-flow rates using the PHF assumes that all movements peak during the same fifteen-minute period, and is therefore a conservative approach.

Determination of Lane Groups for Analysis   This analysis procedure is designed to consider individual intersection approaches, and individual lane groups within approaches. It is, therefore, necessary to determine appropriate lane groups for analysis.

A lane group is defined as one or more lanes on an intersection approach serving one or more traffic movements. Segmenting the intersection into lane groups is usually a relatively obvious process that considers both the geometry of the intersection and the distribution of traffic movements. In general the smallest number of lane groups is used that adequately describes the operation of the intersection. The following guidelines may be applied:

1. An exclusive left-turn lane or lanes should be designated as a separate lane group. The same is true of an exclusive right-turn lane.
2. On approaches with exclusive left-turn and/or right-turn lanes, all other lanes on the approach would generally be included in a single lane group.
3. Where an approach with more than one lane includes a lane that may be used by both left-turning vehicles and through vehicles, it is necessary to determine whether conditions permit equilibrium conditions to exist, or whether there are so many left turns that the lane essentially acts as an exclusive left-turn lane

A simple technique is used to make this determination. The left-turn flow rate is converted to an approximate equivalent flow of through vehicles:

$$v_{LE} = v_L \times \frac{1,800}{1,400 - v_o}$$

where

v_{LE} = approximate equivalent left-turn flow rate, vph
v_L = actual left-turn flow rate, vph
v_o = total opposing flow rate

When v_o is equal to or greater than 1,400 vph, v_{LE} has no meaning. In such cases left-turn movement against the opposing flow is not feasible, and inclusion of a protected left-turn phase in the signal cycle should be considered.

It is assumed that under the most extreme conditions, the equivalent left-turn flow, v_{LE}, completely occupies the leftmost lane of the approach. Remaining flow is then assumed to use remaining lanes equally. If the equivalent flow rate in the leftmost lane exceeds the average flow rate in remaining lanes, then it is assumed that the lane acts as an exclusive left-turn lane, and a separate lane group is established. If the equivalent left-lane flow rate is less than the average flow rate in remaining lanes, it is assumed that through vehicles will share the left lane to establish equilibrium, and the entire approach is considered a single-lane group. Thus if:

$$v_{LE} \geq (v - v_L)/(N - 1)$$

where

v = total flow rate on the approach
N = total number of lanes on the approach

then assume the left lane acts as an exclusive left-turn lane, and analyze the lane as a separate lane group. If:

$$v_{LE} < (v - v_L)/(N - 1)$$

Then assume that shared use of the left lane will take place. Include the lane as part of the total approach for analysis.

Where two or more lanes are included in a lane group for analysis purposes, all subsequent computations treat these lanes as a single entity. Figure 4–27 illustrates some common lane group schemes for analysis.

The operation of a shared left-turn and through lane with permitted left-turn phasing is complex. Left-turning vehicles execute their turning maneuvers through gaps in the opposing traffic stream. The first gap, however, does not appear until the queue of opposing vehicles clears the intersection. If a left turn arrives during the interval in which the opposing queue is clearing, it blocks the lane *for both through and turning vehicles* until the first gap appears. Thereafter left-turn vehicles may move through gaps in the opposing traffic stream until the green phase ends, at which time as many as two left-turning vehicles may be able

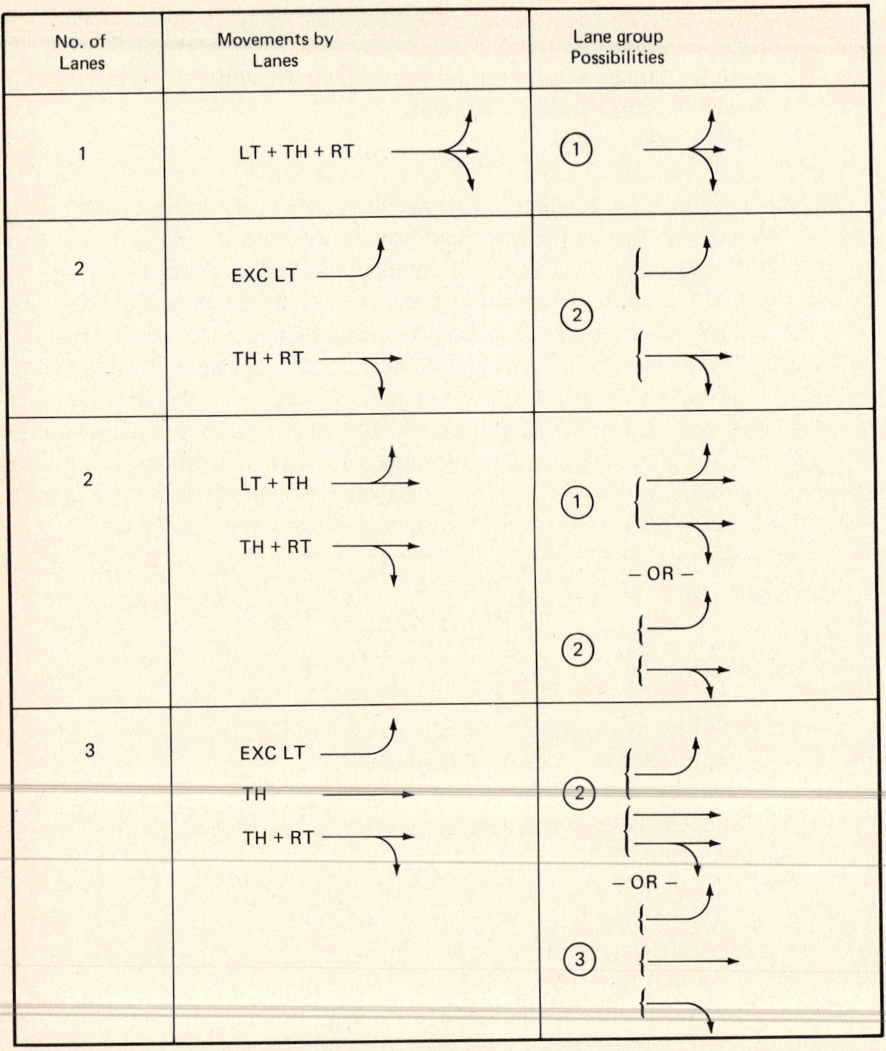

Figure 4–27 Typical Lane Groups for Analysis
(*Source:* Highway Capacity Manual 1985, Special Report 209. Washington D.C.: Transportation Research Board, National Research Council.)

to execute turns during the change interval. Any lane blockages or congestion in the shared lane will influence lane distribution, as vehicles move to adjacent lanes to avoid delays. An additional factor also influences lane distribution, that is, should through vehicle arrive at the intersection at the time a gap appears in the opposing traffic stream, no left-turning vehicle will be able to use it. A large number of through vehicles in the shared lane may block so many of the available gaps that insufficient capacity for left-turning vehicles remains. The interaction of all these mechanisms results in vehicles establishing an equilibrium through their

Table 4–47 Lane-Utilization Factors

Number of Through Lanes in Group (Excluding Lanes used by Left-Turning Vehicles)	Lane-Utilization Factor, U
1	1.00
2	1.05
≥ 3	1.10

(*Source:* Highway Capacity Manual 1985, Special Report 209. Washington D.C.: Transportation Research Board, National Research Council.)

selection of lanes. The analysis procedures attempt to address this equilibrium state, and allow approaches containing shared left-turn and through lanes to be analyzed as a single-lane group.

Adjustment for Lane Distribution The volumes have now been adjusted to peak fifteen-minute flow rates, and lane groups for analysis have been established. Flow rates in each lane group are now adjusted to reflect unequal lane usage. Where more than one lane exists, flow will not divide equally. The lane-utilization adjustment illustrated in Table 4–47 reflects this, and increases the analysis flow rate to reflect the flow in the lane with the highest usage. Thus

$$v = v_p \times U$$

where

$$v = \text{adjusted demand flow rate for the lane group, vph}$$
$$v_p = \text{unadjusted demand flow rate for the lane group, vph}$$
$$U = \text{lane-utilization factor}$$

The lane-utilization factor is only used when it is desirable to analyze the worst of two or more through lanes. Where average conditions for the lane group are desired, the factor is set at 1.00. The factor may also be set at 1.00 when the saturation ratio for the lane group approaches 1.0, as lanes tend to be more equally utilized in such situations. When used the factor assumes that the most heavily used lane in a group of two serves 52.5 percent of the total flow, while the most heavily used lane in a group of three serves 36.7 percent of the total flow.

Saturation Flow Module

This module computes a saturation flow rate for each lane group. The saturation flow rate is the flow in vehicles per hour that could be accommodated by the lane group, assuming that the green phase was always available to the approach—that is, that the green ratio (g/C) was 1.00. Computations begin with the selection

Table 4–48   Adjustment Factor for Lane Width

Lane Width (Feet)	8	9	10	11	12	13	14	15	≥ 16
Lane-width factor, f_w	0.87	0.90	0.93	0.97	1.00	1.03	1.07	1.10	Use two lanes

(*Source:* Highway Capacity Manual 1985, Special Report 209. Washington D.C.: Transportation Research Board, National Research Council.)

of an "ideal" saturation flow rate, usually 1,800 passenger cars per hour of green time per lane (pcphgpl), and adjust this value for a variety of prevailing conditions that are not ideal.

$$s = s_o \; N \; f_w \; f_{HV} \; f_g \; f_p \; f_{bb} \; f_a \; f_{RT} \; f_{LT}$$

where

$\quad s \;\; = \;\;$ saturation flow rate for the subject lane group, expressed as a total for all lanes in the lane group under prevailing conditons, in vphg

$\quad s_o \;\; = \;\;$ ideal saturation flow rate per lane, usually 1,800 pcphgpl

$\quad N \;\; = \;\;$ number of lanes in the lane group

$\quad f_w \;\; = \;\;$ adjustment factor for lane width, 12-foot lanes are standard; given in Table 4–48.

$\quad f_{HV} \;\; = \;\;$ adjustment factor for heavy vehicles in the traffic stream; given in Table 4–49.

$\quad f_g \;\; = \;\;$ adjustment factor for approach grade; given in Table 4–50.

$\quad f_p \;\; = \;\;$ adjustment factor for the existence of a parking lane adjacent to the lane group and the parking activity in that lane; given in Table 4–51.

$\quad f_{bb} \;\; = \;\;$ adjustment factor for the blocking effect of local buses stopping within the intersection area; given in Table 4–52.

$\quad f_a \;\; = \;\;$ adjustment factor for area type; given in Table 4–53.

$\quad f_{RT} \;\; = \;\;$ adjustment factor for right turns in the lane group; given in Table 4–54.

$\quad f_{LT} \;\; = \;\;$ adjustment factor for left turns in the lane group; given in Table 4–55, or computed as described in following sections.

Table 4–49   Adjustment Factor for Heavy Vehicles

Percent Heavy Vehicles (%HV)	0	2	4	6	8	10	15	20	25	30
Heavy-vehicle factor, f_{HV}	1.00	0.99	0.98	0.97	0.96	0.95	0.93	0.91	0.89	0.87

(*Source:* Highway Capacity Manual 1985, Special Report 209. Washington D.C.: Transportation Research Board, National Research Council.)

Table 4–50 Adjustment Factor for Grade

Grade (percent)	Downhill			Level	Uphill		
	−6	−4	−2	0	+2	+4	+6
Grade factor, f_g	1.03	1.02	1.01	1.00	0.99	0.98	0.97

(*Source:* Highway Capacity Manual 1985, Special Report 209. Washington D.C.: Transportation Research Board, National Research Council.)

Table 4–51 Adjustment Factor for Parking, f_p

Number of Lanes in Lane Group	No Pkg	Number of Parking Maneuvers per Hour, N_m				
		0	10	20	30	40
1	1.00	0.90	0.85	0.80	0.75	0.70
2	1.00	0.95	0.92	0.89	0.87	0.85
3	1.00	0.97	0.95	0.93	0.91	0.89

(*Source:* Highway Capacity Manual 1985, Special Report 209. Washington D.C.: Transportation Research Board, National Research Council.)

Table 4–52 Adjustment Factor for Bus Blockage, f_{bb}

Number of Lanes in Lane Group	Number of Buses Stopping per Hour, N_B				
	0	10	20	30	40
1	1.00	0.96	0.92	0.88	0.83
2	1.00	0.98	0.96	0.94	0.92
3	1.00	0.99	0.97	0.96	0.94

(*Source:* Highway Capacity Manual 1985, Special Report 209. Washington D.C.: Transportation Research Board, National Research Council.)

Table 4–53 Adjustment Factor for Area Type

Type of Area	Factor, f_a
CBD	0.90
All other areas	1.00

(*Source:* Highway Capacity Manual 1985, Special Report 209. Washington D.C.: Transportation Research Board, National Research Council.)

Table 4–54 Adjustment Factor for Right Turns

Case	Type of Lane Group	Right-Turn Factors, f_{RT}
1	EXCLUSIVE RT LANE; PROTECTED RT PHASING	0.85
2	EXCLUSIVE RT LANE; PERMITTED RT PHASING	$f_{RT} = 0.85 - (\text{PEDS}/2{,}100)$ PEDS ≤ 1,700 $f_{RT} = 0.05$ PEDS > 1,700

Number of Conflicting Pedestrians (PEDS)	0	(low) 50	100	(mod) 200	300	(high) 400	500
Factor	0.85	0.83	0.80	0.75	0.71	0.66	0.61

Number of Conflicting Pedestrians (PEDS)	600	(low) 800	1,000	(mod) 1,200	1,400	(high) 1,600	≥ 1,700
Factor	0.56	0.47	0.37	0.28	0.18	0.05	0.05

3 EXCLUSIVE RT LANE; PROTECTED + PERMITTED PHASING

$f_{RT} = 0.85 - (1 - P_{RTA})\,(PEDS/2{,}100)$

$f_{RT} = 0.05$ (minimum)

Number of Conflicting Pedestrians (PEDS)	PROP. OF RT USING PROTECTED PHASE, P_{RTA}					
	0.00	0.20	0.40	0.60	0.80	1.00
0	0.85	0.85	0.85	0.85	0.85	0.85
50 (low)	0.83	0.83	0.84	0.84	0.85	0.85
100	0.80	0.81	0.82	0.83	0.84	0.85
200 (mod)	0.75	0.77	0.79	0.81	0.83	0.85
300	0.71	0.74	0.76	0.79	0.82	0.85
400 (high)	0.66	0.70	0.74	0.77	0.81	0.85
600	0.56	0.62	0.68	0.74	0.79	0.85
800	0.47	0.55	0.62	0.70	0.77	0.85
1,000	0.37	0.47	0.56	0.66	0.75	0.85
1,400	0.18	0.32	0.45	0.58	0.72	0.85
≥ 1,700	0.05	0.20	0.36	0.53	0.69	0.85

4 SHARED RT LANE; PROTECTED PHASING

$f_{RT} = 1.0 - 0.15\,P_{RT}$

Prop. of RT in Lane, P_{RT}	0.00	0.20	0.40	0.60	0.80	1.00
Factor	1.00	0.97	0.94	0.91	0.88	0.85

Table 4–54 (continued)

Case	Type of Lane Group	Right-Turn Factors, f_{RT}
5	SHARED RT LANE; PERMITTED PHASING	$f_{RT} = 1.0 - P_{RT}[0.15 + (PEDS/2,100)]$ $f_{RT} = 0.05$ (minimum)

Number of Conflicting Pedestrians (PEDS)	PROP. OF RT IN LANE, P_{RT}					
	0.00	0.20	0.40	0.60	0.80	1.00
0	1.00	0.97	0.94	0.91	0.88	0.85
50 (low)	1.00	0.97	0.93	0.90	0.86	0.83
100	1.00	0.96	0.92	0.88	0.84	0.80
200 (mod)	1.00	0.95	0.90	0.85	0.80	0.75
400 (high)	1.00	0.93	0.86	0.80	0.73	0.66
600	1.00	0.91	0.83	0.74	0.65	0.56
800	1.00	0.89	0.79	0.68	0.58	0.47
1,000	1.00	0.87	0.75	0.62	0.50	0.37
1,400	1.00	0.84	0.67	0.51	0.35	0.18
≥ 1,700	1.00	0.81	0.62	0.42	0.23	0.05

6 SHARED RT LANE; PROTECTED + PERMITTED PHASING

$f_{RT} = 1.0 - P_{RT}[0.15 + (PEDS/2,100)(1 - P_{RTA})]$

$f_{RT} = 0.05$ (minimum)

Proportion RTs Using Prot. Phase P_{RTA}	Number of Conflicting Pedestrians (PEDS)	PROPORTION OF RTS IN SHARED LANE, P_{RT}					
		0.00	0.20	0.40	0.60	0.80	1.00
0.00	all			Same as Case 5			
0.20	0	1.00	0.97	0.94	0.91	0.88	0.85
	50	1.00	0.97	0.93	0.90	0.86	0.83
	200	1.00	0.95	0.91	0.86	0.82	0.77
	400	1.00	0.94	0.88	0.82	0.76	0.70
	600	1.00	0.92	0.85	0.77	0.70	0.62
	1,000	1.00	0.89	0.79	0.68	0.58	0.47
	1,400	1.00	0.86	0.73	0.59	0.45	0.32
	≥ 1,700	1.00	0.81	0.62	0.42	0.23	0.20
0.40	0	1.00	0.97	0.94	0.91	0.88	0.85
	50	1.00	0.97	0.97	0.93	0.87	0.84
	200	1.00	0.96	0.92	0.88	0.83	0.79
	400	1.00	0.95	0.89	0.84	0.79	0.74
	600	1.00	0.94	0.87	0.81	0.74	0.68
	1,000	1.00	0.91	0.83	0.74	0.65	0.56
	1,400	1.00	0.89	0.78	0.67	0.56	0.45
	≥ 1,700	1.00	0.87	0.75	0.62	0.49	0.36

Table 4–54 (continued)

Case	Type of Lane Group	Right-Turn Factors, f_{RT}						
6	SHARED RT LANE; PROTECTED + PERMITTED PHASING	$f_{RT} = 1.0 - P_{RT}[0.15 + (PEDS/2{,}100)(1 - P_{RTA})]$ $f_{RT} = 0.05$ (minimum)						

Proportion RTs Using Prot. Phase P_{RTA}	Number of Conflicting Pedestrians (PEDS)	PROPORTION OF RTS IN SHARED LANE, P_{RT}					
		0.00	0.20	0.40	0.60	0.80	1.00
0.60	0	1.00	0.97	0.94	0.91	0.88	0.85
	50	1.00	0.97	0.94	0.90	0.87	0.84
	200	1.00	0.96	0.92	0.89	0.85	0.81
	400	1.00	0.95	0.91	0.86	0.82	0.77
	600	1.00	0.95	0.89	0.84	0.79	0.74
	1,000	1.00	0.93	0.86	0.80	0.73	0.66
	1,400	1.00	0.92	0.83	0.75	0.67	0.58
	≥ 1,700	1.00	0.91	0.81	0.72	0.62	0.53
0.80	0	1.00	0.97	0.94	0.91	0.88	0.85
	50	1.00	0.97	0.94	0.91	0.88	0.85
	200	1.00	0.97	0.93	0.90	0.86	0.83
	400	1.00	0.96	0.92	0.89	0.85	0.81
	600	1.00	0.96	0.92	0.88	0.83	0.79
	1,000	1.00	0.95	0.90	0.85	0.80	0.75
	1,400	1.00	0.94	0.89	0.83	0.77	0.72
	≥ 1,700	1.00	0.94	0.88	0.81	0.75	0.69
1.00	all	Same as Case 4					

7 SINGLE LANE APPROXIMATION

$$f_{RT} = 0.90 - P_{RT}[0.135 + (PEDS/2100)]$$
$$f_{RT} = 0.05 \quad \text{(minimum)}$$

Number of Conflicting Pedestrians (PEDS)	PROPORTION OF RTS IN SINGLE LANE, P_{RT}					
	0.00	0.20	0.40	0.60	0.80	1.00
0	1.00	0.87	0.85	0.82	0.79	0.77
50 (low)	1.00	0.87	0.84	0.81	0.77	0.74
100	1.00	0.86	0.83	0.79	0.76	0.72
200 (mod)	1.00	0.86	0.81	0.77	0.72	0.68
300	1.00	0.85	0.79	0.74	0.69	0.64
400 (high)	1.00	0.84	0.78	0.72	0.65	0.59
600	1.00	0.82	0.74	0.66	0.59	0.51
800	1.00	0.80	0.71	0.61	0.52	0.42
1,000	1.00	0.79	0.67	0.56	0.45	0.34
1,200	1.00	0.77	0.64	0.51	0.38	0.25
1,400	1.00	0.75	0.61	0.46	0.31	0.16
≥ 1,700	1.00	0.73	0.55	0.38	0.21	0.05

8 DOUBLE EXCLUSIVE RT LANE: PROTECTED PHASING

0.75

(*Source:* Highway Capacity Manual 1985, Special Report 209. Washington D.C.: Transportation Research Board, National Research Council.)

Table 4–55 Adjustment Factors for Left Turns

Case	Type of Lane Group	Left-Turn Factors, f_{LT}					
1	EXCLUSIVE LT LANE; PROTECTED RT PHASING	0.95					
2	EXCLUSIVE LT LANE; PERMITTED PHASING	Special Procedure					
3	EXCLUSIVE LT LANE; PROTECTED + PERMITTED PHASING	0.95*					
4	SHARED LT LANE; PROTECTED PHASING	$f_{LT} = 1.0/(1.0 + 0.05P_{LT})$					
		Prop. of LTs in Lane, P_{LT}	0.00	0.20	0.40	0.60	0.80	1.00
		Factor	1.00	0.99	0.98	0.97	0.96	0.95
5	SHARED LT LANE; PERMITTED PHASING	Special Procedure					

6 | SHARED LT LANE; PROTECTED + PERMITTED PHASING

$f_{LT} = (1,400 - V_o)/[(1,400 - V_o) + (235 + 0.435V_o)P_{LT}]$ $V_o \leq 1,220$ vph
$f_{LT} = 1/[1 + 4.525P_{LT}]$ $V_o > 1,220$ vph

Opposing Volume, V_o	PROPORTION OF LEFT TURNS, P_{LT}					
	0.00	0.20	0.40	0.60	0.80	1.00
0	1.00	0.97	0.94	0.91	0.88	0.86
200	1.00	0.95	0.90	0.86	0.82	0.78
400	1.00	0.92	0.85	0.80	0.75	0.70
600	1.00	0.88	0.79	0.72	0.66	0.61
800	1.00	0.83	0.71	0.62	0.55	0.49
1,000	1.00	0.74	0.58	0.48	0.41	0.36
1,200	1.00	0.55	0.38	0.29	0.24	0.20
≥ 1,220	1.00	0.52	0.36	0.27	0.22	0.18

7 | SINGLE LANE APPROXIMATION

Special Procedure

8 | DOUBLE EXCLUSIVE LT LANE; PROTECTED PHASING

0.90

*This value is a starting estimate. Solutions are iterated for this case.

(*Source*: Highway Capacity Manual 1985, Special Report 209. Washington D.C.: Transportation Research Board, National Research Council.)

Where detailed data defining each of the above factors are not available, a default value for s may be taken to be 1,600 vphgpl $\times$ N. When this is done, however, the analysis becomes highly approximate.

Explanation of Adjustment Factors   The use of adjustment factors is similar to that of uninterrupted flow discussed previously. Each factor accounts for the impact of one or several prevailing conditions that are different from the ideal conditions for which the saturation flow rate of 1,800 pcphgpl applies. A brief discussion of each of the factors is contained below.

The *lane-width factor, f_w*, accounts for the deleterious impact of narrow lanes on saturation flow rate, and allows for an increased flow on wide lanes. Twelve-foot lanes are the standard.

The effects of *heavy vehicles* and *grades* are treated by separate factors, f_{HV} and f_g respectively. Their separate treatment recognizes that passenger cars are affected by approach grades, as are heavy vehicles. The *heavy-vehicle factor* adcounts for the additional space occupied by these vehicles, and for the differential in the operating capabilities of heavy vehicles with respect to passenger cars.

The *grade factor* accounts for the effect of grades on the operation of all vehicles.

The *parking factor, f_p*, accounts for the frictional effect of a parking lane on flow in adjacent lanes, as well as for the occasional blocking of an adjacent lane by vehicles moving into and out of parking spaces.

The *bus-blockage factor, f_{bb},* accounts for the impacts of local transit buses stopping to discharge or pick up passengers at a near-side or far-side bus stop.

The *area-type factor, f_a,* accounts for the relative inefficiency of business area intersections in comparison with those in other locations. This is primarily due to the complexity and general congestion of the environment in business areas.

The *right-turn factor, f_{RT},* depends upon a number of variables, including:

1. Whether the right turn is made from an exclusive or shared lane.
2. Type of signal phasing (protected, permitted, or protected plus permitted); a protected right-turn phase has no conflicting pedestrian movements.
3. The volume of pedestrians using the conflicting crosswalk.
4. The proportion of right turns using a shared lane.
5. The proportion of right turns using the protected portion of a protected plus permitted phase.

Item 5 should be determined by field observation, but can be grossly estimated from the signal timing. This is done by assuming that the proportion of right-turning vehicles using the protected phase is approximately equal to the proportion of the turning phase that is protected. Where right turn on red (RTOR) is permitted, the right-turn volume may be reduced by the volume of right-turning vehicles moving on the red phase. This is usually done on the basis of hourly volumes, before converting to flow rates.

The *left-turn factor, f_{LT},* is based upon similar variables, including:

1. Whether the left turns are made from exclusive or shared lanes.
2. Type of phasing (protected, permitted, or protected plus permitted).
3. The proportion of left-turning vehicles using a shared lane.
4. The opposing flow rate when permitted left turns are made.

The turn factors account for the fact that such movements cannot be made at the same saturation flow rates as through movements. They consume more of the available green time, and consequently more of the intersection's available capacity.

Special Procedure: Left-Turn Adjustment Factor for Permitted Phasing

When a lane group includes permitted left turns, the left-turn adjustment factor must be computed using a complex series of equations. The equations approximate the effect of equilibrium flows that result from the interaction of left-turning vehicles, through vehicles, and opposing flows. The procedure is used for all permitted left turns, whether made from an exclusive or shared lane.

The following variables are used in equations determining the left-turn adjustment factor, f_{LT}.

C = cycle length, seconds

g = effective green time, seconds

g_u = portion of green not blocked by the clearing of an opposing queue of vehicles, seconds

g_f = initial portion of green phase, during which through vehicles may move in a shared left-turn/through lane; movement continues until arrival of first left-turning vehicle, which waits until opposing queue clears, blocking the lane for this period; seconds

g_q = portion of green phase blocked to left-turning vehicles by the clearing of an opposing queue of vehicles; $g_q = g - g_u$, seconds

E_L = through-vehicle equivalent for opposed left turns

v = total approach flow rate, vph

v_M = mainline approach flow rate; total approach flow rate less left turns from an exclusive lane or on a one-lane approach, vph; the maximum value of v_M is 1,399; this value is used for all $v_M \geq 1,399$

v_{LT} = left-turn flow rate, vph

p_{LT} = proportion of left turns in approach flow; $p_{LT} = v_{LT}/v$

p_{LT_o} = proportion of left turns in opposing flow

p_L = proportion of left turns in shared median or left-turn lane

p_T = proportion of through vehicles in shared median or left-turn lane

N = number of lanes in lane group or approach

N_o = number of mainline lanes opposing the permissive left turn

v_o = opposing flow rate, discounting left turns from an exclusive lane or one-lane approach; the maximum value of v_o is 1,399; this value is used for all $v_o \geq 1,399$.

s_{op} = saturation flow rate for opposing approach, vphg
Y_o = flow ratio for opposing approach; $Y_o = v_o/s_{op}$
f_s = left-turn saturation factor

The left-turn adjustment factor reflects three component flows during any given green phase: (1) through flow in a shared lane at the start of the green until a left-turning vehicle arrives, blocking the lane while waiting to turn; (2) shared-lane or left-turn lane flow during the unsaturated period of opposing flow; and (3) left turns made at the end of the green phase by vehicles already waiting in the intersection for an appropriate gap in opposing flow.

The computation of an appropriate left-turn adjustment factor proceeds using the following sequence.

1. The saturation flow rate for the opposing flow is estimated as:

$$s_{op} = \frac{1{,}800 \, N_o}{1 + P_{LT_o} (400 + v_M)/(1{,}400 - v_M)}$$

where N_o does not include exclusive left-turn or right-turn lanes on the opposing approach, and v_M is the mainline flow on the subject approach, not including left turns from an exclusive lane or a one-lane approach, and the denominator of the equation represents a weighted average through-vehicle equivalent for the opposing flow.

2. The flow ratio for the opposing flow is then computed as:

$$Y_o = v_o/s_{op}$$

3. The portion of the green phase that is *not* blocked by an opposing queue of vehicles is estimated as:

$$g_u = \frac{C(g/C - Y_o)}{1 - Y_o} = \frac{(g - CY_o)}{1 - Y_o}$$

$$g_u = 0 \quad \text{if} \quad Y_o \geq g/C$$

For there to be any left-turn capacity other than at the end of the green phase, $g_u \geq 0$ and $g/C > Y_o$. The opposing green ratio must exceed the opposing flow ratio.

4. The left-turn saturation factor is calculated from a consideration of the opposing flow as:

$$f_s = 875 - 0.62 v_o/1{,}000$$

where v_o is the total opposing traffic flow. It should include left-turning vehicles only when left turns are made from a shared lane on multilane approach during a permissive phase. Left turns are not included in opposing flow when made from a single-lane approach or from an exclusive left-turn lane.

5. Where the subject left turn is made from a shared lane, the proportion of left-turn flow in the shared lane is determined from:

$$P_L = P_{LT} \left[1 + (N-1)g/(f_s g_u + 4.5) \right]$$

Where the subject left turn is made from an exclusive left-turn lane, $p_L = 1.00$, as 100 percent of the traffic in the lane turns left.

6. The duration of the green phase during which through vehicles may move in a shared lane until a left-turning vehicle arrives is estimated as:

$$g_f = \frac{2 \, p_T}{p_L} \left[1 - p_T^{0.5 g_q} \right]$$

where $g_q = g - g_u$. If a separate left-turn lane is being analyzed, $g_f = 0$.

7. During the portion of the phase when opposing flow is unsaturated, g_u, the approximate through-vehicle equivalent for opposed left turns is:

$$E_L = \frac{1,800}{1,400 - v_o}$$

8. The left-turn factor for a shared left-turn/through lane or an exclusive left-turn lane is then given by:

$$f_m = \frac{g_f}{g} + \frac{g_u}{g} \left\{ \frac{1}{1 + P_L(E_L - 1)} \right\} + \frac{2}{g} \{1 + P_L\}$$

This factor applies only to the single lane from which left turns are made, however. Thus where a left-turn lane is being considered, or for a single-lane approach, $f_{LT} = f_m$. For shared lanes on a multilane approach, the left-turn factor for the lane group or approach is:

$$f_{LT} = (f_m + N - 1)/N$$

This procedure for determining the left-turn factor for permitted left turns is very complex. However, it is a reasonable analytic representation of a complex equilibrium process. It should be noted that exact determination of the left-turn adjustment factor requires that signal timing parameters, specifically cycle length and green times, be known.

Capacity-Analysis Module

Computational results of previous modules are manipulated in this module to compute key capacity variables, including:

1. Flow ratio for each lane group.
2. Capacity of each lane group.
3. The V/C ratio of each lane group.
4. Critical V/C ratio for the overall intersection.

Flow ratios are computed by dividing the adjusted demand flow (v), computed in the volume-adjustment module, by the adjusted saturation flow rate (s), computed in the saturation flow-rate module.

The capacity of each lane group is computed:

$$c_i = s_i \times (g/C)_i$$

If the signal timing is not known, a timing plan will have to be assumed to make these computations.

The V/C ratio for each lane group is computed directly, by dividing the adjusted flows by the capacities computed:

$$X_i = V_i/C_i$$

The final capacity parameter of interest is the critical V/C ratio, X_c, for the intersection. It is computed, as follows:

$$X_c = \sum_i (v/s)_{ci} \times C/(C - L)$$

This ratio indicates the proportion of available capacity that is being utilized by vehicles in critical lane groups. If this ratio exceeds 1.00, one or more of the critical lane groups will be oversaturated. It is an indication that the intersection design, cycle length, phase plan, and/or signal timing is inadequate for the existing or projected demand. A ratio of less than 1.00 indicates that the design, cycle length, and phase plan are adequate to handle all critical flows without demand exceeding capacity, assuming that green times are proportionally assigned. Where phase splits are not proportional, some movement demands may exceed movement capacities even where the critical V/C ratio is less than 1.00.

The computation of the above ratio requires that *critical lane groups* be identified. Where there are no overlapping signal phases in the signal design, the determination of critical lane groups is straightforward. Overlapping phases (concurrent phase timing) complicate matters, and will not be treated in this text. The following guidelines may be used in determining critical lane groups where phases *do not overlap:*

1. There will be one critical lane group for each signal phase.
2. The lane group with the highest flow ratio (v/s) of those lane groups moving in a given signal phase is critical.
3. Where signal timing is to be estimated or assumed, the critical lane groups are those that are used to determine the timing,

Level-of-Service Module

In the level-of-service module, the average stopped delay per vehicle is estimated for each lane group, and averaged for approaches and the intersection as a whole. Level of service is related to the delay value, and is found from Table 4–43.

Delay Assuming Random Arrivals   The delay for each lane group is found using the following relationship:

$$d = 0.38C\,\frac{[1 - g/C]^2}{[1 - (g/C\,(X))]} + 173\,X^2\,[(X - 1) + \sqrt{(X - 1)^2 + (16X/c)}]$$

where

d = average stopped delay per vehicle for the lane group, seconds per vehicle
C = cycle length, seconds
g/C = green ratio for the lane group; the ratio of effective green time to cycle length
X = v/c ratio for the lane group
c = capacity of the lane group

The foregoing equation predicts the average stopped delay per vehicle for an assumed random arrival pattern for approaching vehicles. The first term of the equation accounts for *uniform delay,* that is, the delay that occurs if arrival demand in the subject lane group is uniformly distributed over time. The second terms of the equation accounts for *incremental delay* of random arrivals over uniform arrivals, and for the additional delay due to cycle failures. The equation yields reasonable results for values of X between 0.0 and 1.0. Where oversaturation occurs for long periods (>15 minutes), it is difficult to accurately estimate delay, as spillbacks may extend to adjacent intersections. The equation may be used with caution for values of X up to 1.2, but delay estimates for higher values are not recommended. Oversaturation (i.e., $X > 1.0$) obviously is an undesirable condition that should be corrected if possible.

It is often wise to compute the uniform delay and incremental delay terms as separate values. This allows the analyst to see the relative contribution of individual cycle failures to total delay. Thus:

$$d = d_1 + d_2$$

where

d_1 = first-term uniform delay, seconds per vehicle
d_2 = second-term incremental delay, seconds per vehicle

Progression-Adjustment Factor   As noted the above delay estimate is for an assumed random arrival condition. In most cases arrivals are not random, but rather are platooned as a result of signal progression and other factors. As part of the input data for an analysis, five arrival types were defined, and one would be specified for each lane group. The delay obtained from the above equation is multiplied by the progression adjustment factor, given in Table 4–56.

When signal progression is favorable to the subject lane group, delay will be considerably less than that for random arrivals. Similarly, when signal progression is unfavorable, delay can be considerably higher than that for random arrivals. The variation of delay with progression quality decreases as the v/c ratio (X) approaches 1.00, and is greater for pretimed signals than for other types of signalization.

Delay is a complex variable that is sensitive to a variety of local conditions. These procedures provide reasonable estimates of delay expected for average conditions. They are useful when comparing operational conditions for various geometric or signalization designs. When evaluating existing conditions, it is advisable to measure delay in the field.

Aggregating Delay Estimates   The procedure for delay estimation yields the average stopped delay per vehicle for each lane group. It is desirable to aggregate these values to provide average delay for an intersection approach, and the intersection as a whole. This is done by computing weighted averages, where such lane group delays are weighted by the adjusted flows in the lane groups.

The delay for an approach is computed as:

$$d_A = \sum_i d_i v_i \, / \, \sum_i v_i$$

where

d_A = delay for approach A, seconds per vehicle
d_i = delay for lane group i (on approach A), seconds per vehicle
v_i = adjusted flow for lane group i, vph

Approach delays can be further averaged to provide the average delay for the intersection:

$$d_I = \sum_A d_A v_A \, / \, \sum_A v_A$$

where

d_I = average delay per vehicle for the intersection, seconds per vehicle
v_A = adjusted flow for approach A, vph

Table 4–56 Progression Adjustment Factor, PF

Type of Signal	Lane Group Types	v/c Ratio, X	Arrival Type[a]				
			1	2	3	4	5
Pretimed	TH, RT	≤ 0.6	1.85	1.35	1.00	0.72	0.53
		0.8	1.50	1.22	1.00	0.82	0.67
		1.0	1.40	1.18	1.00	0.90	0.82
Actuated	TH, RT	≤ 0.6	1.54	1.08	0.85	0.62	0.40
		0.8	1.25	0.98	0.85	0.71	0.50
		1.0	1.16	0.94	0.85	0.78	0.61
Semiactuated	Main street TH, RT[b]	≤ 0.6	1.85	1.35	1.00	0.72	0.42
		0.8	1.50	1.22	1.00	0.82	0.53
		1.0	1.40	1.18	1.00	0.90	0.65
Semiactuated	Side street TH, RT[b]	≤ 0.6	1.48	1.18	1.00	0.86	0.70
		0.8	1.20	1.07	1.00	0.98	0.89
		1.0	1.12	1.04	1.00	1.00	1.00
	All LT[c]	All	1.00	1.00	1.00	1.00	1.00

[a]See Table 4–45
[b]Semiactuated signals are typically timed to give all extra green time to the main street. This effect should be taken into account in the allocation of green times.
[c]This category refers to exclusive left-turn lane groups with protected phasing only. When left-turns are included in a lane group encompassing an entire approach, use factor for the overall lane group type. Where heavy Left-turns are intentionally coordinated, apply factors for the appropriate through movement.
(Source: Highway Capacity Manual 1985, Special Report 209. Washington D.C.: Transportation Research Board, National Research Council.)

Level-of-Service Determination   Intersection level of service is directly related to the average stopped delay per vehicle. When delays have been estimated for each lane group, and aggregated for each approach and the intersection as a whole, Table 4–43 is consulted, and the appropriate levels of service are determined.

Analysis and Interpretation of Results

The above operational analysis yields two key results that must be considered:

1. The *V/C* ratios for each lane group, and for the intersection as a whole.
2. Average stopped-time delays for each lane group and approach, and for the intersection as a whole, and the levels of service which correspond.

Any *V/C* ratio greater than 1.00 is an indication of actual or potential breakdowns, and is a condition requiring correction. Where the overall intersection *V/C* ratio is less than 1.00, but some lane groups have *V/C* ratios greater than 1.00, the green time is generally not optimally apportioned, and a retiming using the existing phasing should be attempted.

Example Calculation: Operational Analysis of an Existing Pretimed, Two-Phase Signal

Description   The intersection of Fifth Avenue and Walker Street is illustrated in Figure 4–28, which is the input module worksheet for this calculation. It is a four-leg intersection with a two-phase, pretimed signal on a seventy-second cycle. Walker Street has two lanes in each direction, while Fifth Avenue has one lane in each direction.

The objective is to analyze the capacity and level of service of the existing intersection for a projected set of future demand volumes that will result from new developments in the area, and to recommend changes to the signal and/or geometric design if the current situation is not able to handle the new traffic in an acceptable manner.

Input Module   The input module worksheet for this calculation is shown in Figure 4–28. All relevant volumes and geometric conditions are illustrated in the diagram on the upper half of the worksheet. Other relevant characteristics are shown in the center of the worksheet. The intersection is on level grade, traffic includes 5 percent heavy vehicles on Walker Street and 8 percent on Fifth Avenue, and there are no buses or parking lanes on any of the approaches. Pedestrian volumes are estimated to be 100 pedestrians per hour in all crosswalks, and the peak hour factor is 0.90 for all approaches. As there are no pedestrian push buttons, the minimum green time for pedestrians may be computed from:

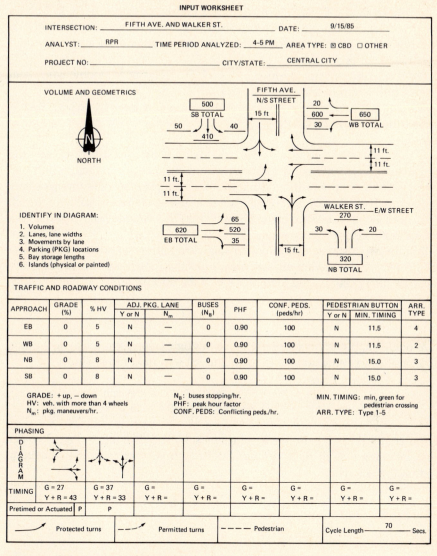

Figure 4–28 Input Module Worksheet for Example Calculation

$$G_p \qquad\qquad = 7.0 + W/4.0 - Y$$
$$G_p \text{ (Walker St.)} = 7.0 + 30/4.0 - 3.0 = 11.5 \text{ seconds}$$
$$G_p \text{ (Fifth Ave.)} = 7.0 + 44/4.0 - 3.0 = 15.0 \text{ seconds}$$

The arrival types are also given: Walker Street is on a progression plan that favors the eastbound approach (type 4) and disadvantages the westbound approach (type 2). Fifth Avenue has essentially random arrivals (type 3).

The signal timing is also illustrated at the bottom of Figure 4–28. It shows a simple two-phase plan, with Walker Street receiving twenty-seven seconds of green time and Fifth Avenue receiving thirty-seven seconds of green time in a seventy-second cycle.

Volume-Adjustment Module The volume-adjustment module worksheet for this calculation is shown in Figure 4–29.

Movement volumes are entered in column 3 from the input worksheet. Each is divided by the PHF of 0.90 to produce the movement flow rate indicated in column 5.

At this point the lane groups for analysis must be established. Clearly the northbound and southbound approaches form one lane group each, as only one lane is present. For the eastbound and westbound approaches, it is now necessary to determine whether or not equilibrium shared-lane operation exists for the left turn, or whether a defacto left-turn lane exists. This is done following the procedure outlined previously in the "Methodology" section.

First the approximate equivalent through-flow rate is computed for both eastbound and westbound left turns, It is assumed that, under the worst conditions, this flow fully occupies the leftmost lane of the approach:

$$v_{LE} = v_L \left[1{,}800/(1{,}400 - v_o) \right]$$

As neither approach includes a left-turn or single lane, v_o is taken to be the total flow on the opposing approach, including left and right turns: Thus:

$$v_{LE} \ (EB) = 72 \left[1{,}800/(1{,}400 - 722) \right] = 191 \text{ vph}$$
$$v_{LE} \ (WB) = 33 \left[1{,}800/(1{,}400 - 689) \right] = 65 \text{ vph}$$

For equilibrium to exist, these values must be less than the average flow per lane assuming that all right-turning and through vehicles must use remaining approach lanes. Thus:

$$v_{LE} < (v - v_L)/(N - 1)$$

and

$$229 < (689 - 72)/(2 - 1) = 617 \text{ vphpl} \quad \text{(OK)}$$
$$99 < (722 - 33)/(2 - 1) = 689 \text{ vphpl} \quad \text{(OK)}$$

Therefore equilibrium will exist on both the eastbound and westbound approaches, and a single-lane group may be established for each. Note that these computations use the flow rates of column 5 on the volume adjustment worksheet, which have already been adjusted for PHF.

The lane-utilization factor is selected from Table 4–47 for Fifth Avenue, with one-lane approaches, the value is 1.00, while for Walker Street, with two-lane

VOLUME ADJUSTMENT WORKSHEET

(1) APPR.	(2) MVT.	(3) MVT. VOLUME (vph)	(4) PEAK HOUR FACTOR PHF	(5) FLOW RATE v_p (vph) (3)÷(4)	(6) LANE GROUP	(7) FLOW RATE IN LANE GROUP (vph)	(8) NUMBER OF LANES N	(9) LANE UTILIZATION FACTOR U	(10) ADJ. FLOW v (vph) (7)×(9)	(11) PROP. OF LT or RT P_{LT} or P_{RT}
EB	LT	65	0.90	72						
	TH	520	0.90	578	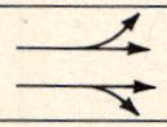	689	2	1.05	723	0.10 LT 0.06 RT
	RT	35	0.90	39						
WB	LT	30	0.90	33						
	TH	600	0.90	667	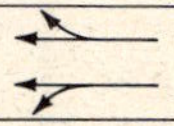	722	2	1.05	758	0.05 LT 0.03 RT
	RT	20	0.90	22						
NB	LT	30	0.90	33						
	TH	270	0.90	300	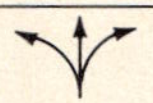	355	1	1.00	355	0.09 LT 0.06 RT
	RT	20	0.90	22						
SB	LT	40	0.90	44						
	TH	410	0.90	456		556	1	1.00	556	0.08 LT 0.10 RT
	RT	50	0.90	56						

Figure 4—29 Volume-Adjustment Worksheet for Example Calculation

SATURATION FLOW ADJUSTMENT WORKSHEET

(1) APPR.	(2) LANE GROUP MOVEMENTS	(3) IDEAL SAT. FLOW pcphgpl	(4) NO. OF LANES N	(5) LANE WIDTH f_w TAB. 4-45	(6) HEAVY VEH f_{MV} TAB. 4-46	(7) GRADE f_g TAB. 4-47	(8) PKG f_p TAB. 4-48	(10) BUS BLOCKAGE f_{bb} TAB. 4-49	(11) AREA TYPE f_a TAB. 4-50	(12) RIGHT TURN f_{RT} TAB. 4-51	(13) LEFT TURN f_{LT} TAB. 4-52	(14) ADJ. SAT. FLOW RATE vphg
EB	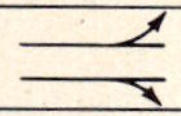	1800	2	0.97	0.975	1.00	1.00	1.00	0.90	0.99	0.78	2366
WB		1800	2	0.97	0.975	1.00	1.00	1.00	0.90	0.99	0.89	2699
NB		1800	1	1.10	0.96	1.00	1.00	1.00	0.90	0.97	0.92	1526
SB		1800	1	1.10	0.96	1.00	1.00	1.00	0.90	0.93	0.99	1575

Figure 4-30 Saturation Flow-Rate Worksheet for Example Calculation

approaches, the value is 1.05. These are entered in column 9 of the worksheet, and are multiplied by the flow rates of column 5 to produce the adjusted flow rates of column 10, that is:

$$v = v_p \times U$$

The proportion of left and/or right turns in the lane group is computed by taking the turning flow rates of column 3 and dividing by the total unadjusted flow in the lane group from column 7.

Saturation Flow-Rate Module   The worksheet for the saturation flow-rate module is shown in Figure 4–30.

Lane-group descriptions are repeated on column 2 of the worksheet. The ideal saturation flow rate will be assumed to be that the usual value of 1,800 pcphgpl. The columns that follow contain the number of lanes in the lane group and all adjustments to the ideal saturation flow rate, as follows:

a. *Number of lanes.* Eastbound and westbound lane groups have two lanes. Northbound and southbound lane groups have one lane.
b. *Lane-width factor.* This factor is selected from Table 4–48. For the 11-foot lanes on Walker Street, the value is 0.97; for the 15-foot lanes on Fifth Avenue, the value is 1.10.
c. *Heavy-vehicle factor.* This factor is found in Table 4–49. For 5 percent heavy vehicles on Walker Street, the value is 0.975 (interpolated between 0.97 and 0.98); for 8 percent heavy vehicles on Fifth Avenue, the value is 0.96.
d. *Grade factor.* Selected from Table 4–50, all values are 1.00, as the grades level for all approaches.
e. *Parking factor.* Found in Table 4–51, all values are 1.00, as no parking lanes exist on any approach.
f. *Bus blockage factor.* This factor is taken from Table 4–52; as there are no buses on any approach, all values are 1.00.
g. *Area-type factor.* This factor is taken from Table 4–53, and is 0.90, as the intersection is located in a CBD.
h. *Right-turn factor.* This factor is taken from Table 4–54. Right turns on Walker Street are permissive from shared lanes (case 5 in Table 4–51), while those from Fifth Avenue are on single-line approaches (case 7 in Table 4–53). The factor is based upon the proportion of right turns in the lane group (see Figure 4–29) and the number of conflicting pedestrians per hour (100 for all approaches, see Figure 4–28).
i. *Left-turn factor.* Left turns from all four approaches are permitted; left-turn factors must be computed using the special procedures for such cases. The supplemental worksheet used for these computations is shown in Figure 4–31. Although lengthy, this worksheet is self-explanatory. Input variables are entered for each approach. They are

selected from the input worksheet and the volume-adjustment work-sheet.

Note that with respect to single-lane approaches, the left-turn flow is discounted when computing mainline and opposing flows for the northbound and south-bound approaches. These resulting factors are entered on the saturation flow-rate worksheet of Figure 4–30. This ideal saturation flow rate is multiplied by all adjustments, with the resulting saturation flow rates for prevailing conditions shown in column 14 of the saturation flow-rate worksheet.

Capacity-Analysis Module   The capacity analysis module worksheet is shown in Figure 4–32.

Lane-group descriptions are repeated again in column 2 of the worksheet. In the subsequent two columns, the adjusted volume for each lane group is entered from the volume adjustment worksheet, and the saturation flow rate is entered from the saturation flow rate worksheet. From these values flow ratios are computed as v/s, and entered in column 5 of the worksheet.

At this point a search is made for the critical lane groups. For Walker Street the east–west street, all lane groups move on the same phase. Thus the maximum flow ratio among the four eastbound and westbound lane groups is critical for the first

Input Variables	EB	WB	NB	SB
Cycle Length, C (secs)	70	70	70	70
Effective Green, g (secs)	27	27	37	37
Number of Lanes, N	2	2	1	1
Flow Rate, v (vph)	689	722	355	556
Flow Rate, v_M (vph)	689	722	322	512
Left-Turn Flow Rate, v_{LT} (vph)	72	33	33	44
Proportion of LT, P_{LT}	0.10	0.05	0.09	0.08
Opposing Lanes, N_o	2	2	1	1
Flow Rate, v_o (vph)	722	689	512	322
Prop. of LT in Opp. Vol., P_{LTO}	0.05	0.10	0.08	0.09

Figure 4–31   Supplemental Worksheet for Computation of Left-Turn Adjustment Factors for Example Calculation

Computations	EB	WB	NB	SB
$S_{op} = \dfrac{1800\ N_o}{1 + P_{LTO}\left[\dfrac{400 + v_M}{1400 - v_M}\right]}$	3342	3090	1709	1648
$Y_o = v_o / S_{op}$	0.22	0.222	0.30	0.20
$g_u = (g - CY_o) / (1 - Y_o)$	14.87	14.73	22.85	28.75
$f_o = (875 - 0.625\ v_o) / 1000$	0.424	0.444	0.56	0.674
$P_L = P_{LT}\left[1 + \dfrac{(N-1)g}{f_s g_u + 4.5}\right]$	0.35	0.172	0.090	0.09
$g_q = g - g_u$	12.13	12.27	14.15	8.25
$P_T = 1 - P_L$	0.65	0.828	0.91	0.91
$g_f = 2\dfrac{P_T}{P_L}\left[1 - P_T^{0.5}\ g_q\right]$	3.45	6.62	9.9	7.37
$E_L = 1800 / (1400 - v_o)$	2.65	2.53	1.58	1.67
$f_m = \dfrac{g_f}{g} + \dfrac{g_u}{g}\left[\dfrac{1}{1 + P_L(E_L - 1)}\right] + \dfrac{2}{g}(1 + P_L)$	0.568	0.780	0.92	0.99
$f_{LT} = (f_m + N - 1) / N$	0.78	0.89	0.92	0.99

Figure 4–31   (continued)

signal phase. This value is the 0.369 ratio on the eastbound lane group. For Fifth Avenue both lane groups move on the same phase, and the critical lane group is the one with the highest flow ratio on the North–South street. This is the south-bound approach, which has a flow ratio of 0.437. Thus the sum of critical lane flow ratios is 0.369 + 0.437 = 0.806.

Green ratios are entered in column 6 of the worksheet, and are found by dividing the effective green time for the lane group by the cycle length. For this calculation it is assumed that the effective green is equal to the actual green, and:

$$g/C \text{ (Walker St.)} = 27/70 = 0.386$$
$$g/C \text{ (Fifth Ave.)} = 37/70 = 0.528$$

CAPACITY ANALYSIS WORKSHEET

LANE GROUP		③ ADJ. VOLUME v (vph)	④ ADJ. SAT FLOW RATE s	⑤ FLOW RATIO v/s ③÷④	⑥ GREEN RATIO g/C	⑦ LANE GROUP CAPACITY c (vph) ④×⑥	⑧ v/c RATIO X ③÷⑦	⑨ CRITICAL ?
① APPR.	② LANE GROUP MOVEMENTS							
EB	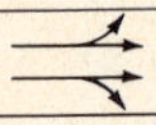	723	2366	0.306	0.386	913	0.791	✓
WB	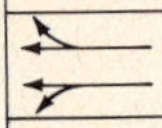	758	2699	0.280	0.386	1041	0.728	
NB	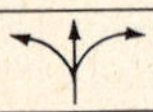	355	1526	0.232	0.528	805	0.44	
SB	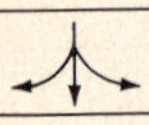	556	1575	0.353	0.528	831	0.66	✓

Cycle Length, C __70__ secs.

Loss Time Per Cycle, L __6__ secs.

$$\sum_i (v/s)_{ci} = .659$$

$$X_c = \frac{\sum_i (v/s)_{ci} \times C}{C - L} = .720$$

Figure 4–32   Capacity-Analysis Module Worksheet for Example Calculation

Lane-group capacities are computed by multiplying the green ratio (g/C) by the saturation flow rate for the lane group (s). Finally, the v/c ratio (X) for each lane group is computed by dividing the adjusted lane group flow rate (v) by the capacity of the lane group (c).

Intersection values are computed at the bottom of Figure 4–32. As the effective green time was assumed equal to actual green time, the lost time is taken as equal to the change intervals, which are assumed to be three seconds per phase. Thus the cycle length is seventy seconds, with six seconds of lost time per cycle.

The critical v/c ratio (X_c) is computed as shown on the worksheet:

$$X_c = \frac{0.659(70)}{70 - 6} = 0.720$$

The results of this module indicate that the existing signal and geometric design of the intersection will be adequate to handle the projected demands, with a reasonable high resulting V/C ratio. The intersection operates at about 90 percent of its capacity for the critical movements, and the eastbound approach operates very near its capacity ($X = 0.956$).

With these results it may be reasoned that green time could be reallocated to produce more equitable operations on all critical movements, but that there is little surplus on any of the critical approach lane groups. Given this result, delay and level of service on these approaches are now considered.

Level-of-Service Module   The level-of-service module worksheet is shown in Figure 4–33. Lane-group descriptions are entered in column 2.

Values of X, g/C, C, and c are entered into columns 3, 4, 5, and 7, respectively, as these will be needed to compute delay. They are obtained from the capacity-analysis worksheet.

The first-term delay is computed:

$$
\begin{aligned}
d_1 &= 0.38\ C\ (1 - g/C)^2/[1 - (g/C)\ (X)] \\
d_1\ (EB) &= 0.38(70)\ (1 - 0.386)^2/[1 - (0.386)\ (0.791)] = 19.44 \text{ seconds} \\
d_1\ (WB) &= 0.38(70)\ (1 - 0.386)^2/[1 - (0.386)\ (0.728)] = 18.05 \text{ seconds} \\
d_1\ (NB) &= 0.38(70)\ (1 - 0.528)^2/[1 - (0.528)\ (0.44)] = 7.41 \text{ seconds} \\
d_1\ (SB) &= 0.38(70)\ (1 - 0.528)^2/[1 - (0.528)\ (0.66)] = 8.48 \text{ seconds}
\end{aligned}
$$

The second-term delay may be computed:

$$
\begin{aligned}
d_2 &= 173\ X^2\ [(X - 1) + \sqrt{[(X - 1)^2 + (16X/c)\,]} \\
d_2\ (EB) &= 1.08 \text{ seconds } (X = 0.791,\ c = 913) \\
d_2\ (WB) &= 0.91 \text{ seconds } (X = 0.728,\ c = 104) \\
d_2\ (NB) &= 0.13 \text{ seconds } (X = 0.44,\ c = 805) \\
d_2\ (SB) &= 1.37 \text{ seconds } (X = 0.66,\ c = 831)
\end{aligned}
$$

These values are entered in the appropriate columns of the level-of-service worksheet. Progression factors are now selected from Table 4–56. For the eastbound approach, the factor is 0.90 (arrival type 4); for the westbound approach, it is 1.18 (arrival type 2); and for the northbound and southbound approaches, it is 1.00 (arrival type 3). The eastbound and westbound factors depend on the v/c ratio. Values were selected for a v/c ratio of 1.0, as both v/c ratios are above 0.80,

LEVEL OF SERVICE WORKSHEET

① APPR.	② LANE GROUP MOVEMENTS	③ v/c RATIO X	④ GREEN RATIO g/C	⑤ CYCLE LENGTH C (secs)	⑥ DELAY d_1 (secs/veh)	⑦ LANE GROUP CAPACITY c (vph)	⑧ DELAY d_2 (secs/veh)	⑨ PROGRESSION FACTOR PF TAB. 4-56	⑩ LANE GROUP DELAY (secs/veh) (⑥+⑧)×⑨	⑪ LANE GROUP LOS TAB. 4-43	⑫ APPROACH DELAY (secs/veh)	⑬ APPR. LOS TAB. 4-43
	LANE GROUP		FIRST TERM DELAY				SECOND TERM DELAY				TOTAL DELAY & LOS	
EB		0.791	0.386	70	19.44	913	1.08	0.82	16.82	C	16.82	C
WB		0.728	0.386	70	18.05	1041	0.91	1.22	25.13	C	23.13	C
NB		0.44	0.528	70	7.41	805	0.13	1.00	7.54	B	7.54	B
SB		0.66	0.528	70	8.48	831	1.37	1.00	9.85	B	9.85	B

INTERSECTION DELAY 15.76 secs/veh   INTERSECTION LOS C

Figure 4–33 Level-of-Service Module Worksheet for Example Calculation

the next lower category. Intermediate values could be interpolated, but the accuracy of the delay prediction usually does not warrant this precision.

The delay in each lane group is now computed as:

$$\text{Delay} = (d_1 + d_2)\, PF$$
$$\text{Delay } (EB) = (19.44 + 1.08)\,(.82) = 16.82, \text{ call it } 16.8 \text{ seconds/vehicle}$$
$$\text{Delay } (WB) = (18.05 + 0.91)\,(1.22) = 23.13, \text{ call it } 23.1 \text{ seconds/vehicle}$$
$$\text{Delay } (NB) = (7.41 + 0.13)\,(1.00) = 7.54, \text{ call it } 7.5 \text{ seconds/vehicle}$$
$$\text{Delay } (SB) = (8.48 + 1.37)\,(1.00) = 9.85, \text{ call it } 9.6 \text{ seconds/vehicle}$$

The average stopped delay per vehicle for the intersection as a whole is now computed as a weighted average of the values for each approach:

$$\text{Delay (int.)} = \frac{(723 \times 16.82) + (758 \times 23.13) + (355 \times 7.54) + (556 \times 9.85)}{723 + 758 + 355 + 556}$$

$$\text{Delay (int.)} = 15.76, \text{ call it } 15.8 \text{ seconds/vehicle}$$

Levels of service may now be assigned by comparing the computed delay values with the criteria of Table 4–43.

An interpretation of the results indicates that the intersection operates at level of service *C* or better on all approaches, with the intersection as a whole operating at level of service *C*. Some reallocation of green time from those approaches operating at level of service *B* might serve to improve operations and further lessen delay on the other two approaches—although the intersection operates well and without significant delay, and has considerable excess capacity capabilities at the moment.

These intersection capacity analysis techniques are involved, complex, and laborious to do by hand calculation. They are included in this text so that the reader has a step-by-step synopsis of state-of-the-art methods that will be used henceforth to compute intersection capacity. Actual calculations will be computerized on a microcomputer disk for use in the near future by the Transportation Research Board. Such further microcomputerized usage will eliminate the need for laborious hand calculations exhibited herein, given the user understands the fundamentals presented. For further computational research and microcomputer documentation, the author suggests the user contact the Transportation Research Board and/or access the forthcoming *1985 Highway Capacity Manual* issued as *Transportation Research Board Special Report 209.*

Highway and Motor Transportation Regulation

The emphasis in this portion of the chapter will be on meaningful consequences of highway transportation and related important regulatory aspects. The legislative background of highway financing is treated in Chapter 13 on transportation policy.

Basic Importance of Highway Transportation

There are two basic characteristics of highway transportation: route and system *flexibility,* and *varying* capital investment possibilities. The highway system is a flexible system in that it has unique, ubiquitous locational flexibility. Likewise it possesses unique capital investment flexibility, in that one can build up the system at a highly variable rate of capital additions, beginning with a path and ultimately evolving the route to a freeway.

Types of Highway Carriers

The motor carriers for hire that use the highway system have several types of operational entities. They are as follows:

1. *Common,* on the open market.
2. *Contract,* contracted out to specific firms.
3. *Private,* for one's own use.

The foregoing environment is somewhat characterized by a number of small firms, often operating at various levels of ease of entry to or exit from the market. This parallels the small-business microeconomic perfect-competition theory of the firm. However, larger firms typically have more route coverage. The industry is regulated by the federal Interstate Commerce Commission (ICC) and state commerce commissions. Before beginning hauling, a carrier must obtain a "Certificate of Convenience and Necessity" from the ICC, which indicates that the intended route service is necessary and the particular carrier is truly filling a market need. All carriers pay for some of their right-of-way and public use requirements through a user's tax on gasoline and oil, license fees, and sales taxes on vehicle parts. This is not enough, obviously, to cover the entire cost of highway facilities, and, therefore, the level of user charge to the truckers is an exceedingly controversial topic, with administrators arguing that adequate user charges are necessary to pay for roadway maintenance and truckers arguing that such charges will be passed on to the consumer, resulting in higher prices.

Rates

These issues are somewhat reflected in the types of rates charged to carry motor freight. There are *class* rates, where different commodity classes are charged specific rates, often cross-classified by distance hauled, and "*distance*" rates, with the most notable being "*tapering*" rates as shown in Figure 4–34. Such rate

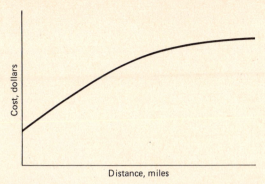

Figure 4–34   Example of a Tapering Truck Rate

structures assure the trucker a fair return for short and medium hauls, and exclude exorbitant costs to the shipper for very-long-distance runs.

Truck Terminals

It is appropriate to describe briefly the place and operating characteristics of truck terminals in motor transportation. Truck terminals play a vital role in the interchange of motor freight from over-the-road transfer to local delivery. The terminals consist of a warehouse or loft-type building, with loading docks and doors to accommodate semitrailer and local delivery trucks. They are divided into four classifications, according to the number of daily dispatches, as follows:

Classification	Number of Dispatches/Day
Small	Less than 20
Medium	More than 20, less than 60
Large	More than 60, less than 120
Major	More than 120

Approximately 15 percent of these dispatches will be by draymen, that is, local delivery trucks taking cargo to its final destination in the area, after off-loading from an over-the-road semitrailer.

Typically several truck terminals tend to cluster in selected areas in a region, often near ports, industrial parks, or the confluence of freeways, to make the best use of delivery paths of finished goods. An efficiently located truck terminal system is vital to freight operations in a metropolitan area. The cargo must be delivered in a timely manner, yet in a traffic pattern such that the presence of a large number of trucks does not totally congest the street system.

A resulting liability of the clustering of many truck terminals is their use of large contiguous acreage that might better be used for industrial and commercial purposes. The four classifications typically require the following acreages.

Classification	Acreage Required
Small	4
Medium	10
Large	25
Major	Greater than 25

Historically small and medium-sized terminals tend to be used to capacity less frequently, and hence they suffer more financial vunerability. Therefore, a major thrust in truck terminal planning is to urge consolidation of many small or medium terminal operators into an integrated terminal, with each operator leasing some space, and thus reducing individual economic risk. This achieves the goal of freeing land formerly occupied by many small and/or medium terminal operators for use by more productive commercial or industrial activities. Due to the economic risks inherent in terminal operation and metropolitan area efforts toward economic development, it is likely that truck terminal planning will receive a great deal of attention in the next decade.

Trucking Deregulation

The Motor Carrier Act of 1980 caused significant shifts in the operating characteristics of the trucking system. The Act has several essential points:

1. It allows virtually total ease of entry to the business, by dropping the ICC Certificate of Public Convenience and Necessity.
2. It substitutes a review of public need for the service in place of the Certificate of Public Convenience and Necessity.
3. It strips all rate restrictions on commodities hauled, and allows the free market economy to determine rate structures

The general thrust of legislation was designed to strip institutional layers of bureaucratic operating practices from the industry, and permit it to operate as a free market, a microeconomic example of perfect competition.

Deregulation, at this point, is not considered a workable solution to the problem. It was initiated in the midst of the economic recession of 1981, and has resulted, concurrently with the economic downturn, in very poor economic and profit results for the industry. The industry's 1982 return on equity was only 5.02 percent, compared with an all-industries national average of 13.22 percent, and many carriers are near bankruptcy.

The flaws appear to be related to poor administration of the Act by the ICC and the timing of its inception. Specifically:

1. The monitoring of specific "certificates of public need" has been argued to have been overly lax, resulting, because of the increased ease of entry provided by the Act, in an excess capacity of small, underfinanced operations, which further dilute the market at a time of economic recession. This has resulted in increased bankruptcies and the pressure of unorthodox rate processes as desperate attempts to stay in business continue by many carriers.
2. The ICC, although allowing freedom of pricing, still requires that rates must cover fixed costs of operation. In light of item 1, this has been violated regularly during the past deregulation period, resulting in discrimination and unreasonable pricing, and driving competition out of business.

In response to dealing with the operational problems resulting from deregulation, the motor carrier industry has taken some major steps, including the following.

1. It has continually sought to maintain the capability for the carriers to band together to set joint or through rates for several combination hauls using several carriers in order to stabilize the earnings–haulage-effort pattern to some extent, and to avoid further rate wars. In reaction to this, the question of antitrust immunity has arisen, as the industry is acting as a cartel in this regard. It is an open question as to whether it will continue to be able to operate under antitrust immunity.
2. The industry has sought, and obtained, legislation allowing larger, heavier trucks, resulting in the capability to haul more volume per threshold movement cost. In the Highway Act of 1982, truck sizes were increased to 80,000 pounds with widths of 104 inches, and the capability to haul tandems or double loads in all states was achieved.

The trucking industry exists in a stage of fragile adjustment to deregulation fostered during a period of economic decline after a significant period of regulatory comfort and stability. Its recovery will be a slow and tenuous one.

Problems

1. A driver is traveling on a rural two-lane highway at 45 mph on a 5 percent downgrade and wet pavement. What is the stopping sight distance? Assume $f = 0.32$.
2. A four-lane (48-foot-wide) highway has a curve with a 1,000-foot radius. What is the proper superelevation for a design speed of 55 mph? Use a friction factor of 0.14.

3. What is the minimum length of spiral required for the curve in Problem 2? Assume $C = 2.0$.

4. What is the stopping sight distance over a crest if the algebraic difference in grades is 6.1 and the length of the curve is 750 feet?

5. Given the following highway characteristics, determine the level of service of the facility.

four-lane divided freeway, two lanes each direction
12-foot lanes
2-foot lateral clearance for an obstruction on one side of roadway only
4 percent grade between one-fourth and one-half mile long
5 percent heavy trucks
50-mph design speed
2,200 vehicles per hour, one direction.
peak-hour factor = 0.80
driver population—weekday commuters

6. A rural two-lane highway in mountainous terrain has a 6 percent grade of one mile. Other characteristics are:

12-foot lanes
8-foot shoulders
60 percent no-passing zone
60/40 directional split
12 percent trucks
6 percent recreational vehicles
2 percent buses
80 percent passenger cars
peak-hour factor = 0.85

What is the maximum volume that can be accommodated on the grade at a speed of 40 mph?

References

Bohman, Raynard F., Jr. *Trucking Deregulation: How Far It Actually Goes.* Gardner, Mass.: Bohman Industrial Traffic Consultants, Inc., 1980.

Chow, Garland. *The Economics of the Motor Freight Industries* Bloomington/Indianapolis: Indiana University, 1978.

Cleveland, Donald E., Editor. *Manual of Traffic Engineering Studies,* 3d ed. Washington, D.C.: Institute of Traffic Engineers, 1964.

Davis, Grant M., Editor. *Collective Ratemaking in the Motor Carrier Industry.* Danville, Ill.: Interstate Printers and Publishers, 1980.

Eastern Transportation Law Seminar, Papers and Proceedings. Washington, D.C.: Association of Interstate Commerce Commission Practitioners, 1980.

Eastern Transportation Law Seminar, Papers and Proceedings. Washington, D.C.: Association of Interstate Commerce Commission Practitioners, 1981.

Haefner, L. E., E. J. Carter, and J. W. Hall. *An Informational Report on Techniques for Evaluating Factors Relevant to Decision Making on Highway Locations.* Washington, D.C.: U.S. Department of Transportation, Federal Highway Administration, December 1972.

Haefner, L. E., E. J. Carter, and J. W. Hall. *Literature References on Techniques for the Evaluation of Factors Relevant to Decision Making on Highway Locations.* Washington, D.C.: U.S. Department of Transportation, Federal Highway Administration, January 1972.

Highway Capacity Manual 1965, Special Report 87. Washington, D.C.: Highway Research Board, 1965.

Highway, Capacity Manual 1985, Transportation Research Circular Number 281. Washington, D.C.: Transportation Research Board, June 1984.

Highway Capacity Manual 1985, Transportation Circular Number 284. Washington, D.C.: Transportation Research Board, October 1984.

Legault, Adrian R. *Highway and Airport Engineering.* Englewood Cliffs, N.J.: Prentice-Hall, 1960.

Lisciandro, Patricia. *Financial Analysis of the Motor Carrier Industry 1982.* Washington, D.C.: American Trucking Association, 1983.

Manual on Uniform Traffic Control Devices for Streets and Highways. Washington, D.C.: Federal Highway Administration, 1970.

Paquette, Radnor, and Leo J. Ritter, Jr. *Highway Engineering,* 2d ed. New York: Ronald Press, 1960.

A Policy on Geometric Design of Highways and Streets. Washington, D.C.: American Association of State Highway Officials, 1984.

A Policy on Geometric Design of Rural Highways 1965. Washington, D.C.: American Association of State Highway Officials, 1966.

Searles, William H., Howard C. Ives, and Philip Kissam. *Field Engineering,* vol. 1. New York: John Wiley, 1980.

"Signalized Intersections," *Highway Capacity Manual 1985,* Chapter 9. Washington, D.C.: Highway Research Board, 1985.

Transportation and Traffic Engineering Handbook. Englewood Cliffs, N.J.: Prentice-Hall (Institute of Traffic Engineers), 1976.

Trucking De-Regulation/Economic Recession: The Facts! Washington, D.C.: Regular Common Carrier Conference, 1983.

Western Transportation Law Seminar, Papers and Proceedings. Kansas City, Mo.: Association of Interstate Commerce Commission Practitioners, 1981.

Western Transportation Law Seminar, Papers and Proceedings. Denver: Association of Interstate Commerce Commission Practitioners, 1982.

5 Rail Transportation Engineering

Rail transportation is one of the oldest, most visible, and dominant forms of transportation in the United States. As discussed in Chapter 2 on history, it has had a formidable impact on the growth and development of the U.S. economic pattern. The past two decades have been ones of turmoil and change for the industry. In this chapter we explore the technological, engineering, and regulatory aspects of rail transportation.

Rail transportation as we know it today is primarily concerned with the movement of great volumes of freight at low rates, competitive with other modes. The recent emphasis has been on the optimum relocation of lines to maximize revenue and reduce high fixed-cost commitments that produce little or no moving revenue.

National Rail Operational Patterns

The location of rail facilities on a regional or national basis attempts to be sensitive to the location of population centers, raw material sites, and manufacturing facilities. The objective is to bring raw materials together for manufacturing and to have an efficient delivery of the finished product to large consumer markets.

Figures 5–1, 5–2, and 5–3 illustrate the major intercity lines in the United States according to professional main- and branch-line intercity standards, which are:

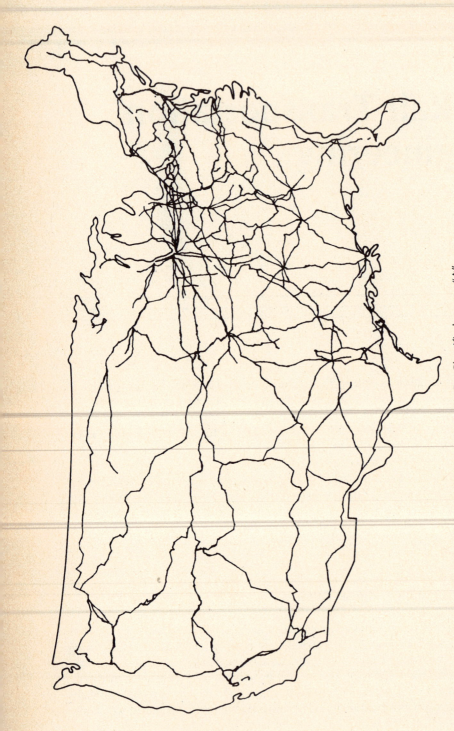

Figure 5–1 *"A" Main-line Track in the United States.* To Be Classified as an "A" Main-line, the Track Has to Carry 20 Million or More Gross Tons of Traffic per Year, Be a major transportation Connective, and/or Be Essential to the National Defense. (*Source:* John H. Armstrong, *The Railroad—What It Does, What It Is,* Omaha, Nebr., Simmons-Boardman, 1978.)

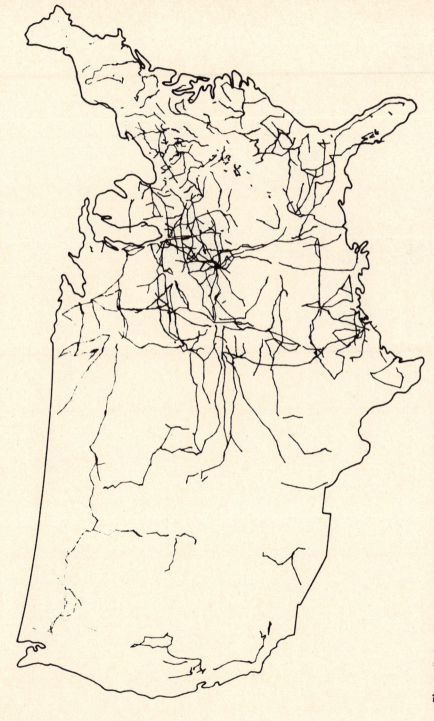

Figure 5–2 *"B" Main-line Track in the United States.* This Is Track Carrying Between 5 and 20 Million Gross Tons of Traffic per Year.

(*Source:* John H. Armstrong, *The Railroad—What It Is, What It Does,* Omaha, Nebr., Simmons-Boardman, 1978.)

Figure 5–3 *"A" Branch-line Track in the United States. This Is Track Carrying Between 1 and 5 Million Gross Tons of Traffic per Year.*

(*Source:* John H. Armstrong. *The Railroad—What It Is, What It Does,* Omaha, Nebr., Simmons-Boardman, 1978.)

"A" Main Line

1. Has traffic density of more than 20 million annual gross tons.
2. Serves a market generating more than 75,000 carloads annually and/or:
3. Provides a through rail corridor designated as essential in the strategic rail corridor network for national defense.

"B" Main Line

1. Carries more than 5 million gross tons annually, but less than 20 million gross tons.

Branch Line

1. Carries more than 1 million gross tons, but less than 5 million gross tons annually.

Table 5–1 provides a composite of the above in the northern hemisphere. Note that light-density lines make up 25 percent of all routes in the United States but handle less than 1 percent of the ton-miles; hence the recent stimulus to consolidate lines and corridors.

For purposes of cost accounting and carrier operations, the Interstate Com-

Table 5–1   The North American Rail Network

		United States	Total North America
Miles of Line			
"First-track" only, excluding rapid-transit, switching and terminal companies, etc. Track over which more than one company operates counted only once. Common-carrier only.			
Standard gage	(4 ft 8½ in. or 1,435 mm)	193,500	250,550
Narrow gage	(3 ft 6 in. or 1,067 mm)	—	725
	(3 ft 0 in. or 914 mm)	10	560
Total		193,510	251,835
Miles of Track			
Including second, third, and fourth tracks; switching and terminal companies, sidings, and yard tracks operated by common-carrier railroad companies.			
Total		311,500	390,600
Ownership—miles of line			
Private companies		191,880	
National (government corporations)		1,250	
Provincial, State, Municipal		380	
Combination		—	

Table 5–2   Class Composition of U.S. Railroads

Effective Date	Class I	Class II	Class III
Jan. 1, 1978	$50 million or more	$5–50 million	Less than $5 million
Jan. 1, 1965	$5 million or more	Less than $5 million	—
Jan. 1, 1956	$3 million or more	Less than $3 million	—
Prior to 1956	$1 million or more	$100,000 but less than $1 million	Less than $100,000

(*Source:* Association of American Railroads, Washington, D.C.)

merce Commission (ICC) identifies individual rail companies as Class I, II, or III, according to their average operating revenues for a three-year period, as illustrated in Table 5–2. For all practical purposes, all major railroads worthy of discussion herein are Class I railroads. As shown in Table 5–3, their miles of road owned and operated have decreased during the 1970–1979 period as they attempt to remove inefficient, unprofitable segments from their systems. Table 5–4 exhibits the comparative amounts of equipment and rolling stock owned by Class I railroads during this period.

Geometric Layout and Right-of-Way

Alignment

Similar in concept to highway alignments discussed in Chapter 4, rail alignment is prescribed to yield a maximum permissible degree of curvature with the following ranges: one–two degrees in flat or gently rolling country; ranging up to

Table 5–3   Mileage of Class I[a] Line-Haul Carriers

Year	Number of Roads	Miles of Road Owned	Miles of Road Operated	Total Mileage Owned (All Tracks)	Total Mileage Operated (All Tracks)
1970	71	176,745	209,836	281,948	346,592
1979	42	157,905	181,870	256,340	302,754[b]

[a]See text for a definition of Class I.
[b]Although the ICC no longer summarizes mileage statistics for switching and terminal companies and other than Class I roads, there are roughly 500 operating railroads, 330,000 miles of owned track, and 350,000 miles of track operated.
Source: Transport Statistics for the Year 1979, Washington, D.C., Interstate Commerce Commission.

Table 5–4 Ownership, Aggregate Carrying Capacity, and Average Capacity Per Car, Class I U.S. Railroads as of January 1

Car Type	Ownership			Aggregate Capacity (tons × 10³)			Average Carrying Capacity (tons)		
	1960	1970	1979	1960	1970	1979	1960	1970	1979
Plain box	655,418	386,499	217,301	32,365	20,720	13,740	49.4	53.6	63.2
Equipped box	50,320	159,574	166,719	2,479	10,169	11,564	49.3	63.7	69.4
Total box	705,738	546,073	384,020	34.843	30.890	25,311	49.4	56.6	65.9
Covered hoppers	61,407	125,867	161,885	4,267	10,641	14,982	69.5	84.5	92.6
Gondolas	271,626	192,238	157,587	16,765	13,423	12,694	61.7	69.8	80.6
Hoppers	490,020	394,204	327,044	29,421	28,207	27,275	60.0	71.6	83.4
Stock	31,470	11,797	*	1,238	487	*	39.4	41.3	*
Flat	51,257	71,498	97,746	2,881	4,732	6,828	56.2	66.2	69.9
Refrigerators	20,173	55,068	68,059	850	3,493	4,779	42.1	63.4	70.2
Tank	*	4,541	2,542	*	262	175	*	57.8	68.9
Others	46,274	36,904	26,491	2,347	2,242	1,698	50.7	60.8	64.1
Total, all types	1,677,965	1,438,190	1,225,374	92,607	94,378	93,962	55.2	65.2	76.7

*Included in others.
(*Source:* Association of American Railroads, Car Service Division, Washington, D.C.)

greater than ten degrees in mountainous country, railyards composed of 10 percent of the trackage having twelve- to forty-degree curves, to accommodate appropriate layout within the site constraints.

Grades

Grades, in consort with the alignments, typically range from 0 to 1 percent on the main line, with 2.5 percent a common maximum in mountainous areas, and approximately 5 percent in logging and mining areas. Grades greater than the foregoing maxima impede the acceleration capabilities of the locomotive, greatly reducing or eliminating motion, and making haulage uneconomical.

Closely related to the percentage of grade content is the length of grades:

1. *Main line*. 0.1 percent per station on crests; 0.05 percent per station on sags.
2. *Minor roads*. 0.2 percent per station on crests; 0.1 percent per station on sags.

These criteria must be met to ensure performance. This is particularly critical in sags because of the presence of slack in the couplings, which introduces jerk and can result in unsafe operating conditions.

These entities are combined to develop appropriate curvature and gradient. A major characteristic of these components is the superelevation or banking and raising of the outer rail to allow safe train operation. The formula for such superelevation is:

$$e = 0.328 \; \frac{V^2}{R}$$

where
    $V =$ velocity, feet per second
    $R =$ radius of curvature, feet

Typical superelevation buildup and runoff are 1 inch per 50 feet of length, with no spirals. Spiral curves, operating with the same formula mechanics illustrated in Chapter 4 for highways, are often used in railroad alignments. Using them allows varying changes in rail curvature, superelevation, and train operating speed. Provision of such spirals allows improved operations in critical areas of topography, and in constricted locations, such as storage and classification yards.

Several operating compromises are made against the above "ideal" *V*. For both high-speed passenger and low-speed freight trains, the theoretical *e* is generally reduced by 3 inches, to allow safety factors on the banked curve for both very slow and very fast train operations.

Roadbed Characteristics

Figure 5–4 exhibits the classic diagram of typical main-line track and ballast structure. The cross section is composed of appropriately compacted earth sub-grade, above which is placed a sub-ballast of pit run gravel, and above that the top ballast of crushed rock or slag found in a two-to-one slope set. The ties are placed 21 inches apart, with dimensions of 8 feet, 6 inches by 7 inches by 9 inches, upon which is placed a 100- or 132-pound rail section. The plates used under the rail above the tie and the joints at rail section ends are either welded or closed by six-hole joint bars with lockwasher bolts. Typical rail is 6 inches high and can be

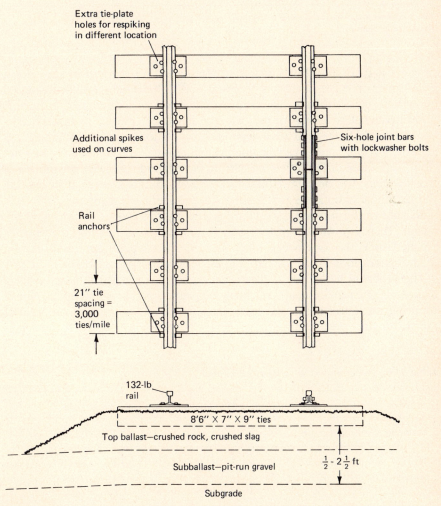

Figure 5–4 Track Structure for Typical Main-Line Track

Table 5–5 Recommended Grading Requirements for Crushed Stone and Crushed Air-Cooled Blast-Furnace Slag

			Percentages by Weight Passing Each Sieve Size						
3 in.	2½ in.	2 in.	1½ in.	1 in.	¾ in.	½ in.	⅜ in.	No. 4	No. 8
100	90–100	......	25–60	......	0–1	0–5			
	100	90–100	35–70	0–15	.....	0–5			
		100	90–100	20–55	0–15	.....	0–5		
			100	90–100	40–75	15–35	0–15	0–5	
			100	90–100	.....	25–60	....	0–10	0–5

(*Source:* Hennes and Ekse, *Fundamentals of Transportation Engineering,* New York, McGraw Hill, 1955. Used by permission.)

expected to carry 600,000,000 gross tons of traffic before wearing out. However, it wears faster on curves. Ballast is necessary to distribute the weight being placed on the ties, yet hold them in place and prevent lateral displacement of the tie itself. Appropriate ballast allows for the "wave of deflection" moving along each axle, approximately 1/100–1/50 inch, depending on car load and track stiffness. It is extremely important to maintain adequate drainage in the ballast so it does not "foul" with loose dirt pumped into it from the subgrade below by the motion of passing trains. Wet or soggy ballast also freezes and causes freeze–thaw heaving similar to that of concrete pavement during temperature changes.

In light of the foregoing, certain material requirements exist for adequate ballast. These are illustrated in Tables 5–5 and 5–6, depending on whether crushed stone, slag, or gravel is used—the only three types of aggregate allowed by the American Railroad Engineering Association (AREA) standards.

The probable life of ties is illustrated on a frequency distribution curve in Figure 5–5. Tie replacement is relatively frequent, depending on weather, type of tie preservative treatment, and loads carried, and is a *major* expense item of railroad engineering. Details of a rail section are shown in Figure 5–6, and details

Table 5–6 Recommended Grading of Gravel for Ballast

Percent Crushed Particles	Percentages by Weight Finer than Each Sieve Size							
	−½ in.	1 in.	½ in.	No. 4	No. 8	No. 16	No. 50	No. 100
0–20	100	80–100	50–85	20–40	15–35	5–25	0–10	0–2
21–40	100	65–100	35–75	10–35	0–10	0–5		
41–100	100	60–95	25–50	0–15	0–5			

(*Source:* Hennes and Ekse, *Fundamentals of Transportation Engineering,* New York, McGraw-Hill, 1955. Used by permission.)

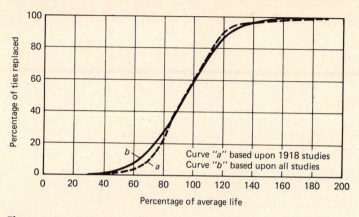

Figure 5–5   Probable Life of Ties

(*Source:* Courtesy U.S. Forest Products Laboratory, Madison, Wis.)

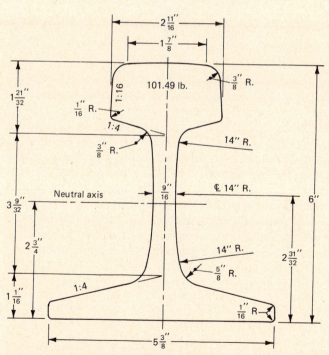

Figure 5–6   A 100-Pound Rail Section

(*Source: Manual for Railway Engineering (Fixed Properties),* American Railway Engineering Association, Chapter 4.

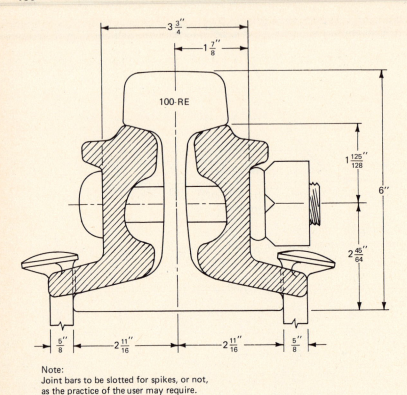

Note:
Joint bars to be slotted for spikes, or not,
as the practice of the user may require.

Figure 5–7   Joint Bar and Assembly for 100-Pound Rail
(*Source: Manual for Railway Engineering (Fixed Properties),* American Railway Engineering Association,
Chapter 4.

of the joint bar in Figure 5–7. The AREA estimates that about 2 million gross tons of
rail with such dimensions are laid annually.

The AREA has set quality standards on ballast as a function of several general
criteria. With regard to the distribution of tie load pressure necessary to produce
the stability discussed, the ballast is the effective medium for achieving this. Using
Talbot's equation, the pressure beneath the centerline of the tie under the rail, P_c,
is a function of unit pressure over the bearing area of the tie, P_a, and the depth h
below that bearing surface, that is,

$$P_c = \frac{16.8\,P_a}{h^{1.25}}$$

where
$\quad P_c$ = pressure in pounds per square inch under the tie centerline
$\quad P_a$ = uniformly distributed pressure over the tie face
$\quad h$ = depth below the face in inches

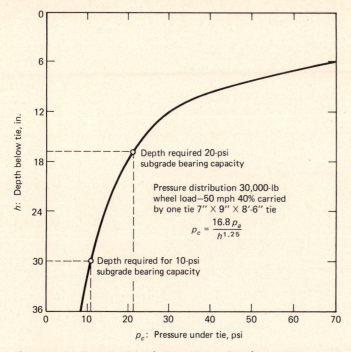

Figure 5–8   Pressure Distribution Versus Depth

(*Source:* William W. Hay, *Railroad Engineering,* 2d ed., New York, John Wiley, 1982. Used by permission.)

However, if the tie pressure P_a (in pounds per square inch) and the bearing capacity of the subgrade, set equal to P_c, are known, then the minimum depth h (in inches) for stability is:

$$h = \left(\frac{16.8 \, P_a}{P_c} \right)^{4/5}$$

The average bearing capacity of a normally firm subgrade soil is taken at 20 pounds per square inch, yielding the relationship in Figure 5–8. Essentially the entire loading and support system relationships are as illustrated in Figure 5–9 which shows the relationship of traffic loading, environmental factors, ballast material, subgrade, and performance.

Switches and Turnouts

The described components operate within a rail *system,* which has several ways of combining design components to maneuver, change direction, and store various train operations. The most elementary of these is the turnout, which is a mechanism that diverts the train from one track to another. The angle of juncture includes an assembly termed the frog, which lets the flanged wheel cross over the

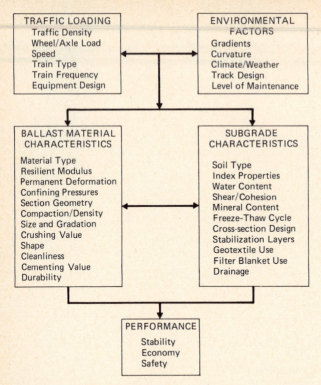

Figure 5–9 Traffic Loading Support Systems Relationship

(*Source:* William W. Hay, *Railroad Engineering,* 2d ed., New York, John Wiley, 1982. Used by permission.)

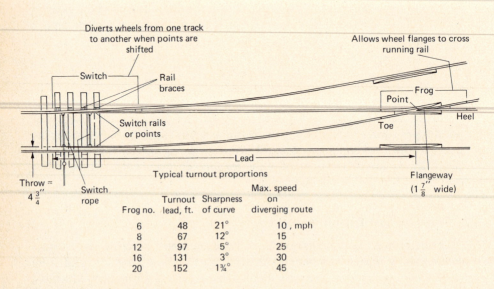

Typical turnout proportions

Frog no.	Turnout lead, ft.	Sharpness of curve	Max. speed on diverging route
6	48	21°	10 , mph
8	67	12°	15
12	97	5°	25
16	131	3°	30
20	152	1¾°	45

Figure 5–10 The Turnout

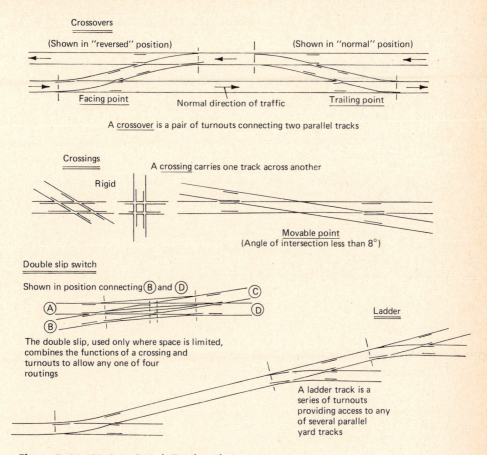

Figure 5–11   Various Switch Trackwork Arrangements

opposite rail. Basic examples are shown in Figure 5–10, designated as no. 6 frog to no. 20 frog—with dimensions as illustrated. There are several complex arrangements of switches, as shown in Figure 5–11, including crossovers, crossings, double slip switches, and ladders. The points of frog at turnouts, crossings, and multiple switches are areas of intense wear and fatigue.

Locomotive Properties:
Types and Characteristics of Power Units

The most important entity in railroad operations is the locomotive and its performance characteristics. Its horsepower and tractive effort are of particular interest. A particular combination of horsepower and tractive effort will determine what a locomotive can do to move trains successfully. Figure 5–12

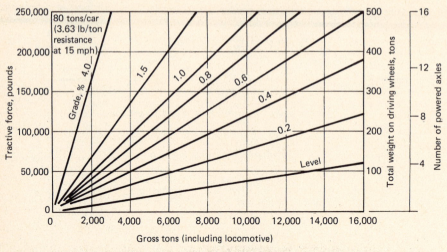

Figure 5–12 Tractive Effort Versus Tonnage and Grade

indicates the tractive force at the driving wheel rim necessary to start and move
tonnage up various grades. This pull is generated by gripping the rails with the
driving wheels. The right side of Figure 5–12 converts this information into
weight of locomotive needed, and typical number of axles. A 250,000-pound
weight is considered the limit for one engine because of the possibility of coupler

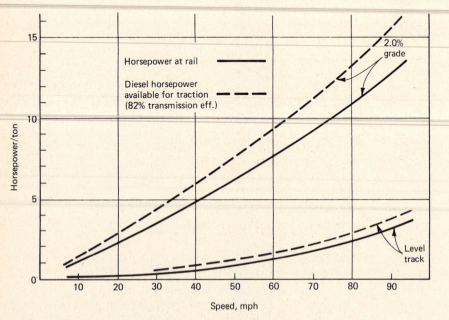

Figure 5–13 Power Required Versus Speed and Grade

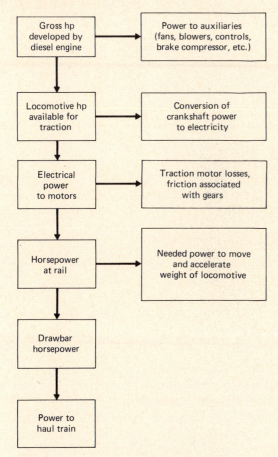

Figure 5–14   Different Horsepower Uses

failure. If more force is needed, a second locomotive, known as a pusher or helper, is used.

Horsepower is a measure of the rate of doing work. To move a train at a desired speed requires a critical horsepower, given the conditions. Figure 5–13 exhibits various levels of horsepower for required speed under various grade conditions. The two set of curves are as follows: The upper curve is the "diesel horsepower available for traction," which is usually given as the locomotive's rating. As shown in Figure 5–14, this is converted in part to electrical usuage to run auxiliaries and then back to tractive force, yielding a final horsepower developed at the rims of driving wheels, usually about 82 percent of diesel horsepower available for traction. Related acceleration, grade, and horsepower combinations are shown in Figure 5–15.

Diesel-electric locomotives operating per the above have a variety of configurations. Only three or four companies manufacture diesel locomotives; Figure

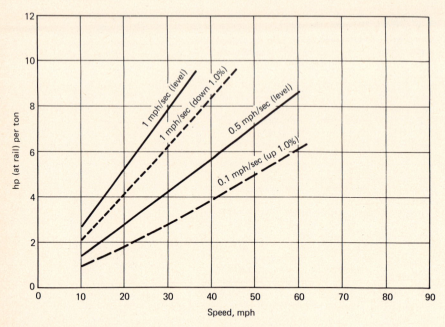

Figure 5–15   Acceleration-Horsepower Requirements

5–16 is a composite of types available. The overwhelming design selection of Class I railroads is types 5, 9, and 10, because of their flexibility, which allows them to be hooked together to handle several types of assignments.

A typical 3,000-horsepower diesel-electric unit exists either in a four-axle or six-axle mode. The latter weighs about 50 percent more. It operates as shown in Figure 5–17. The four axle is superior to speeds of about 23 mph, where it reaches the limit of its reliable traction; from that point on, the six-axle unit excels in hauling capacity. On level track the 3,000-horsepower unit will move the 4,760 gross tons of an average freight train at 34 mph. the majority of rail lines have 0.3 percent predominant grades with minimum desirable speeds of 25 mph. Therefore, the rated haul is usually 2,000–4,000 tons per unit, often resulting in more than one unit for most main-line trains. As units of varying configurations are attached together to function as one locomotive, typical loss of performance of the higher-performance units occur. That is, the maximum speed will be limited to that of the locomotive unit with the lowest gear ratios and lowest performance speed.

Rail Cars

It is important to understand certain dimensional and engineering operating characteristics of cars used in the haulage of rail freight. Car design requires the

	Diagram	Type of locomotive unit	AAR std. Axle-truck designation	Typical horsepower (per unit)
	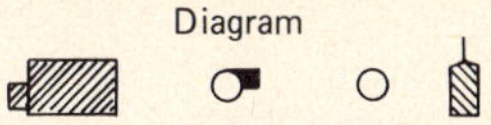 Diesel engine and generator / Powered axle / Idler axle / Steam boiler			
1	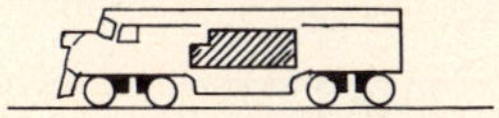	Road freight cab ("A" unit)	B-B	1,350 to 1,750
2	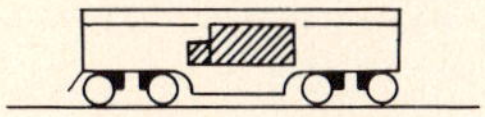	Road freight booster ("B" unit) Hostler controls only	B-B	1,350 to 1,750
3	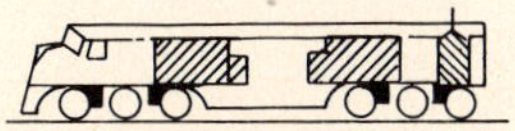	Passenger cab unit ("B" units also used)	A1A-A1A	1,800 to 2,400
4		Light-duty 44-ton switcher	B-B	380
5		Medium/heavy-duty switchers (100 and 125-ton units)	B-B	600
6		"Cow and calf" transfer unit (permanently coupled)	B-B X B-B	1,800 to 2,400
7	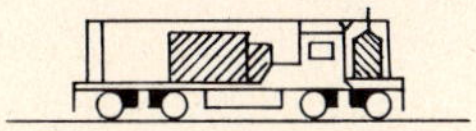	General-purpose road switcher (hood-type car body; steam boiler optional)	B-B	1,000 to 2,000
8	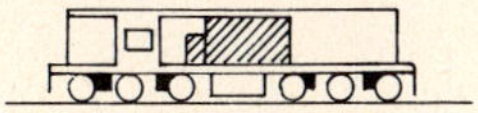	Low-axle-load road switcher	A1A-A1A	1,000 to 1,800
9	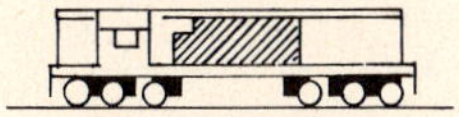	Special-duty six-axle road switcher (later models low nose)	C-C	2,400 to 3,600
10	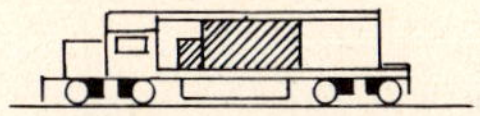	High-horsepower road switcher (low nose)	B-B	2,500 to 3,600
11	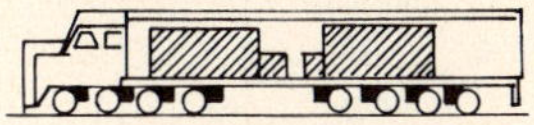	Dual-engine "unit reduction" locomotive (wide-cab hood car body)	D-D (also built as B-B + B-B)	5,000 to 6,600
12	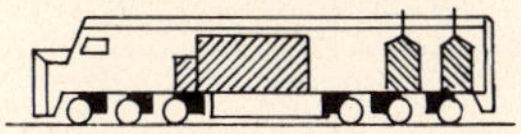	Cowl car body passenger (steam boilers or diesel-electric car heating system)	C-C (also B-B)	3,000 to 3,600

Figure 5–16 Representative Diesel-Electric Locomotive Types

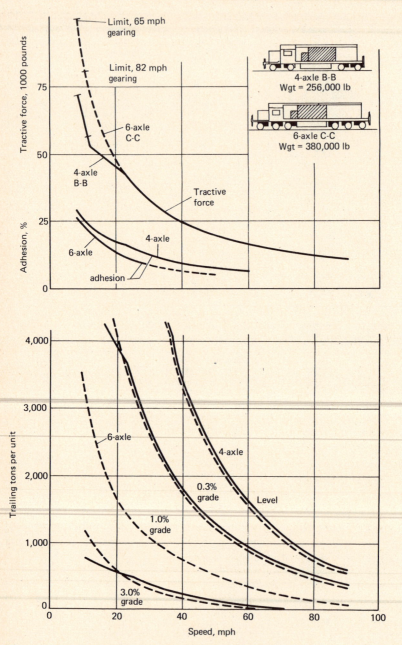

Figure 5–17 Performance Comparisons—3,000-HP Units

ability to compromise between conflicting goals of serviceability requirements and standardization. One needs to be able to get the most efficient loading, transport, and unloading of a particular commodity as much as one needs standardization on dimensions and sizes. Some 2,000,000 cars exist in the North American car fleet. Rigid specifications for car design are administered by the mechanical division of the Association for American Railroads. Nominal car sizes for usage are specified by capacity and come in 30-, 40-, 50-, 70-, 100-, and 125-ton sizes. Most cars are 70–100 tons, with the 70-ton capacity the most significant standard car in the fleet. A schematic of the classical "box" freight car is shown in Figure 5–18.

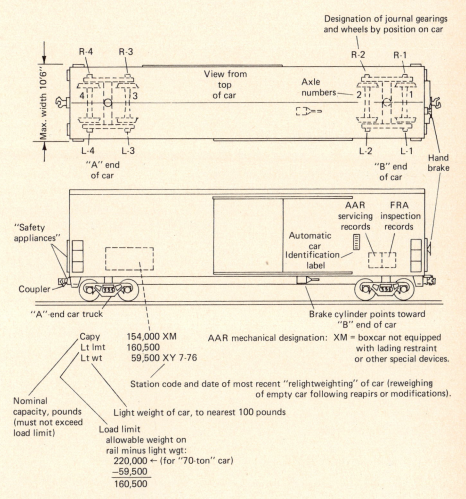

Figure 5–18 The Freight Car

Table 5–7   Statistical Composition of U.S. Freight Cars

Type	Railroad Owned	Car Company or Shipper Owned
Box car	488,000	8,600
Covered hopper	158,000	70,000
Flat car	99,000	42,000
Refrigerator	73,000	28,000
Livestock	4,300	100
Gondola	181,000	5,000
Open hopper	370,000	12,000
Tank	3,000	168,000
Other	30,000	3,000

The fleet exists statistically as shown in Table 5–7. It is composed of eighteen major commodity groups and three general classifications reported in the annual ICC breakdown.

Tractive Effort and Resistance Analysis

Computationally related to our previous graphics of diesel-locomotive tractive effort and horsepower, following is the equation for maximum horsepower, termed *tractive capacity,* which can be developed through rail friction as related to performance speed:

$$P = 4W \frac{V}{3}$$

where

$P =$ diesel locomotive tractive capacity, horsepower
$W =$ total weight supported by the driving wheels, tons
$V =$ velocity, miles per hour

The basic form of tractive resistance is measured in pounds per ton of car weight on tangent, hard track, and is as follows:

$$R = \frac{9.4}{W^{1/2}} + \frac{12.5}{W} + JV + \frac{KAV^2}{Wn}$$

where

W = average weight per axle, tons

J, K = coefficients, depending on type of car

V = speed, mph

A = cross-sectional area of car including the trucks in square feet

n = number of axles per car

Values for these constants are:

1. Locomotives: $J = 0.03$; $k = 0.0024$; $A = 85{-}90$ ft^2
2. Freight cars: $J = 0.045$; $k = 0.0005$; $A = 85{-}90$ ft^2
3. Passenger cars: $J = 0.03$; $k = 0.00034$; $A = 120$ ft^2

AREA uses the following approximation.

$$R' = 2.2T + 121.6C$$

where

R' = total resistance on level tangent, pounds

T = total weight of cars and contents, tons

C = total number of cars in train

Typical values of R are 3–8 pounds per ton in mixed traffic. Tables are employed to find resistance for varying train speeds.

Another type of resistance is *grade* resistance, which is $G = 20$ pounds per ton × percent of grade.

A third type of resistance is *curve* resistance, which is, in general, 0.8 lb/ton/degree of curve. To compensate for changes in alignment and grade, a 0.04–0.05 percent of grade reduction per degree of curvature is introduced into the alignment and profile.

There is also an *accelerating force,* which is the resistance due to inertia while accelerating.

Its general format is:

$$F = 95.5\ Wa$$

where

W = weight, tons of the entire train

a = miles per hour per second

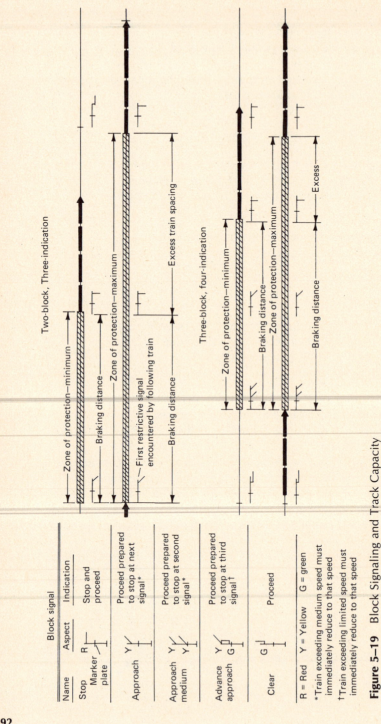

Figure 5–19 Block Signaling and Track Capacity

Signals

It is important to introduce some minimum concepts of railroad traffic control developed by the use of block signals. Much of the U.S. trunk-line roadway operates without signals. However, in congested and frequently traveled main-line areas, it is necessary to divide the line into blocks, which accommodate the typical train length in operation, and do not allow a following train to move into the block until the block is cleared. Thus signals exist not only for safety, but for communication, efficiency, and capacity in operating the railroad. Block signaling can be manual or automatic. When done manually the signals are set by an operator by hand, with written documentation of their time and status of set. In automatic block signaling (ABS), the train itself indicates its presence in the block, with its presence or absence being determined by the track circuit, which engages the appropriate block signal.

The block length must be as long as the longest stopping distance for any train on the route, traveling at its maximum authorized speed. Thus it is desirable to allow trains to progress without the necessity for receiving any approval indication that will require them to slow down prematurely. This requires a train spacing of two block lengths—twice the stopping distance. Therefore, the standard signal system is known as a "two-block/three-indication system" as shown in Figure 5–19. Another three-block/four-indication system is also shown, illustrating the redundancy that can be built into the signal program.

Yards, Switching Districts, and Yard Capacity

Cars are interchanged for loading, unloading, basic directional changes, and train sorting, makeup, and breakup. This is accomplished in a variety of sidetrack, yard, switching district, and classification yard schemes. From the simplest to the most complex, they are described in the following.

Industrial Loading and Unloading These operations, normally known as side-track operations, are necessary to access local cars to their origin point or destination point, resulting in their loading or unloading at industry's door. As shown in Figure 5–20, a variety of patterns of "setouts, runarounds, pickups, and drops" are made with the help of a switch engine. A typical "switching district" involving a multiplicity of such operations in conjunction with making up and breaking up line-haul trains is illustrated in Figure 5–21.

Rail Yard Operations Cars from various components are assembled into "blocks," several of which are then assembled into line-haul trains. Figure 5–21 shows several yards in the switching district. These yards are critical to productivity of the car's travel time. They are expensive, occupy a large area of land, and, through good design, offer an incentive for highly developed industrial parks adjacent to them, taking advantage of immediate accessibility to rail. Their efficient design and service system and capacity levels are crucial to efficient rail

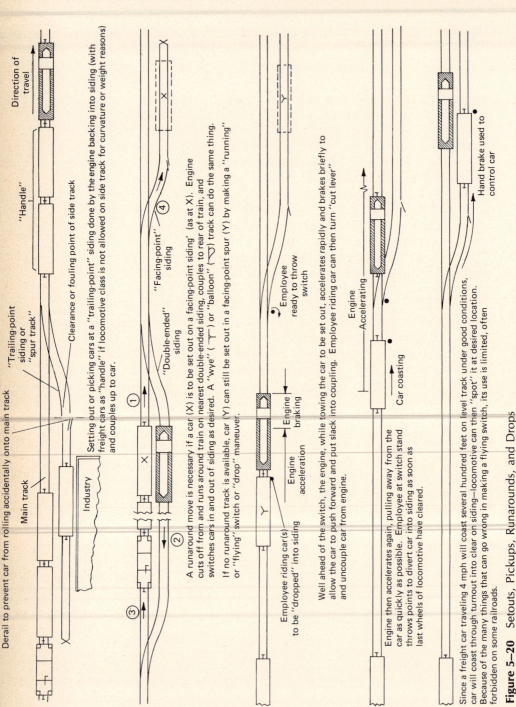

Direction of travel

"Handle"

"Trailing-point siding or spur track"

Clearance or fouling point of side track

Main track

Derail to prevent car from rolling accidentally onto main track

Setting out or picking cars at a "trailing-point" siding done by the engine backing into siding (with freight cars as "handle" if locomotive class is not allowed on side track for curvature or weight reasons) and couples up to car.

Industry

"Double-ended" siding

"Facing-point" siding

A runaround move is necessary if a car (X) is to be set out on a facing-point siding' (as at X). Engine cuts off from and runs around train on nearest double-ended siding, couples to rear of train, and switches cars in and out of siding as desired. A "wye" (⅄) or "balloon" (▽) track can do the same thing.

If no runaround track is available, car (Y) can still be set out in a facing-point spur (Y) by making a "running" or "flying" switch or "drop" maneuver.

Employee riding car(s) to be "dropped" into siding

Engine acceleration

Engine braking

Employee ready to throw switch

Well ahead of the switch, the engine, while towing the car to be set out, accelerates rapidly and brakes briefly to allow the car to push forward and put slack into coupling. Employee riding car can then turn "cut lever" and uncouple car from engine.

Engine Accelerating

Car coasting

Engine then accelerates again, pulling away from the car as quickly as possible. Employee at switch stand throws points to divert car into siding as soon as last wheels of locomotive have cleared.

Hand brake used to control car

Since a freight car traveling 4 mph will coast several hundred feet on level track under good conditions, car will coast through turnout into clear on siding—locomotive can then "spot" it at desired location. Because of the many things that can go wrong in making a flying switch, its use is limited, often forbidden on some railroads.

Figure 5–20 Setouts, Pickups, Runarounds, and Drops
(*Source:* John H. Armstrong, *The Railroad—What It Is, What It Does*, Omaha, Nebr., Simmons-Boardman, 1978.)

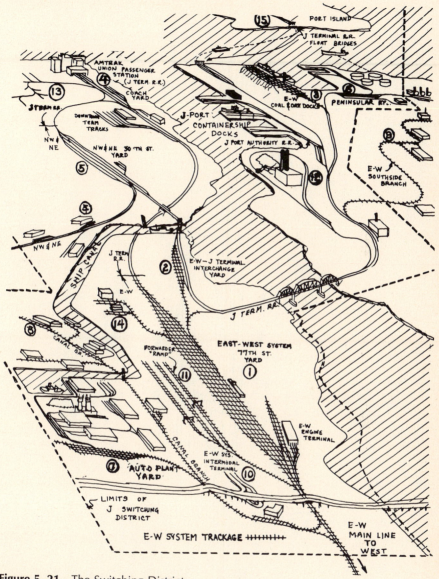

Figure 5–21   The Switching District

(*Source:* John H. Armstrong, *The Railroad—What It Is, What It Does,* Omaha, Nebr., Simmons-Boardman, 1978.)

operations. A typical yard is shown in Figure 5–22 with a diesel shop for engine repair, rip track for car repair, the presence of through tracks, and storage tracks used for storage, spotting, making up, and breaking up trains to various inbound and outbound destinations of the yards.

Operations such as these are known as "flat switching." This is time consuming,

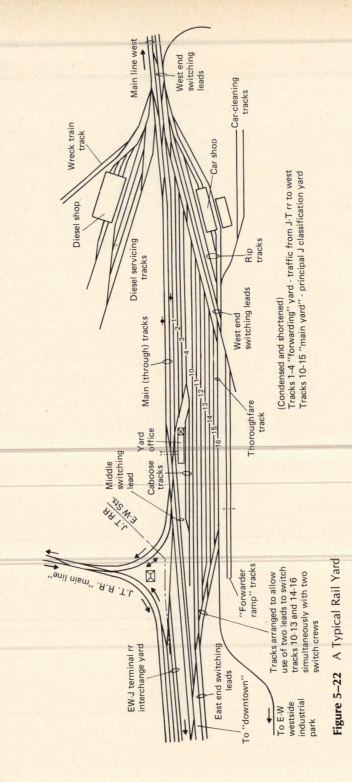

Main line west

West end
switching
leads

Wreck train
track

Diesel shop

Car-cleaning
tracks

Car shop

Diesel servicing
tracks

Rip
tracks

West end
switching leads

Main (through) tracks

4 — 3 — 2 — 1

Thoroughfare
track

12 — 11 — 10

16 — 15 — 14 — 13

Yard
office

Middle
switching
lead

Caboose
tracks

J-T RR
E-W Sts

(Condensed and shortened)
Tracks 1-4 "forwarding" yard - traffic from J-T rr to west
Tracks 10-15 "main yard" - principal J classification yard

J.T. R.R. "main line"

"Forwarder
ramp" tracks

Tracks arranged to allow
use of two leads to switch
tracks 10-13 and 14-16
simultaneously with two
switch crews

EW-J terminal rr
interchange yard

East end switching
leads

To "downtown"

To E-W
westside
industrial
park

Figure 5–22 A Typical Rail Yard

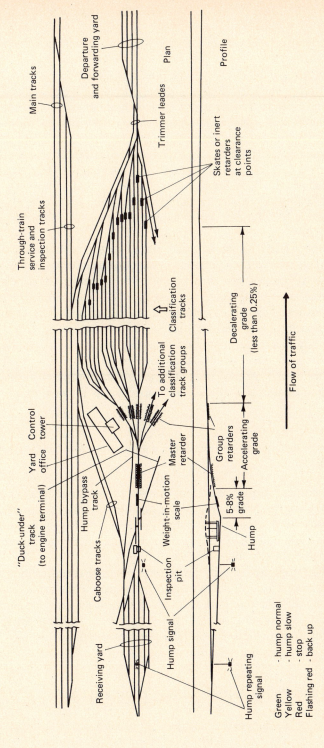

Figure 5–23 Gravity Classification Yard

Main tracks

Departure and forwarding yard

Trimmer leades

Plan

Profile

Through-train service and inspection tracks

Skates or inert retarders at clearance points

Classification tracks

Decelerating grade (less than 0.25%)

To additional classification track groups

Group retarders

Accelerating grade

"Duck-under" track (to engine terminal)

Yard office

Control tower

Master retarder

5–8% grade

Flow of traffic

Hump bypass track

Caboose tracks

Weight-in-motion scale

Hump

Inspection pit

Receiving yard

Hump signal

Hump repeating signal

Green — hump normal
Yellow — hump slow
Red — stop
Flashing red — back up

197

as it is all done by switch engine movement. Where major volumes of cars must be sorted, railroads go to a "hump" yard system, as shown in Figure 5–23, which allows gravity and electronic classification to speed the process.

Moving from right to left in Figure 5–23, cars to be sorted are moved into the receiving yard, and from through trains, engines, and cabooses, are removed. The car's origin/destination is scanned electronically by the tower and pushed up the hump incline. On the down incline of the hump, it is electronically switched into the appropriate track, termed the classification track, or bowl track. At the far end of the yard, these cars are pushed together by a "trim engine," readying the train car components for hook-up and pull-out as a through train to its long-distance destination. Cars can be put over the hump and classified at a rate of 300 per hour. This is considerably faster than flat switching. Some 3,000–5,000 cars are often classified per day.

This concept of *hump* switching makes use of an approach track of 1 percent grade, which interacts with a 4 percent downgrade that lasts 30–50 feet and then runs into a 0.2–0.5 percent classification track. The cars are guided and sorted by remote control, thus allowing train makeup with a minimum of manual or locomotive pusher activity. The typical track spacing in yards is 18 feet of separation with a capacity allowance of 45 feet per car on the tracks.

Rail-yard design raises an important economic issue. The costs of a rail car being in a yard too long are significant, and are a major component of inefficiency and waste in the system, causing late deliveries and inappropriate inventories for the shipper and consignee. Optimal yard capacity C is referred to as:

$$C = 1.10\lambda$$

where λ is the arrival rate of cars per day. For example, if $\lambda = 1,000$ cars/day, then $C = 1,100$ cars.

Thus a 10 percent surplus in capacity is always maintained to allow adequate sorting, processing, and car maneuvering capabilities. This is a fruitful area for research, one where advanced operations research and quantitative methods could be employed, and where the improvement in results would be immediately noticeable to the shipper and consumer.

In general appropriate rail-yard design must optimize coordination with other modes and the opportunity for industrial development in the yard complex. The enormous amount of land required for yard design allows for optimal platting of industrial parks in conjunction with the yard design, yielding productive industrial activity, an improved economic base, increased employment, and positive changes in the tax base for the community.

Regulatory and Policy Aspects of Rail Transportation

There are three fundamental issues worthy of attention with respect to rail regulation and policy: rate structures, ICC formats, and historical legislation.

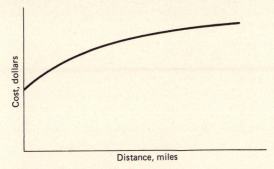

Figure 5–24 Tapering Freight Rates

Rate Structures

The several rail-rate structures in general can be divided into two types — class and commodities. In the former several commodities are grouped as a *class* for similar rate treatment, whereas in the latter, each commodity is classed as a separate pricing item. The rates have historically been set and enforced by the ICC and state commerce commissions. In both types of systems, the following general rate structures prevail.

Distance Composed of price versus distance of haul, this structure is calibrated as tapering, as shown in Figure 5–24 or threshold, as shown in Figure 5–25. In the tapering format, a threshold rate is charged and increases to a maximum and then exists as a flat rate, regardless of distance. A threshold rate system has various price levels of threshold rates for the various distances the commodity travels.

Group Rates This format quotes the same rates for some or all commodities or classes within the same origin–destination pair.

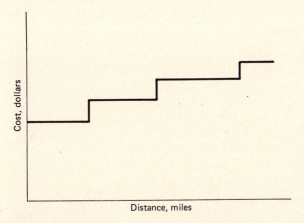

Figure 5–25 Distance Threshold Freight Rates

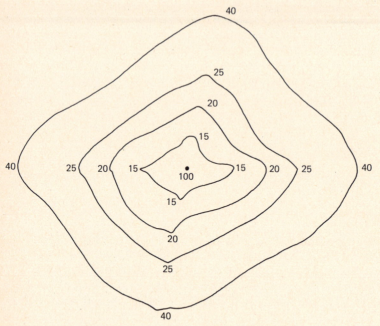

Figure 5–26 Basing Point Pricing and Rate Contour Maps

Basing Point Pricing This format sets one node, typically a major freight interchange zone with a price index of 100. Then, around it, according to length and difficulty of haul, other sites are indexed up or down. A basic rate is established for the 100-point location and all other points are priced up or down according to the index. Thus the whole system may be developed into a rate contour map, as shown in Figure 5–26, yielding comprehensive information about the regional rail pricing structure.

General Regulatory Issues

It should be noted that the rail system has had to pay for its own right-of-way and equipment. This is often considered a disadvantage in competing with other modes, particularly waterways. Further, the ICC has historically been able to require the railroads to maintain service on a line on the basis of "economic convenience and necessity." This has resulted in their subsidizing certain unprofitable operations and has suggested the concept of line, route, and company consolidation. In general situations such as this have resulted in less than profitable operations for the rail sector in the past two decades, and a variety of legislation to correct the situation has resulted.

Relevant Historical Policy Legislation It is impossible to speak of modern rail transportation without paying significant attention to the directions of rail policy in the past twenty years. The time line of Figure 5–27 is a schematic of the

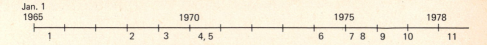

1. High-Speed Ground Transportation Act of 1965.
2. Pennsylvania and New York Central Merger, February 1, 1968.
3. Metroliner service begins in northeast corridor.
4. Penn Central bankruptcy, June 21, 1970.
5. Rail Passenger Service Act, October 30, 1970.
6. Regional Rail Reorganization Act of 1973, January 2, 1974.
7. Preliminary System Plan, United States Railway Association, February 26, 1975.
8. Final System Plan, USRA, July 26, 1975.
9. Railroad Revitalization and Regulatory Reform Act, February 6, 1976.
10. Amtrak Improvement Act.
11. Local Rail Service Assistance Act.

Figure 5–27 A Historical Trajectory of Rail Policy Legislation
(*Source:* L. Hutchins, *1978 Lectures in Transportation,* St. Louis, Mo., Washington University.)

important events to be discussed. The trajectory is an attempt to deal with the economically unsound characteristics of the railroads.

1. *The High-Speed Ground Transportation Act of 1965* formally recognized the need for furthering U.S. rail technology and solving track and train dynamics problems. It developed a research agenda to achieve such goals.
2. *The Pennsylvania and New York Central merger of 1968* signaled the first merger based on a "problem" road and was the forerunner of signals of bankruptcy.
3. *Beginning of Metroliner Service in the Northeast Corridor* was an attempt to stimulate long-distance rail passenger service as private passenger service became unprofitable. It heralded the beginning of the concept of government-subsidized passenger train activity.
4. *The Penn-Central bankruptcy of 1970* signaled the final obvious symptom of a troubled rail industry with low earnings, sluggish management, and overburden of labor problems. It pointed the way toward a need for massive rail reform.
5. *Rail Service Passenger Act of 1970,* as a sequel to the beginning of Metroliner service, yielded the structure of Amtrak as we know it today—a national rail pattern of government-granted and -subsidized passenger service.
6. *The Regional Rail Reorganization Act of 1973* (the "3R Act") attempted to structure operating, engineering, and management financial aid to troubled railroads, and to afford a strategy for them to abandon unprofitable lines.
7. *Preliminary System Plan—United States Railway Administration Act, 1975,* was a plan for governmental takeover and operation of the Penn-Central as a limited freight carrier.
8. *Final System Plan—United States Railway Administration, 1975,* was the

final structure of the foregoing—known now as Conrail—again to minimize further collapse of the Northeast rail freight sector.

9. *Railroad Revitalization Regulation Reform Act of 1976* (the "4R Act") yielded a final system plan of financial assistance and line abandonment for all Class I railroads in the United States.

10. *The Amtrak Improvement Act of 1977* provided an agenda of investment for Amtrak for key corridors, shutting off some others, and furthering the subsidy base for Amtrak passenger operations.

11. *The Local Rail Service Assistance Act* developed a program to ensure adequate transportation service to those commuters whose lines have been abandoned by major railroads, through trucking and other shippers or bus service.

Staggers Rail Deregulation Act　　The major regulatory reform in the past century of railroading was the Staggers Rail Act of 1980. It removed to a large extent the constraints on rates, profits, pricing, and contracts imposed by close regulation by the ICC when dealing with the railroads. The Act's goals were to:

1. Allow railroads to establish reasonable rates and earn adequate revenues.
2. Minimize regulatory control.
3. Ensure competition and prevent unreasonable rates in the absence of competition.
4. Promote safe and energy-efficient transportation.

Specifically the Act allows railroads to charge any given rate, without ICC regulation, provided that:

1. The rate is not below a reasonable minimum, and it contributes to variable cost coverage.
2. The rail carrier does not have market dominance in a haul corridor or pattern. Market dominance is defined as having a corridor revenue/variable cost percentage as follows:
   a. 160 percent through September 30, 1981.
   b. 165 percent through September 30, 1982.
   c. 170 percent through September 30, 1983.
   d. 175 percent or the cost-recovery percentage, whichever is less, through September 30, 1984.
   e. Between 170 and 180 percent for the period after October 1, 1984.

Cost-recovery percentage is the average ratio necessary to create revenue to cover fixed and variable cost, formulated on an industry-wide basis.

Further, the carrier may annually raise rates 6 percent of an adjusted base rate. After 1984 those carriers still not earning adequate revenue are allowed an additional 4 percent annually. Also long-term contracts may be entered into with shippers. All collusion among railroads as to rates, except distinct joint-line service on through routes by two railroads, is prohibited, thus ending "rate bureaus" or pricing cartels as used in the past.

It should be pointed out that the true purpose of the Staggers Rail Act is to "free up" the railroads' pricing capabilities, so they can better compete in a free-market economy without continual regulatory interaction with the ICC. In addition appropriate acceleration steps for prices and rates are stipulated, to allow them to account for the impacts of inflation in attempting to cover fixed and variable costs. In theory the result is to allow them to minimize potentials of bankruptcy, by replenishing their capital and rolling stock, and competing in the marketplace in a more realistic manner. Used with a number of other strategies, particularly mergers and regional rate reorganizations, the Staggers Act will be a hefty strategic tool at the railroads' competitive disposal.

As can be seen from this chapter, railroad transportation is a complex engineering and organizational mode. It represents a temendous capital investment and its technology and regulatory policies have a significant impact on the U.S. economy.

Problems

1. A 50-mile stretch of railroad is in the process of reconstruction. Approximately 150,000 ties are being used in the construction. The ties have a life expectancy of 30 years. How many will have to be replaced after 20 years?
2. The track in the reconstruction problem above is to be constructed such that passenger and freight trains may operate at 60 mph over its entire length. At this speed, what is the maximum allowable degree of curvature?
3. A diesel locomotive is rated at a power of 3,000 hp. If its total weight is 300,000 lb, determine its basic operating speed.
4. A train weighing 700 tons is comprised of ten freight cars of four axles each. What is its tractive resistance at 20 mph? 50mph?
5. a. What is the grade resistance of the cars in Problem 4 on a 3 percent grade?
   b. What is the accelerating force of the same cars, accelerating at 10 miles per hour per second?
6. What is the optimal yard capacity at a railyard handling an average of 20,000 cars per week?

References

Armstrong, John H. *The Railroad—What It Is, What It Does.* Omaha, Nebr.: Simmons-Boardman, 1978.
Final Report: National Transportation Policies Through the Year 2000. Washington, D.C.: National Transportation Policy Study Commission, June 1979.
Hay, William W. *Railroad Engineering,* 2d ed. New York: John Wiley, 1982.

Hammond, Rolt. *Modern Methods of Railway Operation.* London: Frederick Miller, 1968.

Kerr, Arnold D., Editor. *Railroad Track Mechanics and Technology.* Elmsford, N.Y.: Pergamon, 1978.

Moyer, Gerald J., Walter D. Pilkey, and Barbara F. Pilkey, Editors. *Track/Train Dynamics and Design.* Elmsford, N.Y.: Pergamon, 1978.

Railway Age/News, October 27, 1980.

Railway Mechanical Engineering, A Century of Progress. New York: American Society of Mechanical Engineers, 1979.

Raymond, William G., Riggs, Henry E., and Sadler, Walter C. *Elements of Railroad Engineering,* 6th ed. New York: John Wiley, 1947.

Traffic World, "Transportation Week." October 20, 1980.

6 Water Transportation

The water transportation system is a huge and diversified resource for carriage of U.S. freight. Its major physical components include the Deep Water System, the Great Lakes and Coastal System, and the Inland River System. These are illustrated in Figure 6–1.

The Great Lakes System

The Great Lakes System includes the St. Lawrence Seaway, running from Duluth to Chicago and Montreal. The major lakes, as shown in Figure 6–1, are Lakes Huron, Ontario, Erie, Superior, and Michigan. Major expenditures have been made for locks between Lake Superior and Lake Huron and between Lake Erie and Lake Ontario. The lakes' area contains 95,000 square miles of water, with 8,300 miles of shoreline. The 1954 construction of the new St. Lawrence Seaway provides a 27-foot channel between Montreal and Lake Ontario, allowing ocean shipping characteristics to extend into the inland United States.

The Mississippi River System

The Inland Waterway System focuses on the Mississippi River System, also illustrated in Figure 6–1. It reaches from Minneapolis, Minnesota, to the Louisiana delta, with the major tributaries being the Ohio, Missouri, Illinois, and Arkansas

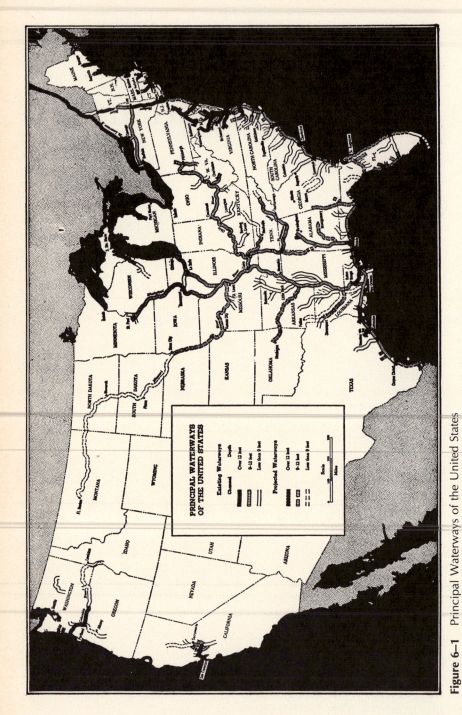

Figure 6–1 Principal Waterways of the United States

(*Source:* President's Water Resources Policy Committee, *A Water Policy for the American People* (Washington, D.C.: U.S. Government Printing Office, 1950), Vol I, pp. 206–7.)

rivers. The Columbia and Williamette rivers in Washington and along the Oregon border complete the major navigable components of the inland waterways.

The *Intracoastal Waterways,* also illustrated in Figure 6–1, consist of a connected series of bays, inlets, and protected channels along the Atlantic and Gulf coasts. Two major components are the Atlantic Intracoastal Waterway, which extends from Massachusetts Bay to Miami, Florida, and the Gulf–Intracoastal Waterway, which extends from St. Marks River, Florida, to the Mexican border.

Cargo Allocations

The Great Lakes typically carry grain, iron ore, and coal. A normal pattern is iron ore to Chicago and Detroit, and from there, finished steel products to international markets, thus making use of the Midwest U.S. transportation system for finished products. Another Great Lakes pattern is grain from Duluth and Lake Superior and Canadian ports to Chicago, and then ultimately to the eastern United States. The inland rivers typically carry petroleum and petroleum products, coal and coke, sand, gravel, crushed rock, machinery, and grain, generally to and from the northern United States to the New Orleans gulf port complex, where cargo loading and unloading for international ocean shipping occur.

Vessel, Barge, and Towboat Characteristics

A variety of ocean-going vessels operate in deep water. Figures 6–2 through 6–6 illustrate a cross section of freighters, tankers, and general cargo vessels; their dimensions are shown in Table 6–1. Almost all of these operate under diesel

Figure 6–2

Figure 6-3 Oil-bulk-ore (OBO) carrier *Eliane*—792 feet long, 106 feet wide, draft 46 feet, 71,060 dwt.

Figure 6–4 Ore carrier *Owari Maru*—849 feet long, 137 feet wide, draft 46 feet, 106,000 dwt.

Figure 6–5   Containership *Sealand Galloway*—942 feet long, 106 feet wide, draft 34 feet, 27,651 dwt.

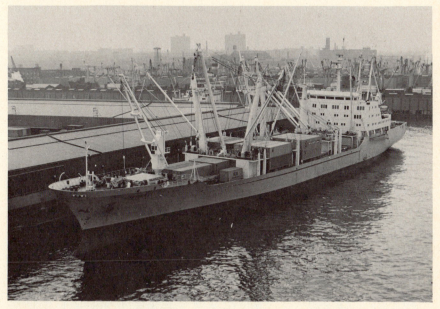

Figure 6-6   Breakbulk cargo ship *Monterrey*—567 feet long, 78 feet wide, draft 33 feet, 15,875 dwt.

Table 6–1 Ocean Going Vessel Dimensions
Largest Vessels and Average Vessel Size in the World Fleet[1]

Vessel Type	Largest Vessels in the World Fleet				Average Vessel Size in the World Fleet				Total Number of Vessels
	Capacity[2] (000's)	Length[3] (ft.)	Beam (ft.)	Draft[4] (ft.)	Capacity[2] (000's)	Length (ft.)	Beam (ft.)	Draft (ft.)	
Breakbulk Freighter	34 dwt	603	84	37	8 dwt	391	55	24	9,924
Partial Containership	31 dwt	600	90	38	11 dwt	444	64	27	1,290
Full Containership	52 dwt	944	106	43	18 dwt	573	79	30	705
Roll-On/Roll-Off	42 dwt	599	106	39	9 dwt	453	69	23	638
Container/Ro-Ro	44 dwt	808	106	38	12 dwt	514	75	25	46
Pallet Carrier	15 dwt	552	85	33	7 dwt	374	60	23	23
Barge Carrier	49 dwt	858	107	40	32 dwt	775	100	32	32

Dry-Bulk Carrier	224 dwt	1,030	164	67	34 dwt	598	84	35	3,912
Combination Carrier	278 dwt	1,109	179	71	106 dwt	805	117	45	239
LNG Tanker	82 dwt	900	138	44	45 dwt	747	109	32	64
LPG Tanker	122 dwt	892	128	54	15 dwt	427	64	25	372
Chemical Tanker	82 dwt	833	113	46	13 dwt	405	60	25	532
General Tanker	556 dwt	1,504	226	81[5]	75 dwt	661	97	38	4,364

[1] As of January 1, 1982, for foreign-flag vessels, and June 1, 1982, for U.S.-flag vessels.

[2] Capacity in terms of thousands of deadweight tons (dwt).

[3] Length shown in length overall (LOA), when available, otherwise length between perpendiculars.

[4] Draft shown is loaded, or load draft.

[5] There are three other tankers in the world fleet having a loaded draft of 94 feet, but they are designed with a lesser length (1,359 ft.), beam (207 ft.), and deadweight (545,000–546,000 dwt).

(Source: A Report to the Congress on the Status of the Public Parts of the United States, Maritime Administration, Office of Port and Intermodal Development and Office of Trade Studies and Statistics, U.S. Dept. of Transportation, Maritime Administration, August 1984.)

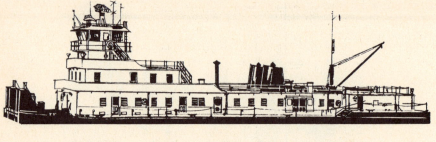

TOWBOATS	Length Feet	Breadth Feet	Draft Feet	Horsepower
	117	30	7.6	1000 to 2000
	142	34	8	2000 to 4000
	160	40	8.6	4000 to 6000

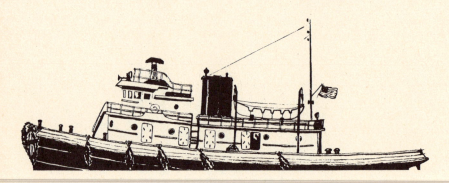

TUGBOATS	Length Feet	Breadth Feet	Draft Feet	Horsepower
	65 to 80	21 to 23	8	350 to 650
	90	24	10 to 11	800 to 1200
	95 to 105	25 to 30	12 to 14	1200 to 3500
	125 to 150	30 to 34	14 to 15	2000 to 4500

Figure 6–7 Inland River Power Units

(*Source:* The American Waterway Operators, Inc., *Big Load Afloat,* Washington, D.C. 1973.)

power, with sophisticated electronic navigation and communication aids. The Great Lakes largely see usage of freighters, ore boats, and tankers.

Likewise the inland river system has a variety of towboat, barge, and service vessels commissioned for usage. The towboats and tugboats have typical dimensions shown in Figure 6–7. The towboats range from 1,000 to 6,000 hp, and tugboats from 350 to 4,500 hp. Tugboats are typically used in coastal harbors, canals, and deep-water ports, and towboats essentially push the barges lashed together in tows to their destination.

The barge sizes and types are illustrated in Figures 6–8 and 6–9. The standard size is 175 by 26 by 9 feet, with a 1,400-ton capacity. The other two sizes, which are becoming more popular, are known as jumbo barges. Open barges typically are

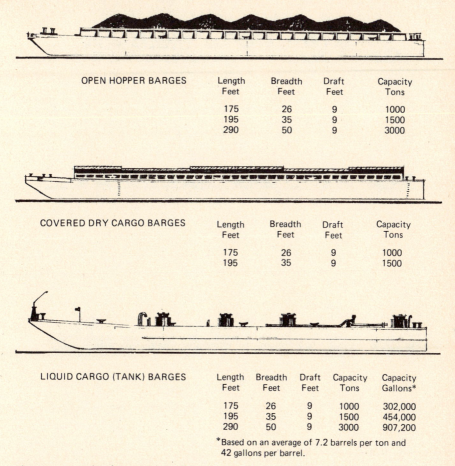

OPEN HOPPER BARGES	Length Feet	Breadth Feet	Draft Feet	Capacity Tons	
	175	26	9	1000	
	195	35	9	1500	
	290	50	9	3000	

COVERED DRY CARGO BARGES	Length Feet	Breadth Feet	Draft Feet	Capacity Tons	
	175	26	9	1000	
	195	35	9	1500	

LIQUID CARGO (TANK) BARGES	Length Feet	Breadth Feet	Draft Feet	Capacity Tons	Capacity Gallons*
	175	26	9	1000	302,000
	195	35	9	1500	454,000
	290	50	9	3000	907,200

*Based on an average of 7.2 barrels per ton and 42 gallons per barrel.

Figure 6–8 Inland River Barge Types
(*Source:* The American Waterway Operators, Inc., *Big Load Afloat,* Washington, D.C. 1973.)

used to carry coal, closed barges to carry grain, and tank barges to carry petroleum and petroleum products and complex liquid chemicals. Deck barges and car floats are used to carry equipment, intermodal cargo, sand, gravel, and refuse.

Lash

Lash (Lighter Aboard Ship) has become an important international cargo component of water transportation. Using barges one half of the dimension of standard U.S. barges, as shown in Figure 6–10, the mother ship carries loaded barges from one national inland river system across the ocean to another national inland river system, requiring only crane off–on loading of the barges to and from the mother vessel.

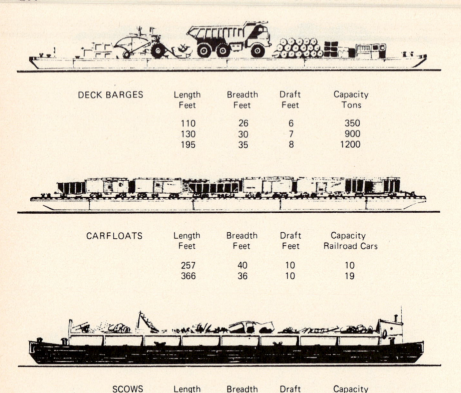

Figure 6–9 for DECK BARGES:

DECK BARGES	Length Feet	Breadth Feet	Draft Feet	Capacity Tons
	110	26	6	350
	130	30	7	900
	195	35	8	1200

CARFLOATS	Length Feet	Breadth Feet	Draft Feet	Capacity Railroad Cars
	257	40	10	10
	366	36	10	19

SCOWS	Length Feet	Breadth Feet	Draft Feet	Capacity Tons
	90	30	9	350
	120	38	11	1000
	130	40	12	1350

Figure 6–9 Inland River Barge Types
(*Source:* The American Waterway Operators, Inc., *Big Load Afloat,* Washington, D.C. 1973.)

Engineering Components of Waterway Systems

There are several basic engineering components of waterway transportation systems that are worthy of presentation. The following sections discuss relevant hydrologic, shoreline, vessel, and port design components employed in water transportation engineering.

Currents and Shoreline Protection

A major component is the *current* of the waterway system, which has an impact on vessel operations. Current is defined as the rate of flow in knots (nautical miles per hour*) and results in two locations related to sediment deposit as shown in

*One nautical mile equals 6,080 feet.

Figure 6–10 The LASH System. Another New Concept in Intermodal Sea Transportation, the Mother Ship Has an Overall Length of 820 Feet and a Dry Cargo Capacity of 20,263 Long Tons of 1,435,500 Cubic Feet of Cargo in 73 LASH Lighters, or 1,650,816 Cubic Feet in 1,498 Standard 20-Foot Containers.
(*Source:* The Americans Waterway Operators, Inc., *Big Load Afloat,* Washington, D.C. 1973.)

Figure 6–11: *shoals,* attributable to the loss of lowered current velocity that causes sediment deposit on the insides of curves of streams, and *pools,* in areas of higher velocity, which result in deeper sections and bank erosion. Severe bank erosion is often prevented by transverse diking, placed longitudially along the pooling shoreline, as shown in Figure 6–12. These typically are constructed of wood or steel piling. Another approach, shown in Figure 6–13, is the treatment of shoreline with paved bank or rip-rap, forming a protective mattress of the shoreline above and below the water surface.

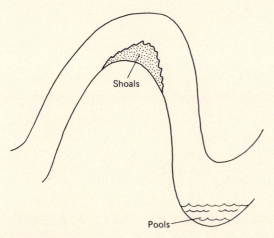

Figure 6–11 Channel Features Related to Sediment Deposit

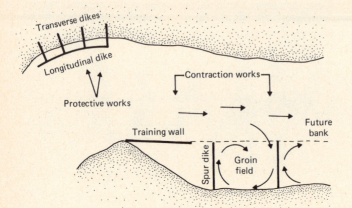

Figure 6–12 Longitudinal and Transverse Diking

(*Source:* Hennes and Ekse, *Fundamentals of Transportation Engineering,* New York, McGraw-Hill 1955. Used by permission.)

An alternate approach, particularly in coastal areas, is the formation of groins, a paving or treating of the coastal bank to stop erosion. As shown in Figures 6–14 and 6–15, a variety of groin designs exist, incorporating sheet pile and timber. The emphasis is on stabilizing the bank or coastline, allowing minimum change in channel and meander patterns. The hydraulic behavior at groins is complex, and performance is a function of wave height, tidal and current influences, and the geometrics of the groin design itself. A variety of seawalls, as shown in Figure 6–16, are used to protect the shoreline from wave-related erosion. The different types of shapes illustrated allow a variety of wave breakup when hitting the shoreline.

Lock and Dam Design

A lock is a chamber that fills with water and hydraulically raises and lowers its elevation to accommodate passage between two waterway levels of different depth and current phenomena. A typical lock, its components, and operation are shown in Figure 6–17. The design criteria are:

1. A minimum filling or emptying period.
2. Minimum disturbance in the approaches.
3. An even distribution of inflow and outflow within the lock, to minimize surging or surf action within the lock.

Lock sizes are set by the conventional barge size, with a width of $W_b + 3$ in feet, where W_b is the beam width of barges, and a length of $L_T + 20$ in feet, where L_T is the conventional length of tow using the lock. Common U.S. barge sizes are

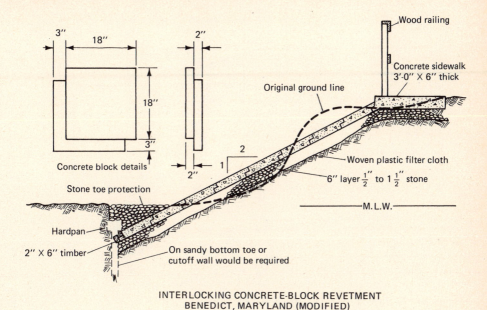

INTERLOCKING CONCRETE-BLOCK REVETMENT
BENEDICT, MARYLAND (MODIFIED)

RIP-RAP REVETMENT
FORT STORY, VIRGINIA

Figure 6–13 Typical Revetments
(Courtesy U.S. Army Corps of Engineers.)

typically 26 by 175 feet, with a 9-foot draft and 1,400-ton capacity. Petroleum or liquid barges are 35 by 195 feet, with a 9-foot draft and 1500-ton capacity. This results in typical lock sizes of 110 by 600 feet and 110 by 1,200 feet. Newer lock design concepts have resulted in some changes in these dimensions.

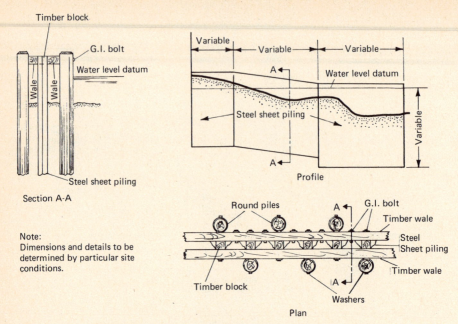

Figure 6–14 Typical Timber–Steel Sheet-Pile Groin.

(*Source:* Philip N. Stoa, *Revised Wave Runup on Smooth Slopes,* Technical Aid No. 78-2, Fort Belvoir, Va., Coastal Engineering Research Center, U.S. Army Corps of Engineers, July 1978.)

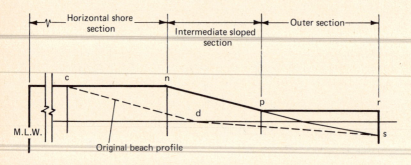

Figure 6–15 Typical Groin Profile

(Courtesy U.S. Army Corps of Engineers.)

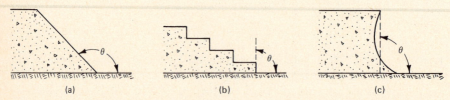

Figure 6–16 Typical Sea Walls (a) Sloping Wall. (b) Stepped Face Wall. (c) Reentrant Face Wall.

218

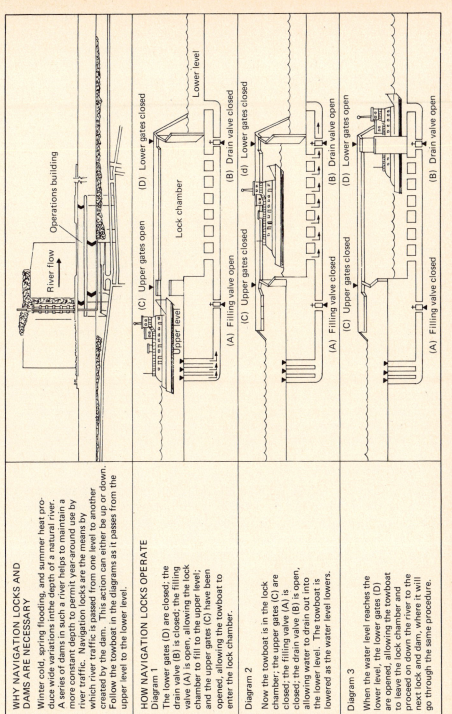

WHY NAVIGATION LOCKS AND
DAMS ARE NECESSARY

Winter cold, spring flooding, and summer heat produce wide variations in the depth of a natural river.
A series of dams in such a river helps to maintain a
more constant depth to permit year-around use by
river traffic. Navigation locks are the means by
which river traffic is passed from one level to another
created by the dam. This action can either be up or down.
Follow the towboat in the diagrams as it passes from the
upper level to the lower level.

HOW NAVIGATION LOCKS OPERATE
Diagram 1

The lower gates (D) are closed; the filling
valve (A) is closed; the filling
valve (A) is open, allowing the lock
chamber to fill to the upper level;
and the upper gates (C) have been
opened, allowing the towboat to
enter the lock chamber.

Diagram 2

Now the towboat is in the lock
chamber; the upper gates (C) are
closed; the filling valve (A) is
closed; the drain valve (B) is open,
allowing water to drain out into
the lower level. The towboat is
lowered as the water level lowers.

Diagram 3

When the water level reaches the
lower level, the lower gates (D)
are opened, allowing the towboat
to leave the lock chamber and
proceed on down the river to the
next lock and dam, where it will
go through the same procedure.

Operations building

River flow

(C) Upper gates open   (D) Lower gates closed

Upper level   Lock chamber   Lower level

(A) Filling valve open   (B) Drain valve closed

(C) Upper gates closed   (d) Lower gates closed

(A) Filling valve closed   (B) Drain valve open

(C) Upper gates closed   (D) Lower gates open

(A) Filling valve closed   (B) Drain valve open

Figure 6–17 Lock Components and Operation
(*Source:* The American Waterway Operators, Inc., *Big Load Afloat*, Washington D.C. 1973.)

219

The U.S. Army Corps of Engineers is the agency authorized to operate, construct, and maintain the lockage system. In response to the barge sizes, it has established the following standard usable lock dimensions:

66-foot width with 400–600-foot length
84-foot width with 600–800–1,200-foot length
110-foot width with 600–800–1,200-foot length

The average lock is designed to accommodate vessel passage in twenty to thirty minutes. Typical passage patterns are as follows:

Width	Length	Tow Pattern (dimensions of 26 by 175 feet per barge)
110	1,200	Four abreast, six long
110	600	Four abreast, three long
110	1,200	Three abreast, three long
110	600	Three abreast, three long

However, with breakup and reassembly of the tow patterns, total preparation, lockage, and departure time is one to one and a half hours per tow. At $200–$400 per hour operating costs, it is obvious that adequate lock design is an integral part of towboat economics.

Dams are similar to locks, and play an important role in providing adequate pools of sufficiently deep water for navigation activities, and acting as a source of flood control by controlling river levels up and down the rivers.

The Buoyage System

Similar to highway signing, appropriate navigation and control systems are necessary for safe and efficient movement of vessels. The navigation system for the United States, enforced by the U.S. Coast Guard, is illustrated in Figure 6–18. Note that the buoyage has adequate markings for starboard (right-hand side), port (left-hand side), and midchannel, and hazards to navigation. As shown in Figure 6–18, the buoys are defined as can or nun buoys, depending on their shape.

Typical vessel steerage systems call for a minimum channel width of one half mile, which allows two vessels to pass within a distance of 100 feet of each other.

Plotting of steerage and appropriate course is accomplished by the use of *charts*. A chart is essentially a map of the ocean and its environs. It includes detailed elements of adjoining land, depth and character of the bottom, navigation aids, and currents.

For ocean and intracoastal waterway systems, these are assembled by the National Oceanic and Atmospheric Services Administration of the Department of Commerce. On inland river systems, they are assembled by the U.S. Army Corps of Engineers. Examples of the chart types are illustrated in Figures 6–19 and 6–20.

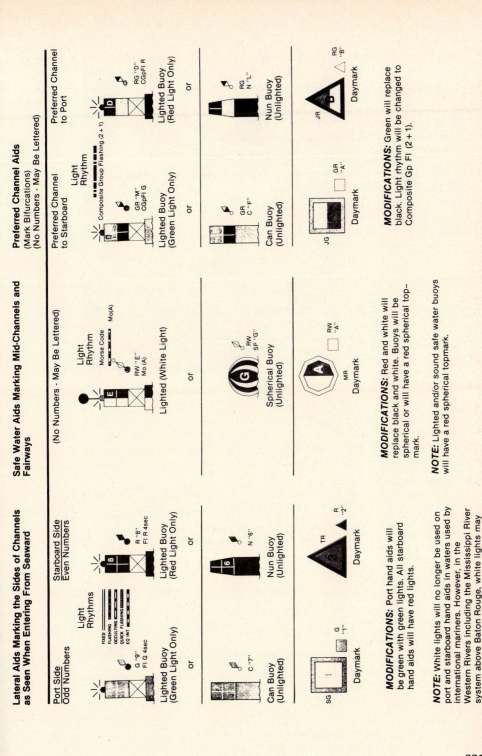

Figure 6–18 Buoyage System of the United States

(*Source*: U.S. Coast Guard, Department of Transportation, 1985.)

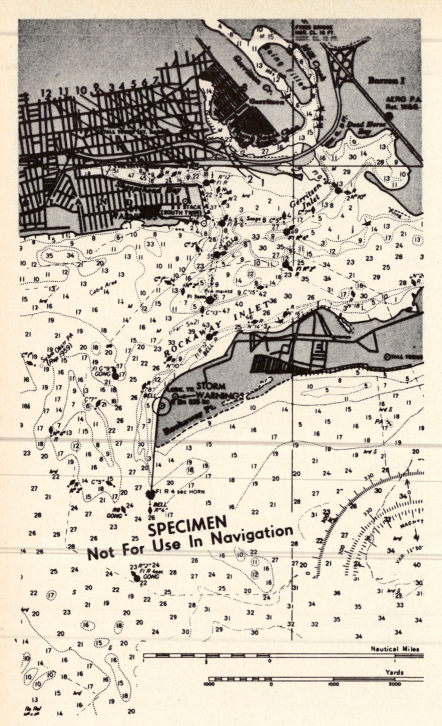

Figure 6–19 Deep-Water Navigation Chart

(*Source:* National Oceanic and Atmospheric Administration and

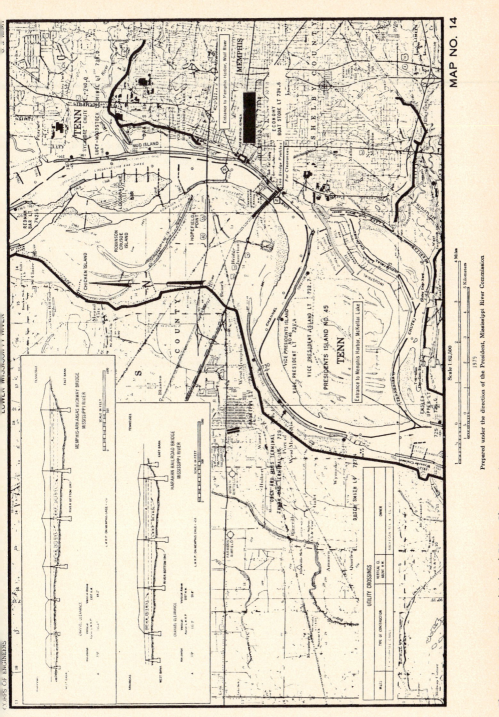

Figure 6–20 Typical Inland River Chart Section
(*Source*: U.S. Army Corps of Engineers.)

Prepared under the direction of the President, Mississippi River Commission

MAP NO. 14

Tides and Tide Tables

For ocean and intracoastal deep-water systems, important components of the transportation environment are the tides and tide tables. *Tide* is defined as the daily rising and falling of the sea. The *rise* of the tides is the amount of rising above the *datum plane* of *mean low water*. All soundings and depth measurements on charts are shown at mean low water. The use of tide tables allows one to refer to key points where time and height of high and low water are given for each day of the year. One can then refer to corrections against those key points for any individual locale. Thus the entire shoreline is effectively tabled by use of the corrections. All of these phenomena are of critical importance in determining design constraints for harbors, channels, and ship and barge performance specifications.

Fleet and Vessel Characteristics

It is important to understand some of the basic naval architecture and engineering power systems involved in water transportation. Figure 6–21 shows the basic parts of a vessel-dimensioning system. There are thirty-two points of vessel referencing. Haulage characteristics are also significant. Several weight and cargo definitions are important:

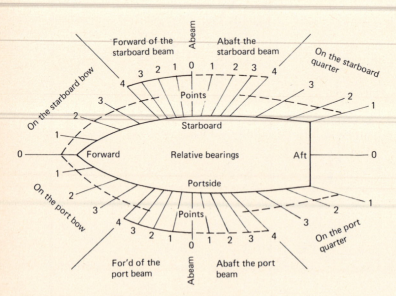

Figure 6–21   Vessel Dimensioning System

Gross tonnage. The internal capacity of the vessel expressed in units of 100 cubic feet. The ton is arbitrarily figured at 100 cubic feet.

Net tonnage or net registered tonnage. Gross tonnage minus all space not available for passenger and cargo carriage. This figure is used for tolling and licensing.

Dead-weight tonnage. The actual carrying capacity of the vessel in long tons.

Displaced tonnage. The actual weight of the vessel and all that is in her.

Draft. The depth to which the vessel sinks into the water.

Buoyancy Criteria

To deal with basic buoyance criteria, one will recall the fresh- and saltwater densities of 62.4 lb/ft³ and 64.0 lb/ft³ respectively.

We then conceive of a basic *LBD block* as shown in Figure 6–22. The LBD block in saltwater weighs $L \times B \times D/2{,}240/64$ long tons. Pertinent displacement space equivalences are that one long ton of saltwater = 35 cubic feet and one long ton of freshwater = 35.9 cubic feet.

The forgoing are related to vessel design within the concept of *streamlining*— that is, the concept of developing a vessel with adequate capacity, but with a shape that is comfortable and efficient to operate. In this regard we define the block coefficient of the vessel as follows:

$$\beta = \frac{\text{Actual underwater volume}}{\text{LBD block}}$$

Obviously the barge has characteristics of shape very similar to the LBD block, and has a β of 0.95. Racing boats and streamlined vessels and ocean racing yachts have much lower β, typically around 0.50. The block coefficient must be considered together with the capacity and size requirements of the vessel.

The related aspect of safe depth of submersion is a function of load, draft, and size of wave to be encountered. We define the *plimsoll line,* the legal and engineering definition of safe depth of submersion, which is located amidships as

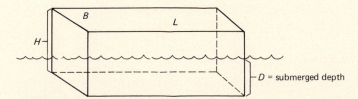

Figure 6–22   LBD Block Concept

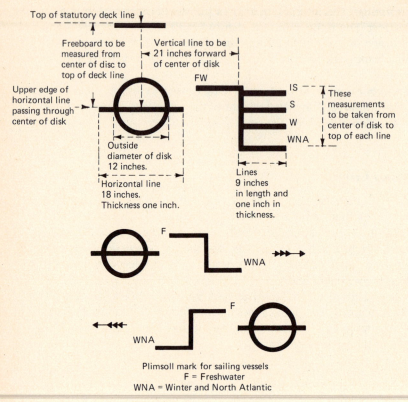

Figure 6–23   Typical Plimsoil Lines

shown in Figure 6–23. Types of displacement influencing the placement of the plimsoll line on the vessel are as follows:

1. Light—crew and supplies only.
2. Loaded—vessel loaded to maximum draft, to deepest load line allowed.
3. Actual—vessel plus tonnage at any time in voyage, varying with fuel, crew, and so on.

$$\text{Loaded} - \text{Light} = \text{Dead-weight tonnage}$$

Resistance to Motion

All of these concepts are brought together in the concept of resistance, the force that must be overcome by the ship's propulsion units to achieve motion. This is compiled as follows:

1. Realization of skin friction, which is the friction of quiet water on the wetted surface of the hull. It approximates 50–85 percent of the total resistance and is

$$R_s = fA_w V^{1.83}$$

where
R_s = skin friction, pounds
f = friction factor, varying from 0.01 for hull length of 20 feet to 0.0085 for 600-foot hulls
V = speed, knots
A_w = wetted surface area, square feet
= $15.6\sqrt{D_s} \times L$

where
D_s = displacement, tons
L = Length, feet

2. In addition to the above are the concepts of *streamline and eddy-current resistance.* These are termed residual resistences, R_v, and

$$R_v = 12.5 \times \beta \times D_s \times \left(\frac{V}{L}\right)^4$$

The term in parentheses represents the effects of bow and stern waves on the system, that is, the amount of chop on the water surface.

3. Finally, the concept of *air resistance:*

$$R_a = CAV^2$$

where
A = cross-sectional area out of water
V = speed, knots
C = drag coefficient = 0.002 percent

4. Thus *total resistance:*

$$R = R_s + R_v + R_a$$

and unit resistance = R/D_s
where D_s is gross loaded displacement

These resistances represent a yardstick for engine design, loading capabilities, and use in different channels and currents.

Table 6–2 Comparison of Commodity Groups Moving Within Mid-America (thousands of tons)

Commodity Group	1976 Tons	Percent of Total		Percent Interstate		Leading States Comprising 50% or More Unless Noted, Arranged in Decreasing Volume		
		1969	1976	1969	1976	Inbound	Outbound	Intrastate
04 Coal and coal products	131,359	27.5	29.7	55.5	57.3	Ohio, Pa., Tenn.	Ky., W.Va., Ill.	Pa., Ala., W.Va
06 Petroleum products and lubricants	87,452	16.3	19.7	85.7	81.6	La., Tenn., Ky.	La., Miss., Ill.	La., Ill., Minn.
01 Cash grains	44,318	5.7	10.0	96.5	95.6	La., Ala., Tenn.	Ill., Minn., Mo.	La., Ala., Ill.
15 Construction materials	42,741	11.2	9.6	39.9	44.9	W.Va., Ill., Tenn.	Ind., Ky., Oh.	Ill., Miss., Ark.
05 Crude petroleum	33,811	16.8	7.6	63.4	45.3	La., Tenn., Miss.	La., Ala., Miss.	La., Ala., Ill.
07 Industrial chemicals	25,673	5.8	5.7	70.0	74.2	Ill., La., Ala.	La., Ill., W.Va.	La., W.Va., Pa
16 Mining products	15,711	4.2	3.5	49.7	45.9	Ill., Ala., Ky.	La., Ala., Ill.	La., Ala., Ill.
08 Agricultural chemicals/fertilizers	13,175	1.8	2.9	93.8	98.1	La., Ill., Iowa	La., Miss., Ark.	La., Miss., Mo.
02 Iron and nonferrous ores	12,363	3.2	2.7	84.6	67.5	Ill., Ohio, Pa.	La., Pa, Ohio	Ala., Ky., Il.

						Origin/Destination		
09 Milled grains and Agricultural products, NEC	7,384	0.6	1.6	81.9	88.8	La., Ala., Tenn.	Ill., Mo., Tenn.	La., Miss., Ala.
20 Waterways improvement materials	7,337	1.8	1.6	70.3	63.3	La., Miss., Tenn.	Ky., Mo., Miss.	La., Mo., Ark.
12 Primary metals	6,339	1.6	1.4	74.5	90.1	Ill., Tenn., La.	La., Pa., Ill.	La., Ill., Pa.
19 Waste and scrap materials, Miscellaneous	5,308	0.9	1.1	16.0	11.9	La., Mo., Ky.	La., Ill. Wis.	La., Il., W.Va.
18 Durable manufactures	2,842	0.4	0.6	25.5	27.9	Ala., La., Ky	La., Tenn., Miss.	La., Ala., Miss.
17 Nondurable manufacturers	2,214	0.3	0.4	85.7	73.6	La., Ohio, Tenn.	La., Miss., Ark.	La., Ala., Ill.
10 Lumber and wood products	1,797	0.4	0.4	32.4	51.5	Miss., Tenn., La.	Ala., La., Tenn.	Ala., Miss., Tenn.
14 Scrap metals	1,558	0.1	0.3	84.0	89.2	Pa., Ill., La.	Ala., Tenn., Ill.	Ill., La., Ala.
11 Sugar and molasses	1,240	0.3	0.2	94.6	90.3	Ill., Iowa, Mo.	La., Minn., Ala.	La., Ill., Ala.
13 Fabricated metals	535	0.1	0.1	83.1	62.6	W.Va., La., Ill.	La., Pa., Ill.	La., Pa., Ill.
03 Aluminum and bauxite	420	0.1	0.0	100.0	100.0	Ark., Ohio, Ill.	La., Ala.	No movement
Total	443,585	100.0	100.0	—	—			

(*Source: Waterborne Commodity Statistics*, U.S. Army Corps of Engineers Analysis of Statistics by Temple, Barker and Sloan.)

Commodity Flow Forecasting

An important part of waterway transportation planning is the analysis and forecasting of traffic to be accommodated on the system. Waterway systems accommodate large bulk cargoes that have little urgency about their movement. As taken from a recent study of waterborne commodities, the predominant haulage is as listed in Table 6–2. Statistics are organized according to two major systems, the U.S. Army Corps of Engineers *Waterborne Carrier Statistics* on a lock-by-lock basis, and the U.S. Department of Commerce Bureau of Economic Analysis Regions of the United States, known as BEARS.

The illustrated commodities usually have to be forecasted for a certain lock reach, or BEAR, or port within a BEAR. Typically this is done by developing a baseline forecast for the area under study, then fine tuning it according to several possible states of the region's economic development over the forecast period. Two examples are relevant here.

The St. Louis Port Region Example

The basic commodities hauled were developed into a baseline forecast by reviewing the industries with a demand for these commodities. Growth rates in each of the industries shown in Table 6–3 were calculated and applied to base-year commodity forecasts to yield future movements. For example, let us assume that the 1972 data base shows a movement of coal from BEAR 114 to BEAR 91. The growth rate to year 2000 in utility earnings in BEAR 91 was calculated. Those growth rates were then applied to the 1972 base-year movement level for coal to develop a movement projection for the year 2000.

Regional Scenarios To facilitate the understanding of origin–destination and commodity flow levels in the St. Louis bistate region, a set of regional scenarios was constructed. Waterborne commodity flows are tied to a great extent

---

Table 6–3 Waterborne Commodity-Related Industries

    I — Grain and grain products
   II — Fertilizers
  III — Chemicals
   IV — Petroleum
    V — Coal
   VI — Aluminum
  VII — Steel
 VIII — Railroad
   IX — International General Cargo

(*Source: Mid-America Ports Study,* vol. 1, U.S. Department of Commerce, New York, Tippetts-Abbett-McCarthy-Stratton, June 1979.)

Table 6–4   Economic Growth States for the St. Louis Metropolitan Area

	Percent Increase	
	1980–1990	*1990–2000*
A. Population		
State 1 Ideal	17.0	13.0
State 2 High	14.0	10.0
State 3 Norm	11.3	7.3
State 4 Low	8.0	6.0
B. Total employment		
State 1 Ideal	28.0	24.0
State 2 High	21.9	17.9
State 3 Norm	15.6	14.1
State 4 Low	11.5	10.5
C. Manufacturing employment		
State 1 Ideal	34.1	26.7
State 2 High	25.1	15.2
State 3 Norm	13.3	11.0
State 4 Low	12.6	9.4
D. Personal income		
State 1 Ideal	143.3	124.0
State 2 High	119.9	110.0
State 3 Norm	98.6	89.5
State 4 Low	62.9	55.3

(*Source:* Real Estate Analysts Limited, July 1979.)

to the demand for raw material inputs to basic industry. Thus an initial examination of regional economic parameters often connected with basic industry allows a starting point from which to refine the macroscale commodity-flow baseline forecast model output referred to above.

As seen in Table 6–4, the ideal, or "economic boom," state shows relatively great increases in regional population, total employment, manufacturing employment, and personal income over a two-decade future period. The high-grown state shows significant, but more realistically attainable, levels of these parameters; the norm state represents status quo without meaningful growth in economic indicators, and the low state depicts the region in decline relative to other national and midwestern economic centers.

Regional Commodity Flow Forecasts   A set of refined St. Louis bistate regional commodity flows based on the above regional economic scenarios was developed as follows:

1. Bureau of Economic Analysis Region (BEAR) regression baseline forecasts of previous metropolitan St. Louis port studies were reviewed for levels of original data aggregation, commodity classification, and statistical quality of variance.
2. Detailed reviews of industrial and port-related market studies and surveys were made to accurately assess target industries of the St. Louis region having an impact on waterborne commodity movement on the river, and responding in a predictable manner to national economic and trade behavior.
3. Detailed interviews were conducted with those barge operators, railroads, trucking and basic industries, and agricultural interests making use of the river and unique intermodal linkages of unit train/unit tow combinations along the St. Louis riverfront.
4. The baseline commodity flows from step 1 were then adjusted to reflect the regional wealth and marketing impacts. Adjustments were made to yield output for three of the four economic states, as illustrated in Table 6–5.
5. At the request of community and industrial interests, the high-growth state was studied in detail, as a basis for design of particular port facilities and development of an industrial incentives strategy.

A review of Table 6–5 in light of the forgoing reveals several results worthy of note:

1. No forecast was made for the ideal or "economic boom" state. It was felt that the number of simultaneous economic-inflation, energy, and international political and trade factors required to be in harmony to achieve such a status was unrealistic, giving no real meaning to such forecast outcome.
2. Forecasts for the other three states clearly exhibit the difference between high and declining regional economic activity and its relation to port development and waterborne commodity flow. The gross total of flows for the high state (71,768,956 short tons) is 23 percent higher than the norm/status quo state (58,135,580 short tons), which is 36 percent higher than the tonnage of the low regional decline state (42,828,903 short tons).
3. Key commodities can be identified from the table that represent response to the unique intermodal–agricultural hinterland location of St. Louis, and/or its strategic position below lock and dam 26, or in response to regional market study indicators. These are:
   Cash grains and grain products
   Coal
   Petroleum and petroleum products
   Chemicals
   Fabricated metals

   For the purposes of port district facility design and future interaction with potential growth industries likely to be attracted to the region, achievement of the high-growth-state economic target and port development was stated as the planning goal for the next twenty years of development.

Table 6–5 Metropolitan St. Louis Bistate Region Waterborne Commodity Flow Projections, 1976–2000 (tonnage in short tons)

Commodity	Year 2000 High-Growth State % Increase	Tonnage	Year 2000 Norm-Growth State % Increase	Tonnage	Year 2000 Low-Growth State % Increase	Tonnage
Cash grains	100	6,918,000	68	4,704,000	55	3,770,000
Iron ore	50	15,000	42	12,600	38	11,400
Metal ores	54	78,945	44	64,326	40	58,478
Coal	372	30,000,000	319	25,725,804	218	17,580,645
Petroleum and petroleum products	66	14,613,663	54	11,956,633	41	9,078,184
Sugar	35	220,000	29	182,285	23	144,571
Grain mill products	45	2,637,000	39	2,285,400	34	1,992,400
Lumber products	90	5,250	80	4,667	68	3,967
Paper products	90	72,000	85	68,000	79	63,200
Chemicals	160	3,427,460	109	2,334,957	90	1,927,946
Iron and steel products	102	1,489,000	85	1,240,833	76	1,109,451
Nonferrous products	84	78,000	78	72,429	68	63,142
Fabricated metal	114	74,000	91	59,070	68	63,142
Mining products	108	5,894,000	90	4,911,666	60	38,947
Nondurable manufactures	60	191,638	48	153,310	66	3,601,889
Durable	100	6,055,000	72	4,359,600	36	114,983
					54	3,269,700
		71,768,956		58,135,580		42,828,903

High is 23 percent higher than norm; norm is 36 percent higher than low.

(Source: Haefner, Lang, and Cronin, "Forecasts of Key Commodities in a Regional Port," Transportation Research Record 855, Washington, D.C., Transportation Research Board, National Academy of Sciences, 1979.)

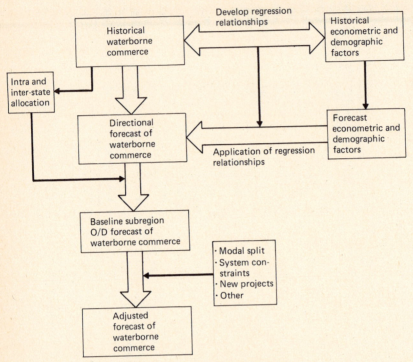

Figure 6–24   Commodity Flow Forecast Methodology
(*Source:* Mid-America Ports Study, Vol. 1, U.S. Department of Commerce, New York, Tippetts-Abbett-McCarthy-Stratton, June 1979.)

Mid-America Port Study

A similar approach using state spaces and econometric forecasts was developed in the Mid-America Port Study; its logic is shown in Figure 6–24. The relationship between econometric factors and specific commodities is shown in Table 6–6. Regressions were built, as shown in the example, for each subregional area, and then tuned for a high- and low-growth scenario, incorporating the economic parameters shown in Table 6–7. Further refinement of the baseline forecasts include taking into account new waterway projects, western coal shipments, lock-capacity constraints, and waterway user charges. Examples of forecasts for high, medium, and low states for all commodities, and related individual commodities, are shown in Figure 6–25 and 6–26.

Port Planning and Engineering

The major creative aspect of waterway transportation is that of port planning and engineering. Whether a deep-water or inland river port, certain objectives and

Table 6–6 Econometrics Utilized for Growth Rates Applied to Initialized 1976 Commodity Movements for All Nonregressible Flows

Group	Commodity Group	Designated Interstate Direction[a] for all Forecasting	Econometric factor[b]
01	Cash grains	In	Grain production
02	Metallic ores	Out	Primary metal productions
03	Nonmetallic ores	In	Primary metal production
04	Coal	Out	Coal production (coal consumption intrastate)
05	Crude petroleum	Out	Petroleum production
06	Petroleum products	In	Petroleum production
07	Industrial chemicals	In	Chemical production
08	Agriculture chemcial/fertilizers	Out	Chemical production
09	Milled grain	In	Food production
10	Lumber/wood	Out	Lumber production
11	Sugar/molasses	In	Food production
12	Primary metals	Out	Primary metal production
13	Fabricated metals	Out	Metal fabrication
14	Scrap metal	Out	Primary metal production
15	Construction material	In	State manufacturing
16	Mining products	Out	State manufacturing
17	Nondurable manufacture	In	State manufacturing
18	Durable manufacture	Out	State manufacturing
19	Waste and scrap	Out	State manufacturing
20	Waterway improvement material	In	State manufacturing

[a]Direction determined by response of regressible flows.
[b]Growth rates were determined on the basis of the log of the econometric regressed against time. The antilog of the slope of this relationship is equivalent to the annual growth rate multiplier.
(*Source:* Temple, Barker & Sloane, Inc.)

Table 6–7 Assumptions for Development of Economic Growth Scenarios

Parameter	Low-Growth Scenario	High-Growth Scenario
Inflation	High rate of inflation (6%)	Low rate of inflation (3½–4%)
Capital investment	Low rate of investment (2½–3%)	High rate of investment (4½%)
Productivity	Low increase in productivity	High increase in productivity
Pollution and vehicle emission control	Stringent enforcement	Limited enforcement

(*Source: Mid-America Ports Study*, vol. 1, U.S. Department of Commerce, New York, Tippetts-Abbett-McCarthy, Stratton, June 1979.)

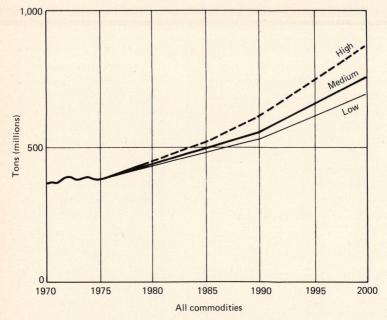

Figure 6–25   High, Medium and Low Baseline Forecasts
(*Source:* Mid-America Ports Study, Vol. 1, U.S. Department of Commerce, New York, Tippetts-Abbett-McCarthy-Stratton, June 1979.)

criteria must be met, and an aggressive study design followed. The objectives of port planning are as follows:

1. To maximize the useful presence of a low-cost mover of bulk freight, that is, the waterway.
2. To provide an efficient point of break-bulk cargo interchange with multimodal surface facilities, that is, rail, highways, and possibly air.
3. To provide an anchor for the region's land-use system.
4. To provide an economic stimulus by being the focal point for water-related basic industry, which groups satellites of related nonbasic industry adjacent to it in industrial parks, providing jobs, tax base, and economic value added.

Criteria for successful port planning include the following:

1. Adequate harbor capacity.
2. Adequate site layout allowing state-of-the-art cargo-handling equipment and efficient modal interchange with surface transportation.
3. Adequate land for industrial expansion.
4. Minimization of environmental degradation.
5. Adequate timing for development.

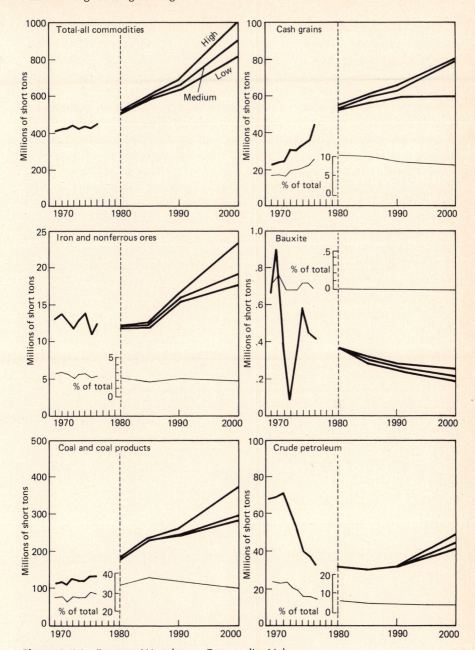

Figure 6–26 Forecast Waterborne Commodity Volumes

(*Source:* Mid-America Ports Study, Vol. 1, U.S. Department of Commerce, New York, Tippetts-Abbett-McCarthy-Stratton, June 1979.)

These objectives and criteria may be viewed in an engineering components/ program budgeting scenario as shown in Figure 6–27. The port and its components may be conceived across several engineering, real estate, financial, and policy subelements, as illustrated for the several port districts of the St. Louis region.

Using this initial organizational base, a typical port engineering study is conceived for one set of districts. A typical study design is illustrated in Figure 6–28. It contains all study activities to meet Environmental Impact Statement issues, develop economic forecasts, and synthesize surface transportation concerns.

From these an engineering site plan of slated improvements is put together. In the most ideal sense, a port should function as a center for multimodal cargo interchange. An excellent example of an idealized system is shown in Figures 6–29 through 6–31. The projects in St. Louis, Missouri and Little Rock, Arkansas, are worthy of note. Both have the following components.

1. Mooring, dockage, or wharfage to facilitate water cargo transfer to rail or truck.
2. Necessary rail trackage.
3. Local traffic circulation.

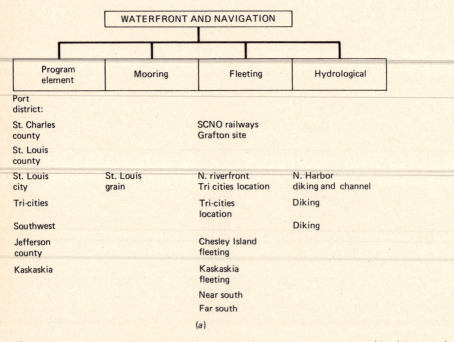

Figure 6–27 A PPBS for a Regional Port: Goal—to Maximize National and Regional Benefits of Port Development

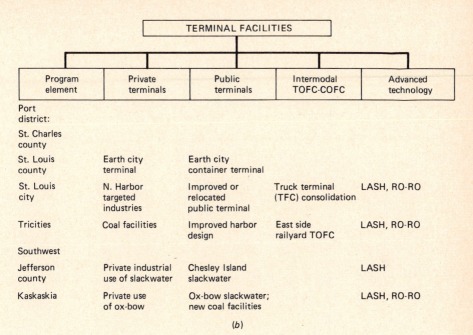

TERMINAL FACILITIES				
Program element	Private terminals	Public terminals	Intermodal TOFC-COFC	Advanced technology

Port district:

St. Charles county

St. Louis county	Earth city terminal	Earth city container terminal		
St. Louis city	N. Harbor targeted industries	Improved or relocated public terminal	Truck terminal (TFC) consolidation	LASH, RO-RO
Tricities	Coal facilities	Improved harbor design	East side railyard TOFC	LASH, RO-RO
Southwest				
Jefferson county	Private industrial use of slackwater	Chesley Island slackwater		LASH
Kaskaskia	Private use of ox-bow	Ox-bow slackwater; new coal facilities		LASH, RO-RO

(b)

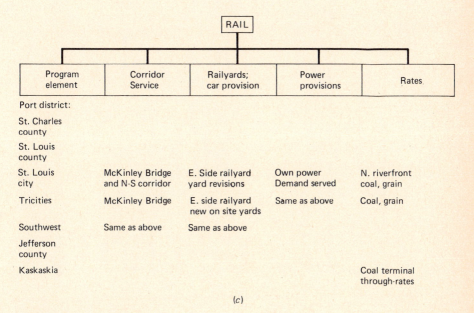

RAIL				
Program element	Corridor Service	Railyards; car provision	Power provisions	Rates

Port district:

St. Charles county

St. Louis county

St. Louis city	McKinley Bridge and N-S corridor	E. Side railyard yard revisions	Own power Demand served	N. riverfront coal, grain
Tricities	McKinley Bridge	E. side railyard new on site yards	Same as above	Coal, grain
Southwest	Same as above	Same as above		
Jefferson county				
Kaskaskia				Coal terminal through-rates

(c)

Figure 6–27 (continued)

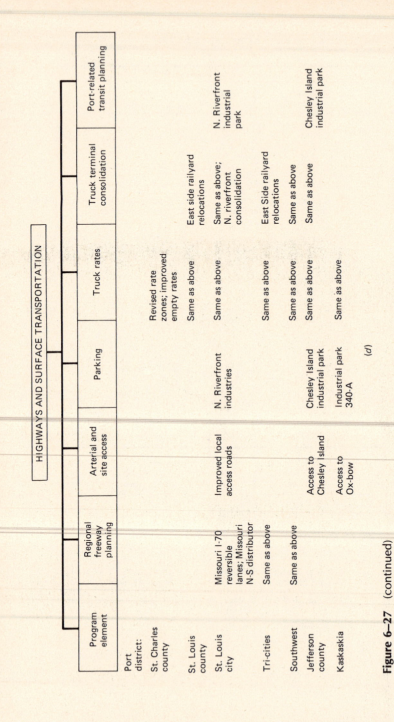

HIGHWAYS AND SURFACE TRANSPORTATION

Program element	Regional freeway planning	Arterial and site access	Parking	Truck rates	Truck terminal consolidation	Port-related transit planning
Port district:						
St. Charles county				Revised rate zones; improved empty rates		
St. Louis county				Same as above	East side railyard relocations	
St. Louis city	Missouri I-70 reversible lanes; Missouri N-S distributor	Improved local access roads	N. Riverfront industries	Same as above	Same as above; N. riverfront consolidation	N. Riverfront industrial park
Tri-cities	Same as above			Same as above	East Side railyard relocations	
Southwest	Same as above			Same as above	Same as above	
Jefferson county		Access to Chesley Island	Chesley Island industrial park	Same as above	Same as above	Chesley Island industrial park
Kaskaskia		Access to Ox-bow	Industrial park 340-A	Same as above		

(*d*)

Figure 6–27 (continued)

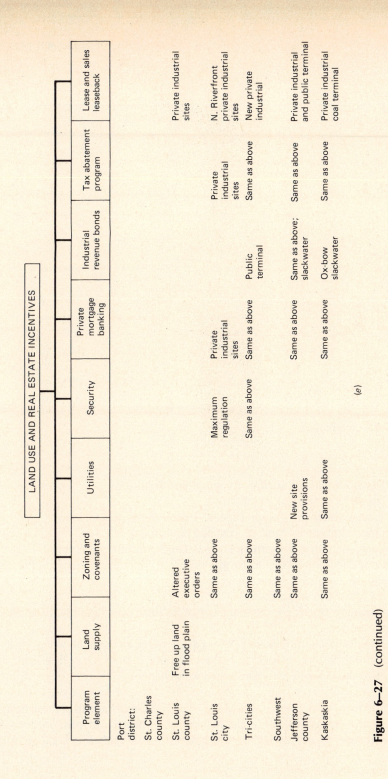

LAND USE AND REAL ESTATE INCENTIVES

Program element	Land supply	Zoning and covenants	Utilities	Security	Private mortgage banking	Industrial revenue bonds	Tax abatement program	Lease and sales leaseback
Port district:								
St. Charles county								
St. Louis county	Free up land in flood plain	Altered executive orders						Private industrial sites
St. Louis city		Same as above		Maximum regulation	Private industrial sites		Private industrial sites	N. Riverfront private industrial sites
Tri-cities		Same as above		Same as above	Same as above	Public terminal	Same as above	New private industrial
Southwest		Same as above	New site provisions					
Jefferson county		Same as above			Same as above	Same as above; slackwater	Same as above	Private industrial and public terminal
Kaskaskia		Same as above	Same as above		Same as above	Ox-bow slackwater	Same as above	Private industrial coal terminal

(e)

Figure 6–27 (continued)

241

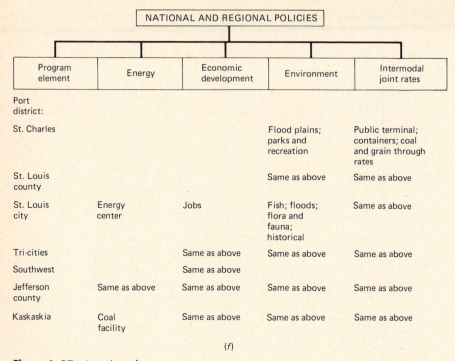

NATIONAL AND REGIONAL POLICIES				
Program element	Energy	Economic development	Environment	Intermodal joint rates

Port district:

St. Charles			Flood plains; parks and recreation	Public terminal; containers; coal and grain through rates
St. Louis county			Same as above	Same as above
St. Louis city	Energy center	Jobs	Fish; floods; flora and fauna; historical	Same as above
Tri-cities		Same as above	Same as above	Same as above
Southwest		Same as above		
Jefferson county	Same as above	Same as above	Same as above	Same as above
Kaskaskia	Coal facility	Same as above	Same as above	Same as above

(f)

Figure 6–27   (continued)

4. Dry bulk storage, such as for grain and fertilizer.
5. Liquid bulk storage—tank farms.
6. Transit sheds for storage of steel, crated items, machinery.
7. Open storage for lumber, covered equipment.
8. Cargo-handling equipment such as fixed and movable cranes.
9. Container capabilities to handle standard containers placed on barges, rail cars, or truck beds.
10. An office for administration.
11. Adequate land for industrial expansion, developing a traffic base for the port.
12. In Little Rock, in Figure 6–30—a slack water channel, allowing for a turning basin to manuever barges, yielding a closed area free from current and drift to isolate cargo interchange.

A typical deep-water port, as shown in Figure 6–32, will have all of these design features, often on much larger scale, in addition to protection from open water. Such protection is developed by the structuring of harbor entrances using

Project Schedule

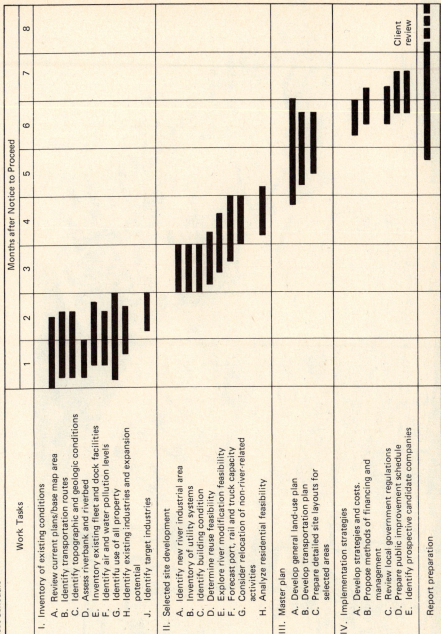

Figure 6–28 Port Engineering Study Design

243

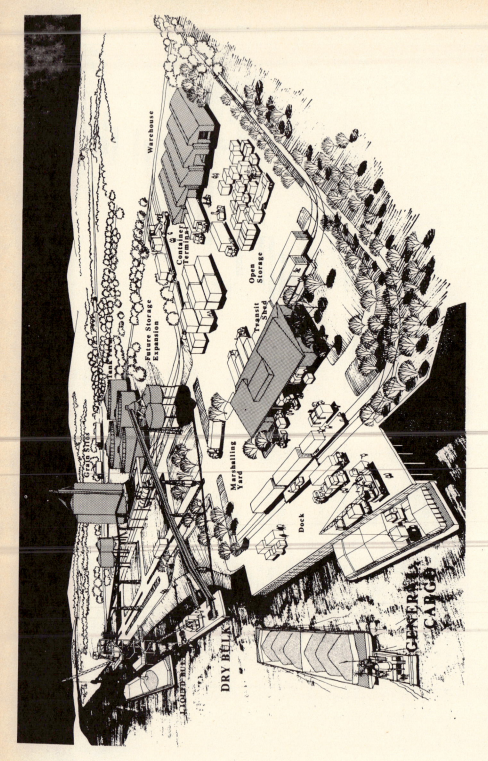

Warehouse

Container Terminal

Future Storage Expansion

Tank Farm

Grain Silos

Open Storage

Transit Shed

Marshalling Yard

Dock

LIQUID BULK

DRY BULK

GENERAL CARGO

Figure 6—29 A Multimodal Distribution Center Plan for the Port of Little Rock, Arkansas

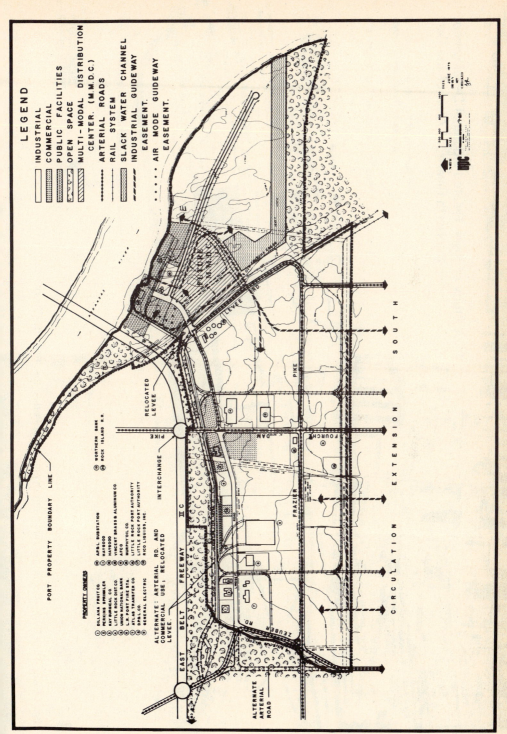

Figure 6–30 Land Use Plan Multi-Modal Distribution Center Port of Little Rock, Arkansas

245

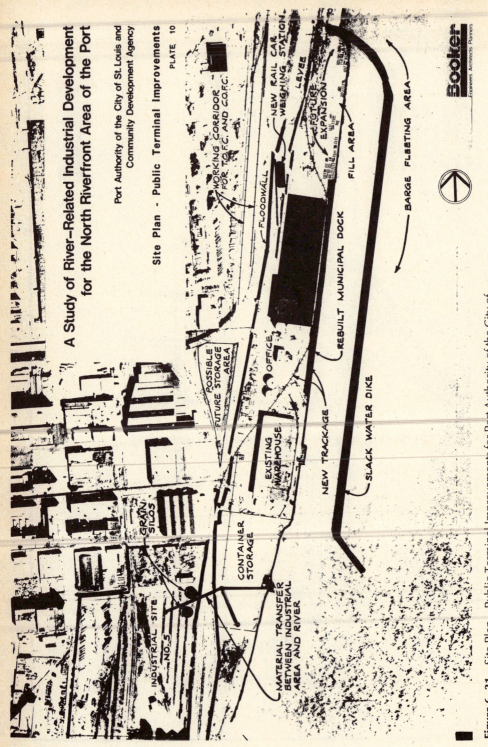

A Study of River–Related Industrial Development for the North Riverfront Area of the Port

Port Authority of the City of St. Louis and Community Development Agency

Site Plan - Public Terminal Improvements

PLATE 10

Booker
Engineers Architects Planners

GRAIN SILOS

INDUSTRIAL SITE NO. 5

POSSIBLE FUTURE STORAGE AREA

WORKING CORRIDOR FOR T.O.F.C. AND C.O.F.C.

FLOODWALL

NEW RAIL CAR WEIGHING STATION

LEVEE

FUTURE EXPANSION

FILL AREA

BARGE FLEETING AREA

OFFICE

EXISTING WAREHOUSE

REBUILT MUNICIPAL DOCK

NEW TRACKAGE

SLACK WATER DIKE

CONTAINER STORAGE

MATERIAL TRANSFER BETWEEN INDUSTRIAL AREA AND RIVER

Figure 6–31   Site Plan—Public Terminal Improvements for Port Authority of the City of St. Louis.

(*Source:* North Riverfront Port Plan; City of St. Louis, Booker Associates.)

246

Figure 6–32 Typical Deep-Water Port Design. The Port Elizabeth Contains Handling Complex of the Port Authority of New York and New Jersey. The largest such facility in the world and one of the first.

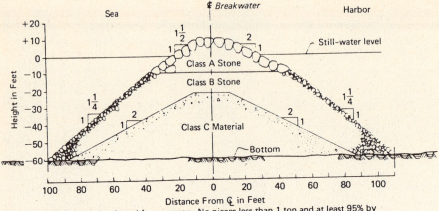

Class A stone is selected from quarry. No pieces less than 1 ton and at least 95% by weight weighing 10 ton or more each.

Class B stone is quarry run. Not more than 25% by weight in pieces less than 20 lbs and not less than 40% in pieces of 1 ton or more.

Class C material is a residuum from quarry operations or a dredged material.

1 ft = 0.3048 m
1 lb = 0.4536 kg
1 ton = 0.907 metric ton

Figure 6–33 Typical Rock Mound Breakwaters

(*Source:* A. D. Quinn, *Design and Construction of Ports and Marine Structures,* 2d ed., New York, McGraw-Hill, 1972. Used by permission.)

breakwaters as shown in Figures 6–33 and 6–34. They are designed to retard wave, tidal current, and wind motion to achieve more placid water inside the harbor zone.

Regulation of Water Carriers

Like railroads and motor carriers, water carriers are subjected to various forms of regulation. Until the Transportation Act of 1940, this was under the jurisdiction of the Federal Maritime Commission. After 1940 foreign deep-water transit continued under the Maritime Commission and the inland water segment was transferred to the Interstate Commerce Commission. The ICC requires a Certificate of Convenience and Necessity for operation, and both deep-water and inland water operations are conceived as either common or contract carriers, as we noted for other modes. However, past this point a major departure exists for operation of inland water carriers.

By the Transportation Act of 1940, new provisions relating to inland water transportation were added as Part III of the Interstate Commerce Act. Most significant is the fact that in this legislative operation, numerous water carriers were made exempt from the Act, most notably bulk carriers. The Act's principal emuneration of exemption are noted in the following:

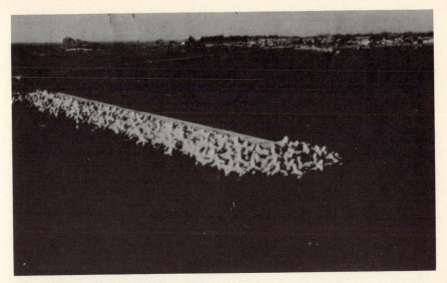

Figure 6–34   Completed Breakwater
(*Source: Shore Protection Manual,* Fort Belvoir, Va., U.S. Coastal Engineering Research Center, U.S. Army Corps of Engineers, 1977.)

1. The transportation of commodities in bulk is exempt "when the cargo space of the vessel in which such commodities are transported is being used for the carrying of not more than three such commodities." The statute then specifies that "two or more vessels while navigated as a unit shall be considered to be a single vessel." Thus if more than three bulk commodities are transported in a single tow consisting of numerous barges, the exemption of the bulk commodities is lost. The Commission held, furthermore, that regulated or nonexempt commodities could not be transported in the same tow as bulk commodities without the latter losing their exemption. This restriction, however, was removed for an experimental three-year period by an amendment to the Act in 1970, thus permitting the transportation of general commodities and bulk commodities in the same tow without loss of the bulk cargo exemption.

2. Transportation of liquid cargoes in bulk in tank vessels is also exempt from regulation.

3. Transportation by contract carriers is exempt when "by reason of the inherent nature of the commodities transported, their requirement of special equipment, or their shipment in bulk," is not actually and substantially competitive with transportation by any common carrier subject to Part I, II, or III of the Act. Contract carriers claiming exemption under this provision must make application to the Commission for such exemption.

4. Private transportation is exempt, since the Act applies only to common and contract carriers; and there is a further exemption of carriers transporting

property of a person who owns all or substantially all of the voting stock of such carrier.

5. An exemption is provided for transportation that is incidental to transportation by railroad, motor carrier, or express company and is in the nature of transfer, collection, or delivery services in terminal areas or has to do with the performance of floatage, car ferry, lighterage, or towage.

In reviewing the above, it is obvious that 90 percent of the domestic water carriage of the nation is exempt from regulation. This lack of regulation as compared with other freight modes is the focus of a major controversy, and is discussed further in the chapter on policy.

Other policy matters and operations are worthy of note in the deep-water and inland water sections. We address two of them: deep-water conference rates and inland waterway user charge policies.

Deep-Water/Ocean Shipping Conference Rates

The Shipping Act of 1916 attempted to control competition by allowing "conferences" and related "conference agreements." These were general understandings among two or more deep-water carriers as to concurrence on rates to be charged, routes or port sailings to be segmented between carriers, or the pooling of earnings. In essence these were oligopolistic cartels to control unprofitable price wars and create a stable, agreed-upon market for all carriers.

The Federal Maritime Commission has deemed that all conferences be open—any U.S. deep-water carrier should be allowed to participate and be admitted to the conference if desired. That is, there shall be no "closed group" of carriers administering the conference policy. This policy concept is probably the only place in contemporary transportation where such cartel price fixing is legally allowed, without sanctioning due to the monopoly antitrust law.

Inland Water Transportation User Charges

A major regulatory issue currently in contention on the Inland Waterway System is that of user charges. As noted from the rail chapter, the rail mode must pay for its right-of-way. It has been suggested that inland waterway operators receive an unfair subsidy in comparison with rail, as their right-of-way—that is, the channel, locks, and dams—are furnished and maintained by the federal government.

It has been suggested by recent Administrations that barge operators pay a user charge to defray such right-of-way and maintenance costs, and bring their operation competitively more in line with rail. Waterway and community interests have fought this, noting that it might cause economic decline of river-related activities and reduce the regional benefits of low-cost water transportation. More will be said about this in Chapter 13 on national transportation policy. However, it is relevant to present the types of user charges under consideration, and the results of one regional study on impacts of user charges on the St. Louis area.

Types of User Charges Examined

The following types of user charges were examined.

Fuel Tax　This is a surcharge placed on the cost of each gallon of diesel fuel pumped for towboat usage.

Congestion Tolls　These refer to fees charged to each tow going through a lock, based on the length of queue existing at the lock upon arrival of the tow, that is, the congestion level at the lock, and the relative degree the presence of an additional tow adds to the congestion.

Segment toll　The waterway system is divided into linear segments of varying length, and capital and operating and maintenance costs on the facility are divided by the number of operators regularly using the facility, with each paying a pro rata share of capital recovery and annual operating and maintenance costs.

Ton-Mile Fee　This is a charge, possibly differentiated by commodity type, for movement of one ton of cargo one mile on the system.

Medallion Charge　A medallion charge is a lump-sum license charge on each towboat, levied once a year, based on horsepower and boat size.

Various combinations of these charges also have been considered in the policy-making process.

Regional Impacts of User Charges

Because of the unique location of the St. Louis region, and its focal point as a center for rail and water transportation, the user charges, in conjunction with the Staggers Rail Act of 1980, will have some meaningful effects on use of St. Louis transportation resources and regional economic strength. Interviews with people in the chemical, steel, petroleum, coal, grain, and terminal industries, and with waterway operators, indicate several findings:

1. With respect to the various fuel tax levels presented in a variety of congressional bills, the waterway carrier community might have some elasticity in internalizing such costs in order to withstand rail competition. Approximately 5 percent of current waterway traffic volumes would be diverted from water to rail at 10¢/gallon fuel tax; 15 percent diversion at 30¢/gallon fuel tax; and 70 percent at 70¢/gallon fuel tax. It is conceded that the 70 cent tax is generally excessive and would cause significant financial hardship for the towing industry in general, incapable of being internalized by even the most financially sound firms. The altered commodity-flow status based solely on the response to fuel tax levels is illustrated in Tables 6–8 and 6–9.

Table 6–8 Effect of User Charges on Commodities Shipped by Barge, Originating from St. Louis Region

Commodity	Year	Total Haul	10 cents		30 cents		70 cents	
			95% by Water	5% Diverted to Rail	85% by Water	15% Diverted to Rail	30% by Water	70% Diverted to Rail
Coal	1978	4,221,051	4,009,998	211,053	3,587,893	633,158	1,266,315	2,954,736
	1980	8,000,000	7,600,000	400,000	6,800,000	1,200,000	2,400,000	5,600,000
	2000	30,000,000	28,500,000	1,500,000	25,500,000	4,500,000	9,000,000	21,000,000
Grain	1978	2,681,946	2,547,849	134,097	2,279,654	402,292	804,584	1,877,362
	1980	3,609,389	3,428,921	180,470	3,067,982	541,409	1,082,817	2,526,574
	2000	6,918,000	6,572,100	345,900	5,880,300	1,037,700	2,075,400	4,842,600
Chemicals	1978	420,216	399,205	21,011	357,184	63,032	126,065	294,151
	1980	458,372	435,453	22,919	389,616	68,756	137,512	320,860
	2000	840,096	798,091	42,005	714,082	126,014	252,029	588,067
Crude petroleum	1978	98,562	93,634	4,928	83,778	14,784	29,569	68,993
	1980	102,997	97,847	5,150	87,547	15,450	30,899	72,098
	2000	132,983	132,983	6,999	125,248	22,103	44,205	103,145
Petroleum and coal products	1978	6,139,041	5,832,089	306,952	5,218,185	920,856	1,041,712	4,297,329
	1980	6,415,298	6,094,533	320,765	5,453,003	962,295	1,924,589	4,490,709
	2000	9,177,866	8,718,973	458,893	7,801,186	1,376,680	2,753,360	6,424,506
Steel products	1978	232,789	221,150	11,636	197,871	34,918	69,837	162,952
	1980	249,852	237,358	12,493	212,374	37,478	74,956	174,896
	2000	418,008	397,108	20,900	355,307	62,701	125,402	292,606

(Source: L. E. Haefner, Principal Investigator, *Inland Waterway System User Charge Impacts on the St. Louis Bi-State Region*, prepared for the Bi-State Development Agency, St. Louis, Mo., Department of Civil Engineering, Washington University, July 31, 1981.)

Table 6–9 Effect of User Charges on Commodities Shipped by Barge, Destined for St. Louis Region

Commodity	Year	Total Haul	10 cents		30 cents		70 cents	
			95% by Water	5% Diverted to Rail	85% by Water	15% Diverted to Rail	30% by Water	70% Diverted to Rail
Coal	1978	1,452,834	1,380,192	72,642	1,234,909	217,925	435,850	1,016,984
	1980	1,838,999	1,747,049	91,950	1,563,149	275,850	551,700	1,287,299
	2000	5,701,215	5,416,154	285,061	4,046,033	855,182	1,710,365	3,990,851
Grain	1978	327,309	310,944	16,365	278,213	49,096	98,193	299,116
	1980	345,868	328,575	17,293	293,988	51,880	103,760	242,108
	2000	531,320	504,754	26,566	451,622	76,698	159,396	371,924
Chemicals	1978	858,135	815,150	42,903	729,345	128,708	257,416	600,637
	1980	936,053	889,250	46,803	795,645	140,408	280,816	655,237
	2000	1,715,583	1,629,804	85,779	1,458,246	257,337	514,675	1,200,908
Crude petroleum	1978	41,205	39,145	2,060	35,024	6,181	12,362	28,884
	1980	42,997	40,847	2,150	36,547	6,450	12,889	30,098
	2000	61,512	58,436	3,076	52,285	9,227	18,454	43,058
Petroleum and coal products	1978	1,716,017	1,630,216	85,801	1,458,614	257,403	514,805	1,201,212
	1980	1,793,237	1,703,575	89,662	1,524,251	268,986	537,971	1,255,266
	2000	2,565,445	2,437,173	128,272	2,180,628	384,817	769,634	1,795,812
Steel products	1978	443,703	421,518	22,185	377,148	66,555	133,111	310,592
	1980	476,226	452,415	23,811	404,792	71,434	142,868	333,350
	2000	801,638	761,556	40,082	681,392	120,246	240,491	561,147

(Source: L. E. Haefner, Principal Investigator, *Inland Waterway System User Charge Impacts on the St. Louis Bi-State Region*, prepared for the Bi-State Development Agency, St. Louis, Mo., Department of Civil Engineering, Washington University, July 31, 1981.)

2. The unanimous conclusion of all industry interviewees was that they would pass all user charge cost increases on to their consumers, maintaining their own profit margins, without altering their current labor force, or undertaking plant relocation away from waterway-related facilities as a specific reaction to the user charge. The high fixed price of plant installation and presence of a ready labor force and tailored terminal facilities render such relocation reactions to the user charge inappropriate.

3. Congestion tolls would be very damaging to the waterway carrier industry and to critical terminal site operations in the St. Louis area. Interviews indicate a 100 percent diversion to rail from water for grain originating above lock and dam 26. This results in some 38,000,000 tons of grain diverted from water to rail, with significant economic hardship for the towing industry, and their incapability to readily develop stable contracts if faced with a congestion toll format. Further, grain terminals in the Tri-City Port District in the confines of lock and dam 27 could face the loss of sixty jobs due to rail diversion of grain under congestion tolls, resulting in an accompanying annual economic loss of $2,300,000 in value added to the region.

4. Consumer energy prices for western coal interchanged to barges at St. Louis could increase. Delivery costs of the long-term target of 12 million tons of coal to the Gulf could range from present projections of $288 million annually to $290 million, $294 million, or $302 million, at levels of 10, 30, and 70 cent fuel taxes. This is likely to occur as captive rail hauls from the West develop a price raise that is some percentage of the increase in price the water carriers will request due to placement of user charges. Interviews indicate that this rail increment is likely to be 93 percent of the water increment.

5. Future port industrial park development plans may be curtailed, as the appraised value of some port-related industrial real estate activities are reduced by a fuel tax, lowering industries' profit by virtue of higher shipping costs. If 30 percent of the industrial land absorption were lost in the St. Louis regional port due to such foreclosure of planned industrial development, the annual economic loss in value added by the year 2000 would be $178,100,000.

6. Segment tolls on the Kaskaskia and Missouri rivers would completely foreclose all planned industrial development. In the case of a planned 400-acre industrial park on the Kaskaskia River by the year 2000, annual value-added loss, depending on the land-use plan options, could range from $27 million to $41 million.

In conclusion a review of this chapter indicates that water transportation is a historically fundamental mode of low-cost bulk freight carriage, allowing international trade and economic stimulation via port and industrial development. It has a sizable technological and labor investment threshold. Although mostly exempt from regulation, its future may be in transition, depending upon the imposition of user charges.

Problems

1. A lock chamber is 600 feet long by 110 feet wide. The difference between upper and lower water pool levels is 20 feet. A lock discharge coefficient of 0.6 is applicable. There are two culverts in the flax of the lock, each 8′ × 12′. It will take 7.5 minutes to lower the level of the water. A tow consisting of 15 open hopper barges 195 feet long by 35 feet wide, operating three abreast, will pass through this lock. Each barge carries 1400 tons of coal and weighs 600 tons. Each section of tow will requires 5 minutes to enter or exit the lock. How much time will it take for the tow to pass through the lock?
2. An ocean vessel has the following dimensional characteristics:
   length = 850 feet
   beam   = 135 feet
   draft   = 40 feet
   The actual underwater volume is 62,000 cubic feet.
   What is the block coefficient of this vessel?
3. What is the unit resistance to motion for the vessel in Problem 2? The following characteristics apply:
   friction factor   = 0.0080
   operating speed   = 40 knots
   displacement   = 250,000 tons
   cross sectional area out of water = 100,000 square feet

References

Baker, C. C. R., and R. B. Oram. *The Efficient Port.* Elmsford, N.Y.: Pergamon, 1971.

Big Load Afloat, Washington, D.C.: American Waterways Operators, 1973.

Bruun, Per. *Port Engineering,* 3rd ed. Houston: Gulf Publishing Co., 1981.

Development of a Multi-Modal Distribution Center, Port of Little Rock, Ark. The Ozarks Regional Commission for the Urban Programming Corporation of America, 1975.

Final Report: National Transportation Policies Through the Year 2000. Washington, D.C.: National Transportation Policy Study Commission, June 1979.

Haefner, L. E., Donald E. Lang, Sr., and Tom Cronin. "Forecasts of Key Commodities in a Regional Port," *Transportation Research Record 855.* Washington, D.C.: Transportation Research Board and the National Academy of Sciences, 1979.

Haefner, L. E., Principal Investigator. *Inland Waterway System User Charge Impacts on the St. Louis Bi-State Region.* St. Louis, Mo.: Department of Civil Engineering, Washington University, prepared for the Bi-State Development Agency, 1981.

Haefner, L. E., Doug Laird, Barry Rosenberg, and Mike Nobs. "PPBS and Dynamic Programming Techniques in Port Development Capital Budgeting Analysis," *Civil Engineering for Practicing and Design Engineers,* Special Transportation Issue, vol. 1, no. 5, 1982.

Imakita, Junichi. *A Techno-Economic Analysis of the Port Transport System.* New York: Praeger, 1978.

Jansson, Jan Owen, and Dan Schneerson. *Port Economics.* Cambridge, Mass.: MIT Press, 1982.

Mid-America Ports Study, vol. 1, Main Report. New York: Tippetts-Abbett-McCarthy-Stratton, 1979.

Mid-America Ports Study, vol. 2, Final Report. New York: Tippetts-Abbett-McCarthy-Stratton, Chase Econometric Associates, Institute of Public Administration for the U.S. Department of Commerce, Maritime Administration, May 1979.

National Port Assessment, 1980–1990, An Analysis of Future U.S. Port Requirements. Washington, D.C.: U.S. Department of Commerce, Maritime Administration, June 1980.

Planning Criteria for U.S. Port Development. Washington, D.C.: U.S. Department of Commerce, Maritime Administration, December 1977.

The Port of Metropolitan St. Louis, by A. T. Kearney Associates, for the East-West Gateway Coordinating Council. May 1976, Appendix B.

Port Planning Design and Construction, 2d ed. Washington, D.C.: American Association of Port Authorities, 1973.

A Study of River-Related Industrial Development for the North Riverfront Area of the Port, vol. 2. St. Louis, Mo.: Booker Associates, 1980.

Takel, R. E. *Industrial Port Development.* Bristol, England: Scientechnica, 1974.

7 Air Transportation

Air transportation, the most recent mode in modern technology, has vastly changed world travel, presenting the business and recreational communities with significantly improved opportunities to reach distant places in minimum travel time.

Some 9,000 airports serve 90,000 registered U.S. active civil aircraft. The sizes of these airports range from 20 to 10,000 acres of land. They are regulated generally by the Federal Aviation Administration, which implements major policies to guide air transport growth and air traffic control systems in the United States. Two types of airport exist. Those for air carrier operation serve the needs of scheduled air carriers; those for general aviation serve all other civil air carriers, typically air taxi services, and business, agricultural, and industrial transportation. The most common type of operation is that termed *domestic,* which serves the contiguous United States, interisland Hawaii, and Alaska.

Domestic aircraft operations have had a significant impact on the U.S. economy. Civil aviation contributions to GNP have grown considerably faster than those of the other modes and the economy as a whole. Total growth in passenger-miles is shown in Table 7–1, with air travel accounting for 13 percent of the growth. Other signals of growth are indicated in Table 7–2 and Figure 7–1, which illustrate the growth in revenue passengers and revenue passenger-miles, and the trend toward much longer flights as the air mode began to dominate long-distance travel. Table 7–3 also illustrates this dominance of long-distance travel by the air mode for household trips. However, this travel is concentrated in a relatively few

Table 7–1 Domestic Intercity Passenger-Miles by Mode of Travel and Class of Service, 1950–1980, Millions

	1950	1960	1970	1975	1980
Total	458,832	748,121	1,161,335	1,331,093	1,496,787
Total common carriers	55,989	67,521	135,335	167,093	233,387
Airlines	7,954	30,557	104,146	131,728	200,087
Railroads	26,781	17,064	6,179	9,765	6,400
Motor buses	21,254	19,900	25,300	25,600	26,900
Air share, percent	14.2	45.3	76.8	78.8	85.7
Private automobile	402,843	680,600	1,026,000	1,164,000	1,263,400
Common-carrier share of total, percent	12.2	9.0	11.7	12.6	15.6
Air share of total, percent	1.7	4.1	9.0	9.9	13.4

(*Source:* Air Transportation Association of America.)

Table 7–2 World Civil Air Transport Revenue Passengers Carried and Passenger-Miles Flown on Domestic and International Routes

Year	Passengers, thousands	Passenger-miles, millions
1950	31,000	18,000
1960	106,000	68,000
1970	386,000	289,000
1971	411,000	307,000
1972	450,000	348,000
1973	489,000	384,000
1974	515,000	407,000
1975	534,000	433,000
1976	576,000	473,000
1977	610,000	508,000
1978	679,000	582,000
1979	738,000	653,000
1980	734,000	665,000
1985*	974,000	869,000
1990*	1,273,000	1,136,000

*Reflects a projection of an average annual increase of 5.5 percent through 1990.
(*Source:* International Civil Aviation Organization.)

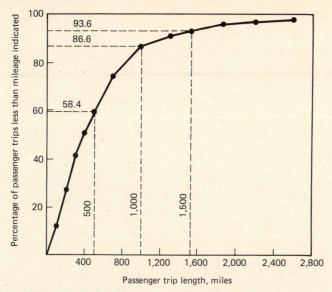

Figure 7–1 Distribution of Passenger-Trip Lengths on Scheduled Domestic Airline Flights in the United States, November 1980. *(Civil Aeronautics Board.)*

large metropolitan cities. Table 7–4 illustrates that the largest fourteen airports accounted for over one half of the air travel enplanements in the United States.

Simultaneously, as air passenger enplanements have grown, so has air freight, as illustrated in Table 7–5. Currently close to 7 million ton-miles of revenue cargo are flown in U.S. domestic scheduled service.

Table 7–3 Household Trips in the United States, 1977

Round-Trip Length, miles	Percent of Trips	Percent by Travel Mode				
		Auto	Bus	Train	Air	Other
200–299	34	93	4	1	1	1
300–399	17	90	4	1	3	1
400–599	17	82	5	1	9	3
600–799	8	70	4	1	21	4
800–999	5	62	4	1	29	4
1,000–1,999	10	48	3	1	42	6
2,000 and over	9	25	2	1	67	5
Total	100	76	4	1	16	3

(Source: Department of Commerce.)

Table 7–4 Passenger Enplanements at Major Airports in the United States, 1978

Cumulative Percent of Passengers Enplaned*	Cumulative Number of Airports	Airport Name
7.78	1	Chicago O'Hare International
14.00	2	Hartsfield–Atlanta International
19.45	3	Los Angeles International
23.71	4	John F. Kennedy International
27.71	5	San Francisco International
31.07	6	Dallas–Fort Worth Regional
34.39	7	Denver Stapleton International
37.37	8	LaGuardia
40.11	9	Miami International
42.51	10	Honolulu International
48.88	13	Detroit Metropolitan
50.53	14	Houston Intercontinental
59.65	20	Newark International
65.60	25	San Diego International
70.21	30	Memphis International
76.28	40	Charlotte Douglas Municipal
80.83	50	Albuquerque International
84.24	60	Rochester–Monroe County
92.07	100	Toledo Express

*Enplaned passengers, total system operations, all services, U.S. certified route carriers (excluding helicopters).
(*Source:* Federal Aviation Administration.)

Table 7–5 Revenue Ton-Miles of Cargo Flown in U.S. Domestic Scheduled Service, Thousands

Year	Mail	Express and Freight	Total
1955	61,233	96,134	157,367
1960	240,572	702,937	943,509
1965	482,977	1,820,154	2,303,131
1970	1,470,131	3,514,066	4,984,197
1975	1,097,297	4,495,309	5,892,066
1980	1,312,910	5,676,593	6,989,503

(*Sources:* Federal Aviation Administration and Air Transportation Association of America.)

Airports have a size classification. This revolves around the term *hub*. A hub is the definition of an area coextensive with the metropolitan area of a single city or of an SMSA. Hubs are classified by the percentage of total enplaned passengers in scheduled domestic air service they serve. Hub classifications are as follows:

Large   ≥ 1.00 percent
Medium = 0.25–0.99 percent
Small   = 0.05–0.24 percent
Nonhub < 0.05 percent

Forecasting Air Travel

The forecast of air traffic, like forecasts for any mode, is critical to the provision of adequate service facilities and the study of the impact of the presence of the mode. Basically forecasts are needed for four reasons:

1. To understand the relative use of the air mode nationally and regionally.
2. To develop manufacturing inventories and strategy.
3. To plan, design, and construct appropriate airport facilities.
4. To calibrate the local, regional, and national impact of air travel and the economy.

Several levels of forecasting are available to any transportation mode, ranging from untutored guesswork to professional judgment to linear regression, logit analysis, market share analysis, and state–space and/or econometric modeling. Air transportation has the opportunity and associated risks of being able to employ all of these in forecasting efforts.

A typical linear regression relevant to issues of forecasting is shown in the following, with the equation:

$$ENP = -75.01 + 1.64\,CMP - 0.04APSU + 1.98PAT - 0.17REL - 5.59STR$$

where

ENP = level of scheduled domestic revenue enplanements, the dependent variable

CMP = number of civilians employed

$APSU$ = annual purchase of automobiles

PAT = private investment in air transportation manufacturing plants, equipment, and so forth

REL = price of air transportation relative to that of other transportation modes

STR = a dummy variable to estimate the impact of strikes on the demand for air travel

Table 7—6 Explanatory Variables Used in Air Transportation Studies to Forecast Aviation and Airport Demand

Factors Analyzed	Explanatory Variables
Market	
Size and traffic potential	Population
	Industrial production
	Personal income
	Total per capita
	Disposable
	Discretionary
	Personal expenditures
	Total
	Travel and recreation
	Propensity for travel
	Leisure time
	Attractions
	Availability
	Interregional linkages:
	Economic
	Social
Transportation	
Accessibility	Distance to airport
	Travel time to airport
Competition	Alternative airports
	Alternative modes of travel:
	Relative cost
	Relative travel time
	Schedule
	Reliability
Cost of air travel	Average fare
	Fare-discounting policies
	Total travel cost
	Value of time
Schedule convenience	Service frequency
	Time of departure
	Necessary connections
Service reliability	On-time performance
	Cancellation history
Transport time	Airport-to-airport time
	Door-to-door time

(*Source:* R. Horonjeff, *Planning and Design of Airports,* New York, McGraw-Hill, 1975. Used by permission.)

A general range of the explanatory variables and dependent variables used in the envelope of modeling techniques is shown in Table 7–6. Different variables and levels of refinement are relevant at different levels of the planning process. These various micro- and macroforecast needs, varying from national airport system needs, through airport planning, to airport-related mass transit forecasts are shown with their required equation forecast variables input in Table 7–7.

Table 7–7 Typical Air Transportation Forecast Variables and Their Use in Aviation and Airport Studies

Application in Planning Studies	*Forecast Variables Required*
Macroforecast	
National airport system needs	Revenue passengers
State or regional airport system needs	Revenue passenger-miles
Airlines	Aircraft fleet:
Aircraft and equipment manufacturers	Air carrier
Investment planning	General aviation
Research and development needs	Composition
Route planning	Size
Work force requirements	Capacity
	Enplaned passengers
	Aircraft operations
	Number of airline pilots and navigators
Microforecast	
Airport Facilities	Aircraft operations:
Airside	Air carrier
Runways	Fleet mix
Taxiways	Capacity
Apron area	Peak hour
Navigational aids	General aviation-based aircraft
General aviation needs	
Landside	Passenger traffic:
Gates	Enplaned
Terminal facilities	Origin, destination
Cargo processing	Connections
Ground access	Freight and cargo tonnage
Curb frontage	Airmail tonnage
Parking	Peaking characteristics
Access highways	Originations
Public transit	Vehicular traffic

(*Source*: R. Horonjeff, *Planning and Design of Airports*, New York, McGraw-Hill, 1975. Used by permission.)

Planning

Planning for air transportation occurs at several hierarchical levels, closely monitored by the FAA. Of most importance in this text are the airport system plan and the airport master plan.

The *airport system plan* is a composite of requirements of facilities needed to meet the aviation demands and activities of a metropolitan area, state, region, or nation. Unlike the plan for an individual facility, it is composed of the needs of several airport facilities within the jurisdiction. It provides broad policies and solutions and suggests a meaningful timing sequence to meet the facility demands. Its major objectives are:

1. To articulate the timing of aviation development in a manner that meets demands without overbuilding.
2. To integrate aviation facilities with the rest of the comprehensive multimodal transportation plan.
3. To protect the environment systematically through the planning policy.
4. To encourage economic development systematically through the presence of air transport facilities.
5. To allow each airport facility to follow its optimal design policy.
6. To develop adequate financing for the plan.
7. To develop an implementation scheme with local governments and citizen groups.

The next level is the individual *airport master plan,* which is the articulation of individual design and construction of a particular airport. Essentially the results of an airport master plan yield specific design recommendations for:

1. The airport component layout:
   Runways
   Terminals
   Taxiways
   Aprons
   Supporting services (emergency facilities, fueling and servicing, concessions)
2. Land use adjacent to the airport.
3. Environmental controls.
4. Economic feasibility analysis of needed airport usage.
5. Financial plan for achievement of the foregoing.
6. A construction schedule.

Airport Layout

Some initial considerations in airport layout and design are the airport's relationship to the community and compatibility with its growth. It is of primary significance that the airport be compatible with, and complementary to, the growth and economic structure of the community, and be integrated with the rest of the transportation system. In this regard, the concept of airport access is a must, through an appropriate planned freeway and rapid transit system, with adequate capacity and interchange facilities. The need for massive engineering investment in airport sites involves initial land acquisition adequate for future growth and control of approach zones and areas of likely runway expansion.

General Site Aspects

Site aspects vary with the general topography encountered. In the case of *elevated sites,* there is less clearing and obstruction and winds are more uniform with generally better visibility. *Valley sites* tend to be more level, with utilities and site installation less costly, and in general may integrate better with ground transportation.

In conjunction with the above, two construction issues emerge: *staged construction programming,* where the long-range concept is implemented through a continuous process of incremental additions of component configurations until the whole is achieved, and *room for expansion,* to the largest forseeable plane size and terminal requirements. Without careful study of these issues, both at the beginning and throughout the planning and design phase, the airport is in danger of becoming ultimately fixed in capacity.

The basic data required to begin preliminary location and siting studies are as follows:

1. Contour maps, with 1 inch = 200 feet in contours of 3–5-foot boundaries.
2. Soil types and details of soil horizons.
3. Initial ideas about runway locations, buildings, and approach-road access.
4. Wind data.

On the basis of these data, several basic types of runway configuration are considered. They are illustrated in Figure 7–2 and discussed in the following.

Aircraft Data Relating to Runway Design

Several specific data items pertaining to the aircraft are necessary for appropriate detailed runway design:

1. Power
2. Cruising speed
3. Landing speed

4. Takeoff distance
5. Landing distance
6. Fuel capacity
7. Wing area, square feet
8. Maximum takeoff gross weight

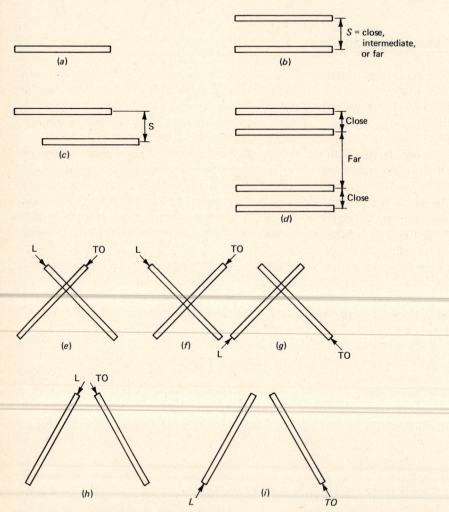

Figure 7–2 Typical Runway Configurations *(a)* Single runway; *(b)* two parallel runways—even threshold; *(c)* two parallel runways—staggered threshold; *(d)* four parallel runways; *(e)* intersecting runways; *(f)* intersecting runways; *(g)* intersecting runways; *(h)* open-V runways; *(i)* open-V runways.

(*Source:* R. Horonjeff, *Planning and Design of Airports*, New York, McGraw-Hill, 1975. Used by permission.)

Table 7–8 Aircraft Classifications

Aircraft Class	Max, Cert. T.O. Weight (lbs)	Number Engines	Wake Turbulence Classification
A	12,500 or less	Single	Small (S)
B	12,500 or less	Multi	Small (S)
C	12,500–300,000	Multi	Large (L)
D	over 300,000	Multi	Heavy (H)

(*Source:* Advisory Circular 150/5060-5, *Airport Capacity and Delay,* Federal Aviation Administration.)

Runway Design and Capacity

A variety of runway types are employed, based on their potential traffic-carrying capabilities, and on the levels of demand forecast for the airport. The combinations of runway shape, configuration, length, and spacing are essentially a function of use by airplanes of various maximum certified takeoff weights, the number of engines, and the type of wake turbulence produced. Table 7–8 illustrates these classifications. For each one percent of grade on the runway, the length is increased by 20 percent. General complementary criteria for grades are as follows:

1. Not in excess of 1.5 percent for a landing strip equal to or less than 3,400 feet.
2. Not in excess of 1 percent for a landing strip greater than 3,400 feet.
3. A 2 percent maximum for small airports for aircraft operating under VFR (visual flight rules).

Capacity Analysis

Capacity analysis of airports for planning and engineering design efforts is based on procedures incorporating the following definitions:

Aircraft Mix— which is the relative percentage of operations conducted by the four classes of aircraft (A, B, C, D) of Table 7–8.

Annual Service Volume (ASV)— ASV is a reasonable estimate of an airport's annual capacity, accounting for differences in runway use, aircraft mix, weather, and so on, typically encountered over a year's time.

Capacity— A measure of the maximum number of aircraft operations which can be accommodated on the airport, or airport component in an hour.

Ceiling and Visibility— for purposes of capacity analysis, VFR, IFR, and PVC relate to the following ceilings and visibilities:

1. Visual flight rule (VFR) conditions occur whenever the cloud ceiling is at least 1,000 feet above ground level and the visibility is at least 3 statute miles.
2. Instrument flight rule (IFR) conditions occur whenever the reported cloud ceiling is at least 500 feet but less than 1,000 feet and/or visibility is at least 1 statute mile but less than 3 statute miles.
3. Poor visibility and Ceiling (PVC) conditions exist whenever the cloud ceiling is less than 500 feet and/or the visibility is less than 1 statute mile.

Delay— Delay is the difference between constrained and unconstrained operating time.

Demand— Demand is the magnitude of aircraft operations to be accommodated in a specified time period.

Mix Index— Mix index is a mathematical expression. It is the percent of Class C aircraft plus 3 times the percent of Class D aircraft, and is written % ($C + 3D$).

Percent Arrivals (PA)— The percent of arrivals is the ratio of arrivals to total operations and is computed as follows:

$$\text{Percent arrivals} = \frac{A + 1/2(T\&G)}{A + DA + (T\&G)} \times 100$$

where

A = number of arriving aircraft in the hour.
DA = number of departing aircraft in the hour.
$T\&G$ = number of touch and go's in the hour.

Percent Touch and Go's— The percent touch and go's is the ratio of landings with an immediate takeoff to total operations and is computed as follows:

$$\text{Percent touch and go's} = \frac{(T\&G)}{A + DA + (T\&G)} \times 100$$

where

A = number of arriving aircraft in the hour.
DA = number of departing aircraft in the hour.
$T\&G$ = number of touch and go's in the hour.

Touch and go operations are normally associated with flight training. The number of these operations usually decreases as the number of air carrier operations increase, as demand for service approaches runway capacity, or as weather conditions deteriorate.

Capacity computations are achieved by associating unique combinations of percent arrivals, percent touch and go's, and annual, daily, and peak hour demand ratios with specific mix indexes, as illustrated in Table 7–9. These combinations

Table 7–9 Operations Assumptions for Capacity Analysis

| | | | Demand Ratios | |
| | | | Annual Demand | Av. Daily Demand[a] |
Mix Index %(C+3D)	Percent Arrivals	Percent Touch & Go	Av. Daily Demand[a]	Av. Peak Hour Demand[a]
0–20	50	0–50	290	9
21–50	50	0–40	300	10
51–80	50	0–20	310	11
81–120	50	0	320	12
121–180	50	0	350	14

[a]In the peak month
(*Source:* Advisory Circular 150/5060-5, *Airport Capacity and Delay,* Federal Aviation Administration.)

have been shown to be empirically accurate. Given the foregoing operating assumptions, Table 7–10 is entered with the appropriate runway configuration and mix index; and hourly capacity in operations per hour under VFR and IFR is obtained, as is annual service volume in operations per year. Nineteen different airport runway configurations are computed, exhaustively illustrating all reasonable layout alternatives.

Aircraft Data Related to Airport Classification and Design

As stated earlier airports are of two general service types: general aviation aircraft and air carrier fleets, which are composed of (1) trunk and continental routes up to 2,000 miles, and (2) long-range intercontinental flights.

From the service perspective, *general aviation* serves flights up to 500 miles—with aircraft of a 12,500-pound maximum takeoff weight and a seating capacity of up to twelve people. The *continental* air-carrier airport is designed to handle planes varying in size from a DC-3, (twenty-one passengers, 64 feet in length, 95-foot wing-span width, 25,000 pounds of takeoff weight) up to Boeing 707, and DC-10 aircraft (length of 100 feet and 107,000 pounds of takeoff weight). The *international* and *intercontinental* airport hubs handle the foregoing plus the Boeing 747, L10-11 complex of aircraft. These 230-foot planes have typical capacities of 500 passengers, and a range of 8,000 miles.

Table 7–10 Capacity and ASV for Long-Range Planning

No.	Runway-use Configuration	Mix Index % (C + 3D)	Hourly Capacity Ops/Hr VFR	IFR	Annual Service Volume Ops/Yr
1.		0 to 20	98	59	230,000
		21 to 50	74	57	195,000
		51 to 80	63	56	205,000
		81 to 120	55	53	210,000
		121 to 180	51	50	240,000
2.	700' to 2499'[a]	0 to 20	197	59	355,000
		21 to 50	145	57	275,000
		51 to 80	121	56	260,000
		81 to 120	105	59	285,000
		121 to 180	94	60	340,000
3.	2500'* to 4299'	0 to 20	197	62	355,000
		21 to 50	149	63	285,000
		51 to 80	126	65	275,000
		81 to 120	111	70	300,000
		121 to 180	103	75	365,000
4.	4300' +	0 to 20	197	119	370,000
		21 to 50	149	113	320,000
		51 to 80	126	111	305,000
		81 to 120	111	105	315,000
		121 to 180	103	99	370,000
5.	700' to 2499' / 700' to 2499'	0 to 20	295	62	385,000
		21 to 50	213	63	305,000
		51 to 80	171	65	285,000
		81 to 120	149	70	310,000
		121 to 180	129	75	375,000
6.	700' to 2499' / 2500' to 3499'	0 to 20	295	62	385,000
		21 to 50	219	63	310,000
		51 to 80	184	65	290,000
		81 to 120	161	70	315,000
		121 to 180	146	75	385,000

[a]Staggered threshold adjustments may apply.

Table 7–10   (continued)

No.	Runway-use Configuration	Mix Index % (C + 3D)	Hourly Capacity Ops/Hr VFR	IFR	Annual Service Volume Ops/Yr
7.	700' to 2499' / 3500' +	0 to 20	295	119	625,000
		21 to 50	219	114	475,000
		51 to 80	184	111	455,000
		81 to 120	161	117	510,000
		121 to 180	146	120	645,000
8.	700' to 2499' / 3500' + / 700' to 2499'	0 to 20	394	119	715,000
		21 to 50	290	114	550,000
		51 to 80	242	111	515,000
		81 to 120	210	117	565,000
		121 to 180	189	120	675,900
9.		0 to 20	98	59	230,000
		21 to 50	77	57	200,000
		51 to 80	77	56	215,000
		81 to 120	76	59	225,000
		121 to 180	72	60	265,000
10.	700' to 2499'ᵃ	0 to 20	197	59	355,000
		21 to 50	145	57	275,000
		51 to 80	121	56	260,000
		81 to 120	105	59	285,000
		121 to 180	94	60	340,000
11.	2500'ᵃ to 4299'	0 to 20	197	62	355,000
		21 to 50	149	63	285,000
		51 to 80	126	65	275,000
		81 to 120	111	70	300,000
		121 to 180	103	75	365,000
12.	4300' +	0 to 20	197	119	370,000
		21 to 50	149	114	320,000
		51 to 80	126	111	305,000
		81 to 120	111	105	315,000
		121 to 180	103	99	370,000

ᵃStaggered threshold adjustments may apply

Table 7–10   (continued)

No.	Runway-use Configuration	Mix Index % (C + 3D)	Hourly Capacity Ops/hr VFR	IFR	Annual Service Volume Ops/Yr
13.		0 to 20	197	59	355,000
		21 to 50	147	57	275,000
		51 to 80	145	56	270,000
		81 to 120	138	59	295,000
		121 to 180	125	60	350,000
14.		0 to 20	150	59	270,000
		21 to 50	108	57	225,000
		51 to 80	85	56	220,000
		81 to 120	77	59	225,000
		121 to 180	73	60	265,000
15.		0 to 20	132	59	260,000
		21 to 50	99	57	220,000
		51 to 80	82	56	215,000
		81 to 120	77	59	225,000
		121 to 180	73	60	265,000
16.		0 to 20	295	59	385,000
		21 to 50	210	57	305,000
		51 to 80	164	56	275,000
		81 to 120	146	59	300,000
		121 to 180	129	60	355,000
17.		0 to 20	197	59	355,000
		21 to 50	145	57	275,000
		51 to 80	121	56	260,000
		81 to 120	105	59	285,000
		121 to 180	94	60	340,000

700' to 2499'

Table 7–10   (continued)

No.	Runway-use Configuration	Mix Index % (C + 3D)	Hourly Capacity Ops/Hr VFR	IFR	Annual Service Volume Ops/Yr
18.	700′ to 2499′ ... 700′ to 2499′	0 to 20	301	59	385,000
		21 to 50	210	57	305,000
		51 to 80	164	56	275,000
		81 to 120	146	59	300,000
		121 to 180	129	60	355,000
19.	700′ to 2499′ ... 700′ to 2499′	0 to 20	264	59	375,000
		21 to 50	193	57	295,000
		51 to 80	158	56	275,000
		81 to 120	146	59	300,000
		121 180	129	60	355,000

(*Source:* Advisory Circular 150/5060-5, *Airport Capacity and Delay,* Federal Aviation Administration.)

Some basic dimensions of these aircraft are important for the engineer to understand in airport layout and engineering. Their dimensional design components and specifications are illustrated in Figure 7–3. Length, wing span, and turning radius are of greatest importance in the geometric layout of airports. Takeoff weight is also important from the viewpoint of pavement design, which is discussed later. The overall characteristics for commercial transport aircraft are shown in Table 7–11, and Table 7–12 lists these characteristics for general aviation aircraft. The largest contributor to design requirements is runway length, which has a significant influence on airport design, size requirements, and geometric configuration.

A further set of relationships of payload to runway length is illustrated in Table 7–13 and Figure 7–4. Table 7–13 shows the average payloads, in tons, of various commercial aircraft; they vary from a low of 2.4 tons for a DC-3 to 48.9 tons for an L10-11-500. To accommodate the latter payload, a relative increase in runway length will be required. Runway length increases hyperbolically, as shown in Figure 7–4, with the largest carrier aircraft requiring 3.5 times the runway needed by the smallest.

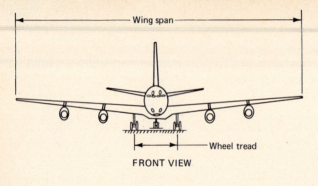

FRONT VIEW

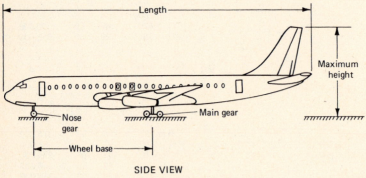

SIDE VIEW

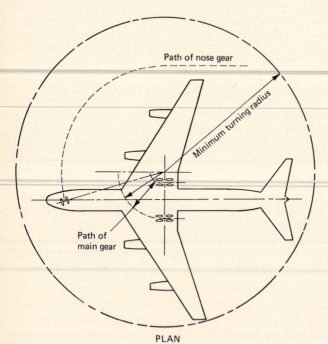

PLAN

Figure 7–3 Definition of Terms Related to Aircraft Dimensions.
(*Source:* R. Horonjeff, *Planning and Design of Airports*, New York, McGraw-Hill, 1975. Used by permission.)

Table 7–11 Characteristics of Principal Transport Aircraft

Aircraft	Manufacturer	Wingspan	Length	Wheel base	Wheel track
DC-9-32	McDonnell-Douglas	93'04"	119'04"	53'02"	16'05"
DC-9-50	McDonnell-Douglas	93'04"	132'00"	60'11"	16'05"
DC-9-80	McDonnell-Douglas	107'10"	135'06"	72'05"	16'08"
DC-8-61	McDonnell-Douglas	148'05"	187'05"	77'06"	20'10"
DC-8-63	McDonnell-Douglas	148'05"	187'05"	77'06"	20'10"
DC-10-10	McDonnell-Douglas	155'04"	182'03"	72'05"	35'00"
DC-10-30	McDonnell-Douglas	161'04"	181'07"	72'05"	35'00"
B-737-200	Boeing	93'00"	100'00"	37'04"	17'02"
B-727-200	Boeing	108'00"	153'02"	63'03"	18'09"
B-720B	Boeing	130'10"	136'09"	50'08"	21'11"
B-707-120B	Boeing	130'10"	145'01"	52'04"	22'01"
B-707-320B	Boeing	142'05"	152'11"	59'00"	22'01"
B-757-200	Boeing	124'06"	153'10"	60'00"	24'00"
B-767-200	Boeing	156'04"	155'00"	64'07"	30'06"
B-747B	Boeing	195'09"	229'02"	84'00"	36'01"
B-747SP	Boeing	195'09"	176'07"	67'04"	36'01"
L-1011-100	Lockheed	155'04"	177'08"	70'00"	36'00"
L-1011-500	Lockheed	155'04"	164'02"	61'08"	36'00"
Caravelle-B	Aerospatiale	112'06"	108'03"	41'00"	17'00"
Trident 2E	Hawker-Siddeley	98'00"	114'09"	44'00"	19'01"
BAC111-200	British Aircraft	88'06"	92'06"	33'01"	14'03"
Super VC-10	British Aircraft	140'00"	171'08"	72'02"	21'05"
A-300	Airbus Industrie	147'01"	175'11"	61'01"	31'06"
A-310	Airbus Industrie	144'00"	153'01"	40'11"	31'06"
Concorde	British Aircraft-Aerospatial	83'10"	202'03"	59'08"	25'04"
Mercure	Dassault	100'02"	111'06"	39'01"	20'04"
Ilyushine-62	U.S.S.R.	141'09"	174'03"	80'04"	22'03"
Tupolev-154	U.S.S.R.	123'02"	157'02"	62'01"	37'09"
Ilyushine-86	U.S.S.R.	157'08"	197'06"	70'00"	36'07"

(*Source:* Manufacturers' data. Reproduced by kind permission of Jane's Publishing Co. Ltd., 13th Floor, 135 West 50th Street, New York 10020.)

Design Standards

Runway orientation is the first major design standard of concern to the FAA. It requires a compass orientation so that aircraft take off or land at least 95 percent of the time with cross-wind components of less than 15 mph. The wind data are put on a compass rose for sixteen points of the compass. Each interval between point

Table 7–12 Characteristics of General Aviation and Short-Haul Passenger Aircraft

Aircraft	Wing Span	Fuselage Length	Wheel Track	Maximum Takeoff Weight, lb	Maximum Number of Seats*	Number and type of Engines	Runway Length, ft
Beech 23 Musketeer	32'09"	25'00"	11'10"	2,200	4	1 P	1,380
Beech V35 Bonanza	33'05"	26'04"	9'07"	3,400	6	1 P	1,320
Beech 58-Baron	37'10"	29'09"	11'00"	6,775	6	2 P	2,380
Beech B80-QueenAir	50'03"	35'06"	12'09"	8,800	11	2 P	1,800
Beech C99	45'10"	44'07"	13'00"	10,900	17	2 TP	2,800
Bellanca 260C	34'02"	22'11"	9'00"	3,000	4	1 P	1,000
Cessna 150	32'08"	23'00"	6'06"	1,600	2	1 P	1,385
Cessna 172 Skyhawk	35'09"	26'11"	7'02"	2,300	4	1 P	1,525
Cessna 182 Skylane	35'10"	28'00"	7'11"	2,950	4	1 P	1,350
Cessna T310	36'11"	29'06"	12'00"	5,500	6	2 P	1,790
Cessna 402	44'01"	36'05"	18'00"	6,850	10	2 P	2,485
Piper PA-23 Aztec	37'02"	30'03"	11'04"	5,200	6	2 P	1,250
Piper PA-28 Cherokee	30'00"	23'06"	10'00"	2,400	4	1 P	1,250

Piper PA-28 Arrow	30'00"	24'02"	10'06"	2,600	4	1 P	1,870
Piper Twin Comanche C	36'00"	25'02"	9'09"	3,600	6	2 P	2,095
Piper PA-31 Navajo	40'08"	32'07"	13'09"	6,500	6	2 P	4,070
Gulfstream II	68'10"	79'11"	13'08"	17,500	22	2 TF	3,550
Metroliner II	46'03"	59'05"	15'00"	12,500	22	2 TF	5,186
Lear Jet 25	35'07"	47'07"	8'03"	15,000	8	2 TJ	4,880
Lockheed Jet Star	54'05"	60'05"	12'03"	42,000	12	4 TJ	4,875
Sabreliner-60	44'05"	48'04"	7'02"	20,000	12	2 TJ	4,430
Jet Falcon 20T	54'03"	60'00"	12'03"	29,100	28	2 TF	
deHavilland TwinOtter	65'00"	51'09"	12'02"	12,500	22	2 TP	1,200
Shorts 330–200	74'08"	58'01"		22,900	32	2 TF	3,880
BAe 146–100	85'05"	78'09"		74,600	84	4 TP	3,530
deHavilland DASH 7	93'00"	80'08"		44,500	52	4 TP	2,260
Fokker F27 Mk500	95'02"	82'03"		45,000	50	2 TP	5,460

*Including pilot.

(*Source:* Manufacturers' data: *Jane's All the World's Aircraft.* Reproduced by kind permission of Jane's Publishing Co. Ltd., 13th Floor, 135 West 50th Street, New York 10020.)

Table 7–13   Average Payload of Transport Aircraft

Aircraft	Payload, tons
DC-3	2.4
DC-4	7.0
DC-7	9.0
B-707-120	17.9
DC-9-80	20.1
DC-8-61	22.0
B-757-200	26.6
DC-10-10	33.0
B-767-200	34.9
A-310	35.2
B-747	44.0
L1011-500	48.9

(*Source:* R. Horonjeff, *Planning and Design of Airports,* New York, McGraw-Hill, 1975. Used by permission.)

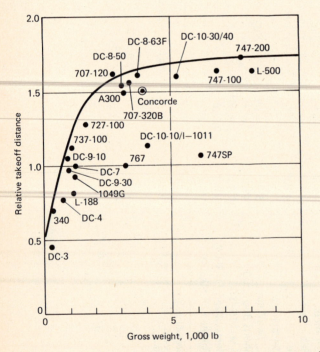

Figure 7–4   Trends in Runway Lengths for Transport Aircraft
(Aerospace Industries Association of America, Inc.)

boundaries covers 22 ½ degrees. The related cross-wind computations are as follows:

$$CW = V \sin \alpha$$

where

CW = cross-wind component
V = Velocity of the wind in mph.
α = angle of wind direction with long axis of the runway

The *coverage* is the sum, in both directions, of the wind velocity assumed to be uniformly distributed over time.

In undetermined or new areas, historical wind data may not be available, and so data are gathered by using information from two or more of the nearest wind-recording stations, if the intervening landscape is level or slightly rolling. If the area is mountainous, this approach is unreliable, and detailed long-term anemometer studies must be done at the proposed location.

Taxiway, Apron, and Terminal Development

The initial ground-side operation of the aircraft upon landing is the use of the taxiway, which is the transition area of ground travel from the runway to the loading area. The most critical aircraft dimensions relating to the ground side are wing span and length. To facilitate ground-side design, the FAA has categorized plans into a *geometric design group,* as illustrated in Table 7–14. The resulting

Table 7–14 FAA Airplane Design Group Classification for Geometric Design for Airports

Airplane Design Group	Wing Span, feet	Typical Aircraft
I	Less than 49	Learjet 24, Rockwell Sabre 75A
II	49 but less than 79	Gulfstream II, Rockwell Sabre 80
III	79 but less than 118	B-727, B-737, BAC1-11, B-757, B-767, Concorde, L-1011, DC-9
IV	118 but less than 171	A-300, A-310, B-707, DC-8
V	171 but less than 197	B-747
VI	197 but less than 262	Future

(*Source:* Federal Aviation Administration.)

Table 7–15   Taxiway Dimensional Standards

	International Civil Aviation Organization				
	A	B	C	D	E
Width, feet					
Pavement	25	35	50[a]	60[b]	75
Safety	45	65	95	140	155
Shoulder			16	33	38
Gradient, percentt					
Pavement, longitudinal					
Maximum	3.0	3.0	1.5	1.5	1.5
Maximum effective					
Maximum change					
Transition curve rate of (slope					
change per 100 feet)	1.2	1.2	1.0	1.0	1.0
Pavement transverse					
Maximum	2.0	2.0	1.5	1.5	1.5
Safety area					
Maximum longitudinal					
Maximum transverse	3.0	3.0	2.5	2.5	2.5

[a]Use width of 60 feet if wheelbase is equal to or greater than 60 feet.
[b]75 feet if outer main gear is greater than 30 feet.
(*Sources:* International Civil Aviation Organization and Federal Aviation Administration.)

taxiway design standards for each of these groups and compositions are illustrated in Table 7–15. In general, since speeds are less than on runways, all geometric controls such as grades, width, and sight distance are relatively less rigorous. A typical detail of taxiway and related exit design with runways is as shown in Figure 7–5, which curve radii as shown in Table 7–16.

Terminal development is also of critical importance in keeping the airport at long-range adequate capacity. General requirements include adequate site parking and traffic circulation. The minimum safety clearance from the centerline of the runway to any building is 200–750 feet, depending on the type of airport. The number of loading areas should also be adequate for the size of airport. They are typically allocated as follows:

6–12 platform areas for small airports
12–20 platform areas for medium airports
20–30 platform areas for major terminals
The loading area diameter is typically 100–200 feet, a function of the wing span.

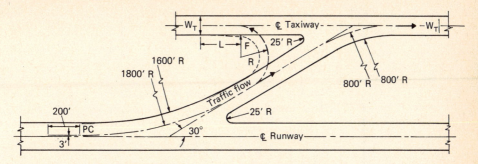

Figure 7–5 Thirty-Degree High-Speed Taxiway Exit for Category C, D, and E Aircraft.
(Federal Aviation Administration)

A good example of interface requirements of the ground-side aned air-side functions and entities is shown in Figure 7–6. Note the necessity to eliminate congestion at points of surface transportation arrival and departure, ticketing and baggage pickup, and loading and unloading of aircraft. There is a need for appropriate passenger amenities, service, and concessions, and adequate parking, access roads, and transit facilities. Adequate short- and long-term parking facilities must be provided, with short-term parking within easy walking distance of the terminal. Appropriate surface transportation shuttles must be available to access long-term parking. The parking facilities must have adequate access and egress ramps, appropriately linked to a freeway and/or arterial road subsystem of adequate capacity. Adequate mass transit systems, through scheduled bus service or a connecting commuter rail link should give travelers ready access to all points in the region from the airport terminal. This is supplemented by taxi service and private limousine services to designated regional activity centers, such as downtown, stadiums, and universities. Typical examples of well-planned terminal facilities are shown in Figures 7–7 and 7–8.

Table 7–16 Radii of Curvature for Transport-Category Aircraft

Taxiing Speed, mph	Radius of Exit Curve, feet
10	50
20	200
30	450
40	800
50	1,250
60	1,800

(Source: Federal Aviation Administration.)

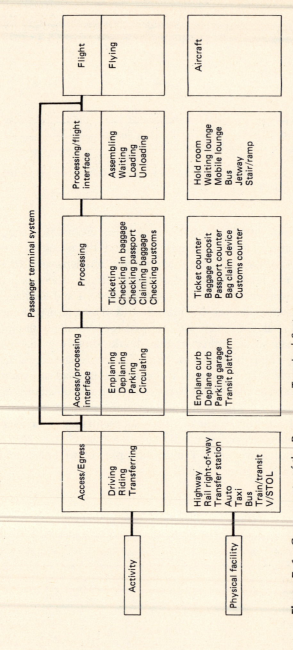

Figure 7–6 Components of the Passenger Terminal System

(*Source:* R. Horonjeff, *Planning and Design of Airports*, New York, McGraw-Hill, 1975. Used by permission.)

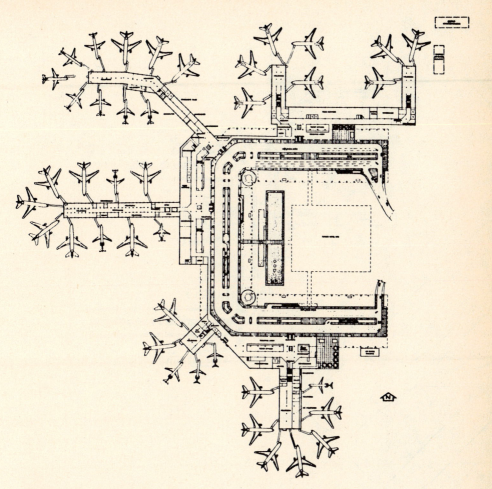

Figure 7–7 Enplaning Level for Proposed Terminal at Fort Lauderdale–Hollywood International Airport.

Airport Pavements

While this section will not substitute for a formal course in pavement design, it does allow the principles of rigid and flexible pavement design to be articulated for airport planning. As shown in Figure 7–9, airport pavement contact areas can be considered as critical, noncritical, and transition areas, with critical areas being responsive load-bearing locations used by the aircraft. As such two sets of pave-

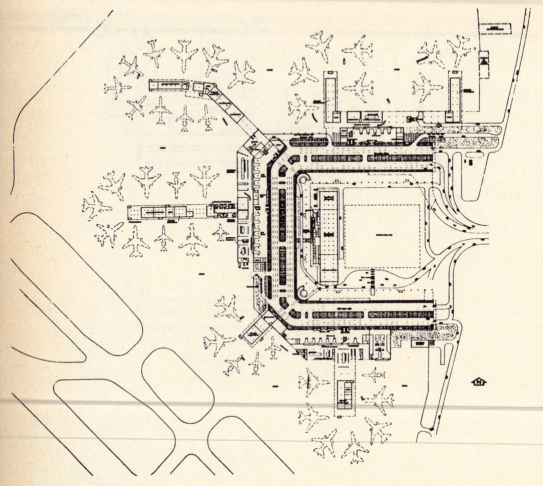

Figure 7–8 Deplaning Level for Proposed Terminal at Fort Lauderdale–Hollywood International Airport.

ment design—one for critical areas and the other for noncritical areas—are developed.

Figures 7–10 through 7–12 show the requirements for flexible pavements, and Figure 7–13 exhibits requirements for rigid pavements. The primary criterion used in these charts is gross aircraft weight, in 1,000-pound increments. For flexible pavement design, the F_Q rating represents the subgrade, drainage, and frost levels of interaction developed in basic soil mechanics, as illustrated in Table 7–17. Thus a solution is effected by choosing the appropriate nomograph for plane weight and soil-frost condition and finding the related critical and noncritical pavement and/or subgrade thickness.

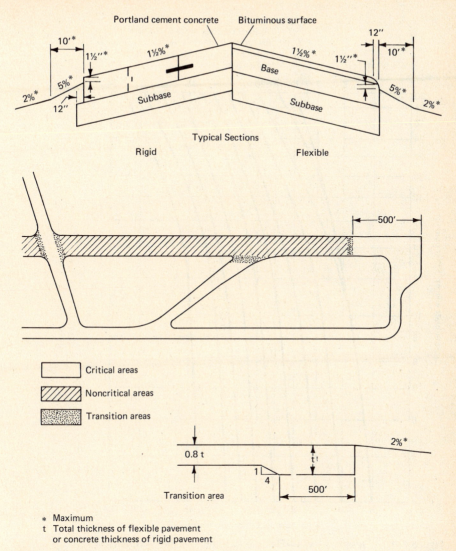

Figure 7–9 Typical Sections and Critical Areas.
(Courtesy FAA.)

Air Traffic Control

Air traffic control is a major air transportation engineering concern. The *airway* is a defined airspace 10 miles wide up to 30,000 feet in altitude. Above that it is 32–40 miles wide. Commercial air carriers' scheduled flights are made on such airways, locked into control that is passed from hub to hub across the flight plan.

Note:
The Fa curve fixes the required base
plus surface course thickness
1″ minimum surface thickness assumed
for Fa curve.

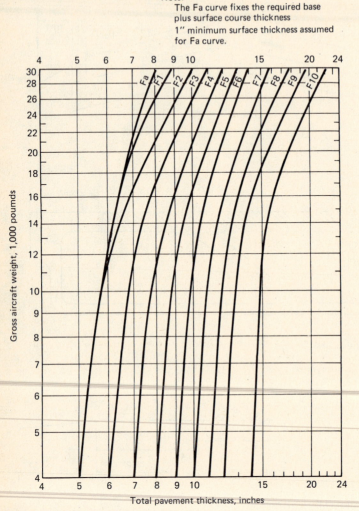

Figure 7–10 Design Curves—Flexible Pavement—Light Aircraft.
(Courtesy Federal Aviation Administration.)

One type of control is *VFR* (visual flight rules), used when the weather is good enough for the aircraft to operate with visual reference to the ground, that is, the "see and be seen" concept. A more sophisticated operation is *IFR* (instrument flight rules), which requires assignment of specific altitudes and routes and much greater minimum separation of aircraft. In IFR the pilot follows a flight plan, with detailed information on airways, altitude, destination, and departure.

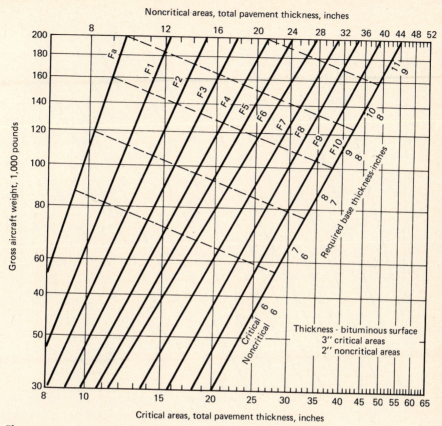

Figure 7–11   Design Curves—Flexible Pavement—Dual Gear.
(Courtesy Federal Aviation Administration.)

Initially the airways were designated or "marked" as follows:

Trunk lines east and west = green
Trunk lines north and south = amber
Secondary lines east and west = red
Secondary lines north and south = blue

Each of these was given a number—green 3, blue 4, and so on. The numbering began at the Canadian border and Pacific Coast, and progressed to the South and East. Each of the designated lines was assigned an altitude level with green and red at odd 1,000-foot intervals eastbound, and even 1000-foot intervals westbound. Amber and blue northbound were given odd 1,000-foot altitudes, and southbound were given even 1,000-foot altitudes.

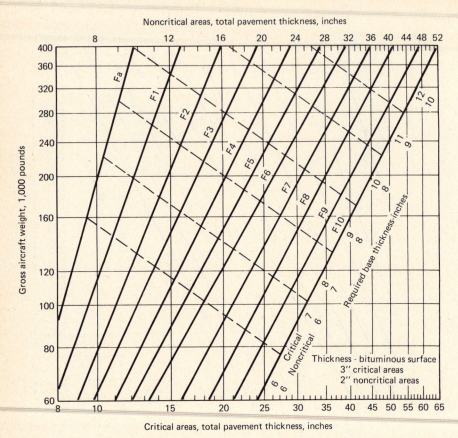

Figure 7–12 Design Curves—Flexible Pavement—Dual-Tandem Gear.
(Courtesy Federal Aviation Administration.)

The color routing system was phased out as ground control and aircraft became better equipped for electronic navigation. The first significant breakthrough allowed the use of *Victor airways*. Victor airways are delineated by boundaries of very-high-frequency omnirange equipment (VOR). Each VOR station has a discrete radio frequency. The pilot tunes to this frequency and files a predesignated course from one VOR to succeeding ones of the prescribed frequency for the flight pattern. The numbering is even numbers east and west, odd numbers north and south. They are designated on charts as V-1, V-2, and so forth. The airway is dimensionally composed of the airspace within parallel lines 4 miles each side of the designated VOR frequency centerline. If two adjacent victor routes are more than 120 miles apart, the space in between is termed a *jet route*.

A *Jet Route* is also delineated by a VOR response system, but with fewer stations, reflecting the fact that the jet is flying at much higher altitudes. Victor routes

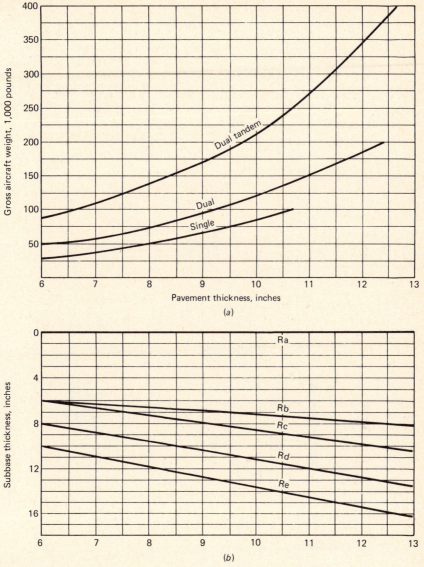

Figure 7–13 Design Curves—Rigid Pavements—Critical Area.
(Courtesy Federal Aviation Administration.)

extend from 1,200 feet above ground up to, but not including, 18,000 feet in altitude. Jet routes extend from 18,000- to 45,000-foot altitudes, also using VOR response. At higher than 45,000 feet, no designated routes exist, and aircraft are handled on an individual basis. Jet routes are designated J-1, J-2, and so on.

Table 7–17 Classification of Soils for Airport Construction[a]

Soil Group	Mechanical Analysis						Subgrade Class			
	Retained on No. 10 Sieve,[b] %	Coarse Sands, Pass No. 10, Ret. No. 60, %	Fine Sand, Pass No. 60, Ret. No. 270, %	Combined Silt and Clay, Pass No. 270, %	Liquid Limit	Plasticity Index	Good Drainage		Poor Drainage	
		Material finer than No. 10 sieve					No Frost	Severe Frost	No Frost	Severe Frost
E-1	0–45	40+	60–	15–	25–	6–	Fa / Ra	Fa / Ra	Fa / Ra	Fa / Ra
E-2	0–45	15+	85–	25–	25–	6–	Fa / Ra	Fa / Ra	F1 / Ra	F2 / Ra
E-3	0–45	...	...	25–	25–	6–	F1 / Ra	F1 / Ra	F2 / Ra	F2 / Ra
E-4	0–45	...	...	35–	35–	10–	F1 / Ra	F1 / Ra	F2 / Rb	F3 / Rb
E-5	0–55	...	...	45–	40–	15–	F1 / Ra	F2 / Rb	F3 / Rb	F4 / Rb
E-6	0–55	...	...	45+	40–	10–	F2 / Rb	F3 / Rb	F4 / Rb	F5 / Rc

E-7.........	0–55	⋯	45+	⋯	50–	10–30	F3 Rb	F4 Rb	F5 Rb	F6 Rc
E-8.........	0–55	⋯	45+	⋯	60–	15–40	F4 Rb	F5 Rc	F6 Rc	F7 Rd
E-9.........	0–55	⋯	45+	⋯	40+	30–	F5 Rc	F6 Rc	F7 Rc	F8 Rd
E10.........	0–55	⋯	45+	⋯	70–	20–50	F5 Rc	F6 Rc	F7 Rc	F8 Rd
E-11.........	0–55	⋯	45+	⋯	80–	30+	F6 Rd	F7 Rd	F8 Rd	F9 Rd
E-12.........	0–55	⋯	45+	⋯	80+	⋯	F7 Rd	F8 Re	F9 Re	F10 Re
E-13	Muck and peat—field examination						Not suitable for subgrade			

aUnited States Federal Aviation Administration system.

bClassification is based on sieve analysis of the portion of the sample passing the no. 10 sieve. When a sample contains material coarser than the no. 10 sieve in amounts equal to or greater than the maximum limit shown in the table, a raise in classification may be allowed provided the coarse material is reasonably sound and fairly well graded. (*Source:* Hennes and Ekse, *Fundamentals of Transportation Engineering,* New York, McGraw-Hill, 1955. Used by permission.)

Environmental Impact Assessment

The Airport and Airway Development Act of 1970 and the Environmental Policy Act of 1969 both require the formal study of environmental factors in airport system planning and individual airport planning and design. The federal government will administer, through FAA and EPA, the review of an Environmental Impact Statement for any airport that is using public monies and is likely to have any impact on public welfare. This includes virtually all airport planning done in the United States today. The findings must address the following:

1. The environmental impact of the proposed development.
2. Any adverse environmental effects that cannot be avoided if the project is implemented.
3. Alternatives to the proposed development, including the null or no-build/do-nothing alternative.
4. Relationship of local short-term use of the environment to its long-term maintenance and enhancement of productivity.
5. Any irreversible environmental damages and irretrievable commitments of resources that would be involved in the proposed development, if it should be implemented.
6. Growth-inducing impacts.
7. Any and all measures designed to minimize impact.

These issues must be addressed for each proposed alternative with regard to the following:

Air quality
Water quality
Noise
Esthetics
Cultural and historical impacts
Residential, commercial, and industrial land use and relocation
Neighborhood disruption
Economic impacts—jobs, tax base, value added
Demographic shifts
Wetlands and flood control
Impacts on flora and fauna

As in dealing with other modes, environmental impact assessment for airport planning and airport system plans is expensive, and will be submitted for citizen participation through public hearings. This is a major determinant of whether or not the airport and/or airport system plan will be implemented.

Marking and Lighting

Lighting and marking at a modern airport are an important design and operational issue, and may make a significant difference in operational safety. The objectives of a lighting and marking system are:

1. To provide ground-to-air visual information required during landing.
2. To provide the visual requirements for takeoff.
3. To provide visual guidance for taxiing.

To provide the foregoing, the following are developed:

1. Approach lighting.
2. Runway threshold lighting.
3. Runway edge lighting.
4. Runway centerline and touchdown zone lights.
5. Taxiway edge and centerline lighting.
6. Taxiway guidance sign system.

Approach Lighting   The type of approach lighting used in the United States is that termed "standard configuration A," illustrated in Figure 7–14. In this system a series of red lights and flashers appears 3,000 feet in advance of the runway, as

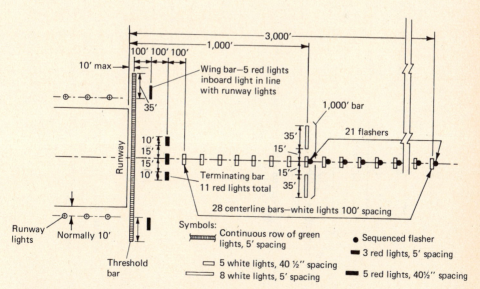

Figure 7–14   Standard Configuration A Approach Light System.
(*Source:* Federal Aviation Administration, Advisory Circular AC 150/5300-2C.)

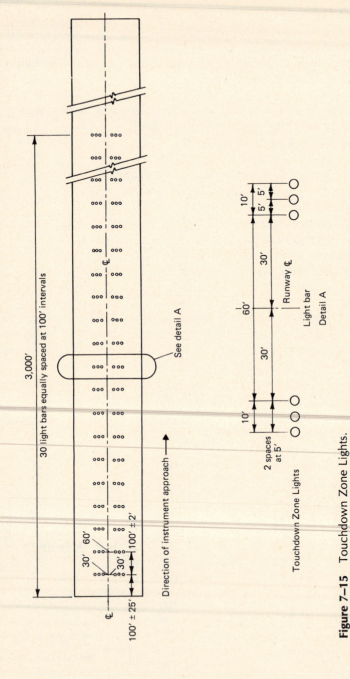

Figure 7–15 Touchdown Zone Lights.

(*Source:* Advisory Circular 150/5340-4C, "Installation Details for Runway Centerline and Touchdown Zone Lighting Systems," Federal Aviation Administration, May 6, 1976.)

illustrated. This is designed to give the pilot a continuing orientation as to the location of the runway on the aircraft's final approach path.

Threshold Lights   These lights, as illustrated in the figure, are a set of semiflush green lights extending across the width of the runway. They are designed to show the pilot the last decision point prior to aborting a landing and executing a "missed approach."

Runway Lights   These lights are located along the edge of pavement, 200 feet apart, within 10 feet of the pavement. They are white, and project beams down the runway, yielding edge markings for the lane of runway travel.

Runway Centerline and Touchdown Zone Lights   To help define the runway center, green lights are installed on the centerline 50 feet apart. For 3,000 feet past the threshold light line, white lights are placed across the runway at 100-foot intervals. These are both illustrated in Figure 7–15.

Taxiway Edge Lights   As on the runway, taxiway edge lights are placed as lane boundary markers. They are typically 200 feet on each side of the runway and are blue in color.

Taxiway Centerline Lights   To show the travel path of the taxiway better, centerline lights are used, spaced between 25 and 100 feet apart, depending on the geometric layout of the taxiway. These lights are also white.

Conventional Marking

The conventional airport marker system is shown in Figure 7–16. It includes boundary markers to afford visibility for the aircraft on approach, and the standard segmented circle, which allows the airport to be divided up in an orderly manner for ground markings. Also note the traffic pattern and landing strip indicators. Related numbering is illustrated in Figure 7–17, and is used in conjunction with landing strip indicators to allocate runway designations.

Economic and Regulatory Aspects

The economic advantages of air travel are significant. They include exceptional speed, frequency of departure and service, and the capability to transport people and freight to remote and thinly settled areas, often inaccessible by other means. Its disadvantages are high cost, some hazard in flight, and unreliability due to the weather. Passenger service classes include first class and coach, with the latter offering lower fares but fewer amenities.

The rate system typically tapers with distance, as shown in Figure 7–18. In addition, other rate patterns also are seen, including *directional,* wherein a particular destination or area (e.g., Tampa, Florida, or the South in general) may have bargain rates to stimulate traffic, or *deferred,* wherein rates change as a function of available space.

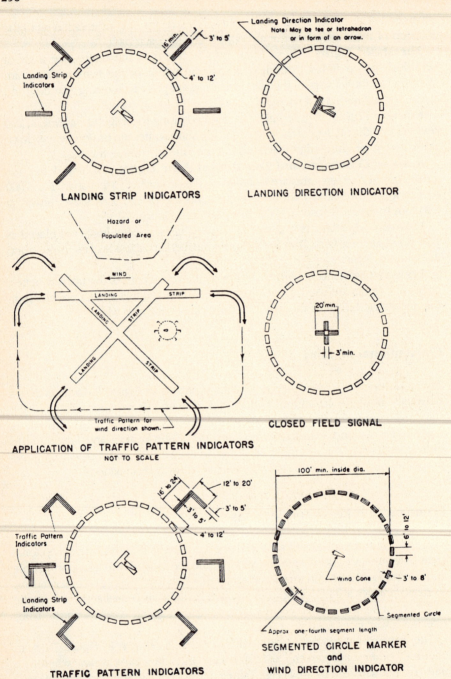

Figure 7–16   Segmented-Circle Airport Marker System.

(Courtesy FAA.)

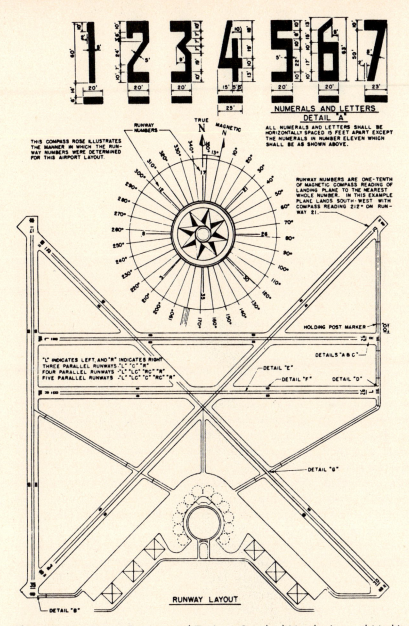

Figure 7–17 Airport Runway and Taxiway Standard Numbering and Marking.
(Courtesy FAA.)

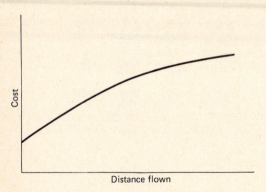

Figure 7–18 Tapering Air-Fare Rates

   Much traditional rate practice has changed, however, as a result of the Comprehensive Airline Deregulation Act of 1981. A forerunner of this deregulation was the subsidy issue, which we now examine in some detail prior to commenting on deregulation.

   The airlines have been given free use of the airways, of which the navigation systems are federally maintained. They do, however, make payments for airport use in the form of airport landing fees. Up to 1985, they have been regulated by the Civil Aeronautics Board (CAB), which has functioned for the air mode in a manner similar to that of the ICC for surface transportation. The CAB has regulated rate and route structures and entry into and exit from the market. Subsequent to 1985, air-carrier regulation has been transfered to the FAA, as part of the deregulation emphasis discussed later. A related aspect is the concept of the *Certificate of Proof.* Before beginning a new service, an air carrier must file proof of "convenience and necessity," that is, that there would not be cheap, adequate service on the route without the new carrier. Major issues surround this concept of convenience and necessity. Basically, what is adequate? Too few carriers result in a monopoly on a route, driving rates up. Too many result in overcompetition and loss. If one carrier wishes to leave the route and it is not permitted to do so, we have overregulation.

   A corrollary to the foregoing is compulsory route extensions, to the detriment of the carrier. The issue of new service with lower development rates is also a relevant one, particularly with regard to the impact of rate changes as the route matures. In essence the entire question of regulation of rates, routes, and their cancellation and sustenance is crucial in viewing the industry with respect to its status in relation to precontrol of entry, free competition versus monopoly, and over- versus underregulation.

   In light of the history of the CAB regarding overregulation, the Administration pushed for passage of the *Comprehensive Airline Deregulation Act of 1981.* This Act frees the carrier from filing a certificate of proof to enter or leave a market or route, and permits the carrier to set whatever fare is considered necessary in order to compete with other carriers. This has opened the airline system to a "free market/perfectly competitive economic model."

The results, however, and the Act's interpretation by professionals have been mixed. It has definitely increased route opportunities and has lowered fares for consumers. However, as the price wars persist, many carriers have approached bankruptcy, with two bankruptcies occurring at the time of this writing. It is not clear what the long-term impact of deregulation will be for the economy as a whole. Bankruptcies of large air carrier corporations have rippling effects on the manufacturing and service industry, the investment market, and the GNP. Some form of re-regulation and price–distance–route controls may have to be instituted. More will be said about the general topic of transport deregulation in Chapter 13 on policy.

In conclusion it should be noted that air transportation has an important impact on our economy and life-styles, and provides international mobility. It is a complex operation requiring massive investment, close coordination with surface transportation, and a compatible interface with community growth and economic development patterns.

Problems

1. Determine the optimum orientation of a single runway to accommodate scheduled air carrier operation under the wind conditions summarized in Table 7–18 and shown in Figure 7–19.

2. In Problem 1, further assume a runway is currently located in the orientation of N 26°E as shown and that a second runway is located in the orientation of N 81°W. What 15 mph cross-wind protection is offered by the first runway? What additional coverage is offered by the second runway?

3. The same airport in Problems 1 and 2 has the following subgrade soil characteristics: 20 percent of soil retained on No. 10 sieve; 52 percent combined silt and clay; liquid limit of 41; and plasticity index of 35. Drainage is good and there is no frost. What is the required thickness of flexible pavement in critical areas for aircraft weighing a maximum of 320,000 pounds with dual-tandem gears?

4. What would the minimum thickness be for rigid pavement rather than flexible pavement in Problem 3?

5. An airport has a single runway with a full-length parallel taxiway and entrance–exit taxiways. All required navigational and air traffic aids exist or will exist, and there are no foreseeable airspace limitations. The airport has a forecasted demand of 230,000 annual operation by the year 1990. The demand consists of 41 percent small aircraft (one-half of these are single engine), 55 percent large

Table 7–18   Wind Coverage Problem C.E. 565 1980
Data From Wind Records at the Wood County Airport, Parkersburg, W. Va.
5 years–1950–1954, Inclusive—Percentages of Total Winds

Direc-tion	Wind Velocity Groups				
	5–9 mph	10–14 mph	15–29 mph	Over 30 mph	Total
N	1.670%	0.516%	0.114%	0.002%	2.302%
NNE	2.014%	0.477%	0.078%	0.002%	2.571%
NE	1.770%	0.288%	0.039%	0.000%	2.097%
ENE	0.885%	0.148%	0.018%	0.000%	1.051%
E	2.058%	0.272%	0.027%	0.002%	2.359%
ESE	2.054%	0.176%	0.021%	0.000%	2.251%
SE	1.428%	0.256%	0.087%	0.000%	1.771%
SSE	1.508%	0.701%	0.653%	0.009%	2.871%
S	2.272%	1.191%	0.869%	0.007%	4.339%
SSW	4.379%	2.467%	2.033%	0.041%	8.920%
SW	4.429%	2.514%	2.559%	0.046%	9.548%
WSW	2.891%	3.252%	4.550%	0.055%	10.748%
W	1.470%	1.330%	1.851%	0.041%	4.692%
WNW	1.743%	1.474%	1.549%	0.027%	4.793%
NW	2.138%	0.974%	0.460%	0.000%	3.572%
NNW	2.166%	0.952%	0.303%	0.002%	3.423%
Total	34.875%	16.988%	15.211%	0.234%	67.308%

Calms 0–4 mph	32.692%

Grand Total	100.000%

aircraft, and 4 percent heavy aircraft. Air carrier operations predominate and touch and go operations are nominal. Do the following: (1) Calculate existing runway capacity. (2) If additional capacity is needed to accommodate demand, identify alternative two-runway configurations that will accommodate the demand.

References

Air Transportation Regulatory Reform. Washington, D.C.: American Enterprise Institute for Public Policy, 1978.

Air Travel Forecasting, 1965–1975. Saugatuck, Conn.: ENO Foundation for Highway Traffic Control, 1975.

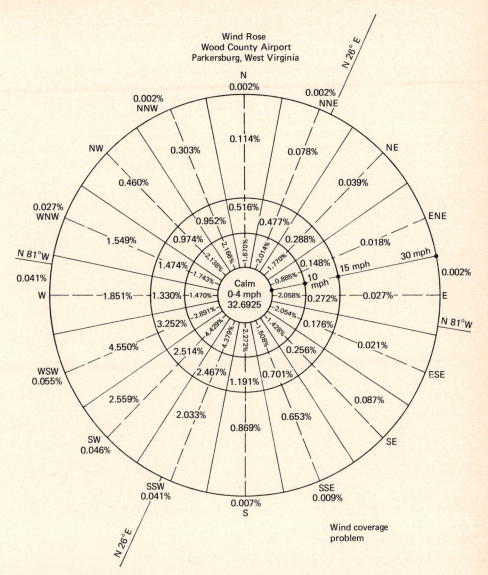

Figure 7–19 Wind Rose Wood County Airport, Parkersburg, West Virginia

Ashford, Norman, and Paul H. Wright. *Airport Engineering*. New York: John Wiley, 1979.

Campbell, George E. *Airport Management and Operations*. Baton Rouge, La.: Claitor's Publishing Division, 1977.

DeNeufville, Richard. *Airport Systems Planning*. Cambridge, Mass.: MIT Press, 1974.

Final Report: National Transportation Policies Through the Year 2000. Washington, D.C.: National Transportation Policy Study Commission, June 1979.

Graham, David R., and Daniel P. Kaplan. *Competition and the Airlines: An Evaluation of Deregulation,* Washington, D.C.: Office of Economic Analysis (staff report), Civil Aeronautics Board, December 1982.

Horonjeff, Cobert. *The Planning and Design of Airports.* New York: McGraw-Hill, 1962, 1975, 1982.

Howard, George P., Editor. *Airport Economic Planning.* Cambridge, Mass.: MIT Press, 1974.

Legault, Adrian R. *Highway and Airport Engineering.* Englewood Cliffs, N.J.: Prentice-Hall, 1960.

Wiley, John R. *Airport Administration.* Westport, Conn.: ENO Foundation for Transportation, 1981.

8 Pipelines

Pipelines provide an effective method for the continuous movement of bulk crude and refined liquid products. Because of relative cheapness in movement costs, they have become a dominant vehicle for moving petroleum and gasses from the extracting field to the market. However, this ease of operation is offset by construction costs and related environmental problems with pipeline construction and the presence of pipeline routes in and around urban areas.

The impact of the use of pipelines on petroleum installations is shown in Table 8–1. In billions of ton-miles, they now carry some 51 percent of the U.S. petroleum product market.

Geographically their distribution is as illustrated in Figures 8–1 through 8–3. The supply of crude oil as of December 1977 is shown in Figure 8–1; note the major imports entering from the Gulf, and major domestic fields in Texas and Alaska. Figure 8–2 illustrates the hierarchy of producing and refining areas, and Figure 8–3 indicates the capacities of the national pipeline system. It should be noted from the latter two illustrations that the fundamental corridor of refineries and pipeline capacity lies in a general northeasterly direction, funneling products from the Southwest and the Gulf to midwestern and northeastern industrial centers.

Several engineering and operational procedures of pipeline transportation are worthy of discussion. The first is that of system definition. The types of lines are:

Table 8–1 Modal Characteristics Related to Pipelines Total Petroleum Products Carried in Domestic Transportation and Percent of Total Carried by Each Mode of Transportation In Billions of Ton Miles

Year	Total Petroleum Products Ton Miles	Pipelines[a]		Water Carriers		Motor Carriers[b]		Railroads	
		Ton Miles	Percent Of Total	Ton Miles	Percent Of Total	Ton Miles	Percent Of Total	Ton Miles	Percent Of Total
1972	476.8	191.3	40.1	254	53.3	22	4.6	9.5	2.0
1973	480.4	205	42.7	238	49.5	23.7	4.9	13.7	2.9
1974	488.8[d]	203[d]	41.5[d]	244	49.9[d]	27.7[d]	5.7[d]	14.1	2.9
1975	515.2	219	42.5	257.4	50.0	26.2	5.1	12.6	2.4
1976	523.9[d]	212[d]	40.5[d]	269.1	51.4[d]	30.4	5.8	12.4	2.3
1977	530.9[d]	219.4	41.3[d]	270.2	50.9[d]	27.6[d]	5.2[d]	13.7	2.6
1978	536.7[d]	226.3	42.2	269.3	50.2[d]	28.6[d]	5.3[d]	12.5	2.3
1979	534.2	236.1	44.2	257.4	48.2	27.8	5.2	12.9	2.4
1980	492.3[d]	225.6[d]	45.8	230.4	46.8	24.3	5.0	12.0[d]	2.4
1981	477.7	230.6	48.3	212.3	44.4	22.7	4.8	12.1	2.5
1982	448.4	231.0[c]	51.5	184.2	41.4	20.7	4.6	12.5	2.8

[a]The amounts carried by pipeline are based on ton-miles of crude and petroleum products for Federally regulated pipelines (84 percent) plus an estimated breakdown of crude and petroleum products for the ton-miles for pipelines not federally regulated (16 percent).
[b]The amounts carried by motor carriers are estimates.
[c]Preliminary.
[d]Revised.
(*Source:* Association of Oil Pipelines, Washington, D.C.)

1. *Gathering line* is a line that can be transported to new and present drilling sites. These lines are often placed on the ground and moved from well to well as the need arises. The common pipe sizes are 2 and 4 inches and they lead to larger mains or field storage facilities.
2. *Trunk line* is the core in-ground pipeline designed to transfer bulk volumes of oil from field storage to refineries. The diameter of such lines historically has been 6–12 inches, although experiments have begun with much larger bulk pipe sizes to accommodate larger throughput. Examples of typical trunk-line routings and related storage and refinery hubs are given in Figures 8–4 and 8–5. Major refinery locales are shown in Figure 8–6.

Storage takes place at three locations in the pipeline hierarchy:

1. In tanks at the gathering trunk-line locations.
2. At major trunk-line junctions.
3. At terminals, at ports, and railroads, where interaction with other modes occurs.

Tank farms, also known as control stations or station manifolds, are clusters of tank storage with pumping and switching instrumentation that permits the operator to:

1. Transfer oil from any producing field to any tank.
2. Transfer oil from one tank to another, or to another tank locale.
3. Transfer oil from any tank to a main line.
4. Bypass all tanks in the station and feed oil production from any field directly through trunk lines.

Criteria for Construction

Due to the many complexities of pipeline construction and operation, some specific construction criteria are paramount:

1. An analysis of the area or extent of the producing field and expected longevity of oil supply, that is, determination of the producing life of the field.
2. Number and expected output of wells, a function of the amount of drilling necessary for complete development of the field.
3. A forecast of production rates expressed in barrels per day for the life of the field.
4. Determination of investment, construction, operating, and maintenance costs for the life of the pipeline project, particularly as compared with other available transport.
5. Assessment of environmental problems; analysis of ways of mitigating environmental impacts.

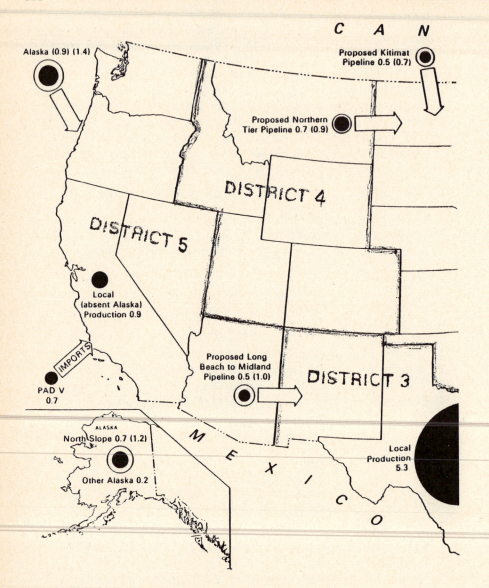

Figure 8–1   Crude Oil Supplies (Millions of Barrels per Day)

(*Source:* Department of Energy, Monthly Energy Reports, July 1976–June 1977. API Refinery Reports, *Oil and Gas Journal,* December 12, 1977.)

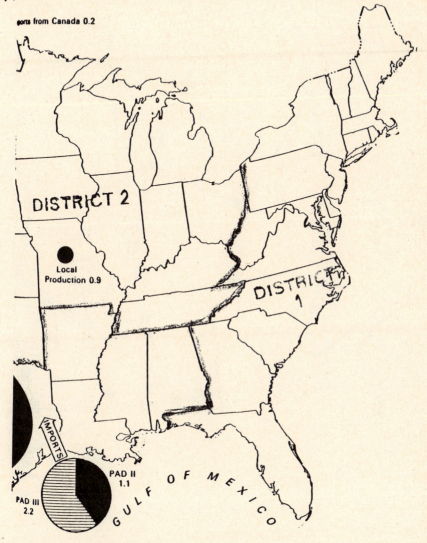

A D A

ports from Canada 0.2

DISTRICT 2

Local
Production 0.9

DISTRICT 1

IMPORTS

PAD II
1.1

PAD III
2.2

GULF OF MEXICO

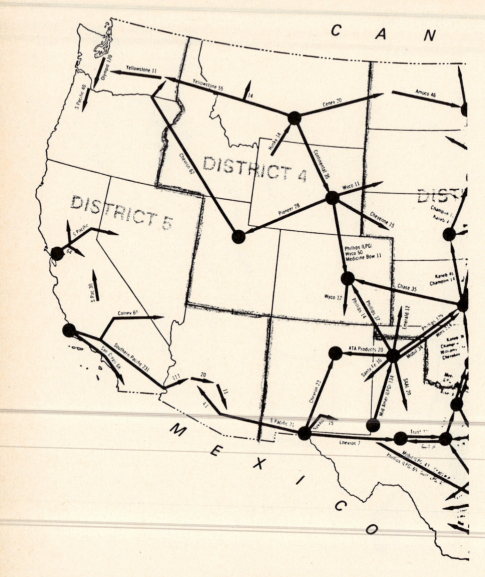

Figure 8–2   Product Pipeline Capacities, 1975 (Thousands of Barrels Daily)
(*Source:* Federal Energy Administration, Office of Oil and Gas.)

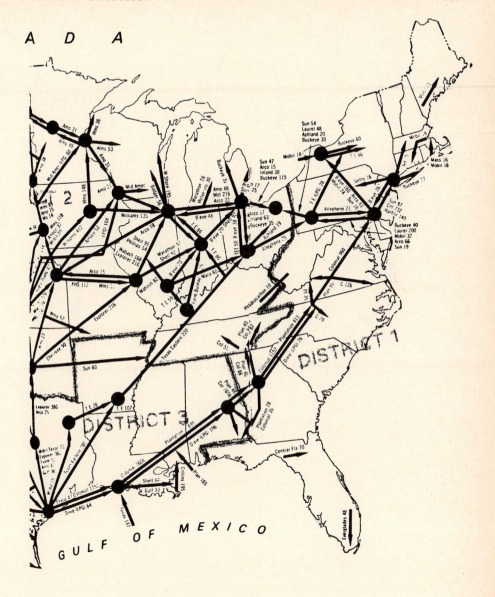

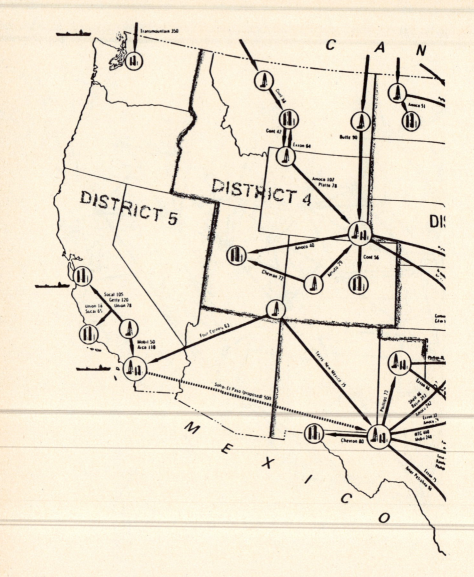

Figure 8–3 Crude Oil Pipeline Capacities, 1975 (Thousands of Barrels Daily)
(*Source:* Federal Energy Administration, Office of Oil and Gas.)

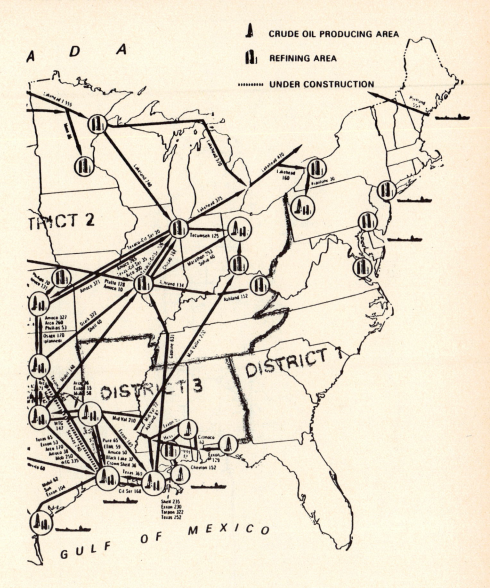

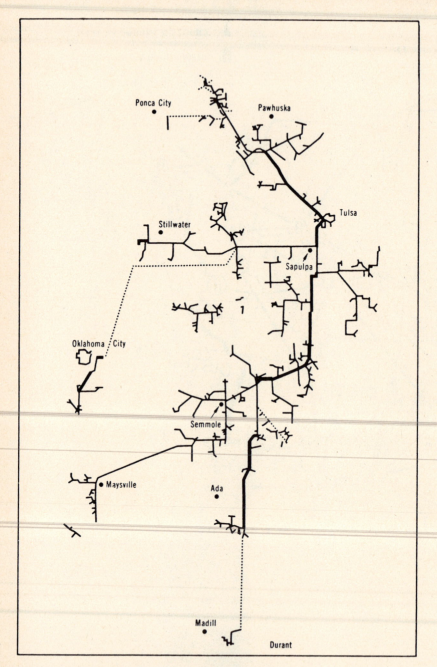

Figure 8–4   Map of Midcontinent Oil Pipeline

(*Source:* Mid-Continent Petroleum Corporation Annual Report 1949, *Oil Pipelines and Public Policy,* American Institute for Public Policy Research, 1979. Reprinted by permission.)

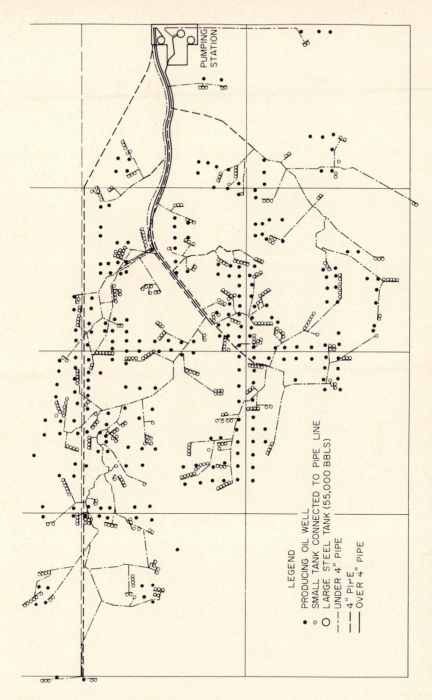

LEGEND

• PRODUCING OIL WELL
○ SMALL TANK CONNECTED TO PIPE LINE
Ⓞ LARGE STEEL TANK (55,000 BBLS)
–·–·– UNDER 4" PIPE
– – – 4" PIPE
——— OVER 4" PIPE

PUMPING STATION

Figure 8–5 Sketch of a Typical Petroleum Gathering Line System
(Prepared by National Resources Planning Board.)

313

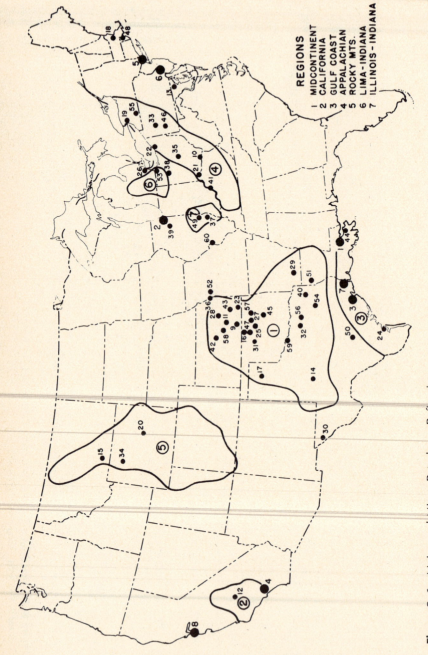

Figure 8–6 Major and Minor Petroleum Refineries

(Prepared by National Resources Committee.)

REGIONS

1 MIDCONTINENT
2 CALIFORNIA
3 GULF COAST
4 APPALACHIAN
5 ROCKY MTS.
6 LIMA–INDIANA
7 ILLINOIS–INDIANA

Petroleum Transport—Fluid Flow Characteristics

As might be recalled from hydraulics, the categories of laminar flow, partially turbulent flow, and turbulent flow have points of transition. At some critical velocity, flow changes from nonturbulent to turbulent, and the range slightly above critical velocity is known as partially turbulent.

The Reynolds number N is a good index of turbulence state. In round pipes this is:

$$N = \frac{vd\,\gamma}{\mu g}$$

where

v = mean velocity of flow

d = diameter of pipe

$\dfrac{\gamma}{g}$ = mass density

μ = absolute viscosity of fluid

Viscosity is essentially the shearing resistance of the fluid. Absolute viscosity is the force required to displace two opposite faces of a unit cube of fluid at a unit rate of speed. It is expressed in dyne-seconds per square centimeter, known as *poises*. It may also be expressed in pounds/second/square foot: 1 poise = 0.002089 lb/sec/ft^2. Using the Saybolt Universal Viscometer, absolute viscosity in poises may be determined empirically from:

$$\mu = G\left(0.0022t - \frac{1.8}{t}\right)$$

where G is the specific gravity of the fluid, and t is saybolt seconds.

Some examples of absolute viscosities of various fluid mediums are given in Table 8–2. Empirical history yields a Reynolds number at a critical velocity of

Table 8–2 Absolute Viscosity in Pound-Seconds Per Square Foot

Fluid	32°F	68°F	122°F	212°F	Sp gr at 68°F
Air	0.00000036	0.00000038	0.00000041	0.00000046	0.0012
Water	0.00003739	0.00002089	0.00001149	0.00000593	0.998
Linseed oil	. . .	0.00079382	0.00037602	0.00013578	0.930
Heavy fuel oil	. . .	0.025±	0.0036±	. . .	0.990

(*Source:* Charles W. Harris, *Hydraulics,* New York, John Wiley, 1944. Used by permission.)

2,000. Therefore, if the Reynolds number of the liquid is less than 2,000, the flow will be laminar. If the Reynolds number is greater than 3,000, the fluid flow will be turbulent. The 2,000–3,000 zone is nebulous, based on the smoothness or roughness of pipe.

If the Reynolds number is less than 2,000, the loss of pressure is attributable strictly to the viscous shearing resistance of the fluid. The resulting pressure drop in pipe of length l (in feet) is:

$$p = \frac{32\ vl}{d^2}\ \mu\ .$$

where p is the pressure drop in pounds per square foot. Lost head is described as the pressure drop p divided by the unit weight of the fluid. Unit weight is discussed later.

When turbulent flow occurs, however, the Darcy formula with an appropriate friction factor must be used to determine the head loss, computed as follows:

$$h' = f\ \frac{lv^2}{d2g}$$

f, the friction factor, is a function mainly of pipe roughness, but also is influenced by pipe size and velocity. The relationship between f and N, the Reynolds number, is empirically valid enough to be used as an appropriate indication for

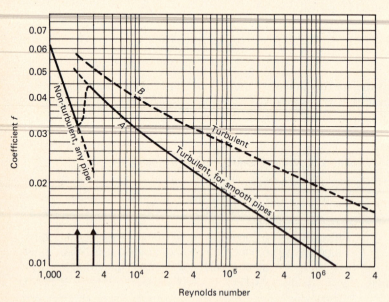

Figure 8–7 Friction Factor f for Partially Turbulent Flow of Fluids.
(*Source:* Charles W. Harris, *Hydraulics,* New York, John Wiley, 1944. Used by permission.)

what f should be in the equation in order to compute h'. Thus one may use the graph of Figure 8–7. The band between A and B includes the majority of viscous oils in the petroleum market flowing through high-quality cored steel pipelines with smooth inner-wall construction. The entire above analysis is necessary in order to ascertain the pressure required to transport oils of various qualities across various grades and cross sections of pipeline of various dimensions.

Carrying the discussion further, the unit weight of the oil must be considered. This is expressed in terms of the API (American Petroleum Institute) gravity scale. This yields a *gravity number,* expressed in degrees API, which increases as the specific gravity decreases, with the specific gravity of water defined arbitrarily as 10. That is:

$$°API = \frac{141.5}{sp. \ gr.} - 131.5$$

and

$$Sp. \ gr. = \frac{141.5}{°API + 131.5}$$

The envelope of specific gravity, unit weight, and pressure relationships discussed previously is exhibited at 60°F in Table 8–3.

Table 8–3 Specific-Gravity, Unit-Weight, and Pressure Relationships Corresponding to API Gravity Scale at 60°F

°API	Sp gr	Lb/cu ft	Lb/gal	Lb/bbl	Psi/ft of head
5	1.037	64.6	8.64	362.6	0.455
10	1.000	62.3	8.33	349.8	0.433
15	0.9659	60.2	8.04	337.8	0.418
20	0.9340	58.2	7.78	326.7	0.404
25	0.9042	56.3	7.53	316.2	0.391
30	0.8762	54.6	7.30	306.4	0.379
35	0.8498	52.9	7.08	297.2	0.368
40	0.8251	51.4	6.87	288.5	0.357
45	0.8017	49.9	6.68	280.4	0.347
50	0.7796	48.6	6.49	272.6	0.337
55	0.7587	47.3	6.32	265.3	0.328
60	0.7389	46.0	6.15	258.3	0.320
65	0.7201	44.8	5.99	251.7	0.311
70	0.7022	43.7	5.85	245.5	0.305

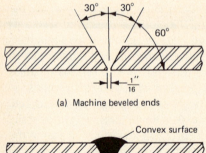

(a) Machine beveled ends

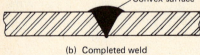

(b) Completed weld

Figure 8–8 Welded Pipe Joint

Pipe Construction Characteristics

Among standard characteristics of pipeline construction are that the average section is 20 feet long, sometimes it is furnished in "double sections" of 40 feet, with joint types as shown in Figure 8–8. A major requirement is that the welded joint *must* develop to the full specified tensile strength of the pipe. Although pipe can be made from a variety of materials, the petroleum pipe considered here for trunk line and tank farm use is restricted to high-quality cased steel with smooth inner walls. Gathering pipe is typically movable plastic, which is highly flexible.

As should be obvious from the discussion of pressure characteristics, pipe of maximum strength is required where maximum pressure occurs, such as at joints where oil leaves the pumping station or tank. Lighter pipe of lower strength can be used at other locations where pressures are low, thus achieving construction cost savings. These types of trade-offs of installation costs versus use and pressure potentials over the design life must be considered at the planning stage to achieve cost effectiveness with safety.

Economic and Regulatory Aspects of Pipelines

With regard to pipeline regulation, we shall concern ourselves with the following usage types.

1. Crude oil pipelines associated with oil companies.
2. Gasoline, or final-product lines, also associated with oil companies.
3. Slurry pipelines, such as for coal slurry.
4. Natural gas pipelines.

The major economic issue, regardless of the regulatory aspects, is the necessity for recognizing, anticipating, and dealing with shifts in the market. Refineries are extremely expensive to build and represent very large fixed costs in unremovable and nonconvertible equipment. Therefore, the effort is made to optimize refinery location, by placing them near the urban market, and requiring the high-value finished gasoline and petroleum products to travel only short distances to the consumer. This concept works in consort with the fact that pipelines are cheaper forms of transport for petroleum than rail, but more expensive than water. However, because of their design and the capability of developing a customized right-of-way that theoretically is idealized as to their origin–destination, pipelines are often superior to water routings. To take advantage of this, pipeline rates are often set in the range of 38–40 percent of rail rates for crude oil, giving pipelines a truly competitive position versus rail and water.

Working against the economic operating environment are several issues of control and regulation. The most apparent is the setting of high rates for independent operators' usage of pipelines owned by major oil companies. Such tactics attempt to force the independents out of business. There are many examples of major oil companies early in the century charging excessive rates to use their pipelines and thus squeezing small independents out of business. Small companies usually did not have the capital to build their own pipelines.

The major regulatory thrusts in dealing with such companies began in 1906 with the *Hepburn Act,* which brought pipelines under the aegis of the ICC and formally declared them common carriers. Another regulatory device was the *Cole Act,* passed in 1941 and active until 1946. This Act declared that anything hauled via pipeline for national defense had the power of eminent domain to yield takings and easements for construction. Eminent domain is now statutorily attached to pipeline construction in many states.

The main issue has been the need for separation of the large oil companies and pipelines to permit a competitive position from which to serve all segments of the petroleum production market.

Regardless of the Hepburn Act, abuses of the tactical use of company-owned pipelines still exist, although they are designated common carriers. Two mechanisms make this possible—the minimum tender provisions and increased rates. Under minimum tender a pipeline company sets a minimum oil production shippage level that must be hauled for the independent. Trunk lines often require a batch of 25,000–100,000 barrels to transport. This forces the small company that cannot meet the minimum tender out of the market by virtue of the fact that no pipeline shipping options are available to it. The second approach is simply to charge higher rates to the independents, cutting their profits and ultimately forcing bankruptcy.

In general control of pipelines by the ICC is less exhaustive than control over the railroads. The most significant differences are:

1. The "commodities clause" does not apply to pipelines as it does to rail.
2. There is no control over construction of new lines or extensions to existing lines.
3. There is no control over abandonment of lines.

4. There is no control over the security issues of pipeline companies.
5. There is no regulation of consolidation and acquisition of control; however, the pipelines are subject to antipooling provisions of the law.

The pipelines and the "commodities clause" are of great relevance. There is much interest in legally preventing the pipelines from hauling their own products, requiring the complete separation of the oil production and refining functions from that of oil transportation. Many believe that this would reinsure competition. However, others feel this could be achieved by stronger ICC action and enforcement of existing laws.

Problems

1. A crude fuel oil with a specific gravity of 0.93 has an absolute viscosity of 0.30 poise. What is the viscosity, expressed in Saybolt seconds, t?
2. An oil with a mean velocity of flow of 0.3 ft/sec is transported through a round 12 inch pipe. If its mass density is 75 lb/ft^3 and its absolute viscosity is 0.25 poise, is the flow turbulent or nonturbulent?
3. In Problem 2 above, what is the pressure drop over one mile?
4. Determine the gravity number of heavy fuel oil at 68°F.
5. The oil in Problem 2 is pumped by a 200 psi pump between two points, A and B. Point A is located at an elevation 300 feet above point B. If the pipeline is at a constant downgrade between the two points, how far away may point B be located in order to receive the oil?

References

Hennes, Robert G., and Martin I. Ekse. *Fundamentals of Transportation Engineering.* New York: McGraw-Hill, 1955.

Locklin, D. Philip. *Economics of Transportation,* 5th ed. Homewood, Ill.: Richard D. Irwin, 1960.

Mitchell, Edward J., Editor. *Oil Pipelines and Public Policy.* Washington, D.C.: American Enterprise Institute for Public Policy Research, 1979.

Paquette, Rodnor, Norman J. Ashford, and Paul H. Wright. *Transportation Engineering, Planning and Design,* 2d ed. New York: John Wiley, 1982.

Transport of Solid Commodities via Freight Pipelines. Washington, D.C.: U.S. Department of Transportation, Office of University Research, July 1976.

Woebert, George S., Jr. *U.S. Oil Pipe Lines.* Washington, D.C.: American Petroleum Institute, 1979.

Yu, Jason C. *Transportation Engineering.* New York: Elsevier North Holland, 1982.

9 Urban Transportation Planning

The Urban Transportation Plan has become one of the major technical endeavors in transportation engineering. It is complex and costly, and requires input from the technical, social, economic, and citizen sectors. Figure 9–1 delineates the general activities that urban transportation plans follow. The effort can be divided into a *demand* side and a *supply and evaluation* side. On the demand side, we are interested in tools and techniques that provide reasonably accurate information on the forecasted level of demand for travel some ten to twenty years hence. On the supply side, we are interested in the formatting and decisions with respect to which set of transportation improvements will best satisfy that demand. Therefore by making use of much of the study design information of Chapter 3, the general urban transportation modeling process illustrated in Figure 9–2, consisting of entities termed trip generation, trip distribution, traffic assignment, and modal split, is employed to yield demand results. We now examine these entities in detail.

Trip Generation

The initial modeling effort is to forecast the number of trips twenty years hence. The economic, population, and land-use forecast information is used, formatted according to the zones of the origin–destination study of Chapter 3. Appropriate

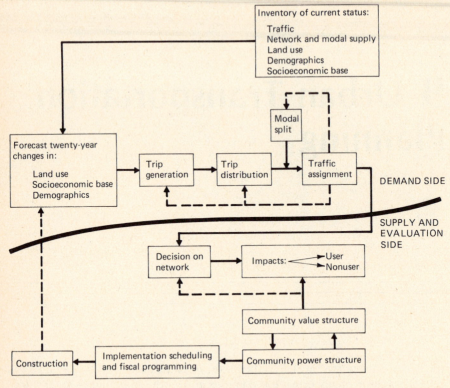

Figure 9–1   Overview of Urban Transportation Planning Structure

mathematical modeling of this information allows the following trips to be forecasted:

Residential trip generation
Home based to work
Home based to nonwork
Non-home-based/nonresidential trip generation
Commercial truck trips to zone
Taxi trips to zone

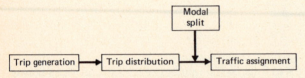

Figure 9–2   The Urban Transportation Planning Modeling Process

Table 9–1   Example of Linear Regression Residential Trip Generation Output

$$T_i = 37.6 + 1.75H_i + 2.39C_i + 1.88W_i$$

where

    T_i = number of work trips produced by zone i
    H_i = number of households in zone i
    C_i = number of cars owned by households in zone i
    W_i = number of workers resident in zone i

(*Source:* Peter R. Stopher and Arnim H. Meyburg, *Urban Transportation Modeling and Planning*, Lexington, Mass., Lexington Books, D. C. Heath, 1975. Used by permission.)

As stated above the assumption is that trip making is a function of the characteristics describing the socioeconomic status of households in a zone or neighborhood. Therefore, relevant zone parameters are:

Residential density
Median income
Mean car ownership
Number of workers per household
Number of people per household
Mean stage in family life cycle
Distance from the CBD

Although several trip generation analysis techniques exist, the traditional approach has been to forecast the above as variables in a multiple regression model.[1]

These variables are regressed in equation form to develop a relationship between trip density and the stimuli. As such:

$$Y = a + b_1 X_1 + b_2 X_2 + b_3 X_3 + \cdots b_n X_n$$

This results in a dependent variable Y, which is either total trips for the zone or can be expressed as trip rate = totals/households in the zone. A typical example of regression results from this operation is illustrated in Table 9–1. Several issues surround the use of the trip generation equation format. It should be noted that this output is extremely sensitive to the zone size. An overly large zone induces so

[1]For a review of a variety of trip generation techniques, including cross-classification approaches, the author suggests the text *Analysis of Travel Demand*, by Shuldini and Oi, Evanston, Illinois, Northwestern University Press, 1962, and *Urban Transportation Planning and Modeling*, by Stopher and Meyburg, Lexington, Mass., D. C. Heath, 1975.

much heterogeneity in socioeconomic status that meaningful forecasting is lost in the variance of output. At the other extreme, sampling of each individual's trip mechanisms in lieu of zoned forecasting is extremely expensive.

Similar equations may be built for nonresidential trip generation, expressed as:

$$Y = \text{trips}/10{,}000 \text{ employees}$$

or

$$Y = \text{trips/employee}$$

or

$$Y = \text{trips}/10{,}000 \text{ square feet of nonresidential floor space}$$

The equation is judged as to quality by the R^2 level, which exists between $0 < R^2 < 1.00$ and measures the closeness of fit of the regressed forecast line to the data. Graphic examples of good and poor fits are shown in Figure 9–3. In addition to the zonal and quantitative issues, it is *always* necessary to review a trip generation equation from the perspective of "Is it a logical equation?" That is, is there a fundamental plausible relationship between the set of independent variables and the dependent variable results they are forecasted to have caused. Without inquiring as to this logic, it may be possible to have an arbitrary combination of unrelated variables yield a consistently high R^2 for a dependent variable. This results in an equation with good quantitative quality, but of no meaning. It is termed "spurious correlation." The trip production output of the equations is used as input to the next model, termed trip distribution.

Trip Distribution

Having ascertained the forecast number of trips in a zone, the next question is: How are these trips distributed over the region? This question is treated by a set of trip distribution computations. These computations utilize the general gravity model concept of travel and interaction across distance, namely:

$$T_{ij} = \frac{P_i P_j}{d_{ij}^k}$$

which states that travel between zone i and zone j is a direct function of population or other stimuli at both i and j (P_i and P_j), and inversely proportional to the friction of distance between i and j, raised to some power k (d_{ij}^k).

Moving from the above concept and making use of specific aspects of previous

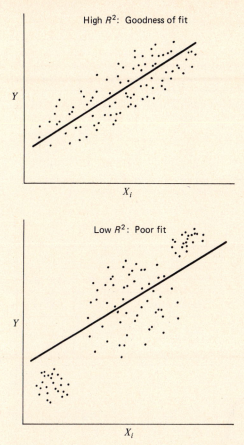

Figure 9–3 Examples of Goodness-of-Fit Plots

trip generation, we develop the following. Outputs of residential trip generation are trip production from a zone P_i, and nonresidential trip generation into a zone is defined as trip attractions by zone A_j. Thus we theorize that the production and attractions are distributed across the region in a series of zonal interchanges, T_{ij}, as shown in Table 9–2, by virtue of a computational procedure based on the above gravity model. We now describe the mechanics of this computational procedure, reformatting the gravity model as follows:

(a) $$T_{ij} = \frac{P_i A_j f(r_{ij}^n) k_{ij}}{\sum_j A_j f(r_{ij}^n) k_{ij}}$$

(b) $$\sum_j T_{ij} = P_i$$

(c) $$\sum_i T_{ij} = A_j$$

Table 9–2 Final Forecast Trip-Interchange Matrix

From Zone	To Zone				
	1	2	3	4	O_i
1	403	171	235	139	948
2	77	565	69	294	1,005
3	287	190	220	649	1,346
4	94	449	361	308	1,212
A_j	861	1,375	885	1,390	4,511

(*Source:* Stopher and Meyburg, *Urban Transportation Modeling and Planning,* Lexington, Mass., D. C. Heath, 1975. Used by permission.)

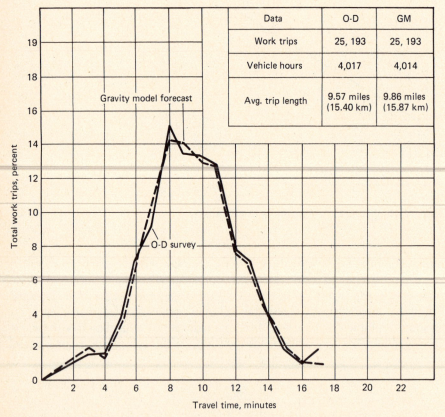

Figure 9–4 Origin–Destination and Gravity Model Trip-Length Frequency Distributions, Sioux Falls, South Dakota, 1956.

(*Source:* "Traffic Assignment and Distribution for Small Urban Areas," Washington, D.C., Bureau of Public Roads, U.S. Department of Commerce, 1965.)

Equation (a) states that trips from i to j are a direct function of possible production at i, attractions at j, the friction of distance from i to j, and an inverse function of attractions to all zones and their frictions of distance. The k_{ij} term is a specific zone-to-zone adjustment factor that permits incorporation of certain social, geographical, and economic characteristics that may affect travel patterns and that are not otherwise accounted for in the gravity model formulation.

The model works by calibrating n in the friction-of-distance formula, using travel time to the nth power, and revising n over a number of iterations until the current origin–destination trip-length frequency is matched by the forecast trip-length frequency resulting from the distribution computation. The result is a forecast matrix of T_{ij} that satisfies requirements and has a forecast trip-length frequency curve that matches the current trip-length frequency curve. An example of the final T_{ij} matrix output is as shown in Table 9–2. The matching frequency curves are illustrated in Figure 9–4.

One of the criticisms of this model is that forecast output matches existing statistical behavior, and the modeling does not allow room for new technology or consumer tastes that might result in different trip-length frequency behavior across zones of travelers in the region. A second criticism is that the computations are very mechanistic, forcing closure and allowing little room for logic in their operation. These are relevant points. The k_{ij} term is often set at varying levels, to force closure of the models. Meaningful interpretation of k_{ij} is questionable, other than to act as a closure variable. The actual adjustment of $f(r_{ij}^{n})$ after each iteration is achieved as follows:

$$f_{adj.} = f_{used} \times \frac{OD\%}{GM\%}$$

where:

$f_{adj.}$ = adjusted travel time factor, $f(r_{ij}^{n})$
f_{used} = travel time factor $f(r_{ij}^{n})$ used in the previous interation.
$OD\%$ = percentage of origin–destination survey trips of a specific length
$GM\%$ = percentage of gravity model trips of a specific length from the iteration run being analyzed

Traffic Assignment

Having established T_{ij}, the gross amount of travel between zones, we now ask the question: What routes do these trips take? In traffic assignment we attempt to answer this question by actually loading the trips onto the current highway network, seeing where the traffic load exceeds capacity, and reformatting several network options under consideration for future construction to be able to handle the forecasted load. Traffic assignment proceeds according to one of the following approaches.

1. All or nothing, no capacity restraint.
2. Capacity restrained.
3. Diversion curve.

The second approach, *capacity restrained,* is the conventional approach used in regional modeling. It is built by supplementing the all-or-nothing concept.

All or Nothing

In all or nothing the following steps are followed:

1. A given origin–destination or forecast T_{ij} is found to exist.
2. A search of the routes for the above *i-j* movement is made, and using design speeds for the various routes searched, the minimum-time path is found.
3. All *i-j* volumes are loaded on the minimum-time path origin–destination route, with no capacity criteria.

As can be seen the foregoing is simplistic, due to the lack of capacity analysis applied to the loading. Placing all volumes on the minimum-time path typically will cause overloading and congestion feedback, resulting in a travel time that is not "minimum." As such the mechanics of this technology do not account for diverting traffic to other routes in the origin–destination corridor.

Capacity Restraint

Capacity restraint builds on the foregoing approach to yield a realistic assignment concept. Its algorithm is illustrated in Figure 9–5. Computation mechanisms result in continually recomputing travel time on the basis of the loaded network, and redistributing the traffic on the basis of new travel times. The formula for redistribution is:

$$T_i = T_o [1 + 0.15 (V/C)^4]$$

where
$$T_i = \text{current iteration minimum-time path}$$
$$T_o = \text{previous iteration minimum-time path}$$
$$V/C = \text{volume-to-capacity ratio of current minimum-time path}$$

Iterations of the algorithm in Figure 9–5 are run until two successive iterations yield the same results, meaning that final equilibrium of traffic loads and travel times over the network has been achieved and results cannot be improved upon for the network being tested.

The congestion is explicitly handled in the $(V/C)^4$ term of the formula. The

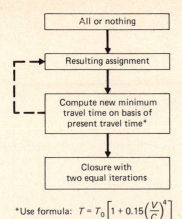

*Use formula: $T = T_0\left[1 + 0.15\left(\frac{V}{C}\right)^4\right]$

Figure 9–5 Capacity Restrained
Traffic Assignment Algorithm

traffic is "spread" over several routes in the network, based on the relative travel time equilibria, resulting in a more accurate picture of route usage. Typically several candidate freeway systems will be employed and tested, taking links in and out of the system until a network is found that performs best with respect to traffic criteria. An example of an existing forecast network is shown in Figure 9–6.

Diversion Curves

A diversion curve, as illustrated in Figure 9–7, is a historical ratio of traffic use of two different facilities, based on their travel time ratio. It is often used for analyzing parallel facilities in a common origin–destination corridor, or facilities of similar functional class. If the diversion curves are on the basis of locally historically accurate analysis, they are likely to be valid for that region, but they may not be transferable to another region.

Modal Split

Modal split attempts to answer the question: How many trips will be via transit versus how many will be via auto? Mode split techniques are divided into two classes: *trip-end models,* which precede the trip distribution and predict mode split in total trips generated zone to zone, and *trip interchange models,* which predict by mode k after the ij interchange is determined, that is, T_{ijk}.

Modeling techniques for these algorithms are much more varied than for other travel demand components. Trip-end models typically work with socioeconomic aspects of the trip-maker that are more refined than those for trip generation, such as refined analysis of income levels and age groups. Typically a highly refined

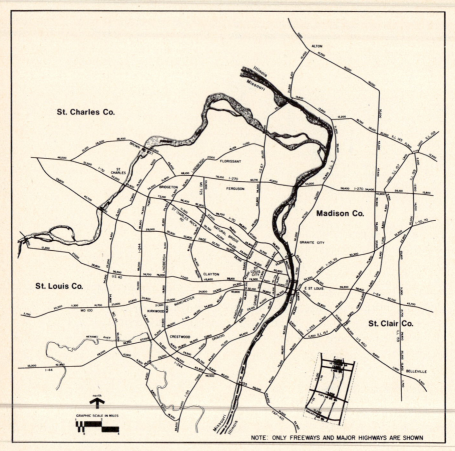

Figure 9–6   A Forecast Network Daily Traffic Volumes on the 1995 Highway System
(*Source:* East-West Gateway Coordinating Council, St. Louis, Mo.)

regression is used, as shown in Table 9–3. The trip interchange models concentrate more on the comparative system performance format of the modes, relying on differential impacts of waiting times, walking time, parking costs, and so on, as illustrated in Table 9–4 and Figure 9–8 for the Washington, D.C., modal split analysis. As shown in Figure 9–9, use of diversion curves to format comparisons are a common technique.

Most modal split studies are built specifically for the region under study, contrary to the rather rigid format imposed on all regions by the trip generation, distribution, and traffic assignment algorithms.

As one can see at the conclusion of the travel demand phase, a set of forecasted trips has been generated for each zone in the region. They have been distributed to all other zones in the region, with their choice of mode, and all auto trips have

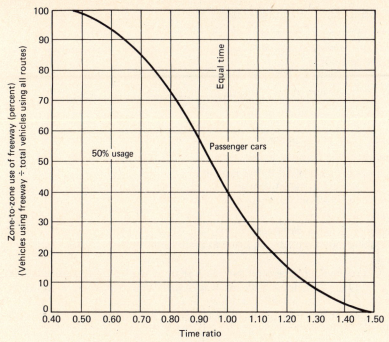

Figure 9–7   Travel Time Ratio Diversion Curve

(*Source:* "Traffic Assignment and Distribution for Small Urban Areas," Washington, D.C., Bureau of Public Roads, U.S. Department of Commerce, 1965.)

Table 9–3   A Trip-End Modal Split Model

$$Y = -2.6466 + 3.7084 \ln P + 0.3912 \ln E$$
$$+ 2.3757 \ln T + 0.4918 \ln U - 0.9708 \ln M$$

where

Y = percentage of person trips on transit
P = population over five years old (in 10,000s)
T = transit-service factor
E = economic factor
U = land-use distribution factor
M = urbanized land area, square miles

(*Source:* Stopher and Meyburg, *Urban Transportation Modeling and Planning*, Lexington, Mass., Lexington Books, 1975. Used by permission.)

Table 9–4   Composition of Trip Interchange, Modal Split Model

---

1. *Relative door-to-door travel time.* The ratio of travel time by public transit to travel time by private auto:

$$\text{Travel time ratio} = \frac{X_1 + X_2 + X_3 + X_4 + X_5}{X_6 + X_7 + X_8}$$

where
   X_1 = time spent in transit vehicle
   X_2 = transfer time between transit vehicles
   X_3 = time spent waiting for transit vehicle
   X_4 = walking time to transit vehicle
   X_5 = walking time from transit vehicle
   X_6 = auto driving time
   X_7 = parking delay at destination
   X_8 = walking time from parking place to destination

   The effect of travel time ratio on the transit share of work trips in peak hours for Washington, D.C., Philadelphia, Pennsylvania, and Toronto, Canada, is shown in Figure 9–8.

2. *Relative travel cost.* The ratio of out-of-pocket travel cost via transit to the travel cost via auto:

$$\text{Travel cost ratio} = \frac{X_9}{(X_{10} + X_{11} + 0.5X_{12})/X_{13}}$$

where
   X_9 = transit fare
   X_{10} = cost of gasoline
   X_{11} = cost of oil change and lubrication
   X_{12} = parking cost of destination
   X_{13} = average car occupancy

3. *Economic status of trip-maker.* The use of both automobile and transit is a function of income. As the income increases, automobile ownership increases and the use of transit decreases.

4. *Relative travel service.* Many factors affect the level of service, but most of them are difficult to quantify. Only excess travel time, that is, the time spent outside the vehicle during a trip (walking, waiting, and transfer time for transit, and parking delay and access time to parking place for automobiles) is used in a ratio form as follows:

$$\text{Travel service ratio} = \frac{X_2 + X_3 + X_4 + X_5}{X_7 + X_8}$$

where the X values have been previously defined.

(*Source:* M. J. Fertel, et al., *Modal-Split Documentation of Nine Methods for Estimating Transit Usage,* Washington, D.C., U.S. Bureau of Public Roads, 1966.)

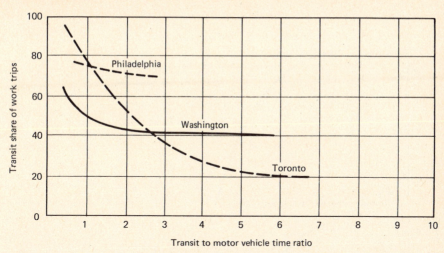

Figure 9–8   Travel Time Ratio Diversion Curve for Work Trips in Peak Periods.
(*Source:* From M. J. Fertal, et al., *Modal Split-Documentation of Nine Methods for Estimating Transit Usage,* Washington, D.C., U.S. Bureau of Public Roads, 1966.)

been assigned to major routes. The knowledge of location-specific forecast demand is such that alternatives may be generated to serve the demand. The alternatives may be evaluated against several criteria. At this point we turn our attention to the supply side of Figure 9–1, and review the various evaluation methods open to us.

Supply and Evaluation Techniques

A set of transportation alternatives are postulated to meet the demand requirements developed above. Evaluation of the so-called "best" or preferred system is necessary. There may be several perspectives as to which is "best," and all perspectives may have to be synthesized in some manner to yield a solution that can be implemented. We thus examine the supply and evaluation of alternatives from several fundamental perspectives:

1. Economic analysis
2. Environmental impact
3. Citizen participation
4. Implementation and financing trajectories

User Evaluation—Traditional Engineering–Economic Evaluation Techniques

The engineering-economic evaluation techniques are noted in standard texts, and have become traditional instruments of evaluation in public works and

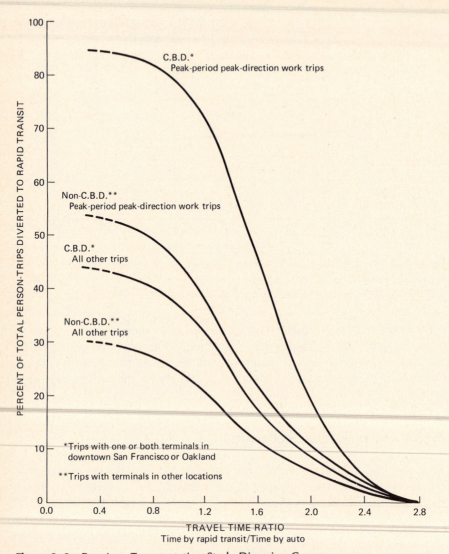

Figure 9–9 Bay Area Transportation Study Diversion Curves
(*Source:* Stapher and Meyburg, *Urban Transportation Planning & Modelling,* Lexington, Mass., D.C. Heath, 1975.)

private investment decisions. They typically work with mutually exclusive alternatives, and the primary choice variable is monetary cost or benefit or some function thereof, developed through the several criteria discussed here.

Minimum Average Annual Cost   The choice variable is $TC_{j,\bar{t}}$:

$$TC_{j,\bar{t}} = (crf_{i,n})\, C_j + O_{j,\bar{t}} + U_{j,\bar{t}} + A_{j,\bar{t}}$$

where

$(crf_{j,n})C$ = annualized capital costs
$O_{j,\bar{t}}$ = annualized operating and maintenance costs in average year $\bar{t}$
$U_{j,\bar{t}}$ = annualized vehicle and user operating costs in average year $\bar{t}$
$A_{j,\bar{t}}$ = annualized accident costs in average year $\bar{t}$
n = service life
i = interest rate
crf = capital recovery factor
j = design alternative j for a site

In this method all benefits are assumed equal, and the minimum cost transportation alternative is chosen for execution. Obviously the assumption of equal benefits of all design alternatives is questionable in most cases. An example of use is shown in Table 9–5.

Table 9–5 Minimum Average Annual Cost Example

Three transit improvement programs have been proposed for a transit district. Capital costs, annual maintenance expenses, and user costs are as follows:

	Alternative A	Alternative B	Alternative C
Capital cost	$2,500,000	$2,000,000	$3,000,000
Maintenance	400,000	500,000	350,000
User costs	1,000,000	1,500,000	1,250,000

The interest rate is 10% and the expected life is 15 years.

The average annual cost $TC_{j,t}$ is given by the equation

$$TC_{j,t} = (crf_{i,n})C_j + O_{j,t} + U_{j,t} + A_{j,t}$$

Alternative A: $TC_{j,t}$ = $2,500,000 \dfrac{i(1 + i)^n}{(1 + i)^n - 1}$ + 400,000 + 1,000,000 + 0

= 2,500,000 (0.1315) + 400,000 + 1,000,000

= \$1,728,800

Alternative B: $TC_{j,t}$ = (2,000,000)(0.1315) + 500,000 + 1,500,000

= \$2,263,000

Alternative C: $TC_{j,t}$ = (3,000,000)(0.1315) + 350,000 + 1,250,000

= 1,994,500

Alternative A represents the minimum average annual cost.

Table 9–6 Benefit–Cost Ratio Example

Continuing the previous example, the benefit–cost ratio of each alternative may be found from the equation:

$$\frac{B_j}{C_j} = \frac{R_{\bar{\imath}} - R_{j\bar{\imath}}}{TC_{j,t} - TC_{\bar{\imath}}}$$

where $R_{\bar{\imath}}$ = annual user cost for present facility
$R_{j,\bar{\imath}}$ = annual user cost for jth proposed facility
$T_{j,\bar{\imath}}$ = annualized capital cost and annual maintenance cost for jth proposed facility
$TC_{\bar{\imath}}$ = annualized capital cost and annual maintenance cost for current facility

In this case: $R_{\bar{\imath}}$ = 1,600,000
$TC_{\bar{\imath}}$ = 650,000

Alternative A: $\dfrac{B}{C}$ = $\dfrac{1,600,000 - 1,000,000}{[(\text{crf})(2,500,000) + 400,000] - 650,000}$

$$= \frac{600,000}{78,750} = 7.62$$

Alternative B: $\dfrac{B}{C}$ = $\dfrac{1,600,000 - 1,500,000}{[(\text{crf})(2,000,000) + 500,000] - 650,000}$

$$= \frac{100,000}{113,000} = 0.88$$

Alternative C: $\dfrac{B}{C}$ = $\dfrac{1,600,000 - 1,250,000}{[(\text{crf})(3,000,000) + 350,000] - 650,000}$

$$= \frac{350,000}{94,500} = 3.70$$

Clearly, Alternative A has the highest benefit–cost ratio.

Benefit–Cost Ratio   This method develops a ratio from the dollar savings in user costs resulting from the transportation alternative, divided by the difference between the total annual costs of the proposed alternative and the present configuration. That is:

$$B_j/C_j = \frac{R_{\bar{\imath}} - R_{j\bar{\imath}}}{TC_{j,t} - TC_{\bar{\imath}}}$$

where

$R_{\bar{i}}$ = total annual user costs for the present facility

$R_{j,\bar{i}}$ = total annual user costs for the proposed facility

$TC_{j,\bar{i}}$ = $(crf_{i,n})C_j + O_{j,\bar{i}}$, total annualized capital, operating and maintenance costs for the proposed facility

$TC_{\bar{i}}$ = $O_{\bar{i}}$, total operating and maintenance costs for the present facility

Problems associated with this method include the inability to quantify some benefits, such as comfort and convenience, environmental and regional impacts, and the difficulty of the nontechnical decision maker in understanding this method. An example is worked through in Table 9–6.

Net Benefits   This method takes the difference of the sum of the discounted benefits for each year of the project life minus the sum of discounted costs for each year of the project life:

$$NB_j = \left[\sum_{t=0}^{n} (pwf_{i,t}) (R_t - R_{j,t}) \right] - \left[\sum_{t=0}^{n} (pwf_{i,t}) (TC_{j,t}) \right]$$

where $pwf_{i,t}$ = present worth factor for interest i in year t and R, R_j, and TC are as defined before. The alternative with the highest positive net benefits is chosen. An example is presented in Table 9–7. This method is the most pleasing of all forms, because of its ease in being readily understood, the ability to include any elements that can be monetized, and the fact that there are no rigid requirements to compare entities and identical project lives.

Any capital improvement will have certain multidimensional cost and effectiveness outputs, and not all of these can be evaluated quantitatively or monetarily. In particular the concept of evaluating a transportation alternative decision process in purely monetary terms can be disputed on several grounds. To place a dollar value on certain results of the transportation decision such as human life and cultural and amenity attributes is erroneous, from the points of view of worth to society and complex life-style relationships, both of which are themselves multidimensional, and require an analytic approach properly tempered with humanism.

Given such complex multidimensional decision characteristics, it is worthwhile to consider further aspects of our analysis on the basis of incorporating present criteria and evaluation techniques into structures that deal with multidimensional considerations in transportation alternatives investment.

Nonuser Evaluation—Environmental Impact

In addition to affecting the user, the transportation alternatives generated may have substantial nonuser impacts relevant to the community at large, such as impacts on tax base, employment, air quality, noise, and flora and fauna modifications. Perhaps the most comprehensive concept to address the entire nonuser issue is the *Environmental Impact Statement* required for any public works

Table 9–7 Net Benefits Example

The following alternatives exist for an intersection currently under study. The net benefits of each alternative are computed as follows:

Alternative	Capital Cost	Annual Maintenance Cost	Annual Cost Due to Accidents	Annual User Costs
Current Facility	0	$15,000	$150,000	$1,350,000
Alternative A:				
Minor reconstruction				
striping	$ 450,000	$17,000	$ 65,000	$1,112,000
street repair				
Alternative B:				
Major reconstruction	$1,250,000	$30,000	$ 21,000	$1,055,000
channelization				
signalization				

Assume an interest rate of 10% over 15 years.

$$\sum_{t=0}^{15} (pwf_{10\%,15yrs}) = \sum_{t=0}^{15} \frac{1}{(i+1)^t} = 7.6061$$

$$crf = \frac{i(1+i)^n}{(1+i)^n - 1} = 0.13147$$

Annualized Capital Cost

Alternative A: $= crf\,(450,000)$
          $= 0.13147\,(450,000) = 59,161$
Alternative B: $= crf\,(1,250,000)$
          $= 0.13147\,(1,250,000) = 164,337$

Alternative A:
$NB_A = 7.6061(1,350,000 - 1,112,000) - 7.6061(59,161 + 65,000 + 17,000)$
   $= \$736,567$

Alternative B:
$NB_B = 7.6061(1,350,000 - 1,055,000) - 7.6061(164,337 + 21,000 + 30,000)$
   $= \$605,924$

Clearly Alternative A is the best choice.

facility using federal funds. It is the outgrowth of the 1970 National Environmental Policy Act and the Clean Air Act. The impact statement is employed at the planning and design levels, and subjects each set of alternatives generated that require federal funds to a comprehensive investigation for potential environmental impacts. The impact statement must provide information on the following nonuser impacts of facilities.

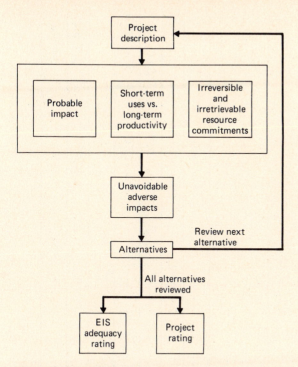

Figure 9–10 Environmental Impact Statement Review Process
(Courtesy Federal Highway Administration and Urban Mass Transportation Administration.)

Air quality
Noise
Wetlands and floodplain management
Water pollution
Land-use changes and relocation
Neighborhood disruption
Flora and fauna
Property values
Tax base
Employment
Historical and cultural impacts
Esthetic impacts

No specified evaluation procedure is required for each impact. It is expected that state-of-the art techniques will be used in studying each individual impact. The prescribed study and review process is outlined in Figure 9–10. An overview of relevant study elements and their likely criteria for a vast array of regional case study transportation alternatives is exhibited in Table 9–8. Transportation engi-

Table 9-8 Environmental Impact Components and Criteria

		Railway		
		Light Rail	Rapid Rail	Commuter Rail
Operating Cost (per car mile, $)		4.06–8.24	3.70–5.08	4.81–11.35
Land Cost per mile (million per mile, $)[a]	CBD	4.47	4.47	4.47
	Fringe	3.37	3.37	3.37
	Residential	2.85	2.83	2.83
Construction Cost (million per mile, $)	At Grade	0.4–2.0	4.8–16.0	6.6–9.4
	Elevated	7.9–19.2	9.8–19.0	13.2–18.6
	Cut & cover downtown	—	89.0–130.0	89.0–130.0
	Cut & cover fringe	—	37.0–89.0	37.0–89.0
Station Cost (million/each)	Subway	17.0–22.0	11.0–14.0	11.0–14.0
	At-grade	0.1–0.3	3.9–5.2	3.9–5.2
	Elevated	1.3–4.7	4.4–5.8	4.4–5.8

	II Bus
	Local (1,000–3,000 vehicles) 2.97–3.39 per bus mile
Operating Cost, $	
Busway Land Cost (million per mile, $)[a]	
CBD	5.41
Fringe	4.88
Residential	4.35
Busway Construction Cost at grade[a]	
CBD	5.93
Fringe	5.72
Residential	4.00

[a]One million population or greater.

Table 9–8 (continued)

		III Highway System						
		Freeway 13.1			Arterial 20.9			
		N	R	W	N	R	W	
Operating Cost (40 mph, cents per vehicle mile)								
Land Cost (million per lane, $)[a]	CDB	2.89	2.71	1.33	1.45	0.38	0.92	
	Fringe	1.87	0.84	0.90	1.09	0.30	0.66	
	Residential	1.67	0.68	0.78	0.60	0.28	0.45	
Construction cost[b] (million per lane mile, $)	CBD	2.97	3.08	3.30	1.19	1.03	1.09	
	Fringe	2.45	1.77	2.71	0.94	0.92	1.01	
	Residential	1.85	1.57	2.07	0.86	0.82	1.01	
Annual cost of Maintenance, $		8,828 per lane mile			3,383 per lane mile			

IV
New Technology—Personal Rapid Transit (PRT)

Operating Cost, $ 0.96–3.21 per vehicle mile

Capital Cost, $ 7–30 million per lane mile

[a] One million population or greater.
[b] 500,000–1,000,000 population.
N—New road.
R—Reconstruction.
W—Major widening.

342

Transportation Alternatives

Energy Consumption	I Railway			II Bus (30 mph, 3% grade)		III Highway	
	Electric Light Rail Transit per Car Mile	Electric Rapid Rail	Diesel Commuter Rail per Car Mile	Local Bus	Exclusive Busway	Freeway	Arterial
Coal	4.55–10.20 pounds	4.55–10.20 pounds	—	—	—	—	—
No. 6 Fuel Oil	0.41–0.46 gallons	0.41–0.46 gallons	—	—	—	—	—
Diesel Fuel	0.44–0.49 gallons	0.44–0.49 gallons	1.4–2.4 gallons	0.317 gallon per vehicle mile	0.123 gal per vehicle mile	—	—
Gasoline	0.49–0.55 gallons	0.49–0.55 gallons	—	0.093 to 0.154 gallon per vehicle mile	—	0.042–0.053 gallon per vehicle mile	0.067–0.069 gallon per vehicle mile
Furnace Oil	0.45–0.50 gallons	0.45–0.50 gallons	—	—	—	—	—
Kerosene	0.46–0.55 gallons	0.46–0.55 gallons	—	—	—	—	—

Table 9–8 (continued)

| | Transportation Alternatives | | | | | | |
| | *I* Railway | | | *II* Bus (30 mph, 3% grade) | | *III* Highway | |
Energy Consumption	Electric Light Rail Transit per Car Mile	Electric Rapid Rail	Diesel Commuter Rail per Car Mile	Local Bus	Exclusive Busway	Freeway	Arterial
Natural gas	52.0–66.0 cubic feet	52.0–66.0 cubic feet	—	—	—	—	—
Manufactured gas	100.0–164.0 cubic feet	100.0–164.0 cubic feet	—	—	—	—	—
Electricity	6.6 kw.h per car mile	6.6 kw.h per car mile	10.1 kw.h[a] per car mile	—	—	—	—

Transportation Alternatives

Pollutant	I Railway			II Bus		III Highways (Composite of Freeways and Service Arterials (mph))	
	Electric Light Rail Transit	Electric Rapid Rail	Diesel Commuter Rail	Line Haul Service Arterial	Exclusive Busway	Autos	Trucks
Carbon Monoxide (CO)	0.1558 gram/car-mile	0.2011 gram/car-mile	30.8 gram/mile	10.90 g per mile	10.54 g per mile	31.60 gram/mile	58.59 gram/mile
Hydrocarbons (HC)	0.1294 gram/car-mile	0.1669 gram/car-mile	22.0 gram/mile	14.70 g per mile	11.69 g per mile	4.61 g per mile	7.06 g per mile
Oxides of Nitrogen (NOX)	10.0822 gram/car-mile	13.0092 gram/car-mile	33.0 gram/mile	13.84 g per mile	8.53 g per mile	3.89 g per mile	9.75 g per mile
Oxides of Sulfur (SOX)	25.4779 gram/car-mile	32.9305 gram/car-mile	28.6 gram/mile	—	—	—	—
Aldehydes	0.0181 gram/car-mile	0.0235 gram/car-mile	1.8 gram/mile	NA	NA	—	—
Particulates	50.2519 gram/car-mile	64.9590 gram/car-mile	11.0 gram/mile	NA	NA	—	—

Table 9–8 (continued)

Pollutant	Transportation Alternatives						
	I			II		III	
	Railway			Bus		Highways (Composite of Freeways and Service Arterials (mph))	
	Electric Light Rail Transit	Electric Rapid Rail	Diesel Commuter Rail	Line Haul Service Arterial	Exclusive Busway	Autos	Trucks
Organic Acids	—	—	3.1 gram/mile	NA	—	—	—
Noise In vehicle	60.–72 DBA	61–72 DBA	70–75 DBA	82–96 DBA	82–96 DBA	50–76 DBA	—
At station	68–80 DBA	78–108 DBA	80–90 DBA	88–102 DBA heavy traffic	88–102 DBA	66–82 DBA 20 ft away	

[a] kw.h = kilo-watt-hour

(*Source:* Urban Mass Transportation Administration U.S. Department of Transportation.)

neers have found that a wide variety of levels of sophistication exist across the several impacts. Air quality and economic impacts are subject to readily usable computational techniques, as is noise analysis. However, esthetic and cultural–historical impacts are often much more subjective and lack conciseness in their evaluation. This leads us to the next issue, that of citizen participation in assessing the impacts.

Citizen Participation Citizen participation in transportation systems evaluation is an outgrowth of the movement leading to the National Environmental Policy Act of 1970, wherein citizens declared that public works facilities, in addition to serving the user, must fit the desires, value system, and governmental mechanics of the community. Since then a variety of forms of citizens' input into nonuser and environmental impact statement review have become apparent.

The most general of these responses in the public hearing, which is called to examine transportation alternatives at their various stages (planning, preliminary design, final design) and allow citizens to voice their views as to acceptability and modification. Well-structured hearings provide a method of documenting concerned groups' input. If ill structured, they are a source of unfocused criticism resulting in harrassment rather than solution of transportation and public works problems. Hearings seldom work in a vacuum. As shown in Figure 9–1, the transportation planner is called upon to be a technical mediator, dealing with several groups representing various facets of the power structure in the community. If the elected officials are truly representative of their constitutiencies' views, the engineer may spend much time with them; if they are not, the engineer will ferret out the "power elite," the subgroup of citizens who represent various viewpoints and deal with them. The engineer's job will be to fashion a set of transportation alternatives before and during the hearing that has consensus to go forward for financing and implementation.

Illustrative Nonuser Evaluation Techniques Incorporating Environmental Impact Statements—The Value Matrix The foregoing is more easily achieved if the transportation engineer has some conceptual construct from which to develop interaction with the user and nonuser environmental impact perspective. In Table 9–9 we offer a typical example using a technique termed the value matrix, which allows assessment of various citizen group perspectives on transportation planning alternatives. The citizen group is asked to weigh the relative importance of each impact on a 0–100-point scale, with all weights summing to 100 points. Then:

$$S_k = \sum_{x=1}^{M} r_x^k W_x$$

where

S_k = score of transportation alternative k; $k = 1, \ldots, n$ alternatives

r_x^k = rank value of that alternative k, for impact criteria x, impacts $x = 1, \ldots, M$.

Table 9–9 A Value Matrix Example

The three alternative transit improvement plans have the following impact evaluation matrix:

		Alternative		
Impact	Weight	A	B	C
Capital cost	40	$2.5M	$2.0M	$3.0M
Air quality	25	78T/day	68T/day	88T/day
Noise	10	40 dBA	20 dBA	25 DBA
Travel time	25	30 min.	45 min.	40 min.

A value matrix may be set up as follows:

		Alternative					
Impact	Weight	A	pts.	B	pts.	C	pts.
Capital cost	40	$2.5M	20	$2.0M	40	$3.0M	0
Air quality	25	68T/day	25	78T/day	12.5	88T/day	0
Noise	10	40 dBA	0	20 dBA	10	25 dBA	7.5
Travel time	25	30 min.	25	45 min.	0	40 min.	8.3
Total Pts.			70		62.5		15.8

Points are assigned by the best choice receiving the maximum value, the worst choice receiving no points, and other values are interpolated linearly.

Clearly, Alternative A is best.

W_x = weighting of impact criteria x by citizens group

$$0 \leqslant W_x \leqslant 100; \quad \sum_{\forall x} W_x = 100 \text{ points}$$

S_k^* = the optimal alternative = Max S_k

Implementation, Funding, and Financing Structures

It is important to assess our current position in the transportation plan. Referring again to Figure 9–1, inventory has been completed, and socioeconomic forecasts have been made, as have trip generation, distribution, mode split, and assignment. A series of select transportation plan alternatives have been offered to meet this travel demand, and have been evaluated from a user/economic analysis point of view and a nonuser environmental impact perspective, and citizens have

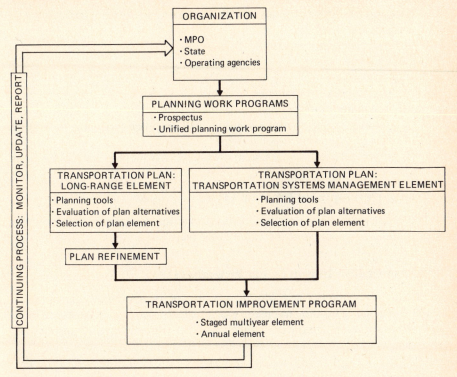

Figure 9–11   Organization of Principal Tasks of a Metropolitan Planning Organization (MPO).

(*Source: An Introduction to Urban Travel Demand Forecasting,* Washington, D.C., FHWA and UMTA, 1977.)

made their feelings known through subgroup activity within the planning process, with elected officials, and at the hearings. A final decision on a twenty-year transportation plan and its network and policy components has been reached. This section reviews what, by federal mandate, that plan must contain, and how it gets from plan to funding to construction. Figure 9–11 illustrates the fundamentals of the following components.

Components of the Transportation Plan   Under current DOT guidelines, the plan must contain the following.

1. A twenty-year long-range general set of capital and noncapital transportation alternatives to satisfy the stated planning goals, conceived as the transportation plan.
2. Related to noncapital alternatives, a *transportation systems management plan,* which is a set of no or low capital alternatives capable of helping to solve the congestion and accessibility problems facing the region. Not all

low and noncapital options will be relevant to any region, but all must be considered. They are:

a. Staggered work hours
b. Auto-free zones
c. Car pooling
d. Altered parking strategies
e. Designated transit lanes
f. Low-cost traffic operations and circulation procedures, that is, striping, marking, one-way street systems.
g. Improved traffic signal systems—control, phasing, and interconnections.

Transit Development Program (TDP)

This is a revolving five-year pragmatic effort to improve transit systems where applicable in the context of the twenty-year plan.

Transportation Improvement Program (TIP)

This is a revolving five-year *specific* schedule of transportation improvements and sequencing of funding to ensure that *specific* project components are being prioritized and completed within the trajectory of the twenty-year transportation program.

Unified Work Program (UWP)

This is the annual listing of specific projects and related funds sought, categorized by local and federal matching share of resources. It is submitted annually to the Regional Transportation Planning Agency Policy Advisory Committee, reviewed by it, and sent to the Department of Transportation for final review and appropriation of funds. As funds are appropriated and returned to the Regional Transportation Planning Agency, design of the projects and their construction and opening for use are scheduled.

In conclusion, one can see that urban transportation planning is a complex array of interacting components, utilizing socioeconomic, political, technological, mathematical, traffic engineering, and construction factors to yield a composite, implementable transportation plan.

Problems

1. A transportation zone in a growing urban area has the following characteristics: 2,516 households; 4,530 automobiles owned; and 750 workers resident. Using the example regression equation in Table 9–1, compute the number of work trips produced by this zone.

2. Two highway improvement programs have been proposed for consideration. Alternative A has a capital cost of $6,000,000, an annual maintenance cost of $800,000, and an estimated annual user cost of $1,100,000. Alternative B has a capital cost of $7,000,000, an annual maintenance cost of $600,000, and an annual user cost of $1,500,000. Accident costs for both projects are expected to be $500,000 annually. Interest over the 20-year life of the project is expected to be 12 percent. What are the annual costs of each alternative?

3. Find the benefit–cost ratio for each alternative in Problem 2. Assume $TC_{j,0} = $3,500,000$ and $U_{j,0} = \$2,500,000$.

4. A river operator is considering buying 30 new barges at a price of $250,000 each. These barges are expected to last 20 years and have no salvage value at the end of their life. Maintenance costs are $2,500 per barge per year. Income attributable to each barge is $40,000 annually. What is the rate of return on this investment?

5. Three alternatives are proposed for a freeway expansion program. The appropriate costs are listed below. Determine the net benefits of each.

Scheme	Capital Costs	Annual Maintenance Cost	Annual User Costs
No change	$ 0	$250,000	$8,000,000
A	6,500,000	170,000	6,500,000
B	10,200,000	100,000	5,600,000
C	17,500,000	90,000	4,500,000

Assume an interest rate of 10% over 30 years.

6. An agency is studying three alternative transit improvements to a region. The systems have the following impact evaluation matrix:

Impact	Weight	Alternative 1	Alternative 2	Alternative 3
Travel Time	25	15 min.	10 min.	20 min
Capital Cost	30	$30M	$40M	$25M
Air Quality	30	8 g/day	6 g/day	9 g/day
Noise	15	30 dBA	20 dBA	10 dBA

Apply a value matrix approach to determine which alternative is best. What approach should be taken if only $35M is available for the project?

References

Cleveland, Donald E., Editor. *Manual of Traffic Engineering Studies,* 3d ed. Washington, D.C.: Institute of Traffic Engineers, 1964.

Department of Transportation Organization Directory. Washington, D.C.: U.S. Government Printing Office, February 1984.

Haefner, L. E., E. J. Carter, and J. W. Hall. *An Informational Report on Techniques for Evaluating Factors Relevant to Decision Making on Highway Locations.* Washington, D.C.: U.S. Department of Transportation, Federal Highway Administration, December 1972.

Haefner, L. E., E. J. Carter, and J. W. Hall. *Literature References on Techniques for the Evaluation of Factors Relevant to Decision Making on Highway Locations.* Washington, D.C.: U.S. Department of Transportation, Federal Highway Administration, January 1972.

Meyburg, Arnim H., and Peter R. Stopher. *Urban Transportation Modeling and Planning.* Lexington, Mass.: Lexington Books, 1975.

Morlok, Edward K. *Introduction to Transportation Engineering and Planning.* New York: McGraw-Hill, 1978.

Yarjani, Bigan. Technology Assessment of Transportation System Investments (doctoral dissertation). St. Louis, Mo.: Department of Civil Engineering, Washington University, December 1979.

Yu, Jason C. *Transportation Engineering.* New York: Elsevier North Holland, 1982.

10 Mass Transit

Urban public transportation, or as it is often popularly called, "mass transit," is a mode of passenger transportation that is open to public use. It employs large rubber-tired or rail vehicles (bus or commuter rail) singly or together in a variety of right-of-way concepts. The traveler is one of many on a vehicle catering to several common points of origin and destination.

Objectives of Mass Transportation

The objectives of mass transportation are several. They are:

1. To provide a method of conveyance for those who cannot afford an automobile, or those whose age and/or physical condition does not make auto travel possible (children, the elderly, indigent, handicapped).
2. To provide large-scale access to major generators of employment and recreation and social events (the central business district, stadiums, office and industrial parks, recreational areas).
3. To complement auto travel.
4. Through use of transit, and in certain auto-free zones, to reduce congestion, air pollution, noise, and the need for parking space.
5. To yield accessibility to all socioeconomic strata of the population, thus creating opportunities for employment by providing a reasonably priced transportation system to and from work.

353

6. Through accessibility, to help ensure the viability of real estate investments in key locations, thus improving the area's economic structure, tax base, and regional wealth.
7. To aid in the achievement of compatible integration of transportation and land-use planning in a region.

Conventional Transit Types

To achieve the foregoing, an entire spectrum of transit technology is available. Specific types include:

1. *Conventional bus.* Operating in mixed street traffic, making scheduled stops over a delineated route.
2. *Conventional express bus.* A bus route in mixed traffic with a single or few origins, and a single or few destinations. This is a line-haul operation without intervening stops. The operation is designed to have minimum points of boarding and alighting activity, similar to an over-the-road bus trip. It is typically between outlying areas and points of employment or activity concentration, such as suburb to central business district, or suburb to stadium or theater.
3. *Conventional bus with priority treatment system.* Wherein components of the bus system receive favorable design or operations treatment in the system, such as continuous right turns, right turns on red, a separate turning lane, or favorable signal timing for bus-use lanes.
4. *Exclusive bus lane.* A delineated lane on an arterial or a freeway dedicated only to bus use. Typically this is found only during morning and evening rush hours.
5. *Bus rapid system.* A dedicated, fully access-controlled right-of-way, which is used only for buses, traveling at high speeds and with very close headways. These systems are designed to freeway standards, with two or three lanes, reversible during peaks, and are often set in the closed medians of freeway systems.
6. *Light rail transit.* A set of small, lighter weight rail cars, capable of traveling on lightweight rail guideways (38 pounds per running yard). This rail may be mixed in with city streets, adjacent and parallel to arterials and freeways, and on isolated rail rights-of-way, sometimes using freight rail corridors. Typical train size is two to four vehicles.
7. *Heavy rail transit, commuter rail, and/or rail rapid transit.* These consist of heavy high-capacity rail rapid transit trains of three to six cars serving a dedicated rail route network; there is no intermingling of the rail with the street system at surface, except within freeway rights-of-way and over or under the street right-of-way due to air rights or subway tunneling.
8. *Para transit.* This is a general term for surface bus service that does not fit any of the conventional modes, is small in capacity (six to twelve persons),

and may deviate from standard route coverage. The most typical of these is demand-responsive transportation, where a small van picks up passengers in order of their request for service. The van's destination may be a common drop point, such as a shopping center or a bus stop or station for conventional bus or rail service, thus acting as a feeder to the system.

Patterns of Route Coverage

Each of the foregoing achieves a different type of route coverage and is best deployed to meet a particular demand pattern.

Para Transit   Used in low-density areas to pick up and distribute riders where conventional bus sizes would be uneconomical or inoperable due to street dimensions and configuration.

Conventional Bus   Used in typical grid patterns where demand is ubiquitously spread over the area, and density of pickup is medium to high.

Conventional Bus Express Operations, Bus Priority on Freeway, or Bus Rapid   Used where there is a consistently high demand for service to and from specific points and an obvious corridor of demand can be established. It may be employed in lieu of building a rail transit corridor, because of the lower cost of using existing rights-of-way.

Light Rail Transit   May be employed where medium radial corridor demand exists, and some flexibility of usage of present rail tracks exists and/or some flexibility of operating rail into the surface street system is possible.

Heavy Rail or Regional Rail Rapid Transit   Exists when significantly high corridor or radial demand density is well established over long line lengths with many stops and the very high cost may be justified by ridership. Few, if any, new startups of heavy rail exist today due to the costs per mile of right-of-way and construction.

Thus it should be apparent that the viability and "correct fit" of a particular transit system to a region is very sensitive to the land-use density question. Generally low- to medium-density and sprawl land-use patterns lend themselves to a flexible bus system. Corridor-established heavy radial densities lend themselves to a light rail/heavy rail or bus rapid system, depending on the costs of construction.

Performance Characteristics

All of the systems have different dimensions, capacities, and performance characteristics. The wide range in dimensions is illustrated in Table 10–1. Note that the unit capacity of operation varies widely, from ten to sixteen persons for a van to a maximum of 1,600 to 3,000 persons for a single regional commuter rail train, thus relating to the previous discussion of density, demand, and service provisions.

In addition to the dimensions are the characteristics of acceleration, decelera-

Table 10–1 Ranges of Geometric Dimensions and Passenger Capacities of Transit Vehicles

Transit Vehicle Type	Length ft / m	Width ft / m	Height ft / m	Design Capacity of Single Unit			Design Capacity of Maximum Train	
				Seats	Standees	Total Passengers	Cars	Total Passengers
Van	15–18 / 4.5–5.5	5.5–7.2 / 1.7–2.2	7–9 / 2.0–2.8	10–16	—	10–16	—	—
Minibus	18–25 / 5.5–7.6	6.5–8.0 / 2.0–2.4	7.5–10 / 2.3–3.0	15–25	0–15	15–40	—	—
Transit bus								
Single unit	25–40 / 7.6–12.2	7.5–8.5 / 2.3–2.6	9–11 / 2.8–3.4	30–55	10–75	40–115	—	—
Articulated	54–60 / 16.5–18.3	8.0–8.5 / 2.4–2.6	9.5–10.5 / 2.9–3.2	35–75	30–125	95–185	—	—
Double deck	30–40 / 9.1–12.2	7.5–8.5 / 2.3–2.6	13–14.5 / 4.0–4.4	50–85	15–50	90–130	—	—
Streetcar								
Single unit	40–55 / 12.2–16.8	6.5–9.0 / 2.0–2.7	10–11 / 3.0–3.4	20–60	40–80	75–130	3	225–400
Articulated	60–90 / 18.3–27.4	7.5–9.5 / 2.3–2.9	10–11 / 3.0–3.4	30–85	120–200	100–275	3	300–825

Rail transit car							
Steel wheel	45–75	8.5–11.0	10–13	40–85	50–250	100–330	8–10	1,000–2,700
Rubber-tired	13.7–23.0	2.6–3.4	3.0–4.0	35–55	70–130	110–170	9	1,000–1,500
	48–60	8.0–9.5	11–12					

Commuter railroad car							
Regular	15.2–18.3	2.4–2.9	3.4–3.7	80–110	20–120	100–200	10	1,000–2,000
	65–85	9.5–10.5	12					
Double deck	20.0–26.0	3.0–3.2	3.7	110–165	20–150	160–270	10	1,600–2,700
	65–85	10	14–16					
	20.0–26.0	3.0	4.3–4.8					

(*Source:* Compiled from Traffic and Transportation Engineering Handbook, Institute of Transportation Engineers, Englewood Cliffs, N.J., Prentice-Hall, 1982; originally synthesized from *Lea Transit Compendium* vol. II, nos. 5, 6, 9 (1975), vol. III, nos. 5, 6, 9 (1976–77); M. A. Sulkin and D. R. Miller, *Some State-of-the Art Characteristics of Rubber-tired Rapid Transit,* Pasadena, Calif., 27th California Transportation and Public Works Conference, 1975; and other various data and performance specifications sources.)

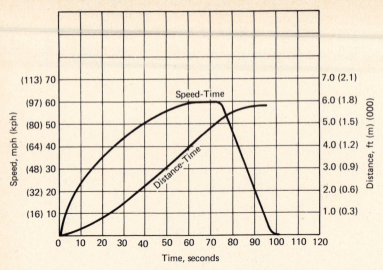

Figure 10–1 Speed–Time–Distance Performance Curves, Typical Standard City–Suburban Transit Bus. Schematic Representation for Full Seated Load on Level, Tangent Road; Eight-Cylinder Engine; VH-8V Transmission.

(*Source: Transportation and Traffic Engineering Handbook,* Institute of Transportation Engineers, Englewood Cliffs, N.J., Prentice-Hall, 1976. Reprinted by permission of Institute of Transportation Engineers. Originally taken from General Motors Corporation.)

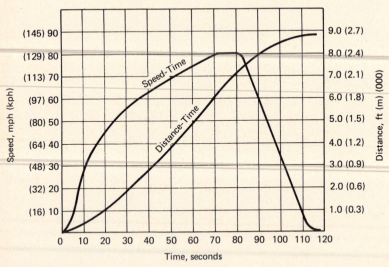

Figure 10–2 Speed–Time–Distance Performance Curves, Four-Car San Francisco Bay Area Rapid Transit (BART) District Train. Schematic Representation for Full Seated Load on Level, Tangent Track.

(*Source: Transportation and Traffic Engineering Handbook,* Institute of Transportation Engineers, Englewood Cliffs, N.J., Prentice-Hall, 1976. Reprinted by permission of Institute of Transportation Engineers. Originally taken from Parsons Brinckerhoff Tudor Bechtel, General Engineering Consultants to BART.)

Table 10–2   Vehicle Velocities

Transit Vehicle and Service Type	Typical Maximum Performance Speeds [mph (kph)]	Typical Platform Speeds [mph (kph)]
Local bus, urban	50–65 (80–105)	8–14 (13–23)
Limited-stop bus, urban	50–65 (80–105)	12–18 (19–29)
Express bus, urban	50–65 (80–105)	16–32 (26–51)
Intercity bus	60–75 (97–120)	25–55 (40–88)
School bus	50–70 (80–113)	10–20 (16–32)
Local tram, urban	40–60 (64–97)	8–15 (13–24)
Express tram, urban	50–65 (80–105)	15–35 (24–56)
Rapid transit, urban	50–70 (80–113)	15–35 (24–56)
Rapid transit, regional	70–85 (113–137)	35–55 (56–88)
Commuter railroad	70–100 (113–145)	25–65 (40–105)
Rapid transit, superregional	120–160 (193–257)	80–120 (129–193)

(*Source: Transportation and Traffic Engineering Handbook,* Institute of Transportation Engineers, 1976. Englewood Cliffs, N.J., Prentice-Hall, Reprinted by permission of Institute of Transportation Engineers.)

tion, and jerk. The service rates of these in transit must be such that the standing passenger can tolerate them without disruption or injury if he or she is not holding on to a hand grip. Acceleration and deceleration rates of 3.0–3.5 mph per second are the upper limits; a preferred jerk rate is 2.0 mph per second and a maximum allowable jerk rate is 3.0 mph per second. Curves illustrating typical speed–time–distance relationships for bus and rail facilities are shown in Figures 10–1 and 10–2.

Speed performance of the system also is important. Table 10–2 exhibits the wide variety of speeds associated with the various technologies. Platform speed is defined as the typical daily operating speed, excluding terminal layovers. Schedule speed is defined as platform speed plus terminal layovers; it is 5–15 percent slower than the foregoing speeds, and is used to schedule a system's performance.

An appropriate equation to compute platform speed is:

$$S = \frac{D}{T + \dfrac{D}{C} + C\left(\dfrac{1}{2a} + \dfrac{1}{2d}\right)}$$

where
S = average transit vehicle speed
T = stop time at stations or stops
C = cruising speed
a = rate of acceleration
d = rate of deceleration
D = average distance between stations

Since transit vehicles are required to come to stops more frequently than most other types of vehicles, the adhesion parameters are of significance. Thus we are interested in the maximum force that can be transferred between wheels and guideway surface as expressed:

$$F = \mu \times W_n$$

where
F = friction force; same units as W_n
μ = dimensionless friction or adhesion coefficient
W_n = force normal to the guideway surface

On level surfaces W_n is the gross weight of the vehicle.

Passenger Travel Time and System Performance

As in other systems, attempts should be made to minimize passenger travel time, in order to offer optimum service. In addition to speed characteristics, the frequency and spacing of stops will influence this by determining the passenger access time. A conceptual diagram illustrating this is presented in Figure 10–3. Optimum spacing of stations with respect to demand density is necessary to minimize travel time. Table 10–3 illustrates relationships of typical vehicle velocities and stop spacings for CBD- and non-CBD-oriented routings. Closely related to this is the behavior of most riders with respect to access. Table 10–4 shows typical access performances of commuters. In light of such performance and the land-use density in a suburb, the Route Density Accessibility Standards of Table 10–5 have been developed. A smiliar concern is time lost in system performance due to boarding and alighting. Table 10–6 illustrates a range of 1.0–8.0 seconds lost per passenger as a function of various fare-paying strategies.

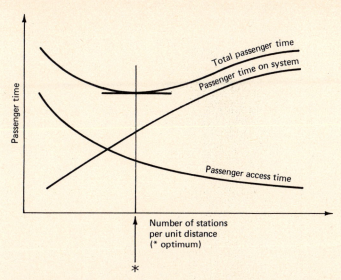

Figure 10–3   Passenger Travel Time as a Function of Station Spacing Along a Route

[*Source:* V. R. Vuchic, *Interstation Spacing for Line-Haul Passenger Transportation,* Graduate Report, Berkeley Calif., University of California, (Institute of Transportation and Traffic Engineers), 1966, Figure 11.]

Capacities

The major engineering performance measures ultimately focus on *capacity*—or output of the planned system. Line capacity C is generally the maximum number of units that can be transported on a line past a fixed point during one hour under a given set of conditions. Component parameters include:

$$\text{Service frequency } f = \frac{3{,}600}{h}$$

where

h = headway between units
f_{max} = line capacity

$$f_{max} = \frac{3{,}600}{h_{min.}}$$

Vehicle line capacity c is the maximum number of vehicles that can pass a fixed point. For single-unit vehicles:

$$c = f_{max}$$

Table 10–3 Typical Vehicle Velocities and Stop Spacings

Transit Vehicle and Service Type	Maximum Performance Speeds mph (km/h)	Platform Speeds mph (km/h)	Linear Stop Spacing		
			CBDs ft (m)	Non-CBD	
				Traditional Practice ft (m)	Some Modern Systems with Longer Stop Spacings ft (m)
Urban bus					
Local	50–65 (80–105)	8–14 (13–23)	500–1000 (150–300)	500–800 (150–250)	1,000–1,500 (300–460)
Limited stop	50–65 (80–105)	12–18 (20–30)	500–1000 (150–300)	1,200–3,000 (360–900)	2,000–5,000 (600–1,500)
Express	50–65 (80–105)	16–32 (25–50)	*	4,000–30,000 (1,200–9,000)	5,000–15,000 (1,500–45,000)
Streetcar, local	40–60 (65–95)	8–15 (13–25)	500–1,000 (150–300)	500–800 (150–250)	1,000–1,500 (300–460)
Light rail transit	50–65 (85–105)	15–35 (25–55)	1,000–2,000 (300–600)	—	2,000–5,000 (600–1500)
Heavy rail transit	50–70 (80–110)	15–35 (25–55)	1,000–2,500 (300–750)	1,700–3,500 (500–1,000)	3,500–8,000 (1,000–2,500)
Regional rapid transit	70–85 (110–135)	35–55 (55–90)	2,000–3,000 (600–900)	—	6,000–30,000 (1,800–9,000)
Commuter railroad	70–100 (100–160)	25–65 (40–105)	*	4,000–15,000 (1,200–4,500)	8,000–30,000 (2,500–9,000)

*Usually stops at only one or two terminals in or adjacent to CBD.
(*Source: Transportation and Traffic Engineering Handbook*, Institute of Transportation Engineers, Englewood Cliffs, N.J., Prentice-Hall, 1982. Reprinted by permission of Institute of Transportation Engineers.)

Table 10–4 Typical Maximum Distance Traveled to Reach Urban Transit Stops and Stations

Access Mode	Most Patrons mi (km)	Some Patrons mi (km)
Walk	0.4–0.6 (0.6–1.0)	0.6–1.0 (1.0–1.6)
Bicycle	1.0–2.0 (1.6–3.2)	2.0–3.0 (3.2–4.8)
Feeder transit; motorcycle	2.0–4.0 (3.2–6.4)	4.0–8.0 (6.4–13.0)
Auto		
Kiss-ride; taxi	3.0–4.0 (4.8–6.4)	4.0–6.0 (6.4–9.7)
Park ride	4.0–6.0 (6.4–9.7)	6.0–10.0 (9.7–16.0)

(*Source: Transportation and Traffic Engineering Handbook,* Institute of Transportation Engineers, Englewood Cliffs, N.J., Prentice-Hall, 1982. Reprinted by permission of Institute of Transportation Engineers. Originally taken from Henry D. Quinby, "Coordinated Highway Transit Interchange Stations," *Origin and Destination: Methods and Evaluation,* Highway Research Record 114, Washington, D.C., Highway Research Board, 1966, pp. 99–121.)

Table 10–5 Accessibility Standards for Urban Transit

Population Density thousands/mi^2 (thousands/km^2)	Average Route Spacing		Route Density route-mi/mi^2 (route-km/km^2)
	Radial Routes mi (km)	Circumferential Routes mi (km)	
Over 12 (Over 4.6)	0.40 (0.65)	0.60 (1.00)	4.00 (2.50)
10–12 (3.9–4.6)	0.50 (0.80)	0.75 (1.20)	3.33 (2.00)
8–10 (3.1–3.9)	0.60 (1.00)	0.90 (1.50)	2.67 (1.67)
6–8 (2.3–3.1)	0.80 (1.25)	1.20 (2.00)	2.00 (1.25)
4–6 (1.5–2.3)	1.00 (1.60)	1.50 (2.40)	2.67 (1.00)
2–4 (0.8–1.5)	1.00 (1.60)	—	1.00 (0.60)
Under 2 (Under 0.8)	2.00 (3.20)	—	0.50 (0.30)

(*Source: Transportation and Traffic Engineering Handbook,* Institute of Transportation Engineers, Englewood Cliffs, N.J., Prentice-Hall, 1982. Reprinted by permission of Institute of Transportation Engineers.)

Table 10-6 Average Boarding and Alighting Intervals for Transit Vehicles

Operation	Physical Conditions	Operational Conditions	Seconds/ Passenger/ Lane[a]
Boarding	High-level platform (rapid transit)	Fares paid at fare gates	1.0
		Fares paid off vehicle (at fare gates or by passes)	2.0
	Low-level or no platform (buses and streetcars)	Single-coin or token fare paid on vehicle	3.0[b]
		Multiple-coin fare paid on vehicle	4.0[b]
		Zone fares prepaid; tickets registered on vehicle	4.0–6.0
		Zone fares paid on vehicle	6.0–8.0[b]
Alighting	High-level platform	No ticket checking at vehicle doors	1.0
	Low-level or no platform	No ticket checking at vehicle doors	1.7
		Ticket checking or issue of transfers at vehicle doors	2.5–4.0

[a]A lane represents one file of persons, 22–24 in. (55–60 cm) wide. Assumes that all lanes are used equally; however, allowance is usually made for the fact that whereas some lanes are used to capacity, others operate below that flow rate.
[b]Where "exact fares" are required and drivers do not make change, times may be somewhat less.
(*Source: Transportation and Traffic Engineering Handbook,* Institute of Transportation Engineers, Englewood Cliffs, N.J., Prentice-Hall, 1982. Reprinted by permission of Institute of Transportation Engineers. Originally taken from H. S. Levinson, et al., *Bus Use of Highway: Planning and Design Guidelines,* National Cooperative Highway Research Program Report 155, Washington, D.C., Transportation Research Board, 1975.)

For train units:

$$c = nf_{max}$$

where n is the number of vehicles per train unit.

Maximum offered line capacity C (offered in passenger spaces per hour), known as "line capacity," is the product of c and C_v, where C_v is vehicle capacity in persons. That is:

$$C = cC_v = nf_{max} C_v$$

which can also be expressed as a function of

$$C = \frac{3,600 n C_v}{h_{min}}$$

Thus two capacities can be expressed for transit: way capacity C_w, a function of h_{wmin} and station capacity C_s, a function of h_{smin}. Thus, $C = \min(C_w, C_s)$.

Scheduled line capacity is the number of spaces available for a given schedule. The scheduled line capacity utilization coefficient δ is the ratio of offered line capacity C_o to scheduled capacity and is

$$\delta = \frac{C_o}{C}$$

The utilization coefficient is the ratio of actual volume to provided capacity and is defined as:

$$\alpha = \frac{P}{C_o}$$

and is also known as the load factor, where P is the number of passengers transported past a point during one hour.

Thus volume transported during one hour is:

$$\alpha C_o = \alpha \delta C$$

These computations are developed for various types of systems, as shown in Table 10–7. Resulting general capacities for the various systems are illustrated in Table 10–8.

Rail rapid transit scheduling must be sensitive to dwell times at stations, and the relationship of safety between following trains, and to cruise speed acceleration and deceleration rates of consecutive trains. Therefore, the required capacity of the station and the system are often studied with the aid of a performance time–space diagram, as shown in Figure 10–4, to detail the trains' performance.

Scheduling of Service

Closely related to the foregoing is the actual development of service schedules on a route once its likely capacity and load factors have been found. Scheduling employs the following procedure:

1. Determine the peak hour of passenger demand.
2. Obtain the demand on the maximum link within this system = P_{max}.

Table 10–7 Typical Minimum Average Headways, and Resulting Units or Trains per Hour, per Moving Lane or Track in One Direction of Travel (During the Peak Fifteen Minutes of the Peak Hour)

Vehicle and Facility Type	Passenger Stops Along or Affecting Route Section Involved	Headways (in sec)	Resulting Nos. of Units or Trains per Hour
1. Buses in mixed street traffic	Yes	40–60	90–60
2. Buses in exclusive street lane	Yes	30–50	120–72
3. Buses in mixed freeway traffic	Yes	40–60	90–60
4. Buses in mixed freeway traffic	No	10–30	360–120
5. Buses in exclusive busway	Yes	25–35	144–103
6. Buses in exclusive busway	No	10–30	360–120
7. Trams in mixed street traffic	Yes	25–40	144–90
8. Trams in mixed street traffic	Yes	50–60	72–60
9. Trams in reserved street medians	Yes	25–40	144–90
10. Trams in reserved street medians	Yes	50–60	72–60
11. Trams in exclusive right-of-way	Yes	20–40	180–90
12. Trams in exclusive right-of-way	Yes	40–120	90–30
13. Trams in exclusive right-of-way	No	10–30	360–120
14. Trams in exclusive right-of-way	No	60–80	60–45
15. Urban-regional rapid transit	Yes	90–120	40–30
16. Urban-regional rapid transit	No	60–80	60–45
17. Commuter railroad	Yes	120–240	30–15
18. Superregional rapid transit	Yes	240–360	15–10

(*Source: Transportation and Traffic Engineering Handbook,* Institute of Transportation Engineers, Englewood Cliffs, N.J., Prentice-Hall, 1976. Reprinted by permission of Institute of Transportation Engineers.)

3. Determine a reasonable cycle time for the route (travel time for one round trip and suitable recovery time for late arrival and operator rest).

4. Define a proposed headway and load factor.

Table 10–8 Passenger Capacities per Lane or Track, Expressed in Typical Ranges (Hourly rate, in One Direction of Travel, During the Peak Fifteen Minutes of the Peak Hour)

Transit Vehicle and Facility Type	Seated Only	Total Seated Plus Standing
1. Minibus–midibus		
a. In mixed street traffic	900– 2,300	1,500– 4,000
b. In exclusive street lane	1,100– 3,000	1,800– 5,400
2. City–suburban transit bus, nonarticulated		
a. In mixed street traffic	1,800– 5,000	2,700– 9,000
b. In exclusive street lane	2,200– 6,600	3,200–12,000
c. In mixed freeway traffic	1,800– 5,000	2,700– 9,000
d. In exclusive busway	3,100– 7,900	4,600–14,400
3. City–suburban transit bus, articulated		
a. In mixed street traffic	2,100– 6,700	6,000–15,300
b. In exclusive street lane	2,500– 9,000	7,200–20,400
c. In mixed freeway traffic	2,100– 6,700	6,000–15,300
d. In exclusive busway	3,600– 9,000	10,300–20,400
4. City–suburban transit bus, doubledeck		
a. In mixed street traffic	3,000– 6,700	3,900– 8,100
b. In exclusive street lane	3,600– 9,000	4,700–10,800
c. In mixed freeway traffic	3,000– 6,700	3,900– 8,100
d. In exclusive busway	5,200–10,800	6,700–13,000
5. Intercity bus		
a. In mixed street traffic	1,800– 4,500	2,400– 6,300
b. In mixed freeway traffic	1,800– 4,500	2,400– 6,300
c. In exclusive busway	3,100– 7,200	4,100–10,100
6. School bus		
a. In mixed street traffic	1,200– 5,800	1,200– 5,800
b. In mixed freeway traffic	1,200– 5,800	1,200– 5,800

(*Source: Transportation and Traffic Engineering Handbook,* Institute of Transportation Engineers, Englewood Cliffs, N.J., Prentice-Hall, 1976. Reprinted by permission of Institute of Transportation Engineers.)

5. From the load factor, calculate passengers per transit unit (C_v).

6. Develop a first estimate of operable headway =

$$\frac{C_v}{P_{max}}$$

7. Then develop a first estimate of number of transit units required:

$$N = \frac{T}{h}$$

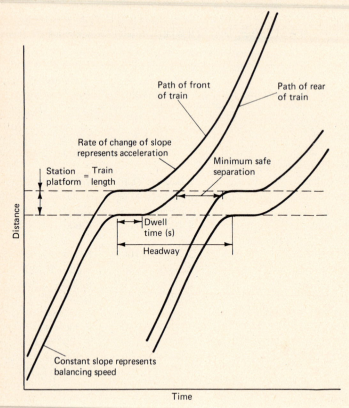

Figure 10–4 Distance–Time Diagram for Rapid Transit Train Headway and Frequency Analysis.

(Source: Transportation and Traffic Engineering Handbook, Institute of Transportation Engineers, Englewood Cliffs, N.J., Prentice-Hall, 1982. Reprinted by permission of Institute of Transportation Engineers.)

8. Increase N to next highest integer N' and recalculate new headway h':

$$h' = \frac{T}{N'}$$

Round headway to acceptable value for safety and schedule coordination, and call this h''.
9. Develop final cycle time $T' = n \times h''$.
10. Prepare time table, vehicle assignments, and operator assignments (run cutting) based on labor agreements.

Economic Aspects of Transit Systems

An initial introduction to economic concepts of transit systems should be directed to adequate measures of merit for the system. Three general perspectives must be addressed: efficiency, effectiveness, and a combination of the two. Table 10–9 illustrates the entire envelope of performance indices. Efficiency measures focus on cost, labor productivity, vehicle utilization, and energy efficiency. Effectiveness measures focus on service utilization, accessibility, and generic quality of service.

Table 10–9 System Performance Indicators

Indicator	Construction	Focus
Efficiency		
Operating cost per revenue vehicle-mile	$\dfrac{\text{Total operating costs}}{\text{Total revenue vehicle-miles}}$	Cost efficiency
Operating cost per revenue vehicle-hours	$\dfrac{\text{Total operating costs}}{\text{Total revenue vehicle-hours}}$	
Revenue vehicle-hours per employee	$\dfrac{\text{Total revenue vehicle-hours}}{\text{Total system employees}}$	Labor productivity
Revenue vehicle-miles per employee	$\dfrac{\text{Total revenue vehicle-miles}}{\text{Total employees}}$	
Revenue miles per vehicle	$\dfrac{\text{Total vehicle-miles}}{\text{Total vehicles}}$	Vehicle utilization
Revenue hours per vehicle	$\dfrac{\text{Total revenue vehicle-hours}}{\text{Total revenue vehicles}}$	
Total passengers per vehicle	$\dfrac{\text{Total passengers}}{\text{Total vehicles}}$	
Energy consumption per revenue vehicle-mile	$\dfrac{\text{Total energy consumption}}{\text{Total revenue vehicle-miles}}$	Energy efficiency
Energy consumption per revenue vehicle-hour	$\dfrac{\text{Total energy consumption}}{\text{Total revenue vehicle-hours}}$	

Table 10–9   (continued)

Indicator	Construction	Focus
Effectiveness		
Revenue passengers per revenue vehicle-mile	$\dfrac{\text{Total revenue passengers}}{\text{Total revenue vehicle miles}}$	Service utilization measures
Revenue passengers per service area population	$\dfrac{\text{Total passenger trips}}{\text{Total population of service area}}$	Service utilization measures
Percentage of population served	$\dfrac{\text{Total service area population}}{\text{Total coverage area population}}$	Accessibility
System reliability	$\dfrac{\text{Total trips on time}}{\text{Total trips}}$	Quality of service
Vehicle revenue miles per square mile of served area	$\dfrac{\text{Total vehicle revenue miles}}{\text{Total square miles of served area}}$	Quality of service
Efficiency/Effectiveness		
Operating ratio	$\dfrac{\text{Total operating revenues}}{\text{Total operating costs}}$	Financial performance
Cost per passenger trip	$\dfrac{\text{Total operating costs}}{\text{Total passenger trips}}$	Financial performance
Cost per passenger-mile	$\dfrac{\text{Total operating costs}}{\text{Total passenger miles}}$	Financial performance

(*Source:* G. J. Fielding, et al., *Development of Performance Indicators for Transit,* Irvine, Calif., Institute of Transportation Studies, School of Social Sciences, University of California, UMTA, UC/PT. Inc., and APTA, 1977. *Proceedings of the First National Conference on Transit Performance. Norfolk, Virginia,* Washington, D.C., UMTA.)

Financial performance centers on combining efficiency and effectiveness measures to yield operating ratios, cost per passenger trip, and cost per passenger-mile, resulting in a basis upon which to do long-range economic and system planning. In a typical transit system, these indices will be available weekly and monthly, and summarized seasonally and annually. They will also be used as targets in transportation planning of alternative strategies relating to alteration of size, composition, and pattern of routing and scheduling of the transit fleet.

Table 10–10 Unit Operating Expenses, Chicago Transit Authority, 1977

Vehicle Type	Expense/Vehicle		
	mi	km	Percent of Total
Motor buses			
Maintenance of plant and equipment	$0.61	$0.38	22.3
Operating and garage expense, fuel	0.13	0.08	4.8
Transportation, including drivers	1.59	0.99	58.2
Administrative, and misc.	0.27	0.17	9.9
Depreciation	0.13	0.08	4.8
Total	$2.73	$1.70	100.0
Rail rapid transit			
Maintenance of way and structures	$0.40	$0.25	16.1
Maintenance of equipment	0.41	0.25	16.5
Power	0.13	0.08	5.3
Transportation, including train crews	0.99	0.62	39.9
Administrative, and misc.	0.28	0.17	11.3
Depreciation	0.27	0.17	10.9
Total	$2.48	$1.54	100.0

(*Source:* Chicago Transit Authority.)

Cost Components

Costs for operation of transit systems have escalated rapidly in the past decade. Table 10–10 illustrates the unit operating expenses of the Chicago Transit Authority (CTA), which are typical of large urban systems. Note that labor and maintenance yield the major variable cost components. Labor is the primary escalation factor, with an 80 percent increase in constant dollars of labor costs from 1951 to 1973.

Capital costs for systems are significant, especially for rail systems. These costs are illustrated in Table 10–11. The costs of heavy rail in dense areas are staggering, as high as $30 million per mile in certain areas. This almost entirely precludes new startups. Likewise, Table 10–12 illustrates the significant cost of vehicles. These costs are roughly 200–250 percent of the cost of similar vehicles in 1970. Transit in any form is an expensive system.

Fare Structure

Three general types of fares exist: a *flat* fare, which is the same throughout the network; fares *graduated* by distance traveled from start to finish, and fares

Table 10–11   Capital Costs of Infrastructure for Two-Track Rail Systems, United States, 1974

Location Alignment	Typical Costs ($ × 10^6$)			
	Guideway		Stations Each	Yards and Shops Each
	per mile	per km		
Light rail systems				
Suburban				
At grade	2.9–5.3	1.8–3.3	0.02–2.8	12.0–45.4
Elevated	5.1–11.3	3.2–7.0	0.2–3.5	—
Depressed	6.5–15.2	4.0–9.5	0.2–3.6	—
Urban				
At grade	4.1–7.3	2.6–4.5	0.02–0.06	12.0–45.4
Elevated	18.1–23.7	11.2–4.7	0.2–0.7	—
Cut-and-cover	32.7–40.3	20.3–25.0	0.4–1.0	—
Core				
Elevated	19.5–27.8	12.1–17.3	1.3–4.6	—
Cut-and-cover	34.1–44.4	21.2–27.6	1.8–7.6	—
Heavy rail systems				
Surburban				
At grade	3.4–8.4	2.1–5.2	0.4–4.2	11.1–40.7
Elevated	5.2–13.1	3.2–8.1	0.7–5.2	—
Depressed	6.6–17.0	4.1–0.6	0.9–5.5	—
Urban				
Elevated	18.2–25.5	11.3–15.9	1.0–2.9	—
Cut-and-cover	32.8–42.1	20.4–26.2	4.0–10.0	—
Core				
Elevated	19.6–29.6	12.2–18.4	1.4–4.7	—
Cut-and-cover	34.2–46.2	21.2–28.7	5.0–12.0	—

(*Source*: Dyer, T. K. *Rail Transit System Cost Study,* Report No. DOT-TSC-UMTA-75-22, Rev. 1, Washington, D.C., U.S. Urban Mass Transportation Administration, March 1977, Table 1–2.)

geographically *zoned* over the network. Very refined geographic zone fares operate similarly to a linear graduated fare. A good example of a progressive zone fare is shown in Figure 10–5.

The zonation of fares is a continual concern between the system and its riders. Attempts must be made to maximize revenue, while maintaining equity among passengers and keeping the fare at an affordable level. Ticketing and fare-

Table 10–12 Capital Costs of Selected Urban Transit Vehicles, United States

Vehicle	Typical Cost ($ × 10³)	Year
Light rail vehicle, articulated	645	1977
Heavy rail transit car	475–730	1976–1977
Bus with air conditioning		
Articulated, 60 ft (18.3 m)	180	1977
Standard, 40 ft (12.2 m)	95–117	1979
Standard, 35 ft (10.7 m)	85	1979
Minibus, 25 ft (7.6 m)	52	1977

(*Source:* (a) Richard J. Barkers Associates, Inc., *The U.S. and International Market for Rail Equipment,* Report UMTA-DC-06-0213-78-1, Washington, D.C., U.S. Urban Mass Transportation Administration, March 1978; (b) new reports in *Passenger Transport* and various surveys.)

collection systems must not become too complex and burdensome to the system, rider, or transit operator. Various special incentive fares may be used in conjunction with promoting the system and improving its ridership, such as flat-rate season passes to theater and sporting events, rides to school, and weekend shopping passes.

Resulting Economic Conditions of Transit

Up to the early 1950s, many transit systems were owned by private operating companies and franchises. As costs soared and auto usage increased to the point where the bulk of ridership remaining was transit captive, these systems were liquidated to become public, and "public transit" as we know it today came into existence. As costs continued to climb, particularly for labor, and the need remained to keep ridership affordable, transit began to find itself unable to pay for its services out of revenues collected at the fare box. This resulted in illustrations of financial distress as depicted in Figures 10–6 and 10–7 and yielded cost-effectiveness envelopes as shown in Figures 10–8 and 10–9. Clearly these illustrate an industry headed toward bankruptcy, unless there was some form of governmental intervention.

These facts were recognized in the early 1960s. The federal and state sectors began to view transit as somewhat of a welfare tool, permitting autoless individuals to become mobile and thus be able to take advantage of gainful employment opportunities. To that end the system was to be kept in financial balance by the use of subsidies. In 1964 and 1968 federal funds were set aside to subsidize capital and operating costs subject to matching ratios from local entities, usually through sales and property taxes.

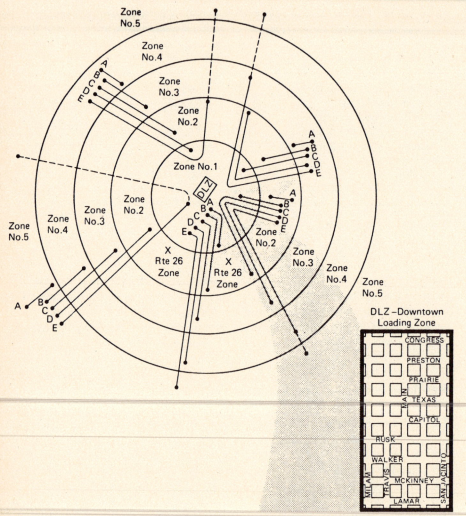

A — Ride within any one zone	30¢ or 1 token
B — Ride crossing any one zone line	35¢ or 1 token and 5¢
C — Ride crossing any two zone lines	40¢ or 1 token and 10¢
D — Ride crossing any three zone lines	45¢ or 1 token and 15¢
E — Ride crossing any four zone lines	50¢ or 1 token and 20¢

– – – (No additional fare after crossing four zone lines)
An additional 5¢ deposit is required for transfers issued to adult passengers.
Students and children are not subject to zone fare charges or transfer deposits.

Figure 10–5   Zone Fare Using Concentric Rings, Houston (Texas) Rapid Transit Lines,
Inc. Adult Fares and Zone Fare System Examples.

(*Source:* Rapid Transit Lines, Inc., Houston, Texas.)

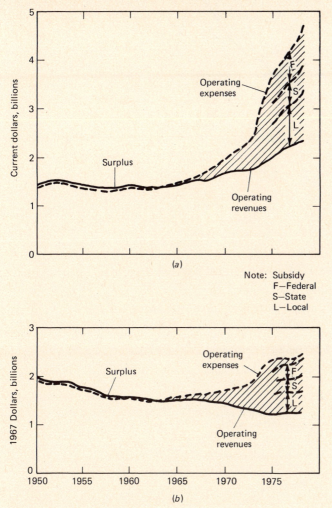

Figure 10–6   Transit Operating Revenues and Expenses. United States, 1950–1978. (Upper Graph in Current Dollars; Lower Graph in 1967 Dollars.)

(*Source:* Transportation and Traffic Engineering Handbook, Institute of Transportation Engineers, Englewood Cliffs, N.J., Prentice-Hall, 1982. Reprinted by permission of Institute of Transportation Engineers.)

Subsequently the federal sector ordered a cessation of new transit line investments and purchases of equipment that involved excessive capital intensity and expense. The result was a minimum of light and heavy rail corridor construction in the past decade, and a very refined review of all equipment expenses proposed by systems. During recent periods of inflation/recession, local governments have found it difficult to develop the local match. The subject of

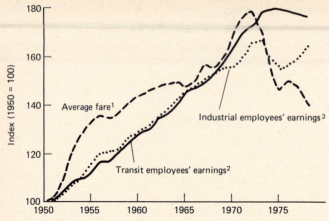

[1]Average fare in constant cents; includes transfer and zone
charges, reduced fares, and fare-free rides.
    Index 100 = 10.02 cents at 1950 dollar levels.

[2]Average annual earnings of all transit industry employees
in constant dollars.
    Index 100 = $3,480 at 1950 dollar levels.

[3]Average annual earnings of all US industry employees in constant
dollars.
    Index 100 = $3,000 at 1950 dollar levels.

Figure 10–7   Trends in Transit Fares and Employee Earnings, United States, 1950–1978.

[*Source: Transit Fact Book,* annual publication, Washington, D.C., American Public Transit Association; *Historical Statistics of the United States, Colonial Times to 1970* (Series D722), Washington, D.C., U.S. Bureau of the Census, 1975; *Statistical Abstract of the United States 1978,* Table 686, Washington, D.C., U.S. Bureau of the Census.]

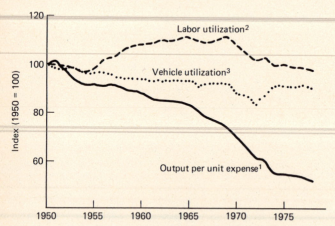

[1]Vehicle - miles (*vehicle - km*) per constant dollar of operating expense.
    Index 100 = 2.17 veh-mi (*3.49 veh - km*) per 1950 dollar.

[2]Vehicle - miles (*vehicle - km*) per employee.
    Index 100 = 12.5 veh-mi (*20 veh - km*) per employee.

[3]Vehicle - miles (*vehicle - km*) per vehicle owned or leased.
    Index 100 = 34,900 miles (*56,000 km*) per vehicle.

Figure 10–8   Trends in Efficiency Indicators, United States, 1950–1978.

(*Source: Transit Fact Book,* annual publication, Washington, D.C., American Public Transit Association.)

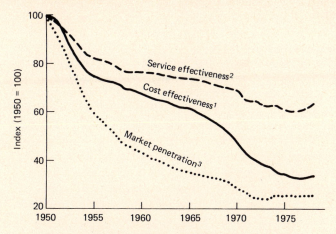

¹ Revenue passengers per constant dollar of operating expenses.
  Index 100 = 10 psgrs per 1950 dollar.

² Revenue passengers per vehicle-mile (*vehicle - km*)
  Index 100 = 4.6 psgrs/veh-mi (*2.9 pagrs/veh - km*).

³ Revenue passengers per annum per capita of urban population.
  Index 100 = 140 psgrs/annum per capita.

Figure 10–9   Trends in Effectiveness Indicators, United States, 1950–1978.
(*Source: Transit Fact Book,* annual publication, Washington, D.C., American Public Transit Association.)

subsidies, their amount and matching ratio, is a continual controversy throughout the government and transportation communities. More will be developed on this topic in the chapter on policy.

Joint Development—Value Capture

Two concepts are relevant in discussing the capability of transit to recover its costs and generate economic development. One is the concept of *joint development,* where a transit station in a major region of activity is physically connected within the conglomeration of several high-quality commercial and office land uses designed to stimulate travel interchange and accessibility to office and commercial activity.

The other related concept is that of *value capture.* Where it can be illustrated that real estate values and commercial and industrial earnings on a property are increased by the presence of transit, a transit district tax is levied on owners of such income-producing properties. This results in the value captured by the presence of transit being returned in some measure to the system, resulting in more money to sustain transit operations.

Innovations in Transit

It is important to acknowledge some of the innovations in transit technology in the past decade. Two major innovations are *personal rapid transit* (PRT) and dual-mode operation. Personal rapid transit is the use of small (three-to-twelve passenger) high-speed electronically operated vehicles to transport people, as shown in Figures 10–10 and 10–11. Their use allows people to be carried to select designations in a complex site. The costs are exorbitant—in the range of $19–$22 million per mile.

Another innovative concept under test, illustrated in Figure 10–12 is *dual-mode operation,* a bus with both rail wheels and rubber-tired wheels. Its function is to perform local surface bus pickup tasks, then access a rail head and make a rail line haul to a major transit center in the CBD. Although this concept involves high vehicle development costs, it warrants consideration in view of its potential for flexibility—the ability to serve a variety of densities in one continual vehicle operation cycle.

In a like manner, the concepts of para transit, demand-responsive transportation, and car and van pooling may be considered institutional innovation, as compared with the conventional transit planning of a decade ago. All these efforts are attempts to provide flexible access to meet low-density ridership pickup needs, and to reduce auto usage by pooling riders and thus reducing pollution, energy requirements, and congestion. Their relevance to the planning process was discussed in Chapter 9 on urban transportation planning. The energy implications of such programs are discussed in Chapter 12.

Fitting the Hierarchy Together

It should be obvious that no single type of transit is "optimum." That is, a specific transit system type fits a particular class of densities. As cities become more complex, they typically cannot be characterized simply as "urban sprawl" or "high-density corridors," but rather as a mix of varying density concentrations. Hence any modern transit system must concern itself with the development and investment of a variety of the transit subsystems described in this chapter, resulting in an economic and service mix that is optimal and cost effective. This is difficult to attain and requires a continual monitoring of land-use and socioeconomic changes in the population, demand levels, ridership, route patterns, and costs of service provision. It is only in continually attempting to understand and search for this "optimal mix" that transit can be the cost-effective provider of services to those who require it and participate in the development of a region.

Problems

1. A transit line in a small city consists of 20 stops. The average stop time for each stop is 45 seconds. The vehicle's cruising speed is 30 mph. Acceleration and

Figure 10–10 Personal Rapid Transit Operational Features

(*Source:* Automated Transportation Systems, Inc., Minneapolis, Minnesota, 1985.)

Figure 10–11 Additional Personal Rapid Transit Operational Features
(*Source:* Automated Transportation Systems, Inc., Minneapolis, Minnesota, 1985.)

System	Suburban collection/distribution	Guideway line haul	CBD collection/distribution
Pallet			
Auto highway			
New small vehicles			

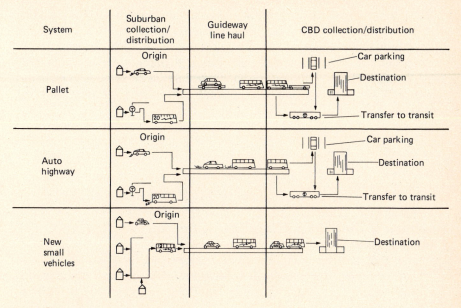

Figure 10–12 Typical Dual Mode Trips

(*Source:* E. J. Anderson and Sherry H. Romig, *Personal Rapid Transit II*, Minneapolis, University of Minnesota Press, 1974. Reprinted by permission.)

deceleration is 2 mph per second. The average distance between stops is one-quarter mile. What is the average transit vehicle speed for this route?

2. A rapid transit train serves a metropolitan area during peak hours at 5-minute headways. Each train has 10 passenger vehicles and each vehicle can accommodate 30 passengers. What is the line capacity of this service?

3. A transit operator's records show a certain bus route is operating at an average speed of approximately 8 mph. The operator knows that the average distance between stops is 800 feet and buses accelerate at a rate of 2.5 feet per second and decelerate at a rate of 2.0 feet per second. If the average cruising speed of the bus is 28 mph., what is the average stop time?

4. A rail transit operator must revise rail rapid transit schedules to meet new passenger demands. Passenger demands are highest in the afternoon and are summarized by 15-minute periods as follows:

Time	Demand (Passengers)	Time	Demand (Passengers)
3:45 – 4:00	575	5:00 – 5:15	800
4:00 – 4:15	625	5:15 – 5:30	750
4:15 – 4:30	680	5:30 – 5:45	625
4:30 – 4:45	700	5:45 – 6:00	600
4:45 – 5:00	750		

The operator owns rail cars that hold a maximum of 45 passengers (standing capacity). These cars may be run in units of a minimum of 4 vehicles and maximum of 12 vehicles. Minimum acceptable headways for safety purposes are 5 minutes. Cycle time for the peak route is 90 minutes. A load factor of 0.85 is desirable. How should the operator schedule transit services to meet this demand? What is the maximum acceptable headway if the operator runs 12 car trains?

References

Cleveland, Donald E., Editor. *Manual of Traffic Engineering Studies,* 3d ed. Washington, D.C.: Institute of Traffic Engineers, 1964.

Department of Transportation Organization Directory. Washington, D.C.: U.S. Government Printing Office, February 1984.

Haefner, L. E., E. J. Carter, and J. W. Hall. *An Informational Report on Techniques for Evaluating Factors Relevant to Decision Making on Highway Locations.* Washington, D.C.: U.S. Department of Transportation, Federal Highway Administration, December 1972.

Haefner, L. E., E. J. Carter, and J. W. Hall. *Literature References on Techniques for the Evaluation of Factors Relevant to Decision Making on Highway Locations.* Washington, D.C.: U.S. Department of Transportation, Federal Highway Administration, January 1972.

Meyburg, Arnim H., and Peter R. Stopher. *Urban Transportation Modeling and Planning.* Lexington, Mass.: Lexington Books, 1975.

Morlok, Edward K. *Introduction to Transportation Engineering and Planning.* New York: McGraw-Hill, 1978.

Vuchic, Vukan. *Urban Public Transportation.* Englewood Cliffs, N.J.: Prentice-Hall, 1981.

Yarjani, Bigan. Technology Assessment of Transportation System Investments (doctoral dissertation). St. Louis, Mo.: Department of Civil Engineering, Washington University, December 1979.

Yu, Jason C. *Transportation Engineering.* New York: Elsevier North Holland, 1982.

11 Federal and State Organizational Structures and Studies

This chapter discusses and illustrates the typical state and federal organizational frameworks within which transportation engineering is performed. We are concerned with state structures, the federal structure, and related studies of importance in the historical state-federal interface.

State Transportation Structures

The typical state transportation organizational structure is keyed to two basic issues: (1) degree of relationship of the state transportation agency to the governor and the legislature, and (2) whether the agency is truly multimodal. The typical department, in addition to a state-level cabinet head, called the State Secretary of Transportation, will be responsible to a commission, or to a blue-ribbon committee jointly responsible to the governor and the legislature, often termed the State Transportation Study Commission. This general relationship is illustrated in Figure 11–1.

Similarly the state may have two different perspectives in this regard. If the state historically has had a strong highway department, then its organizational structure will be as appears in Figure 11–2, with emphasis on materials, design, construction, and right-of-way.

On the other hand, if the department is a strong multimodal department of transportation, its structure will be much more complex and exist as shown in

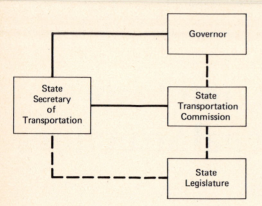

Figure 11–1   Relationship of State Department
of Transportation to Other Entities

Figure 11–3. This type of department will have modal structures, or departments for rail, water, air, and urban transit, in addition to the traditional highway mode, and have a complete demand, forecasting, planning, and research division in addition to the cabinet offices and a legal division. Table 11–1 shows the 1978 modal composition of all the different state agencies in the United States.

A further issue in state operations is the concept of strong versus weak district offices. The district office in a highway department or department of transportation plays a key role in achieving the local implementation and operation of the transportation system. The critical question is the level of policy-making authority the district engineer has at the district level. At a strong district-level operation, as shown in Figure 11–4, the district engineer has very broad policy or goal statements from the cabinet office level as a guide and he operates with substantial authority on policy items. At the other extreme, as illustrated in Figure 11–5, a weak district engineer may be required to pass all of the policy discussions to the state cabinet office for analysis prior to rendering a conclusion for a problem at the local level.

The U.S. Department of Transportation

The U.S. Department of Transportation is the federal cabinet office responsible for the administration of transportation policy across the United States. It is headed by a Presidentially appointed cabinet officer, the Secretary of Transportation, and has a multimodal scope, encompassing air, rail, water, and highway, and safety and environmental functions. It has a complex organizational structure covering the design, planning, construction, and research aspects of all of the

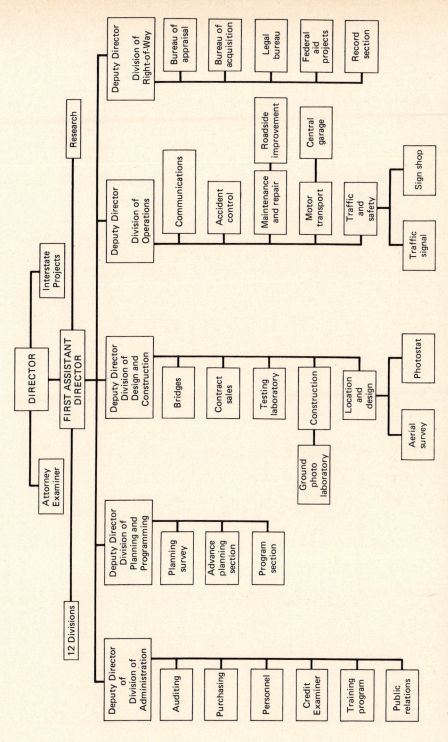

Figure 11–2 Organization Chart of the Original Ohio Department of Highways
(*Source:* Ohio Department of Highways, now Ohio Department of Transportation.)

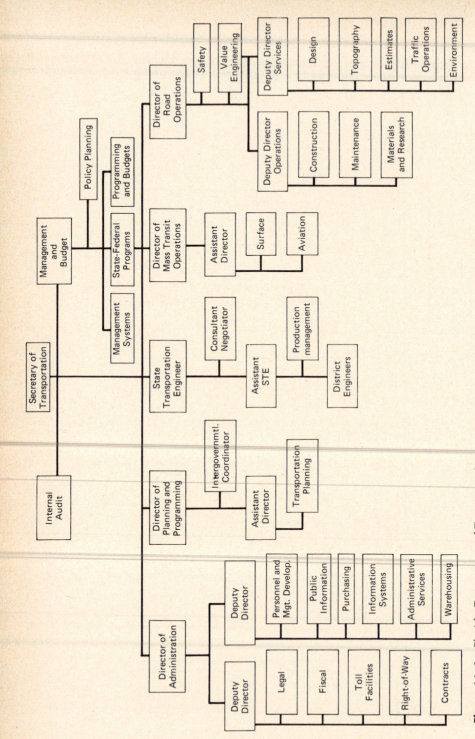

Figure 11–3 Florida Department of Transportation
(*Source:* Florida Department of Transportation.)

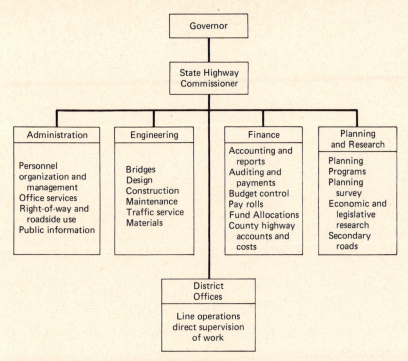

Figure 11–4 Typical Organization of a State Highway Department with a Strong District Organization.

(*Source: Transportation and Traffic Engineering Handbook,* Institute of Transportation Engineers, Englewood Cliffs, N.J., Prentice-Hall, 1982. Reprinted by permission.)

federal transportation activities and their relationship to the states. This structure is shown in Figure 11–6, and its operational and modal components are organized as illustrated in Figures 11–7 through 11–15. In addition to the modal administrations and their departments, the Secretary of Transportation office structure is itself quite complex, as shown in Figure 11–7. In addition to a Deputy Secretary, it contains a legal staff under the general counsel, and an Assistant Secretary and staffs for policy, budget and programs, governmental affairs, auditing, and inspection and administration.

Pertinent Historical
State/Federal Studies and Interaction

The state historically has chosen to deal with broad, multimodal policy studies, leaving the deployment of urban transportation planning at the metropolitan level. Such broad state study processes have often focused on rail-line abandon-

Table 11–1 Department of Transportation Functions by State 1978[a]

State	Aeronautics	Highway	Rail	Waterway or Ports	Transit	Regulation	Highway Patrol	Motor Vehicle	Other
Alaska	X	X		X	X				Public facilities
Arizona	X	X	P		P			X	
Arkansas	X^{b,c}	X	P	P	P				Toll roads
California	X^{b,c}	X	X^c	P	X^{b,c}	Weight	T		Ferries, toll bridges
Connecticut	X	X		X	X				
Delaware	X	X	X		X				Toll roads
Dist. of Columbia	X	X			T			X	
Florida	X	X	P T	P	X	T			Toll facilities
Georgia	X	X	P T	X	X	T			Toll roads
Hawaii	X	X	T	X	X		T	X	
Idaho	X	X	P		P T	Weight/size			Highway safety
Illinois	X	X	T X	P T	X P T	T	T		Safety
Iowa	X	X	X	P T	X P T	X		X	Toll bridges
Kansas	X	X	P	P	X	T			
Kentucky	X	X	P	P	T X	X	T	X	Toll facilities

State												Notes
Louisiana	X				P			X	Weight		X		Ferries, toll bridges
Maine	X			X		T		X		T			
Maryland	X			X		T		X	P		X		Toll facilities and safety
Massachusetts	X			X		X P		X				T	Toll roads
Michigan	X			X		X		X			X		Toll bridges
Minnesota	X			X		X		X	X		X		
Missouri	X			X		X		X	X		X		
New Jersey	P	T		X				X	In process Enforcement		X		
New Mexico	X			X				X					
New York	X	T		X		X		T	X	T	T		
North Carolina	X^c	P	T	X		P			Weight	P T	X^c	X^e	Ferries
Ohio	X			X			T		X	T	X		Toll facilities
Oklahoma	X	P	T	X		P							
Oregon	X			X		P			P	P T			
Pennsylvania	X	P	T	X P		X		X	P T	P T	X	X^e	Parks; Toll facilities
Puerto Rico	X			X				X			X		Toll roads
Rhode Island	X		X^c	X				X^c	X		X		Highway and safety

389

Table 11-1 (continued)

	Aeronautics	Highway	Rail	Waterway or Ports	Transit	Regulation	Highway Patrol	Motor Vehicle	Other
South Dakota	X	X	P		T	X[d]	X[e]		
Tennessee	X	X		X	X				
Texas		X			P T			X	Ferries
Utah	X	X	Safety		T	Motor carriers			
Vermont	X	X	X	X	X	X		X	
Virginia	X	X			X			X	Toll roads
Washington	X	X	P		P T	Weight			Ferries, toll bridges
Wisconsin	X	X		P	X	X	X	X	

aP, planning only; T, technical assistance; X, financial control or responsibility.
bCapital improvements only.
cPartial funding.
dHighway and airports only, exclusive of motor vehicles.
eFrom highway revenues; under Department of Public Safety.
(*Source: Transportation and Traffic Engineering Handbook*, Institute of Transportation Engineers, Englewood Cliffs, N.J., Prentice-Hall, 1982. Reprinted by permission. Orginally taken from the Iowa Department of Transportation.)

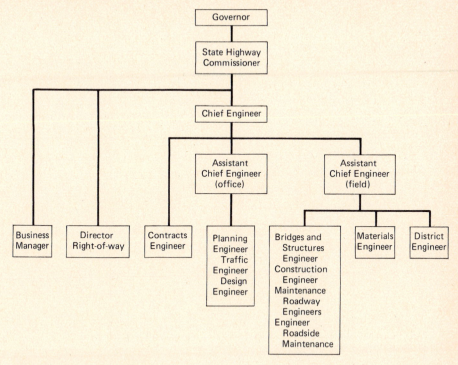

Figure 11–5 Typical Organization of a State Highway Department with a Strong Headquarters Organization.

(*Source: Transportation and Traffic Engineering Handbook,* Institute of Transportation Engineers, Englewood Cliffs, N.J., Prentice-Hall, 1982. Reprinted by permission.)

ment, user charges on the waterways, air commuter processes and patterns, and statewide highway financing. The state/federal interaction study process, which was the backbone for all of these, is worthy of description. It formed the national data base for state and federal policy studies and is known as the *1970 State Needs and Capital Improvement Program.* Under section 17 of the 1968 Federal Highway Act, each state was required to produce a statewide needs and capital improvement program in 1970, to be updated in 1972. The structure of the study was as illustrated in Figure 11–16.

After a local review of goals, objectives, and level of service criteria, the various modes (highway, air, rail, water) would be studied and inventoried across the following city classifications: more than 250,000 population; 50,000–250,000 population; 5,000–50,000 population; and less than 5,000 population. For these, all deficiencies were to be noted in terms of immediate need, needs within five years, and needs by ten years hence. Simultaneously a set of solutions or capital improvements was to be developed to form a Capital Improvement Program to

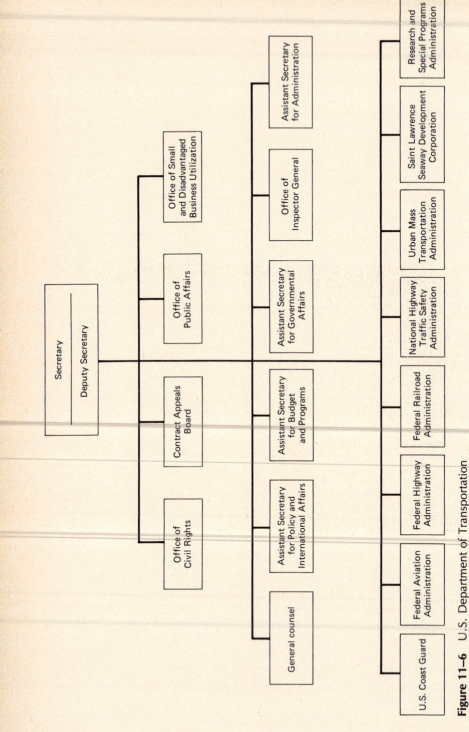

Figure 11–6 U.S. Department of Transportation

(*Source:* U.S. Department of Transportation.)

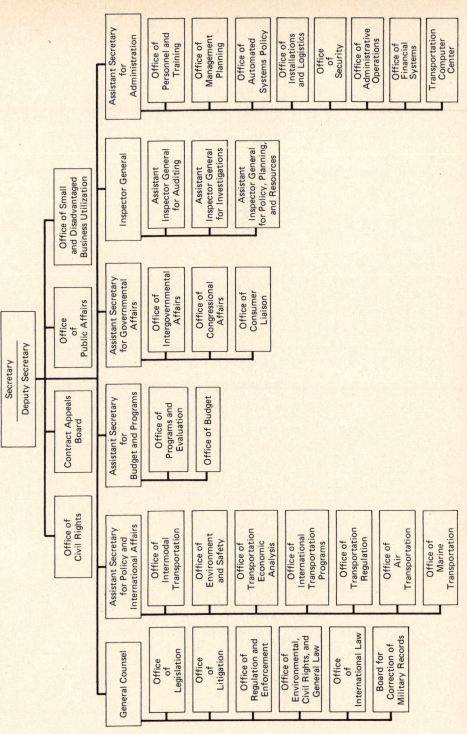

Figure 11–7 U.S. Department of Transportation, Office of the Secretary

(*Source:* U.S. Department of Transportation.)

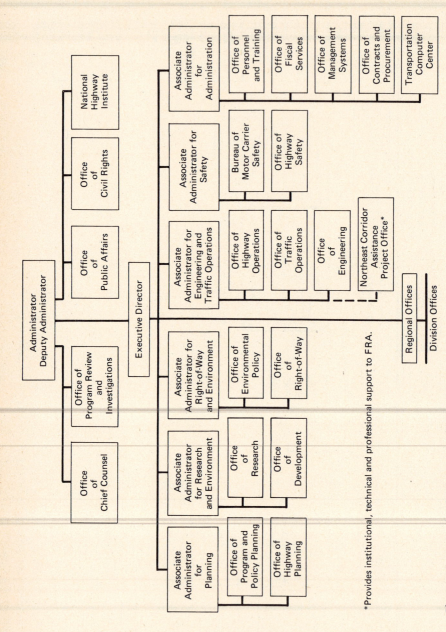

Figure 11–8 Federal Highway Administration

(*Source:* U.S. Department of Transportation.)

*Provides institutional, technical and professional support to FRA.

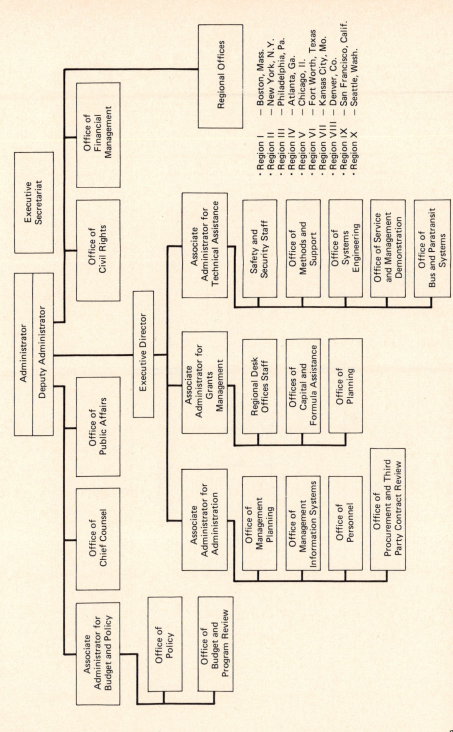

Figure 11–9 Urban Mass Transportation Administration

(*Source:* U.S. Department of Transportation.)

395

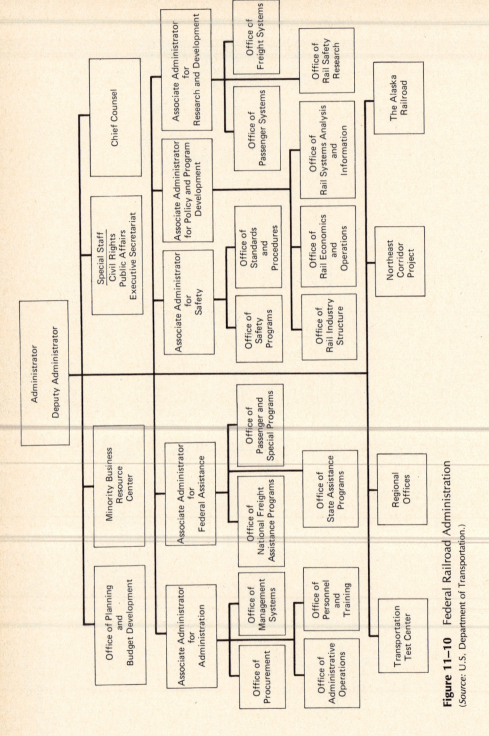

Figure 11–10 Federal Railroad Administration

(*Source:* U.S. Department of Transportation.)

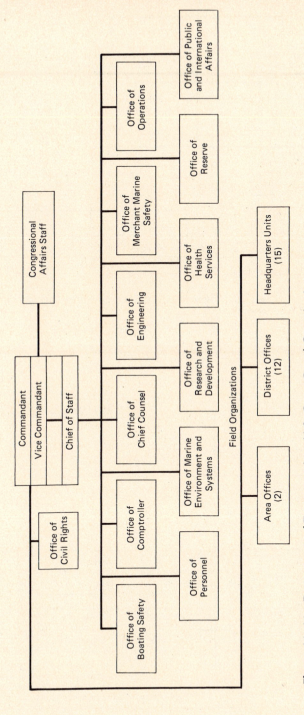

Figure 11–11 Department of Transportation, U.S. Coast Guard Organization

(*Source:* U.S. Department of Transportation.)

The chart shows the following organizational structure:

- Commandant
- Vice Commandant
- Chief of Staff
- Congressional Affairs Staff
- Office of Civil Rights
- Office of Boating Safety
- Office of Personnel
- Office of Comptroller
- Office of Marine Environment and Systems
- Office of Chief Counsel
- Office of Research and Development
- Office of Engineering
- Office of Health Services
- Office of Merchant Marine Safety
- Office of Reserve
- Office of Operations
- Office of Public and International Affairs

Field Organizations
- Area Offices (2)
- District Offices (12)
- Headquarters Units (15)

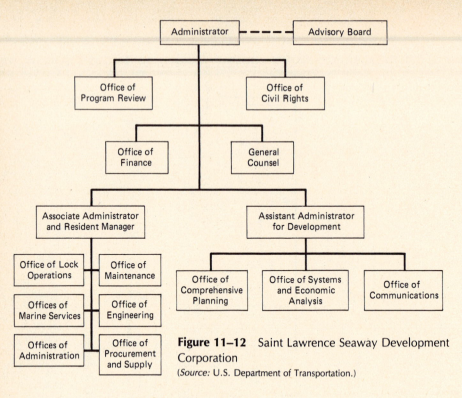

Figure 11–12 Saint Lawrence Seaway Development Corporation

(*Source:* U.S. Department of Transportation.)

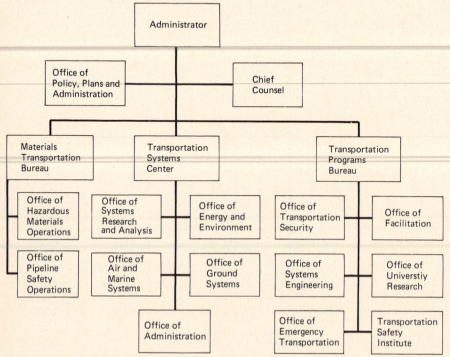

Figure 11–13 Research and Special Programs Administration

(*Source:* U.S. Department of Transportation.)

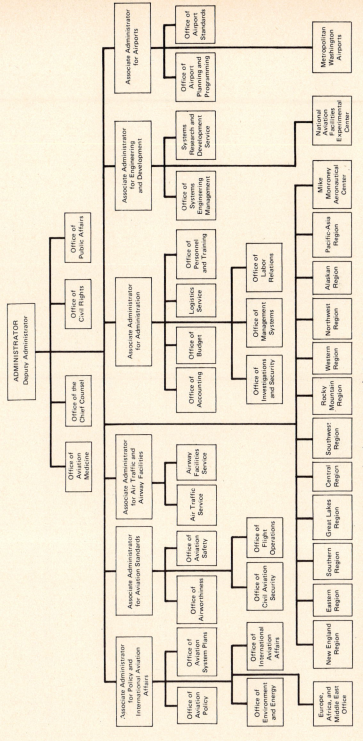

Figure 11–14 Department of Transportation, Federal Aviation Administration

(*Source*: U.S. Department of Transportation.)

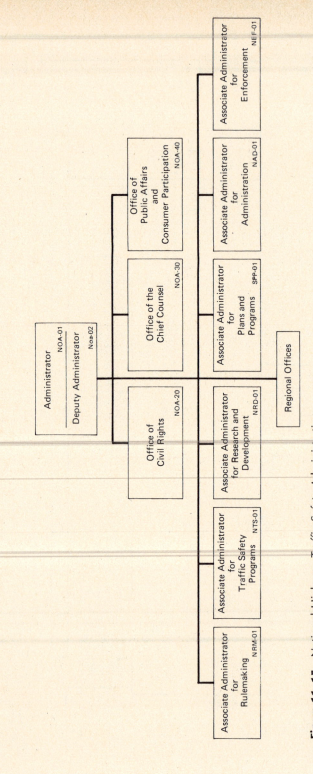

Figure 11–15   National Highway Traffic Safety Administration.
(*Source:* U.S. Department of Transportation.)

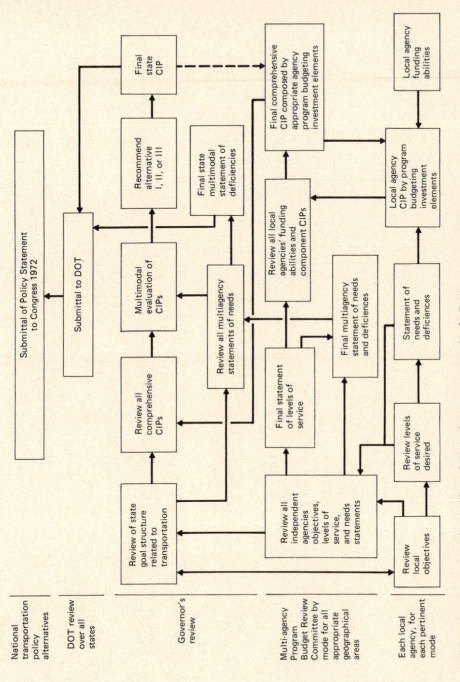

Figure 11–16 Statewide Needs and Capital Improvements Study Design

(*Source:* Carter, Haefner, and Johnson, "Emerging Analysis Issues in Statewide Transportation Studies," Paper Presented to the Transportation Research Forum, 1971.)

National transportation policy alternatives

DOT review over all states

Governor's review

Multi-agency Program Budget Review Committee by mode for all appropriate geographical areas

Each local agency, for each pertinent mode

Submittal of Policy Statement to Congress 1972

Submittal to DOT

Final state CIP

Recommend alternative I, II, or III

Final state multimodal statement of deficiencies

Multimodal evaluation of CIPs

Review all comprehensive CIPs

Review of state goal structure related to transportation

Review all multiagency statements of needs

Final statement of levels of service

Review all independent agencies objectives, levels of service, and needs statements

Final comprehensive CIP composed by appropriate agency program budgeting investment elements

Review all local agencies' funding abilities and component CIPs

Final multiagency statement of needs and deficiencies

Review levels of service desired

Review local objectives

Local agency funding abilities

Local agency CIP by program budgeting investment elements

Statement of needs and deficiencies

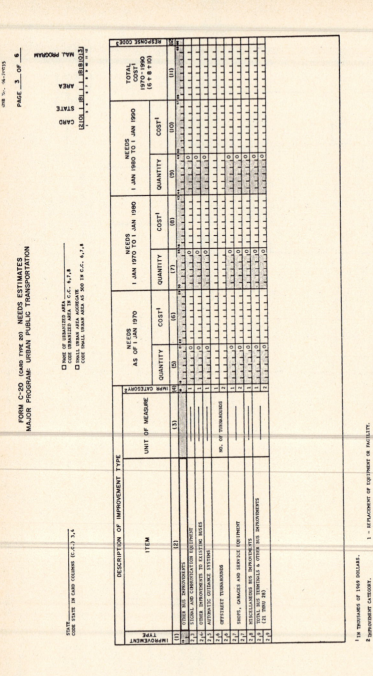

Figure 11–17 Form C-20 (Card Type 20) Needs Estimates; Major Program: Urban Public Transportation

(*Source:* U.S. Department of Transportation.)

402

FORM C-17 (CARD TYPE 17) CAPITAL IMPROVEMENT PROGRAMS
FEDERAL FUNDING ALTERNATIVE ____
PERIOD COVERED FY 19___ - 19___

MAJOR PROGRAM: URBAN PUBLIC TRANSPORTATION

OMB No. 04-70035
PAGE 2 OF 4

STATE
CODE STATE IN CARD COLUMNS (C.C.) 3,4
☐ NAME OF URBANIZED AREA — CODE URBANIZED AREA IN C.C. 6,7,8
☐ SMALL URBAN AREA AGGREGATE — CODE SMALL URBAN AREA AS 900 IN C.C. 6,7,8

IMPROVEMENT TYPE	ITEM	UNIT OF MEASURE	QUANTITY		COSTS AND FUNDS					
			REPLACEMENT OF EQUIPMENT OR FACILITY	NET ADDITIONS OF EQUIPMENT OR CONSTRUCTION ON NEW LOCATION	TOTAL COST[1]	FEDERAL AID FUNDS[1]	STATE/LOCAL FUNDS ON FEDERAL AID PROJECTS[1]	PRIVATE FUNDS ON FEDERAL AID PROJECTS[1]	STATE/LOCAL FUNDS ON NON-FEDERAL AID PROJECTS[1]	PRIVATE FUNDS ON NON-FEDERAL AID PROJECTS[1]
(1)	(2)	(3)	(4)	(5)	(6)	(7)	(8)	(9)	(10)	(11)
0,1	EXCLUSIVE BUSWAY	ROUTE MILES								
	TRANSIT BUSES									
0,2	BUSES: UNDER 11 SEAT CAPACITY	NO. OF BUSES								
0,3	BUSES: 11 - 25 SEAT CAPACITY	NO. OF BUSES								
0,4	BUSES: 26 - 50 SEAT CAPACITY	NO. OF BUSES								
0,5	BUSES: OVER 50 SEAT CAPACITY	NO. OF BUSES								
0,6	TOTAL TRANSIT BUSES (02 - 05)									
	INTRA-CITY BUS TERMINALS AND SHELTERS									
2,1	INTRA-CITY BUS TERMINALS	PASSENGERS/HR.								
2,2	BUS SHELTERS	NO. OF SHELTERS								
	OTHER BUS IMPROVEMENTS									
2,3	SIGNAL AND COMMUNICATION EQUIPMENT									
2,4	OTHER IMPROVEMENTS TO EXISTING BUSES									
2,5	AUTOMATIC GUIDANCE SYSTEMS									
2,6	OFFSTREET TURNAROUNDS	NO. OF TURNAROUNDS								
2,7	SHOPS, GARAGES AND SERVICE EQUIPMENT									
2,8	MISCELLANEOUS BUS IMPROVEMENTS									
2,9	TOTAL BUS TERMINALS AND OTHER BUS IMPROVEMENTS (21 - 28)									

[1] IN THOUSANDS OF 1969 DOLLARS.

[2] RESPONSE CODE (SEE APPENDIX G, MANUAL I FOR DETAILED EXPLANATION).
1 = FULL INFORMATION.
2 = PARTIAL INFORMATION (9 FILL UNUSED FIELDS).
3 = NO INFORMATION AVAILABLE AT THIS TIME.

Figure 11–18 Form C-17 (Card Type 17) Captial Improvement Programs; Federal Funding Alternative, Period Covered FY 19XX-19XY Major Program: Urban Public Transportation

(Source: U.S. Department of Transportation.)

403

FORM C-20 (CARD TYPE 20) NEEDS ESTIMATES
MAJOR PROGRAM: URBAN PUBLIC TRANSPORTATION

STATE OKLAHOMA
CODE STATE IN CARD COLUMNS (C.C.) 3,4

STATE [2|0]

CARD [2|0] |B| | |B|B|0|3|

MAJ. PROGRAM

NAME OF URBANIZED AREA OKLAHOMA CITY
☐ CODE URBANIZED AREA IN C.C. 6,7,8
☐ SMALL URBAN AREA AGGREGATE — CODE SMALL URBAN AREA AS 500 IN C.C. 6,7,8

Improvement Type (1)	Item (2)	Unit of Measure (3)	Impr Category[2] (4)	Needs As of 1 Jan 1970 Quantity (5)	Cost[1] (6)	Needs 1 Jan 1970 to 1 Jan 1980 Quantity (7)	Cost[1] (8)	Needs 1 Jan 1980 to 1 Jan 1990 Quantity (9)	Cost[1] (10)	Total Cost[1] 1970-1990 (6+8+10) (11)	Response Code[3]
01	Exclusive Busway	Route Miles									
01	Transit Buses										
02	Buses: Under 11 Seat Capacity	No. of Buses	1							1.502	
02	Buses: 11 - 25 Seat Capacity	No. of Buses	1			10	150	10	150	1.502	
03	Buses: 26 - 50 Seat Capacity	No. of Buses	2	41	1435	25	875	72	2520	483.0	
04	Buses: Over 50 Seat Capacity	No. of Buses	1			10	210			210.0	
05		No. of Buses	2								
06	Total Transit Buses (02 thru 05)		1	41	1435	10	1235	10	2470	6340	
21	Intra-City Bus Terminals & Shelters										
21	Intra-City Bus Terminals	Passengers/hr.	1								
22	Bus Shelters	No. of Shelters	2	6	25	5	25			502	

[1] IN THOUSANDS OF 1969 DOLLARS.

[2] IMPROVEMENT CATEGORY.
  1 = REPLACEMENT OF EQUIPMENT OR FACILITY.
  2 = NET ADDITIONS OF EQUIPMENT OR CONSTRUCTION ON NEW LOCATION.
  3 = SUM OF 1 AND 2 (USED ONLY FOR MAJOR PROGRAM TOTALS).

[3] RESPONSE CODE (SEE APPENDIX G, MANUAL A FOR DETAILED EXPLANATION).
  1 = FULL INFORMATION.
  2 = PARTIAL INFORMATION (9 FILL UNUSED FIELDS).
  3 = NO INFORMATION AVAILABLE AT THIS TIME.

404

FORM C-20 (CARD TYPE 20) NEEDS ESTIMATES
MAJOR PROGRAM: URBAN PUBLIC TRANSPORTATION

STATE _DELAHOMA_
CODE STATE IN CARD COLUMNS (C.C.) 3,4

NAME OF URBANIZED AREA _OKLAHOMA CITY_
☑ CODE URBANIZED AREA IN C.C. 6,7,8
☐ SMALL URBAN AREA AGGREGATE
☐ CODE SMALL URBAN AREA AS 500 IN C.C. 6,7,8

CARD [20] AREA [B] MAJ. PROGRAM [B|B|0|3]

IMPROVEMENT TYPE	ITEM	UNIT OF MEASURE	IMPR CATEGORY[2]	NEEDS AS OF 1 JAN 1970		NEEDS 1 JAN 1970 TO 1 JAN 1980		NEEDS 1 JAN 1980 TO 1 JAN 1990		TOTAL COST[1] 1970-1990 (6+8+10)	RESPONSE CODE[3]
(1)	(2)	(3)	(4)	QUANTITY (5)	COST[1] (6)	QUANTITY (7)	COST[1] (8)	QUANTITY (9)	COST[1] (10)	(11)	(12)
2.3	OTHER BUS IMPROVEMENTS		1	0		0		0		100.2	
2.4	SIGNAL AND COMMUNICATION EQUIPMENT		1	0	150	0	50	0	50		
2.4	OTHER IMPROVEMENTS TO EXISTING BUSES		1	0	240	0		0			
2.5	AUTOMATIC GUIDANCE SYSTEMS		1	0	240	0		0			
2.6	OFFSTREET TURNAROUNDS	NO. OF TURNAROUNDS	2	0							
2.7	SHOPS, GARAGES AND SERVICE EQUIPMENT		2	0	150	0	187	0	408	1,502	
2.8	MISCELLANEOUS BUS IMPROVEMENTS		1	0	240	0	347	0	458	8,251	
2.9	TOTAL BUS TERMINALS & OTHER BUS IMPROVEMENTS (21 THRU 28)		2	0	175					100.2	

[1]IN THOUSANDS OF 1969 DOLLARS.

[2]IMPROVEMENT CATEGORY.
1 = REPLACEMENT OF EQUIPMENT OR FACILITY.
2 = NET ADDITIONS OF EQUIPMENT OR CONSTRUCTION ON NEW LOCATION.
3 = SUM OF 1 AND 2 (USED ONLY FOR MAJOR PROGRAM TOTALS).

[3]RESPONSE CODE (SEE APPENDIX G, MANUAL A FOR DETAILED EXPLANATION).
1 = FULL INFORMATION.
2 = PARTIAL INFORMATION (9 FILL UNUSED FIELDS).
3 = NO INFORMATION AVAILABLE AT THIS TIME.

Figure 11–19 Form C-20 (Card Type 20) Needs Estimates; Major Program: Urban Public Transportation

(*Source:* 1970 State Needs and Capital Improvement Programs, U.S. Department of Transportation.)

FORM C-17 (CARD TYPE 17) CAPITAL IMPROVEMENT PROGRAMS
FEDERAL FUNDING ALTERNATIVE
PERIOD COVERED FY 19 _79_ - 19 _89_
MAJOR PROGRAM: URBAN PUBLIC TRANSPORTATION

NAME OF URBANIZED AREA _OKLAHOMA CITY_
☑ CODE URBANIZED AREA IN C.C. 6,7,8
☐ CODE SMALL URBAN AREA AGGREGATE
☐ CODE SMALL URBAN AREA AS 300 IN C.C. 6,7,8

STATE _OKLAHOMA_
CODE STATE IN CARD COLUMNS (C.C.) 3,4

IMPROVEMENT TYPE (1)	ITEM (2)	UNIT OF MEASURE (3)	QUANTITY: REPLACEMENT OF EQUIPMENT ON FACILITY (4)	QUANTITY: NET ADDITIONS OF EQUIPMENT OR CONSTRUCTION ON NEW LOCATION (5)	TOTAL COST (6)	FEDERAL AID FUNDS (7)	STATE/LOCAL FUNDS ON FEDERAL AID PROJECTS (8)	PRIVATE FUNDS ON FEDERAL AID PROJECTS (9)	STATE/LOCAL FUNDS ON NON-FEDERAL AID PROJECTS (10)	PRIVATE FUNDS ON NON-FEDERAL AID PROJECTS (11)	RESPONSE CODE (12)
0,1	EXCLUSIVE BUSWAY	ROUTE MILES									
	TRANSIT BUSES										
0,2	BUSES: UNDER 11 SEAT CAPACITY	NO. OF BUSES									
0,3	BUSES: 11 - 25 SEAT CAPACITY	NO. OF BUSES		10	150	100	50				2
0,4	BUSES: 26 - 50 SEAT CAPACITY	NO. OF BUSES	72		2520	1680	840				1
0,5	BUSES: OVER 50 SEAT CAPACITY	NO. OF BUSES									
0,6	TOTAL TRANSIT BUSES (02 - 05)				2670	1780	890				2
2,1	INTRA-CITY BUS TERMINALS AND SHELTERS										
	INTRA-CITY BUS TERMINALS	PASSENGERS/HR.									
2,2	BUS SHELTERS	NO. OF SHELTERS									
	OTHER BUS IMPROVEMENTS										
2,3	SIGNAL AND COMMUNICATION EQUIPMENT				50	33	17				2
2,4	OTHER IMPROVEMENTS TO EXISTING BUSES										
2,5	AUTOMATIC GUIDANCE SYSTEMS										
2,6	OFFSTREET TURNAROUNDS	NO. OF TURNAROUNDS									
2,7	SHOPS, GARAGES AND SERVICE EQUIPMENT										
2,8	MISCELLANEOUS BUS IMPROVEMENTS				408	270	138				1
2,9	TOTAL BUS TERMINALS AND OTHER BUS IMPROVEMENTS (21 - 28)				458	303	155				2

COSTS AND FUNDS

CARD | STATE | AREA | F.P.A. | PERIOD | MAJ. PROGRAM | RESPONSE CODE 2

1 IN THOUSANDS OF 1969 DOLLARS.

2 RESPONSE CODE (SEE APPENDIX G, MANUAL A FOR DETAILED EXPLANATION) 1 = FULL INFORMATION. 3 = PARTIAL INFORMATION (9 FILL UNUSED FIELDS). 9 = NO INFORMATION AVAILABLE AT THIS TIME.

Figure 11–20 Form C-17 (Card Type 17) Capital Improvement Programs; Federal Funding Alternative, Period Covered FY 19XX-19XY; Major Program: Urban Public Transportation

(*Source:* 1970 State Needs and Capital Improvement Programs, U.S. Department of Transportation.)

satisfy the needs. They were formatted as Alternative I, no capital; Alternative II, low capital; or Alternative III, high capital. The alternatives were programmed as to whether they were composed of private, local, state, or federal funds, or combinations of matches thereof. Typical needs and capital improvement forms and table formats to achieve the above are shown in Figures 11–17 and 11–18, respectively. A final list and plan set are shown in Figures 11–19 and 11–20.

As shown in Figure 11–16, all this material ultimately was transmitted via each state to the U.S. Department of Transportation Office of Planning and Policy, where a complete data base was formed for the nation. The report information was used to develop the first multimodal comprehensive Department of Transportation Policy, and presented in Congress to form the Surface Transportation Act of 1972. The study was updated by each state in 1972, then dropped on a formal basis. However, the U.S. Department of Transportation continues to update its data bank on the basis of timely reports from the states, replicating the foregoing process in its legislative activities, and resulting in a national transportation policy implemented by continuous transportation legislation. These legislative trajectories and their policy implications are addressed in detail in Chapter 13. The states, as a result of the stimulus of the original 1970 study, have become comfortable with developing statewide multimodal plans encompassing major issues of highway, rail, air, and water. As such the 1970 Needs and Capital Improvement Program Study was the initial catalyst, and formed the study construct, which truly began federal and state multimodal transportation planning and programming.

References

Carter, Everett C., Lonnie E. Haefner, and Ralph D. Johnson. "Emerging Analysis Issues in Statewide Transportation Studies." *Transportation Research Forum,* October 19, 1971.

Department of Transportation Organization Directory. Washington, D.C.: U.S. Government Printing Office, February 1984.

Final Report: National Transportation Policies Through the Year 2000. Washington, D.C.: National Transportation Policy Study Commission, June 1979.

Cleveland, Donald E., Editor. *Manual of Traffic Engineering Studies,* 3d ed. Washington, D.C.: Institute of Traffic Engineers, 1964.

12 Energy and Transportation

The relationship between transportation and energy use is a significant one. In the past fifteen years, transportation has become a major user of energy, and has had a substantial impact on national energy negotiations in the world market.

The fact that transportation is a primary consumer of energy is borne out by Tables 12–1 and 12–2. Transportation has consistently accounted for one fourth of the nation's energy consumption. Most of the energy source is petroleum, as shown in Table 12–3 and illustrated in Figure 12–1. However, fuel consumption does vary by mode, as shown in Table 12–3, with railroads, air, and water transport consuming large amounts of diesel fuel, and transit using electricity.

Total motor vehicle fuel consumption and travel showed a steady increase to 1973, as illustrated in Table 12–4, when the energy crisis was recognized and steps toward conservation were begun. These steps are discussed later. In a like manner, the transit industry exhibited a similar growth and downturn, as shown in Table 12–5, as run cutting, rescheduling, and other measures were invoked to conserve fuel in the 1970s.

Concurrently prices of all fuel increased dramatically during the past decade, as shown in Table 12–6. All aviation fuels, regular, premium, and unleaded automobile gasoline, and diesel fuels more than doubled in price in five years, while C Bunker marine fuel stayed constant. Regular and premium gasoline price indices rose higher than other key domestic consumables such as food, rent, apparel, and entertainment.

A parallel item of behavior is the fuel efficiency of U.S. passenger cars, as

Table 12–1 Consumption of Energy by End-Use Sector (Quadrillion Btu at Five-Year Intervals 1950–1965 and Annually 1966–1980)

Year	Residential and Commercial	% of Total	Industrial and Misc.	% of Total	Transportation	% of Total	Electrical Utilities	% of Total	Total Energy Consumption
1950	7.58	22.5	12.18	36.2	8.84	26.3	5.03	15.0	33.62
1955	8.47	21.6	13.83	35.3	10.15	25.9	6.73	17.2	39.18
1960	10.42	23.6	14.95	33.9	10.48	23.8	8.23	18.7	44.08
1965	11.94	22.5	17.68	33.4	12.30	23.2	11.07	20.9	52.99
1966	12.42	22.2	18.50	33.0	13.04	23.3	12.03	21.5	55.99
1967	13.02	22.5	18.45	31.9	13.69	23.6	12.73	22.0	57.89
1968	13.44	21.9	19.16	31.2	14.80	24.1	13.92	22.7	61.32
1969	14.01	21.7	19.84	30.7	15.43	23.9	15.25	23.6	64.53
1970	14.35	21.5	20.14	30.1	16.03	24.0	16.29	24.4	66.83
1971	14.59	21.4	19.84	29.0	16.65	24.4	17.22	25.2	68.30
1972	14.96	20.9	20.46	28.6	17.63	24.6	18.58	25.9	71.63
1973	14.66	19.6	21.44	28.7	18.49	24.8	20.01	26.8	74.61
1974	13.95	19.2	20.65	28.4	18.00	24.7	20.16	27.7	72.76
1975	13.61	19.2	18.54	26.2	18.14	25.7	20.42	28.9	70.71
1976	14.39	19.3	19.54	26.2	19.03	25.5	21.55	28.9	74.51
1977	13.93	18.2	19.87	26.0	19.70	25.8	22.82	29.9	76.33
1978	14.13	18.1	19.91	25.5	20.58	26.3	23.52	30.1	78.15
1979	13.13	16.6	21.69	27.5	19.92	24.0	24.23	30.7	78.97
1980p	12.33	16.0	20.62	27.0	18.59	24.4	24.82	32.5	76.27

Note: Sum of components may not total due to independent rounding.
p = preliminary
(Source: U.S. Department of Energy, 1980 Annual Report to Congress, Volume Two, Table 4.)

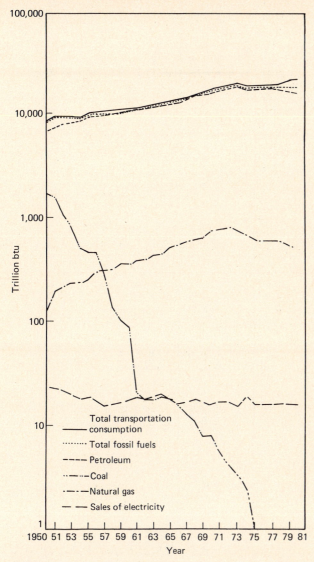

Figure 12–1 Energy Consumption: Transportation Sector, 1950–1980

(*Source:* U.S. Department of Transportation, *National Transportation Statistics,* 1980.)

illustrated in Table 12–7. During the period 1950–1965 it stayed constant at about 15 miles per gallon (mpg). As post-energy-crisis changes were induced in the automotive industry, it gradually improved, climbing to 19.3 mpg in 1979. Graphics of the table are illustrated in Figures 12–2 and 12–3. The associated 1967 cost of operating a standard-size motor vehicle was 2.47 cents per mile, of which gasoline costs accounted for 22 percent. In 1974 these costs accelerated to 4.23

Table 12–2 U.S. Energy Consumption by the Transportation Sector (At Five-Year Intervals 1950–1965 and Annually 1966–1980)

Year	Coal[a] Million Short Tons	Coal[a] Tril-lion[d] Btu	Petroleum Million Barrels	Petroleum Tril-lion[d] Btu	Natural Gas[b] Trillion Cubic Feet	Natural Gas[b] Tril-lion[d] Btu	Total Fossil Fuels Trillion Btu	Sales of Electricity[c] Million Kilowatt Hours	Sales of Electricity[c] Tril-lion[d] Btu	Total Transportation Consumption Tril-lion Btu	Total Transportation Consumption % of Total Gross Energy Consumption	Total Gross Energy Consumption Quadril-lion Btu
1950	63.0	1,651	1,248.3	7,053	0.13	135	8,839	5,881	20.1	8,859	26.4	33.62
1955	17.0	439	1,690.0	9,452	0.25	259	10,150	4,563	15.6	10,166	25.9	39.18
1960	3.0	80	1,862.9	10,041	0.35	362	10,483	4,770	16.3	10,499	23.8	44.08
1965	0.7	19	2,182.7	11,765	0.50	516	12,300	4,652	15.9	12,316	23.2	52.99
1966	0.6	16	2,314.1	12,473	0.54	558	13,047	4,514	15.4	13,062	23.3	55.99
1967	0.5	13	2,427.3	13,095	0.58	599	13,707	4,572	15.6	13,723	23.7	57.89
1968	0.4	11	2,627.9	14,185	0.59	608	14,804	4,540	15.5	14,820	24.2	61.32
1969	0.3	8	2,737.5	14,772	0.63	650	15,430	4,531	15.5	15,446	23.9	64.53
1970	0.3	8	2,832.4	15,284	0.72	742	16,034	4,633	15.8	16,050	24.0	66.83

Year												
1971	5	0.2	2,945.6	15,886	0.74	763	16,654	4,537	15.5	16,670	24.4	68.30
1972	5	0.2	3,122.0	16,831	0.77	791	17,627	4,440	15.1	17,642	24.6	71.63
1973	3	0.1	3,288.7	17,752	0.73	745	18,500	4,186	14.3	18,514	24.8	74.61
1974	3	0.1	3,208.4	17,313	0.67	686	18,002	4,258	14.5	18,017	24.8	72.76
1975	**	*	3,252.2	17,546	0.58	592	18,138	4,273	14.6	18,153	25.7	70.71
1976	**	*	3,422.1	18,479	0.55	560	19,039	4,338	14.8	19,054	25.6	74.51
1977	**	*	3,544.2	19,153	0.53	540	19,693	4,212	14.4	19,707	25.8	76.33
1978	**	*	3,704.8	20,050	0.53	538	20,588	4,336	14.8	20,603	26.4	78.15
1979	**	*	3,566.1	19,310	0.60	611	19,921	4,243	14.5	19,936	25.2	78.97
1980p	**	*	3,323.3e	17,976	0.59	601	18,577	4,288	14.6	18,592	24.4	76.27

Note: Sum of components may not equal due to independent rounding.

p = preliminary e = estimated

*Less than 0.05 million short tons.

**Less than 1 trillion Btu's.

aBituminous coal and lignite only.

bPipeline fuel.

cIncludes only energy used by railroads and railways.

dBtu's derived by multiplying by conversion factors on p. 231 for bituminous coal and lignite consumption by nonutility, p. 230 for natural gas consumption by nonutility, p. 228 for petroleum in transportation use, and p. 227 for electricity consumption, DOE, *1980 Annual Report to Congress, Volume Two.*

(*Source:* U. S. Department of Energy, *1980 Annual Report to Congress, Volume II.* Edison Electric Institute, *Statistical Year Book, 1978, 1971* and *Historical Statistics Through the Year 1970. Sales of Electricity: 1950–1978; Ibid.*)

Table 12–3 Fuel Consumption by Mode of Transportation, 1969–1979

	1969	1970	1971	1972	1973	1974	1975	1976	1977	1978	1979
Class I railroads											
Locomotives											
Diesel oil, gals $\times 10^6$	3,919	3,800	3,819	3,999	4,141	4,112	3,732	3,890	3,982	3,966	4,069
Fuel oil, gals $\times 10^6$	33										
Electricity, kWh $\times 10^6$	610	578	534	435	346	467	422	353	417	331	309
Coal, tons	1,137	1,238	1,191	1,400	1,202	1,160	1,160	1,421	1,569	1,275	1,421
Motor Cars											
Diesel oil, gals $\times 10^6$	5	8	4	3	3	4	4	5	3	2	3
Electricity, kWh $\times 10^6$	538	763	756	715	901	847	857	790	986	991	1,062
Air											
Certified carriers											
Aviation gasoline, gals $\times 10^6$	33	33	12	13	11	7	6	n/a	n/a	n/a	n/a
Jet fuel, gals $\times 10^6$	10,113	10,085	10,140	10,302	10,671	9,546	9,507	9,808[e]	10,268[e]	10,639[e]	11,369[e]
General aviation[c]											
Aviation gasoline, gals $\times 10^6$	522	551	508	584	411	443	412	432	456	518	570
Jet fuel, gals $\times 10^6$	168	208	226	245	304	357	453	495	536	763	736
Highway											
Gasoline, gals $\times 10^6$											
Pass. cars + taxis	62,325	65,649	69,213	73,121	77,619	73,770	76,010	78,398[f]	80,225	83,312	79,793
Motorcycles	123	135	301	342	392	447	447	448[f]	451	463	440
Diesel + gasoline, gals $\times 10^6$											
Commercial buses[b]	657	644	631	561	520	525	553	574	583	615	618
School buses	290	300	316	320	327	333	342	390	401	407	405
Single-unit trucks[a]	16,528	17,237	18,221	22,118	22,755	21,125	21,868	24,914[f]	26,255	27,780	28,544
Combination trucks	8,199	8,363	8,865	8,600	8,860	10,101	9,764	10,975[f]	11,709	12,491	12,315

Water transport											
Residual fuel oil, gals × 10^6	3,506	3,774	3,307	3,273	3,881	3,824	4,060	4,933[r]	5,417	6,615	n/a
Distillate fuel oil, gals × 10^6	793	819	880	929	1,125	1,040	1,098	1,190[r]	1,408	1,579	n/a
Gasoline, gals × 10^6	569	598	645	687	717	697	730	764	774	812	780
Transit											
Electricity, kWh × 10^6											
Rapid transit	2,291	2,261	2,262	2,149	2,098	n/a	n/a	n/a	n/a	n/a	n/a
Surface rail	173	157	153	146	140	n/a	n/a	n/a	n/a	n/a	n/a
Trolley	154	143	141	133	93	n/a	n/a	n/a	n/a	n/a	n/a
Total	2,618	2,561	2,556	2,428	2,331	2,630	2,646	2,576	2,303	2,223	2,473[p]
Gallons of motor fuel, gals × 10^6											
Gasoline	40	37	29	20	12	7	5	5	8	9	9[p]
Diesel oil	274	271	257	253	283	316	365	389	403	422	404[p]
Propane	32	31	27	24	15	3	3	1	1	0	0[p]
Pipelines											
Natural gas, cu. ft. × 10^6	630,962	722,166	742,592	766,156	728,177	668,834	582,963	548,323	532,669	530,151	600,964
Total[d]											
Nonhighway use of gasoline gallons × 10^6	4,105	4,003	3,913	3,824	3,896	3,623	3,642	3,778	3,577	3,645	

r = revised
p = preliminary
n/a = not available
[a] Includes nonfreight truck movements.
[b] Includes intercity and urban buses.
[c] Data for 1969–1972 calculated by method different from that used for 1973–1979 data.
[d] Private, commercial, and public nonhighway use of gasoline.
[e] Includes aviation gasoline.
(*Source:* National Transportation Statistics, Annual Report, DOT-TSC-TSPA-81-8, Washington, D.C., U.S. Government Printing Office, 1981.)

415

Table 12–4   Total Motor Vehicle Fuel Consumption and Travel,* 1969–1979

Year	Number Registered (thou- sands)	Total Vehicle Miles Traveled (millions)	Average Miles Traveled per Vehicle	Average Miles Traveled per Gallon	Total Fuel Con- sumed (millions of gallons)	Average Gallons Con- sumed per Vehicle
1969	107,391	1,070,575	9,969	12.15	88,122	821
1970	111,222	1,120,705	10,076	12.14	92,328	830
1971	116,344	1,186,289	10,198	12.16	97,547	838
1972	122,304	1,268,342	10,370	12.07	105,062	859
1973	129,778	1,308,562	10,083	11.85	110,473	851
1974	134,900	1,285,647	9,530	12.09	106,301	788
1975	137,917	1,330,074	9,644	12.20	108,984	790
1976	143,427	1,411,990	9,844	12.20	115,700	807
1977	148,785	1,476,567	9,926	12.34	119,625	804
1978	153,920	1,548,213	10,059	12.38	125,067	813
1979	159,621	1,529,133	9,580	12.52	122,115	765

*For the fifty states and District of Columbia, includes personal passenger vehicles, buses, and motor trucks. (*Source:* U.S. Department of Transportation, Federal Highway Administration, *Highway Statistics,* Table VM-1, annual issues.)

cents per mile, of which 27 percent was gasoline. These and other summary computations are graphed in Figure 12–4 for vehicles of various sizes. Typically gasoline costs in all cases range between 22 and 27 percent of total costs per mile.

An appropriate parameter to review is that of energy intensiveness, or usage per revenue production in the various modes. Figures 12–5 and 12–6 are excellent illustrations of air, rail, and other passenger modes. With the exception of general aviation and some air cargo movements of the late 1970s, the general trend has been toward lessened energy usage per ton or passenger-mile, resulting from increased emphasis on fuel conservation and improved fuel economy design components and standards.

Pre-Energy-Crisis Behavior

It is important to cast the statistics and user characteristics in a historical context of the U.S. position in the energy community. This is illustrated in Table 12–8. As shown the United States has turned from being a net exporter to being a net importer of petroleum. Further, in the context of the world community, Western Europe, Japan, and the United States are significant importers of petroleum, and

Table 12–5 Motor Fuel and Energy Consumption by the U.S. Transit Industry (at Five-Year Intervals 1950–1965 and Annually 1966–1979)

| Year | Kilowatt-Hours Consumed (In Millions) | | | | Gallons of Motor Fuel Used (In Thousands) | | |
	Heavy Rail	Light Rail	Trolley Coach	Total	Gasoline	Diesel Oil	Propane
1950	2,000	2,410	841	5,251	430,000	98,600	*
1955	1,900	910	720	3,530	246,000	172,600	30,300
1960	2,098	393	417	2,908	153,600	208,100	38,300
1965	2,185	218	181	2,584	91,500	248,400	32,700
1966	2,075	226	166	2,467	76,000	256,000	33,600
1967	2,194	180	157	2,531	57,800	270,300	33,000
1968	2,250	179	157	2,586	45,700	274,200	32,200
1969	2,291	173	154	2,618	40,000	273,800	31,600
1970	2,261	157	143	2,561	37,200	270,600	31,000
1971	2,262	153	141	2,556	29,400	256,800	26,500
1972	2,149	146	133	2,428	19,647	253,250	24,400
1973	2,098	140	93	2,331	12,333	282,620	15,152
1974	n/a	n/a	n/a	2,630	7,457	316,360	3,142
1975	n/a	n/a	n/a	2,646	5,017	365,060	2,559
1976	n/a	n/a	n/a	2,576	5,203	389,187	960
1977	n/a	n/a	n/a	2,303	8,077	402,842	1,196
1978	n/a	n/a	n/a	2,223	9,318	422,017	13
1979[p]	n/a	n/a	n/a	2,473	8,961	403,922	12

n/a = not available
p = preliminary
*Propane included with gasoline.
(*Source:* National Transportation Statistics, Annual Report, DOT-TSC-TSPA-81-8, Washington, D.C., U.S. Government Printing Office, 1981, and American Public Transit Association, *Transit Fact Book,* 1979–1980 Edition, Table 17.)

the Middle East, U.S.S.R., Latin America, and Africa are significant exporters of petroleum. It is the fact that the United States has assumed a position in the net import market that makes our transportation energy position difficult and led to the so-called "crisis" of 1973.

Several important dates and actions characterize the energy crisis of 1973. The increased import requirements and oil usage of a more travel-intensive United States put the country in a vulnerable position. Table 12–9 illustrates the historical time frame of energy crisis activities, beginning in 1973 with White House warnings of American vulnerability. The true origin of the active crisis was the complete Arab oil embargo on October 21, 1973, followed by a U.S. petroleum

Table 12–6 Average Retail Price of Transportation Fuel (¢/Gallon), 1975–1980

| | Aviation Fuels | | | Highway Fuels | | | | Railroad Fuel | | Marine |
| | | Jet Fuel | | Motor Gasoline | | | | | | |
Year	Aviation Gasoline	Naphtha	Kerosene	Regular	Premium	Unleaded	Truck No. 2 Diesel	Diesel	Coal ($/ton)	Bunker "C" Fuel
1975	41.1	30.7	29.8	56.7r	60.9r	57.1	n/a	30.00	16.90	24.66
1976	43.1	31.5	31.2	59.0r	63.6r	61.4r	34.7	32.38	23.22	24.83
1977	47.7	35.0	35.8	62.2r	67.4r	65.6r	39.3	36.38	33.14	27.74
1978	52.1	37.5	38.9	62.6r	69.4r	67.0r	40.2	36.50	*	25.74
1979	69.5	52.3	55.1	85.7	92.2	90.3	62.4	74.80	*	n/a
1980	108.7	87.4	87.0	119.1	128.1	124.5	86.4	n/a	*	n/a

n/a = not available

r = revised

*Coal is no longer used as a railroad fuel.

(*Sources*: National Transportation Statistics, Annual Report, DOT-TSC-TSPA-81-8, Washington, D.C., U.S. Government Printing Office, 1981; Railroad Fuel, 1975–1980: AAR, personal communication based on percentage increase as of January 1; other data: 1975–1977: DOE/EIA, *Monthly Energy Review*, Part 9, January 1980.)

Table 12–7 Average Fuel Efficiency of U.S. Passenger Cars (at Five-Year Intervals 1950–1965 and Annually 1966–1979)

Year	Average Passenger Car Fuel Efficiency[a] (Calendar Year Basis) (mpg)	New Car Fuel Efficiency Big Four[b](Model Year Basis) (mpg)
1950	14.95	16.0
1955	14.53	16.0
1960	14.28	15.5
1965	14.07	15.4
1966	14.00	15.0
1967	13.93	14.6
1968	13.79	14.2
1969	13.63	14.1
1970	13.57	14.1
1971	13.57	13.7
1972	13.49	13.6
1973	13.10	13.3
1974	13.43	12.8
1975	13.53	15.1
1976	13.72	16.5
1977	13.94	17.7
1978	14.06	18.7
1979	14.29[r]	19.3

r = revised
[a]55% city, 45% highway miles sales weighted average.
[b]Big Four = American Motors, Chrysler, Ford, and General Motors (domestic fleet).
(*Source:* U.S. Department of Transportation, Federal Highway Administration, *Highway Statistics,* Table VM-1, annual issues. New car fuel efficiency: U.S. DOT, NHTSA/NRM-20, personal communication.)

allocation plan on November 27, 1973. Development of conservation measures began shortly thereafter, with a voluntary ban on Sunday gasoline sales and the formation of a Federal Energy Administration. This was followed by federal legislation requiring a 55 mph speed limit, and voluntary rationing plans for gasoline by states, the first being Oregon. Although the Arab oil embargo was lifted in March 1974, the result of the crisis and our related actions had seen oil prices double to over a $1 per gallon, and had seen energy and transportation being treated as a serious technical, economic, and diplomatic issue by the nation for the first time in its history. The gas lines, no Sunday sales, rationing, and lack of fuel for trucker haulage of freight were a stimulus to developing a formal agenda for solving the problems.

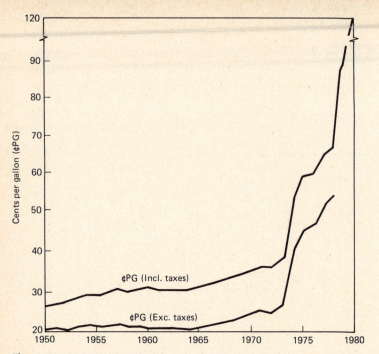

Figure 12–2 Price Trend of Regular-Grade Gasoline Prices, 1950–1980

(*Source:* 1950–1977: *Basic Petroleum Data Book,* Section VI, Table 4.4a. 1978–1980: Platt, *Oil Price Handbook and Oilmanac,* 57th ed., 1980.

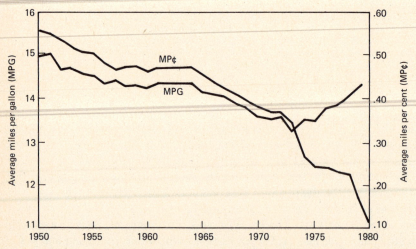

Figure 12–3 Average Fuel Efficiency of U.S. Passenger Cars, 1959–1980 (Average Miles per Gallon and Average Miles per Cent Cost of Gasoline)

(*Source:* MPG, FHWA, *Highway Statistics,* annual issues, Table VM-1. MP¢, U.S. DOT, Transportation Systems Center computation.)

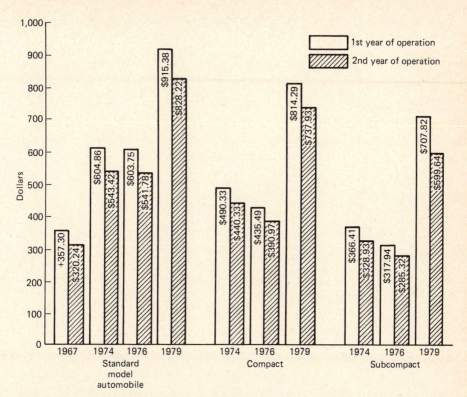

Figure 12–4   Estimated Annual Automobile Gasoline and Oil Costs, Including Taxes, by Size and Year of Operation

(*Source:* National Transportation Statistics, Annual Report, Washington, D.C., U.S. Government Printing Office, DOT-TSC-TSPA-81-8, 1981.)

The Energy Solution Framework

Several engineering, transportation planning, auto industry, and fuel research approaches were developed as short- and long-range energy solutions. They are as follows:

Short-Range Transportation Planning and Regulatory Efforts

Mandatory 55-mph Speed Limit   The legislated 55-mph speed limit was estimated to result in savings in three ways:

1. Reduction in fuel consumption as a function of speed. It was estimated that a 2.9 percent savings in fuel consumption would occur.

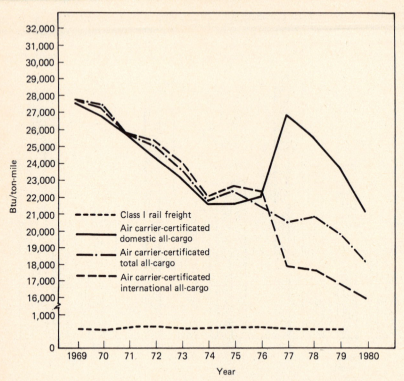

Figure 12–5   Energy Intensiveness by Air and Rail Modes, 1969–1980 (Btu/Ton-Mile)

Table 12–8   Petroleum Imported as a Percent of Petroleum Consumed by Seven World Regions, 1925, 1965, and 1976

	1925	1965	1976
United States	−3.7*	21.0	42.9
Western Europe	100.0	100.0	94.1
Japan	76.9	100.0	100.0
U.S.S.R.	−23.0*	−34.7*	−15.7*
Eastern Europe	−33.3*	46.0	
Latin America	−129.3*	−142.7*	−25.9*
Africa	100.0	−317.3	−421.0*

*A negative means that the region had a net export of petroleum.
(*Source:* Joel Darmstadter, *Energy in the World Economy*, Baltimore, Md., Johns Hopkins Press, 1971. Published for Resources for the Future.)

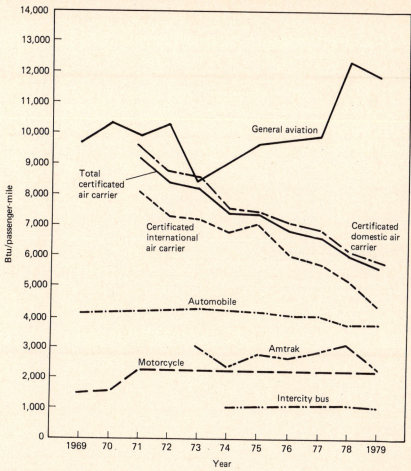

Figure 12–6 Energy Intensiveness by Passenger Modes, 1969–1979 (Btu/Passenger–Mile)

2. Altering the distribution of speeds, resulting in savings as shown in Figure 12–7.
3. Decrease in actual street mileage driven; a decrease of 2.6 percent resulted. In addition, accident rates, particularly fatal accidents, declined.

Car Pools and Car-Pool Incentives

Several programs for car pools were developed as incentives to leave vehicles at home. Among the most prominent were:

1. Employee programs for car pooling, voluntary or required.
2. Employee-sponsored van pools.

Table 12–9 Significant Dates and Events in the 1973–1974 Energy Shortage

April 18, 1973	President Nixon's Energy Message urges conservation and warns of higher prices and shortages.
October 21, 1973	Complete Arab oil embargo in effect.
November, 27, 1973	Official Government Allocation Plan for gasoline and home heating fuel. (President Nixon signs Emergency Petroleum Allocation Act of 1973.)
December 3, 1973	Truckers' strike begins.
December 9, 1973	Official government voluntary ban on Sunday gasoline sales.
December 19, 1973	Federal Energy Administration under William Simon is established.
January 2, 1974	Federal 55-mph speed limit is established under the Emergency Highway Energy Conservation Act.
January 6, 1974	Effective date of the change to nationwide daylight savings time.
January 9, 1974	Oregon first state to implement voluntary odd/even gasoline rationing plan.
March 13, 1974	Arab oil embargo lifted.

(*Source: Energy Conservation in Transportation,* U.S. Department of Transportation, 1976.)

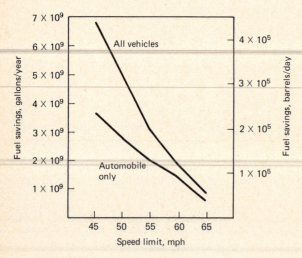

Assumptions

- Strict compliance with speed limit
- 1972 travel on main rural roads
- 1973 speed distributions on main rural roads

Figure 12–7 Theoretical Motor Vehicle Fuel Savings
(*Source: Energy Conservation in Transportation,* U.S. Department of Transportation, 1976.)

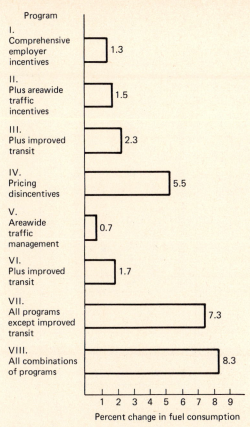

Figure 12–8   Fuel Conservation Potential of Car Pool-Related Program Packages
(*Source: Energy Conservation in Transportation*, U.S. Department of Transportation, 1976.)

3. Car-pool parking subsidies.
4. Elimination of parking for employees or parking surcharges.

Examples of forecasted changes in fuel consumption are shown in Figure 12–8 and Table 12–10.

Actions to Increase Ridership in Public Transit

These actions essentially would achieve the goals of less vehicle-miles of auto travel (VMT), resulting in less fuel usage. In general there are four such strategies:

1. Elimination or reduction of fares.
2. Increase in size of transit fleet.
3. Gasoline price increase, availability decrease.
4. Increase in city commuter parking costs.

Table 12–10 Assessment of Car-Pooling Strategies

| | | | Employer-Based Actions | | | | | |
			Car-pool matching and promotion	Van pools and buses	Financial incentives for van pools	Car-pool cost subsidies	Mandatory car-pool programs	Variable working hours
Assessment	Potential Effectiveness	Effective on an areawide basis						
		Effective within individual market segments	●	●			●	
		Not highly effective vis-à-vis car-pooling and energy conservation						●
	Institutional and Legal Barriers	No major barrier	●					●
		Changes in statutes or regulations required but no major barrier		●	●	●	●	
		Difficult barriers to overcome, requiring long start-up time: potential opposition						
	Public Acceptability	Demonstrated to be acceptable	●	●			●	●
		Potentially acceptable			●			
		Acceptable only as an emergency measure						
		Likely to be widely opposed						

(Source: Energy Conservation in Transportation, U.S. Department of Transportation, 1976.)

| Strategy Classification | | | | | | | | | | | | |
| Parking Availability and Cost | | | | | Traffic Control and Regulation | | | | Travel Cost | | | |
Preferential car-pool parking	Car-pool parking subsidies	Elimination of employee parking subsidies	Parking supply restraint or reduction	Parking tax surcharge	Preferential traffic control	Auto restricted zones	Gasoline rationing	One-day-a-week driving ban	Car-pool tax rebates	Trip tolls	Gasoline price increases	Vehicle ownership taxes
		●				●		●			●	
●	●		●		●	●					●	
				●					●			●
●	●				●					●		
						●					●	
		●	●	●			●	●	●			●
●	●				●					●		
			●			●			●			●
							●	●				
		●		●							●	

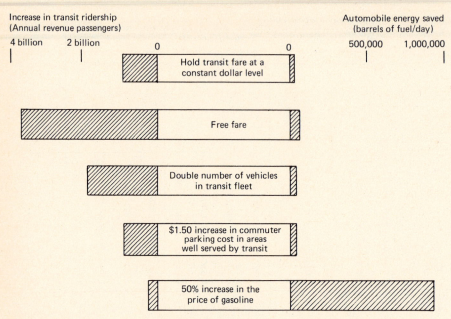

Figure 12–9   Effectiveness of Transit Incentive and Auto Restraint Actions
(*Source: Energy Conservation in Transportation,* U.S. Department of Transportation, 1976.)

This effectiveness is estimated to be as shown in Figure 12–9. Although transit, if implemented, is an effective energy reducer, it is an extremely complex mechanism for which to predict implementation. It is a function of the transportation planning status of the community involved, funding, the highway network, and socioeconomic characteristics of the community. In short conservation through transit will not be easily achieved.

Reduction Efforts in the Freight Movement

As shown in Table 12–11, three operating strategies were proposed to achieve fuel savings in the rail industry. They are reduction in maximum speeds, reduction of horsepower per ton, and both combined. Each results in an approximate 5 percent savings in fuel.

Reduction Related to Aircraft Usage

As shown in Table 12–12, a number of operational procedures were formatted in the aviation industry, ranging from flight reduction to alteration of taxi operation and engine retrofits. Due to the relationship of gross national product and

Table 12–11 Comparison of the Three Alternative Operating Strategies to Achieve Fuel Savings in the Rail Industry

Strategy	Change in Running Time	Change in Fleet Horsepower	Change in Train Speed	Change in Average HP/Ton	Fuel Savings
A: Reduction of maximum speeds allowable	+10%	+5%	17%	0	5%
B: Reduction of horsepower/ton	+5%	−10%	0	−33%	5%
C: Reduction of both maximum speeds and horsepower/ton	+8%	0	−12%	−13%	5%
Baseline	−	−	60 mph	3 hp/ton	−

(*Source:* Adapted from "Fuel Efficiency Improvement in Rail Freight Transportation," Table 4, p. 30. *Energy Conservation in Transportation,* U.S. Department of Transportation, 1976.)

Table 12–12 Major Categories for Fuel Savings in the Domestic Aviation System

1. Reduce the number of flights
   a. Reduce demand, keeping load factors constant.
   b. Increase load factors.
      (1) Across-the-board reductions in capacity.
      (2) Alter time of day distribution of trips.
      (3) Eliminate excess capacity in selected routes.
2. Increase block-to-block fuel efficiency.
   a. Taxiing operations.
   b. In-flight operating procedures and routing.
   c. Fuel conservation in takeoff and landing.
      (1) Reduce air space delays at congested sites.
      (2) Reroute traffic to less congested sites.
   d. Reduce amount of fuel carried.
3. Substitute more fuel-efficient aircraft.
   a. Retrofit existing equipment.
   b. Alter fleet mix.

(*Source: Energy Conservation in Transportation,* U.S. Department of Transportation, 1976.)

national economic wealth to intensity of air travel, any fuel conservation here is likely to be difficult to achieve.

Auto Industry and Regulatory Efforts

The Energy Policy and Conservation Act of 1975 ensured that auto gasoline consumption would be made as low as possible through vehicle design and manufacture. The Act directs the Department of Transportation to establish standards for 1981–1984, which are (1) the maximum feasible average fuel economy level each year, and (2) result in progress toward the 1985 standard. However, the auto manufacturers may use any of several paths to achieve that standard. The standards are:

Year	mpg
1981	22
1982	24
1983	26
1984	27
1985 and thereafter	27.5

The strategies developed are illustrated in Table 12–13. They range from engine items such as acceleration reduction, to design, including reduced weight

Table 12–13 Proposed Options and Percentage Fuel (MPG) Savings

Options	Estimated Savings in Percentages
Acceleration reduction	10
Automatic transmission with lockup torque converter	10
Five-speed manual transmission	5
Improved lubricants	2
Reduced accessory loads	2
Reduced aerodynamic drag	4
Reduced rolling resistance	3
Diesels (or equivalent alternative engine)	20–25
Further weight reduction (additional material substitution and further downsizing, including front wheel drive)	5
Improved spark ignition engines	2–10
Variable displacement engines	3–7
Turbochargers	0–15
Domestic production of captive imports	0–4
Mix shift to 10 percent large, 25 percent intermediate, 25 percent compact, and 40 percent subcompact	5

(*Source: Energy Conservation in Transportation,* U.S. Department of Transportation, 1976.)

and altered transmissions, to fleet mix, and to maintenance, including improved lubricants. As shown the estimated savings range from 2 to 25 percent, with the majority of effort in the 10 percent range. This has caused a complete rethinking of the manufacturing process of the U.S. automobile industry. The result has been down-sized, more efficient cars that are more capable of competing in the international marketplace.

Effective Synthesis

To implement fuel savings, it will be necessary to synthesize the individual efforts into planning strategies. Table 12–14 presents an overview of the synthesis of energy options and their likely impacts and times to achieve results. It should be noted that the first column, ultimate limit, shows that the most promising results in the reduction of VMT are as a result of van and car pooling and improved automobile design. The latter is essentially being achieved by the auto industry. Reducing VMT by using other illustrated components is likely to be difficult to achieve in our highly mobile society.

It is appropriate, however, to consider relevant "packages" that are sensible for a variety of urban communities. Tables 12–15 and 12–16 illustrate minimum, medium, and maximum packages synthesized into the transportation systems management portion of an urban transportation plan to yield a reduction of between 2 and 18 percent for the community.

Long Term—The Search for New Fuels and Resources

While the short- to medium-range planning, regulatory, and design solutions are considered necessary for energy conservation, it is of equal importance to develop new sources of energy for the long-run sustenance of U.S. economic activity. Thus a parallel component of the country's energy policy is the quest for new energy formats and sources. The following are the major thrusts of such long-term technology efforts:

Alaskan Pipeline   The completion of the Alaskan pipeline from Prudhoe Bay should open up vast Alaskan reserves of petroleum to the U.S. continent without major shipping complexities, and put more crude petroleum "on stream" and into the gasoline-pump marketplace much faster.

Improving the Search   The search for known U.S. reserves within the continental United States can be improved by more vigorous exploration, drilling, and secondary recovery activities at lesser known oil locales, such as Kentucky, Tennessee, and California.

Opening Up some Environmentally Sensitive Areas to Drilling   A joint move by the Department of Interior and the EPA has enabled offshore drilling in the Pacific and Atlantic and drilling in certain national park areas heretofore considered taboo by environmentalists.

Table 12–14 Comparison of Transportation Conservation Options

	Fuel Saving (as % of Total Transport Fuel)			Efficiency (Btu per Pas. Mile or Ton-mile)	
	Ultimate Limit	Practical 15-Year Limit	Practical 5-Year Limit	Before Implementation	After Implementation
1. Auto-efficiency improvement	20+	15.3	4.0	4,837	3,289
2. Truck-efficiency improvement	5.4	5.4	2.2	2,714	2,362
3. Speed limits	2.9	2.9	2.9	3,470	3,063
4. Car pooling (work trips)	10.0	5.0	3.0	6,510	3,931
5. Passenger aircraft load factor	8.0	6.2	3.5	8,500	5,859
6. Truck freight-load factor	4.4	4.4	3.9	2,288	1,929
7. Auto (urban) → transit shift	1.8	1.7	1.0	6,510	2,615
8. Auto (intercity) → bus/rail/shift	2.9	1.3	0.5	3,470	1,380
9. Auto (short trips) → walking/ bicycle shift	1.8	0.9	0.5	6,510	700
10. Truck freight → rail shift	1.6	0.6	0.3	1,778	591

Total Investment Billion		Cost Differential (Compared with Present Trend)		Implementation Time to Achieve Maximum Practical Benefit (years)	Travel Time Differential % Change
		User Operating			
$	%	¢ per PM/TM	% Change		
10	+20	−0.5	−10	20	No change
3	+20	−0.3	− 3	15	No change
.02	N/A	−0.15	− 8	3	Up to + 40%
N/A	N/A	−(2 to 4)	−(15 to 35)	2+	+(10 to 40)
neg.	N/A	−1	−(10 to 30)	5	No change
neg	N/A	−1	−10	10	(Unknown)
6.2	1000	depends on fare policies	?	10	+(0 to 200)
6	600	+1.2	+44	15	+(10 to 40)
2	N/A	−3.5	−90	10	−50 to +50
15	50	−2	30	15	+(25 to 100)

N/A = Not applicable.
+ = increase.
− = decrease.
*Proportional to degree of implementation.
(*Source: Energy Conservation in Transportation,* U.S. Department of Transportation, 1976.)

Table 12–14   (continued)

| | Environmental Impact | | |
	Air Quality	Demand for Non fuel Resources	Safety
1. Auto-efficiency improvement	Minor gain	Reduction in use of metals	Minor degradation
2. Truck-efficiency improvement	Minor gain	No change	No change
3. Speed limits	Minor gain	No change	Favorable*
4. Car pooling (work trips)	Favorable*	Negligible	No change
5. Passenger aircraft load factor	Favorable*	Minor reduction in metals	Negligible
6. Truck freight-load factor	Favorable*	Minor reduction in metals	Minor gain*
7. Auto (urban) → transit shift	Favorable*	Minor reduction in metals	Minor gain*
8. Auto (intercity) → bus/rail/shift	Favorable*	Negligible	Favorable*
9. Auto (short trips) → walking/ bicycle shift	Favorable*	Negligible	Unknown
10. Truck freight → rail shift	Favorable*	Negligible	Minor improvement

N/A = Not applicable.
+ = increase.
− = decrease.
*Proportional to degree of implementation.
(*Source: Energy Conservation in Transportation,* U.S. Department of Transportation, 1976.)

Attempts at Oil Shale and Tar Sands Recovery   Some three fourths of the world's oil is permeated in shale and tar sands. Extraction of oil from shale and sand composites is expensive, and as yet has not been proved operationally feasible. Past Administrations have taken a stop-and-go approach to funding, beginning, then stopping, such research efforts by the oil companies. The particular sources of major oil potential of this type are the shale oil reaches in the Colorado Rocky Mountain Range and the tar sand fields of Alberta, Canada. The capital expenditure for a fully operational shale-oil extraction plant has been estimated at $1–$1½ *billion* for a daily output of 100,000 barrels. The yields from different sites vary greatly, and there is very little experience with large-scale extraction from shale other than at the pilot plant/research level. Although still an active research-demonstration issue, with varying political support, this source of possible future energy will not become viable until the extraction price comes down, or oil prices at the pump rise even more dramatically to make this method competitive.

Synthetic Liquid Fuel Derived from Coal   In an approach similar to the foregoing, liquid fuel is catalytically derived from coal, often with hydrogen as the catalyst. The process suffers essentially from similar problems, typically:

1. It takes 1.77 tons of coal to produce the Btu of 1 ton of oil.
2. Efficiency of extraction is between 50 and 60 percent.
3. If significant oil were to be regained from coal, coal output would have to be tripled in a very short time span. It is highly unlikely that the coal production industry is capable of such a dramatic expansion. Such expansion would further lessen our world coal sources significantly.
4. An extraction cost of five to five and a half times the conventional drilling methods appears necessary.

Again, as for shale and tar sands, conventional prices would have to soar to make this process effective, or substantial technological breakthroughs in recovery would have to occur, and massive research and development efforts would have to be funded and subsidized by the government.

Alcohol-Grain or Gasohol Products   The development of grain alcohol fuel as a substitute for gasoline received wide attention during the late 1970s as an alternate fuel source. While still being explored, it has experienced problems because of:

1. Its lack of acceptance by the automotive industry, owing to the necessity to retool engines and the unavailability of data concerning its impact on engine wear.
2. The complexity of the international grain market with its relationships to subsidies, embargoes, and the like, making it difficult for gasohol to be "placed" in the national grain output scenario.

Table 12–15 Packaged Action to Reduce Energy Consumption in a Medium-Sized Urban Area (250,000–1,000,000 Population)

Action Group	Packages		
	Minimum Package*	Medium Package*	Maximum Package*
1. Measures to improve flow of high-occupancy vehicles		Bus-only lanes on streets 0–2%	Bus-only lanes on streets 0–2%
2. Measures to improve total vehicular traffic flow			Eliminate unnecessary traffic control devices, improved signal systems, widening intersections, staggered hours 1–5%
3. Measures to increase car and van occupancy	Car-pool program: Public information, encourage employer programs, car-pool matching guidance, areawide coordination, cost and convenience incentives 6–11%	Car-pool program: Public information, encourage employer programs, car-pool matching guidance, areawide coordination, cost and convenience incentives 6–11%	Car-pool program: Public information, encourage employer programs, car-pool matching guidance, areawide coordination, cost and convenience incentives Neighborhood ride sharing 6–11%
4. Measures to increase transit patronage		Fare reduction in combination with service improvements, traffic-related incentives 5–8%	Fare reduction in combination with service improvements, traffic-related incentives, demand-responsive service 5–10%
5. Measures to encourage walk and bicycle modes		Bicycle storage facilities, bikeway system 1–3%	Bicycle storage facilities, bikeway system, pedestrian mall(s) 1–5%

Measure	Low	Medium	High
6. Measures to improve the efficiency of taxi service and goods movement			
7. Measures to restrict traffic			Autofree zone(s) of pedestrian mall type 0–2%
8. Transportation pricing measures		Parking-related actions 1–3%	Parking-related actions, possible bridge and/or highway tolls, possibly vehicle-related fees 1–10%
9. Measures to reduce the need to travel			Possibly four-day work week, possibly zoning-related changes 1–14%
10. Energy restriction measures	Low level of restriction of quantity of sales on a geographical basis 2–6%	Restriction of quantity of sales on a geographical basis, ban on Sunday and/or Saturday gasoline sales 5–15%	Gas rationing with or without transferable coupons, restriction of quantity on a geographical basis, ban on Sunday and/or Saturday gas sales, reduced speed limits 10–25%
Cumulative energy reduction (Percent)	6–11%	11–18%	18–32%

*The figures given in the upper right-hand corners are expected percent regional energy reductions if only that particular measurement is implemented.
(*Source:* Adam M. Voorhees and Associates, Inc., *Energy Primer: Selected Guidelines to Reduce Energy Consumption Through Transportation Actions,* U.S. Department of Transportation, 1975.)

Table 12–16 Packaged Actions to Reduce Energy Consumption in a Large Urban Area (1,000,000 or more population)

Action Group	Packages		
	Minimum Package*	Medium Package*	Maximum Package*
1. Measures to improve flow of high-occupancy vehicles		Bus-only lanes on streets, reserved lanes, or ramps on existing freeways 1–5%	Bus-only lanes on streets, reserved lanes, or ramps on existing freeways 1–5%
2. Measures to improve total vehicular traffic flow		Staggered work hours 1–2%	Eliminate unnecessary traffic-control devices, ramp metering, and freeway surveillance, widening intersections, staggered work hours 2–6%
3. Measures to increase car and van occupancy	Car-pool program: Public information, encourage employer programs, car-pool matching guidance, areawide coordination, cost, convenience, and travel-time incentives 6–12%	Car-pool program: Public information, encourage employer programs, car-pool matching guidance, areawide coordination, cost, convenience, and travel-time incentives 6–12%	Car-pool program: Public information, encourage employer programs, car-pool matching guidance, areawide coordination, cost, convenience, and travel-time incentives 6–12%
4. Measures to increase transit patronage		Fare reduction in combination with service improvements, park/ride facilities with express bus service, traffic-related incentives 7–10%	Fare reduction in combination with service improvements, park/ride facilities with express bus service, traffic-related incentives, demand-responsive service 8–12%

	2–6% / 1–2% level	5–15% / 1–3% level	10–25% / 1–5% level
5. Measures to encourage use of walk and bike modes		Bicycle-storage facilities, bikeway system 1–3%	Bicycle storage facilities, bikeway system, pedestrian mall(s) 1–5%
6. Measures to improve the efficiency of taxi service and goods movement	High-occupancy taxi operation 1–2%	High-occupancy taxi operation, restrict cruising, truck-loading zones 1–3%	Combination of several truck- and taxi-related actions 1–5%
7. Measures to restrict traffic			Autofree zone(s) of pedestrian mall type 0–2%
8. Transportation pricing measures		Parking-related actions 1–3%	Parking-related actions, possibly bridge and/or highway tolls, possibly vehicle-related fees 1–10%
9. Measures to reduce the need to travel			Possibly four-day work week, possibly zoning-related changes 1–14%
10. Energy restriction measures	Low level of restriction of quantity of sales on a geographical basis 2–6%	Restriction of quantity of sales on a geographical basis, ban on Sunday and/or Saturday gasoline sales 5–15%	Gas rationing with or without transferable coupons, restriction of quantity on a geographical basis, ban on Sunday and/or Saturday gas sales, reduced speed limits 10–25%
Cumulative package energy reduction (percent)	7–12%	12–20%	20–35%

*The figures given in the upper right-hand corners are expected percent regional energy reductions if only that particular measurement is implemented.
(*Source:* Adam M. Voorhees and Associates, Inc., *Energy Primer: Selected Guidelines to Reduce Energy Consumption Through Transportation Actions,* U.S. Department of Transportation, 1975.)

439

Storage Batteries—Electric Vehicles   A recent form of experimentation is the development of "electric cars," that is, vehicles that use an ordinary automobile storage battery instead of gasoline to energize the car's propulsion system. The major problem has been finding a battery complex for the vehicle that has significant range. Typically such efforts require recharging ("refueling") approximately every 200 miles. However, the technique at its current level of operation may allow effective use of a fleet of small vehicles for local operation within a metropolitan area, such as postal vehicles, local delivery trucks, and government staff vehicles. It is contemplated that further research in this area will be active. The objective will be to increase range, allow effective use of larger vehicles, and organize the travel fleet into components that are viable for this type of energy technology. Attempts will be made to render the purchase price of an electric car cost-effective in comparison with a combustion engine.

Projected Energy-Transport Scenarios

Clearly any attempt at forecasting energy-transport scenarios is complex, involving international diplomacy, technological innovation, manufacturing regulations, and transportation planning guidelines. However, on the basis of goals likely to be strived for as a result of the energy crisis and long-range energy planning of the 1970s, Figure 12–10 appears to encompass a plausible economic forecast.

This figure reflects reasonable recent studies made by the Department of Transportation. It assumes a continual growth of 3 percent in average annual real economic growth with current fuel economy standards in effect. Further, it assumes annual growth of VMT will average 2 percent per year. However, fuel consumption by vans, pickups, and light trucks is expected to double by 1985, with an annual growth of service of 4 percent for commercial trucks. The air-mode fuel consumption is expected to grow at 4 percent per annum to 1985. Little growth is expected in the other modes, except for a 3 percent annual growth in rail, to service increased coal transport demand.

It is expected, from a review of Figure 12–10, that all the short-, medium-, and long-range energy conservation practices, searches for new fuel sources, and technological research and development innovation discussed herein will result in a reduction in consumption somewhere around 1985, as shown by the dotted line. This is offset by the likely increase in transportation activity of VMT, ton-miles, and passenger-miles as a result of increasing population and a desired expansion of economic opportunities. Thus should the short-, medium-, and long-range conservation and innovation projects discussed in this chapter be discontinued or prove ineffective, a sharp rise instead of a curved decline may be seen in such graphs in the mid-1980s.

In conclusion, one must be aware of several points worth resummarizing. The United States ignored the dimensions, and limitations, of its transportation energy use into the 1970s. The Middle East crisis and world oil embargo illustrated the

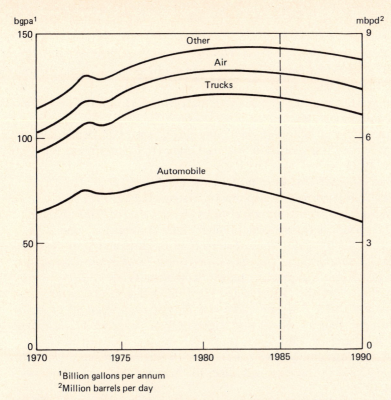

Figure 12–10 Future Transportation Energy Consumption

(*Source:* Adam M. Voorhees and Associates, Inc., Energy Primer: Selected Transportation Topics Guidelines to Reduce Energy Consumption Through Transportation Actions, U.S. Department of Transportation, 1975.)

nation's energy vulnerability, resulting in legislation and a national energy plan. The plan contained short-, medium-, and long-range technological, planning, automotive design, and regulatory components in addition to a long-range incentive for searches for alternative fuels.

However, such long-range alternative fuel research and development is difficult due to conflicting government messages regarding funding, costs of getting past the demonstration stage, likely long-range costs that are significantly higher than conventional costs of producing fuel, and environmental opposition to using known conventional reserves. In light of the foregoing, and as a result of short- and medium-range conservation efforts, increased efficiency in the transport sector is expected, with lessened consumption by the mid-1980s. These short- and medium-range scenarios of conservation will likely have to be rigidly adhered to by the U.S. transportation user and producer, to ensure against dramatic upswings in consumption and increased vulnerability of the U.S. transportation system in the mid–late 1980s.

References

Cornett, Colleen M. *Energy Forecasts Through 2010: The Effect of Efficiency Improvements in the Transportation Sector.* Washington, D.C.: U.S. Government Printing Office, 1981.

Daniels, George H., and Mark H. Rose. *Energy and Transport.* Beverly Hills, Calif.: Sage Publications, 1982.

Energy Conservation in Transportation. Cambridge, Mass.: U.S. Department of Transportation, Transportation Systems Center (U.S. Government Printing Office), 1979.

Energy Primer: Selected Transportation Topics. Cambridge, Mass.: U.S. Department of Transportation, Transportation Systems Center, 1975.

Final Report: National Transportation Policies Through the Year 2000. Washington, D.C.: National Transportation Policy Study Commission, June 1979.

Greene, D. L., T. P. O'Connor, P. D. Patterson, A. B. Rose, and D. B. Shonka. *Regional Transportation Energy Conservation Data Book.* Oak Ridge, Tenn.: Oak Ridge National Laboratory, September 1978.

Hudson, Charles L., Evelyn S. Putnam, and Roy Hildestad. *Vehicle Characterization for the TAPCUT Project: Materials, Energy, and Residuals of Manufacture for Vehicles, Fuels, and Rights-of-Way.* Argonne, Ill.: Argonne National Laboratory, 1981.

Knorr, Rita E., and Marianne Millar. *Projections of Direct Energy Consumption by Mode: 1975–2000 Baseline.* Argonne, Ill.: Argonne, National Laboratory, August 1979.

Kulp, G., D. L. Greene, G. H. Walton, M. J. Collins, D. B. Shonka, and J. L. Blue. *Regional Analyses of Highway Energy Use.* Oak Ridge, Tenn.: Oak Ridge National Laboratory, April 1980.

Kulp, G., D. B. Shonka, and M. C. Holcomb. *Transportation Energy Conservation Data Book: Edition 5.* Oak Ridge, Tenn.: Oak Ridge National Laboratory, November 1981.

Millar, M., J. Bunch, A. Vyas, M. Kaplan, R. Knorr, V. Mendiratta, and C. Saricks. *Baseline Projections of Transportation Energy Consumption by Mode: 1981 Update.* Washington, D.C.: Department of Energy, April 1982.

Mitchell, Edward J., Editor. *Oil Pipelines and Public Policy.* Washington, D.C.: American Enterprise Institute for Public Policy Research, 1979.

National Transportation Statistics, Annual Report. Washington, D.C.: U.S. Government Printing Office, 1981.

Transport and Energy (Report of the Fifty-Second Round Table on Transport Economics). Paris, France: European Conference of Ministers of Transport, 1981.

Wayne, Francis. *Energy for Future Transport.* Hythe, Kent, England: Volturna Press, 1980.

Worldwide Transportation/Energy Demand, 1975–2000, Revised Variflex Model Projections. Oak Ridge, Tenn.: Oak Ridge National Laboratory, March 1980.

13 Transportation Legislation, Financing, and Policy

Introduction

This concluding chapter views the history, development, and current status of the transportation policy formulation process in the United States. In this context present financing, programmatic, legislative, and governmental organizational efforts are examined. Such an examination is crucial in light of the United States' interest in economic development, national defense, and environmental and energy concerns.

Major legislation relating to each mode is reviewed and the findings of the National Transportation Policy Study Commission integrated with the current flow of transportation policy-related items between cabinet agencies and the Congress, the Executive Branch, and the Office of Management and Budget. Finally, we deal with current policy issues relevant to the United States, including deregulation, user charge financing, rail mergers, and, most recently, the concept of rail/barge cartels.

Highway Legislation and Financing

To understand the outgrowth of modern highway legislation, one must review the origin of the highway trust fund. The history of federal aid to highways is complex and dates back to 1893 in the United States, but the main concept of modern legislation began with the *Highway Act of 1940*. This Act gave the Commission of Public Roads the specific authority to develop prioritized "defense highways" when seeking approval for federal aid. By 1941 some 11,300 miles of roads built under federal aid programs existed. Over 40 percent of the funds programmed were directed to defense highway needs. This was furthered by the *Defense Highway Act of 1941*, which developed access to the Pentagon Building.

Another breakthrough occurred with the *Federal Aid Highway Act of 1944*. In section three of the Act, three specific subsections were composed to:

1. Provide an authorization for the Federal Aid Primary Road System.
2. Authorize principal secondary and feeder roads and designate a secondary system.
3. Authorize projects in the Federal Aid System in urban areas of greater than 5,000 population.

This Act also had the key wording that designated the National System of Interstate Highways, which was not to exceed 40,000 miles in extent. The mileage was located and directed to the principal metropolitan areas, and for the purpose of serving national defense. This 1944 Act provided greatly expanded funding and established separate, proportional authorization for primary, secondary, and urban extensions of the primary system—known as the *ABC programs*. The proportion of federal aid—45 percent primary, 30 percent secondary, and 25 percent urban extension—remained the same until 1974.

The next major Act was the *Federal Aid Highway Act of 1956*, which led to the development of the trust fund. Several smaller Acts led up to this Act: *The Revenue Act of 1951*, which imposed an excise tax of 2 cents per gallon on diesel fuel; *The Federal Aid Highway Act of 1952*, which developed a specific separate authorization of $25 million per year for the Interstate System apportioned by mathematical formula; and *The 1955 Highway Act*, which modified the foregoing with an increase in the authorization for the Interstate to $175 million per year, apportioned by formula now weighted by population, increased the Interstate federal share to 60 percent, and increased the research monies that could be accessed under the Act.

This legislation was followed by the results of the Clay Committee Report to President Eisenhower, titled *A Ten Year National Highway Program, A Report to the President*. The report called for, among other things, a vastly expanded program for Federal Aid highways. A detailed study of national highway deficiencies was made, and specific recommendations for financing a program were included. It was in this landmark report that a total of $101 billion in highway needs was identified to modernize the U.S. system. Projected revenues appeared to leave a $54 billion gap in such funds. The committee proposed a Federal Highway Corporation to issue bonds to accelerate the funding needed to complete the system. The bonds were to be serviced and retired using receipts from federal taxes on gasoline and lubricating oil. Thus the proposal of limited borrowing and highway user-fee trust fund redemption of debt was born, the forerunner of the Highway Trust Fund as we know it today.

The report led to the milestone legislation of 1956, which placed the Highway Trust Fund into full operation. Although the mechanics leading up to passage into law are complex, two titles of the Act sum up its thrust.

The Federal Aid Highway Act of 1956

Title I This formally expanded the federal role by developing and defining the Highway Trust Fund as a repository for all dedicated monies from user fees. Title I also increased the size of the Interstate System to 40,000 miles and specified it for an accelerated completion over a thirteen-year period through 1969. Less dramatic increases in funding for the noninterstate portions of the ABC system also were implemented.

Title II *The Highway Revenue Act of 1956* increased some taxes and created new ones. The increase in motor fuel taxes from 2 to 3 cents per gallon was the major change in rate. It should be pointed out that the trust fund is not, per se, a federal assistance program for highways. It is, rather, simply created as a holding device for dedicated funds. Its level may bear little relationship to current or future requirements for highway assistance. However, the trust fund, in the minds of financially conscious highway engineers, is a visible sign of continuity and the fiscal foundation of funding and construction. Its existence has become the prerequisite cornerstone in subsequent highway and transportation legislation. Additional trust fund income measures were introduced in *The Highway Acts of 1959, 1960, and 1961*. This was done by increasing fuel taxes and placing half of the existing auto excise tax into the trust fund. No further significant highway legislation was enacted until 1962, when urban extensions of secondary roads were authorized for inclusion in the Federal Aid System, and emphasis on formalized urban transportation planning surfaced as an item declared to be in the national interest. Approval of urban projects for federal funding was contingent on an effective and active local planning process. To achieve significant analytical results for this, 1.5 percent of federal aid apportionments were transmitted to states for planning and research, known as HP&R money. This became the origin of modern urban transportation planning methodology. The 3-C concept of continuous, comprehensive, and coordinated planning was begun.

The *1963 Federal Aid Act* had one significant item—the mandate by law to forecast traffic growth twenty years in the future as a basis for determining design standards. Remaining Acts were insignificant until 1966. However, in 1966 all revenues from highway-related federal taxes on fuels, tires, new trucks, parts, oils, and heavy vehicles were transferred to the trust fund, and used only for federal programs, thus developing the fund to its current structure.

The next major Act was *The Highway Safety Act of 1966,* the first Act that specifically recognized and reacted to the safety problem. It established a national agency with safety responsibilities, funded it, and developed uniform national safety standards and a drive for reduction in accidents. States not implementing a safety program were assessed a 10 percent penalty against their federal aid apportionments.

This effort was followed by the *Department of Transportation Act of 1966,* which consolidated the Bureau of Public Roads and all other modes under one cabinet agency, the *Department of Transportation.* This was the first modern attempt to consolidate and coordinate effective multimodal planning in the U.S. system of transportation.

From 1968 to the present, the highway Acts have become more complex and cumbersome. The *1968 Act* increased the interstate cost estimate to $56.6 billion, and added 1,500 miles to the system, for a total of 42,500 miles for the proposed network. In addition a revolving right-of-way fund was established, and a major Urban Arterial Funding Program termed TOPICS (Traffic Operations Program to Improve Capacity and Safety) was funded at $200 million per year. Individual property owner relocation assistance was increased up to 100 percent of actual expenses, or a maximum of $25,000.

Major environmental policy and clean air Acts were passed in 1969 and 1970 (which are covered in another section of this chapter). The *Highway Act of 1970* brought changes in perspective with respect to multimodal viewpoints and planning flexibility. The most striking was the concept of trust fund interstate substitution, which allowed local communities to opt for the choice of construction and funding of associated public transportation facilities in conjunction with completion of interstate construction in their community.

In addition a new system was entered into the network, the first since the inception of the ABC system in the 1940s. Specific trust fund authorizations were made for an "urban system" known as *FAU (Federal Aid to Urban Systems)* for high-priority improvements on urban arterials. The matching rate was 70–30 percent, federal and local funds respectively. Relative apportionment was based on the population of the urban area. Further the Act prescribed a uniform 70 percent federal/30 percent local matching ratio for all regular noninterstate programs effective in fiscal 1974, and a 90 percent federal/10 percent local interstate matching ratio.

The 1970 Act also funded two thirds of the National Highway Traffic Safety Administration from the trust fund. A special bridge-replacement program was established to replace important but unsafe bridges, in addition to a rail-crossing program. The 1970 Act was deemed a major departure from previous legislation, resulting in the beginning of new, multimodal perspectives concerning the use of the Highway Trust Fund.

This perspective was continued in the *Highway Act of 1973,* which emphasized an increased urban system funding level for transit projects in lieu of highway projects, and the use of money in "Interstate Transfer" projects, which substituted mass transit projects for unwanted or "nonessential" urban interstate projects. However, funds for such transit projects would be delivered from the General Fund, thus causing no reduction in trust fund levels. The relinquished highway project could be substituted, mile for mile, by another proposed new interstate link, thus allowing, for the first time, limited flexibility in the interstate systems.

The *Budget Act of 1974* was significant in that it removed the unilateral use of executive impoundment by the President to stop apportionment of highway funds. Under the Act's new mechanics, the President must submit a message desiring impoundment to the Congress, which makes the final decision on the floor.

The *1974 Highway Energy Conservation Act* provided a mandated 55-mph speed limit and car-pool incentives. The *Federal Aid Highway Amendment of 1974* liberalized the size and weight provision for trucks, in response to the revenue-haul problems created by the 55 mph limit for truckers. Maximum axle weight was increased to 20,000 pounds, and gross weight to 80,000 pounds.

Following closely on the foregoing, the *Energy Policy and Conservation Act of 1975* set rigorous fuel-economy standards for 1985, requiring auto manufacturers to be able to produce autos with 18.0 mpg capabilities in 1978, increasing to 27.5 mpg by 1985. Auto manufacturers not meeting these standards face civil penalties. The law could have a significant impact on lowering the growth of trust fund revenues in the future.

The *Federal Aid Highway Act of 1976* authorized continuation of construction of the interstate to 1990, an additional eleven years, and provided that 30 percent of available funds would be used to complete "essential" gaps in the first two years. The concept of the trust fund and its use of dedicated revenues was extended for two years. For the first time, assistance was provided for federal maintenance of interstate highways. The *3R Program* called for pavement resurfacing, restoration, and rehabilitation for those portions of the interstate in need, which were more than five years old.

The next major Act was *The Surface Transportation Act of 1978,* which for the first time consolidated all modal legislation into one legislative entity. It will be addressed at the conclusion of the next section, in order better to illustrate the synthesis of surface transportation planning into the 1980s.

Public Transportation Legislation

In a like manner, the public transportation resources have experienced a series of legislative and financing relationships over the years. While not as voluminous as the highway Acts, they are significant to U.S. mobility, and include the following.

The initial thrust for an urban public transportation legislative policy can be traced to *The Housing Act of 1961*. During this period it was clear that the legislative concept of mass transit activity could not pass by itself. It did, however, stand a reasonable chance of passage if included with other domestic aid programs, particularly housing. Thus the mass transit effort was made part of *The Omnibus Housing Act of 1961,* and passed into law on June 30, 1961. Three major provisions existed in this legislation:

1. A total of $25 million was authorized for transit demonstration projects in communities.
2. Transit planning was to be an integral part of the urban transportation planning process.
3. Low-interest loans from the Housing and Home Finance Authority (HHFA) were authorized for local transit systems where repayment was reasonably certain.

As stated earlier section 9 of *The 1962 Highway Act* included the requirement that federal funds be appropriated only to areas involved in comprehensive planning. The goal was for major areas to pay closer attention to their transit systems. As noted in previous chapters, it became clear that public transit systems could not make it on the basis of fare-box receipts alone. The consensus was that subsidy, in some form, was inevitable, resulting in *The Urban Mass Transit Act of 1964.*

This Act was the first milestone in transit legislative history. It called for $75 million in 1965 and $150 million for 1966 and 1967. A program of 70 percent federal/30 percent local matching capital grants was made available to metropolitan areas with operable transit systems and a 3-C planning process. The result was the first large infusion of capital for bus and commuter rail purchases. An amendment to the Act, actually passed in September 1966, allotted money for engineering studies, and developed a $1,500,000 fund for management training purposes in transit agencies. The amendment also developed the *New Systems Research Program,* which encouraged research into and demonstration of more exotic forms of transportation, such as personal rapid transit (PRT), demand-response systems, and dual-mode systems. When the Department of Transportation, (DOT) was made a cabinet-level office in 1967, the administration of the Act was entrusted to the department's Urban Mass Transit Administration (UMTA).

Shortly after the formation of DOT and UMTA, the mayors of large cities and the transit lobby set out to demonstrate the need for more extensive capital support of transit systems in all cities of more than 50,000 population. The *Urban Mass Transit Assistance Act of 1970* became the major capital subsidy stimulus of the decade. The Act provided for a $3.1 billion outlay over the succeeding five years, connecting it entirely to capital acquisition of equipment in major cities on a 70 percent federal/30 percent local matching ratio. This resulted in an era of massive capital purchases of buses, rail cars, and new transit starts for hard rail such as BART and the Washington Metro.

The *Highway Act of 1973* also included provisions important to transit. Among the most important of these was that of operating subsidies, and the goal of capturing some highway trust fund monies. The initial efforts of this Act stimulated major legislation, resulting in *The National Mass Transportation Assistance Act of 1974.* The main provision of this Act was for federal operating assistance, not to exceed 50 percent of total operating costs, but providing such funds in accordance with a national formula based on population and population density. At the local option, the monies could be used for capital or operating aid, on an 80 percent/20 percent basis if capital aid, and 50 percent/50 percent if operating aid.

Finally, as stated earlier, the modal legislation was merged in 1978 to yield *The Surface Transportation Act of 1978,* which attempted to address initially perceived fund needs for both modes. *The Surface Transportation Act of 1978, Title I,* composing the federal aid to highways section, contained, as its critical portion, the development of a formalized comprehensive bridge-replacement program for unsafe and obsolete structures. In addition a car- and van-pooling incentive program employing federal funds was developed as a continuing response to energy crises. Further, a continuing statewide survey of hazardous locations was mandated. An additional $70 million from the trust fund was allocated to highway safety research and development.

The highway revenue portion of the Act, *Title V,* extends for five years the taxes that constitute the highway trust fund. In addition a complete study of each component tax in the trust fund was required by the Secretaries of Treasury and Transportation, to investigate the ease of administration and burdens of compliance with the taxes. A report was to be submitted by April 15, 1982, to the House Ways and Means Committee.

The transit side of the bill has several important features, including, *Title III,* the authorization of grants or loans to assist public bodies in financing new fixed-guideway systems and coordination of highway and transit systems, such as joint development centers.

In addition 1978 legislation extended such grants to communities on the basis of population size and density. Other aspects of the granting process were modified to allow additional sums for urbanized areas of over 750,000 in population and regularly to set aside dedicated funds for bus replacement and rail improvement programs.

Air Transportation Legislation and Financing Programs

The air transportation capital engineering and development programs were the last to receive significant attention and development, awaiting the results of modern intercity air travel and its rising passenger volumes.

The *Civil Aeronautics Act of 1938* was designed to yield some stability and identification of governmental control in the airline industry. The Act created the *Civil Aeronautics Authority* and empowered it with economic regulation of the air transportation community. During its first eighteen months, however, it had extreme organizational difficulties, and under the powers of the Reorganization Act of 1939, President Franklin Roosevelt reorganized it completely. He created two separate agencies, the *Civil Aeronautics Board (CAB)* and the *Civil Aeronautics Administration (CAA),* to be the forerunner of the current Federal Aeronautics Administration. During this period the federal government was authorized to establish, operate, and maintain the airways, but authority for airport develop-ment was totally lacking. The Act did authorize federal expenditures for landing areas and made a national study of airport needs in the United States, suggesting appropriate levels of federal participation in meeting such needs.

The study was completed in 1937 and continuously updated through the war years and up to 1945. This provided the stimulus for the first major legislative entity, *The Federal Airport Act of 1946*. While not of tremendous substance, the Act did pave the way for more direct participation of federal agencies in local airport development. It allowed channeling of federal funds either through the state or directly to a municipality or other political subdivision of government. Further, 35 percent of the fund was made available to the CAA administrator to assist in national airport development.

The procedures of the law guided the nation until the early 1950s, when the Director of the Bureau of the Budget requested a comprehensive review of long-range aviation facility problems. A study plan resulted in 1957, outlining the responsibility for guiding future U.S. civil aviation policy and coordinating efforts at all levels of government. The result of the study and the obvious need to coordinate military and civil aviation facilities resulted in the passage of *The Federal Aviation Act of 1958,* known as *The Airways Modification Act.* This law superseded The Civil Aeronautics Act of 1938 but not The Federal Airport Act of 1946. It concentrated on organizational and bureaucratic changes, which:

1. Retained the Civil Aeronautics Board as an independent agency, keeping all of its present rule-making functions except aviation safety, which was trans-ferred to the FAA (see item 2).
2. Created an independent *Federal Aviation Administration (FAA)* in place of the Civil Aeronautics Administration and the Air Modernization Board. This FAA entity was subsequently made a part of the Department of Transporta-tion when DOT began to function in 1967.

The next important legislation was in direct response to the expanding com-mercial air traffic of the 1960s and related ground transportation and amenity needs at major metropolitan airports. The congressional consensus was that fees collected from the users of airport facilities should be utilized to pay for airport improvements. Thus the concept of establishing a dedicated trust fund similar to the highway trust fund was developed, and resulted in *The Airport and Airway Development and Revenue Acts of 1970 (ADAP)*. These provided for 100 percent federal funding of airport facilities development from a trust fund collected through user landing fees, paid also in part by excise taxes on passenger tickets and air cargo freight movements. The past fourteen years have seen continual updating of the ADAP concept to provide an adequate trust fund for orderly airport development in metropolitan areas.

Water Transportation

Three important Acts relating to water transportation are part of today's national transportation system. The first is *The Transportation Act of 1940,* which specified the mechanics of operation and regulation of the industry. It named the Interstate Commerce Commission as having jurisdiction over coastwise, intercoastal, inland, and Great Lakes common and contract water carriers in interstate and foreign commerce. This gave the ICC regulation over all entities except air after 1940. The Act was a declaration of a national policy of uniform and impartial regulation of all modes subject to specific operating and pricing provisions.

The Act excludes water transportation of bulk commodities from regulation where a contract carrier transports not more than three commodities in the cargo space of a vessel. Liquids are exempt, as is contract carriage under special circumstances of needed equipment, such that the carrier is not competitive with another common carrier.

Although this Act set the tone for water transportation regulation, the few subsequent major acts were responsive to facilities' development and the equity of financing of waterway facilities. One is *The Rivers and Harbors and Flood Control Act of 1970,* which specifies the allocation of responsibilities for the improvement and management of navigation facilities. In the Act $280 million was allocated for navigation improvement and $350 million for flood control, to be administered through the Secretary of the Army, acting through the Office of the Chief of the Corps of Engineers. Subsequent annual appropriations have continued the Corps' responsibility for development and maintenance of the navigable waterway system of the United States.

However, controversy has broadened as to the source of funding for such implementation. The question of whether barge and shipping companies should pay waterway user charges has been an issue for some time. But during the early 1970s this question was closely examined by the government. This scrutiny resulted in *The Inland Waterway Revenue Act of 1978,* which established a fuel tax on commercial users of inland waterways. The tax began at 4 cents per gallon with provision for increases to 10 cents per gallon in 1985, which reflects a recovery level of 20–25 percent of navigation capital, maintenance, and development costs on the system. These monies are placed in an inland waterways trust fund, and provide a dedicated funding source. The desire for higher, more sophisticated user charges continues, dovetailing with several port-development bills.

Railroad Legislation

Modern rail transportation legislation has its origins in *The Transportation Act of 1958,* which reflected the first governmental response to a visibly declining rail system. The rail's share of intercity freight fell from 62.4 percent in 1939 to 41.6

percent in 1967. This led to the development of an Advisory Committee on Rail Transport Policy and Organization. Findings of the committee, in conjunction with congressional hearings and reports, resulted in the passage of *The Transportation Act of 1958*.

The Act provided that the ICC be authorized to guarantee loans to railroads up to a total of $500 million outstanding at any time, to allow the railroads to finance capital investment in roadbed maintenance and equipment used for maintenance. The ICC was also given decision-making power with respect to discontinuance of or changes in passenger trains. By September 1960 a major reduction in passenger train activity had been effected, resulting in the cessation of 136 scheduled passenger runs, with a one-third abandonment of routes nationally. The 1958 Act was, in general, an attempt to begin to deal with the plight of the railroads, both with respect to financial aid and to liberalization of the operational and scheduling regimen. The treatment was incomplete. The worst was yet to come.

The continuing massive decline in passenger haulage by rail service persisted until the late 1960s, when the total number of passenger trains still running was reduced to 500. Clearly total disappearance of the passenger train or government nationalization of service were the options before the Congress in 1970. Preferences expressed on Capitol Hill by DOT resulted in the formation of a federal corporation called *The National Railroad Passenger Corporation (Amtrak)*, established by *The Rail Passenger Service Act of 1970*. Congress provided Amtrak with an outright grant of $40 million to assume and begin operation of the national rail passenger network, reorganizing routes so as to increase revenue as best possible.

Permanent efforts to strengthen Amtrak and expand its route coverage on an "efficient" basis resulted in *The Amtrak Improvement Act of 1973*. Further support for expansion and fiscal strengthening came from the subsequent *Amtrak Improvement Act of 1974*. The high level of $200 million per fiscal year for operations was approved and, in addition, the guaranteed loan volume available was raised to $900 million. The administration of all financial assistance was funneled through the Federal Railroad Administration, now established as a component of DOT.

Throughout 1975 Amtrak remained an operator of passenger trains in legal terms rather than a bona fide "railroad," in that it owned equipment, but not track. In the early 1970s, owing to bankruptcies of some private lines, it did retain some 620 miles of trackage.

The *Amtrak Improvement Act of 1978* has a series of positive and negative elements. A $613 million subsidy for operating expenses and $130 million capital subsidy aided the system's financial status. However, the Act also authorized Amtrak to provide commuter service in agreements with state, local, or regional authorities, placing it in a new, often confusing and bureaucratic area of local A-95 transportation decision making.

The last major Act was the significant *Amtrak Reorganization Act of 1979*. The core of the Act was to greatly increase the subsidy again, with $603.9 million in fiscal 1980, and $675 million in 1985 for operating subsidies, and with capital subsidies of $203 million in 1980, $244 million in 1981, and $254 million in 1982. Along with this subsidy, route capability was to be maintained throughout the system. Subsequent legislation in the 1980s has largely been directed toward route reduction, attempting to reduce or eliminate routes with major deficits in various subregional corridors of the system. Such efforts have largely failed, due to regional political forces.

Amtrak is the most heavily subsidized form of U.S. domestic transportation. The 1982 deficit on the system was approximately $87.6 million. Whether Amtrak is a success or failure is subject to a variety of interpretative perspectives.

The Three- and Four-R Acts

While the passenger roads were being reorganized and nationalized under Amtrak, a similar plight was rapidly eroding the major freight railroads of the Northeast. Essentially the historically powerful freight rail lines of the northeastern United States were going bankrupt. Penn-Central filed for bankruptcy in June 1970. After going into trusteeship, it was still not capable of meeting its fixed costs, and lost substantial amounts of money including $237 million in 1970, $180 million in 1971, and $105 million in 1972. Its roadbed and equipment represented such a massive investment in domestic freight movement that the U.S. government simply could not allow it to go under.

Shocked by the visible insolvency of one of the country's major roads, the U.S. Congress requested the ICC to investigate the viability of all Northeast rail freight carriers. The ICC concluded that northeastern U.S. railroads were in deep trouble and could not be reorganized without federal aid.

In conjunction with further analysis by the ICC and DOT, Congress proceeded to write *The Regional Rail Reorganization Act of 1973,* known as the *3R Act,* which passed in January 1974. The Act formally structured the *United States Railway Association (USRA)* to plan and finance, with the help of DOT and a new rail services planning office of the ICC, a completely restructured and economically viable northeastern freight rail system—to be called and operated as the *Consolidated Rail Corporation (Conrail).*

The *Preliminary 1975 Conrail Plan* emphasized cutting usage on 6,200 miles of light-density lines, unless state and local aid helped in subsidizing the loss. The remaining 15,000-mile main-line operations and roadbed were to be rehabilitated over a fourteen-year period for a total of $7.3 billion, provided by the federal government. In 1976 Conrail began operation of its designated lines, yards, and terminals. The transportation community largely felt that a major private resource had been saved, again through nationalization.

The last significant item of legislation for freight rail in the 1970s was *The Railroad Revitalization and Regulatory Reform Act of 1976,* known as the *4R Act.* It is an important piece of legislation that continues the aid concept of the 3R Act and also sets the stage for limited deregulation. In 1975, as the result of the 3R Act, saving the railroads became a national priority. The 4R Act proposed a variety of aid efforts to continue the thrust of the 3R Act. It allowed further financial assistance for roadbed, track, and operational improvements, by the use of loan guarantees and direct grants. Further, opportunities for mergers were delineated and liberalization of railroad pricing and line abandonments put forth.

As a forerunner to *The Staggers Rail Deregulation Act of 1980,* the 1976 Act states it to be the policy of Congress to "foster competition among all carriers by railroad and other modes of transportation," and "to permit railroads greater freedom to raise or lower rates for rail service in competitive markets." Concurrently Congress limited the authority of the ICC to find rates "unjust and unreasonable." Abandonment of light-density lines without local support was again stressed. This 4R Act was the final source of support offered the rail systems prior to formal deregulation.

Major Environmental Legislation

In response to continuing concern about the impact of transportation systems on the environment, major legislation was enacted to address the issue. The most notable was *The National Environmental Policy Act of 1969,* which is concerned with all federally funded projects with possible environmental impacts, whether or not actual construction is involved. The functional purpose of the Act is to require a detailed statement on projects and proposals that have a potential impact on the human environment. These Environmental Impact Statements must include:

1. The impact on the environment of the proposed action.
2. Any adverse environmental effects.
3. Alternatives to the proposed action.
4. The relationship between short-term uses of the human environment and the maintenance of long-term productivity.
5. Any irreversible, irretrievable commitment of resources.

As should be obvious by now, fulfillment of the requirements of the Act has vastly altered the mechanics of how transportation engineering is practiced today compared with the pre-1970s.

A substantive impact component has always been air quality and pollution. Hence the other primary components of legislation have dealt directly with air quality. Beginning with *The Clean Air Act of 1970,* emission standards for CO_2, NO_x, CO, and particulates were specified for new and age-classified trucks and autos. The *Clean Air Act Amendment of 1977* made these requirements much more precise and specified certain land-use areas that currently do not have violations of "National Ambient Air Quality Standards," as areas of "Prevention of Significant Deterioration" (PSD). Areas currently in violation are designated "nonattainment areas." A "State Implementation Plan" (SIP) is required for every state, designating specific areas and techniques to develop an air quality control plan to meet national air quality standards. The goal of related vehicle emission standards was to eliminate 97 percent of HC and 96 percent of CO by the time the 1980 models appeared. Inability of an area to meet Federal Air Quality Standards carries loss of federal funds for transportation systems as the penalty.

As a concluding commentary on legislation, it is important to present an overview of the wide array, type, and objectives of federal transportation assistance available for programs. Table 13–1 presents the capital, operating, and planning assistance programs currently available, along with their agency sponsorship, representing the federal input into local cooperative transportation programs.

Contemporary National Policy Formats

The National Transportation Policy Study

With the advent of modern technology and pressure for regulatory changes, the nation's leadership, expressed through the Congress, attempted in the 1970s again to address national policy issues through a blue-ribbon study program. However, unlike previous efforts, this study was able to avail itself of modern forecasting techniques, computer simulation and software, and well-researched transportation systems evaluation techniques, in addition to a large professional literature resource.

The study was in response to the population growth of the 1960s and 1970s, the tenuous economic condition of the railroads, a deteriorating infrastructure, a questionable position in international trade, and escalating construction and implementation costs, and a highly complex bureaucracy for carrying out transportation administration. A Blue Ribbon Steering Committee of senators, representatives, and laypeople was chosen to steer the study effort.

The format was to develop a series of forecast scenarios of low growth, medium growth, and high growth of key parameters affecting U.S. transportation needs and policy strategies between 1975 and the year 2000. These are illustrated in Table 13–2. The appropriate supply of transportation investment to the scenario needs was developed as shown in Table 13–3. These represent the true long-range capital needs adequately to address likely ranges of transportation activity into the year 2000. The committee issued several findings and specific recommendations for fundamental revamping of the financing, energy, and regulatory operations of the nation's transportation system. Presented verbatim, they are:

Activity Forecasts

1. Total national domestic person miles of travel are forecast to increase from 2.57 trillion in 1975 to 4.6 trillion in 2000, and may reach as high as 5.04

Table 13–1 Overview of Federal Assistance Programs

Type of Assistance	Objectives	Agency
Boating safety—special services, disseminate information, training	Improve safe operations of watercraft.	U.S. Coast Guard
Aviation education—counseling, disseminate information	Aviation education, Kindergarten through university.	Federal Aviation Administration (FAA)
Airport Development Aid Program (ADAP)—50 to 90% project grants, counseling	Assist public agencies to develop adequate nationwide system of public airports.	FAA
Highway research planning and construction (Federal-aid Highway Program)—formula grants and project grants, 70 to 90%	Assist state highway agencies to construct and rehabilitate interstate, primary, secondary, and urban highways; provide for disaster repairs, improve safety.	Federal Highway Administration (FHWA)
Highway beautification—control of outdoor advertising, junkyards; 75% grants	Beautify highways and their vicinities.	FHWA
Railroad safety—investigation of complaints, providing state participation in enforcement and promotion of safe practices with projects grants-in-aid	Reduce rail accidents, deaths, and injuries to employees and public, and general damage and damage involving carriers of hazardous materials.	Federal Railroad Administration (FRA)
Local rail service assistance—National Rail Service Continuation Grants, formula grants	Avoid local hardship due to sudden abandonment of rail service.	FRA
Railroad rehabilitation improvement—guarantee of obligations, guaranteed/insured loans	Financial assistance for acquisition or rehabilitation of rail facilities or equipment.	FRA
Urban Mass Transportation Capital Improvement Grants—project grants, up to 80%	Acquisition, construction, reconstruction, improvement of facilities and equipment for mass transport use; coordinate with highway and other modes.	Urban Mass Transportation Administration (UMTA)

Urban Mass Transportation Capital Improvement Loans—direct loans	As above.	UMTA
Urban Mass Transportation Grants for University Research and Training—project grants	Research, investigations into urban transportation problems.	UMTA
Urban Mass Transportation Managerial Training Grants—75% project grants; $12,000 maximum	Fellowships for training managerial, technical, and professional personnel in urban mass transportation field.	UMTA
Mass Transportation Technology (R&D Program)—project and research grants; 50 to 100%	Develop, test, demonstrate new facilities, equipment, techniques, methods to reduce transportation problems; improve mass transportation service.	UMTA
Urban Mass Transportation Technology Studies Grants—80% project grants	Assist in planning, engineering, design of urban mass transportation projects; other urban transportation system studies.	UMTA
Urban Mass Transportation Demonstration Grants (Service and Methods Demonstration Program)—project and research grants; 50 to 100%	Demonstrate innovative urban mass transportation service techniques.	UMTA
Urban Mass Transportation Capital and Operating Assistance Formula Grants—formula grants, up to 50% of operating deficit, up to 80% of construction costs	Help finance acquisition, construction, improvement of mass transportation facilities and equipment; help pay operating expenses to improve or continue service.	UMTA
State and community highway safety—formula grants, up to 70%	Coordinated national highway safety program to reduce accidents.	FHWA, National Highway Traffic Safety Administration
Gas pipeline safety—formula grants	Develop and maintain state gas pipeline safety programs.	U.S. DOT, Office of Pipeline Safety Operations, Materials Transportation Bureau, Research and Special Programs Directorate

(*Source: Transportation and Traffic Engineering Handbook*, Institute of Transportation Engineers, Englewood Cliffs, N.J., Prentice-Hall, 1982. Reprinted by permission of Institute of Transportation Engineers.)

Table 13–2 National Overview, by Scenario (1975, 1985, and 2000)

	Years			
	1975	1985	2000	2000/1975
Low-Growth Scenario				
GNP (billions of 1975 dollars)	1,529	2,034	2,342	1.53
Population (millions)	214	229	246	1.15
Households (millions)	71	79	89	1.25
Civilian labor force (millions)	95	105	117	1.23
Disposable personal income per capita (1975 dollars)	5,078	6,195	6,688	1.32
Person-miles (trillions)	2.6	3.2	4.2	1.62
Ton-miles, (trillions)	2.4	3.1	4.0	1.67
Energy consumed by transportation (quads)	17.4	16.8	18.6	1.07
Highway fatalities (thousands)	46.0	47.7	56.1	1.22
Metric tons of air pollutants in urban areas (millions)	50.8	37.5	31.3	0.62
Medium-Growth Scenario				
GNP (billions of 1975 dollars)	1,529	2,276	3,588	2.35
Population (millions)	214	233	260	1.21
Households (millions)	71	90	104	1.46
Civilian labor force (millions)	95	109	124	1.31
Disposable personal income per capita (1975 dollars)	5,078	6,853	9,826	1.94
Person-miles (trillions)	2.6	3.3	4.6	1.77
Ton-miles (trillions)	2.4	3.5	6.3	2.63
Energy consumed by transportation (quads)	17.4	17.7	22.3	1.28
Highway fatalities (thousands)	46.0	53.4	66.9	1.45
Metric tons of air pollutants in urban areas (millions)	50.8	38.8	38.6	0.76
High-Growth Scenario				
GNP (billions of 1975 dollars)	1,529	2,418	4,474	2.93
Population (millions)	214	229	246	1.15
Households (millions)	71	92	105	1.48
Civilian labor force (millions)	95	110	124	1.31
Disposable personal income per capita (1975 dollars)	5,078	7,429	13,051	2.57
Person-miles (trillions)	2.6	3.4	5.0	1.92
Ton-miles (trillions)	2.4	3.8	7.7	3.21
Energy consumed by transportation (quads)	17.4	19.5	26.3	1.51
Highway fatalities (thousands)	46.0	55.2	75.2	1.63
Metric tons of air pollutants in urban areas (millions)	50.8	39.4	44.0	0.87

(*Source:* National Transportation Policy Study Commission, *Final Report.*)

trillion. This represents increases of 81 percent and 96 percent respectively. At the lower figure, the urban local market leads the growth with a 95 percent increase while under the higher scenario the intercity market will lead the growth with a 119 percent increase.

2. Total national domestic freight ton-miles are forecast to increase from 2.361 trillion in 1975 to 6.264 trillion in 2000, and may reach as high as 7.687 trillion. This represents increases of 165 and 226 percent respectively, with the urban market leading the growth in both cases with increases of 207 percent and 314 percent respectively.

Capital Needs

3. Based on these activity forecasts, the country will most likely need $4.2 trillion in capital investment in constant 1975 dollars through the year 2000, and may need as much as $4.6 trillion.

4. Of the total capital needs, it is projected that various levels of government will be required to spend $1.242 trillion and may need to spend as much as $1.292 trillion.

5. For the year 2000 itself, total federal, state, and local government transportation outlays are projected to be $105.4 billion in constant 1975 dollars, and may range as high as $109.7 billion as compared to $37.06 billion in 1975.

6. Of the total government transportation outlays in the year 2000, it is projected that general revenue requirements will be $70.8 billion and may be as high as $72.8 billion as compared to $17.5 billion in 1975.

Energy Related

7. The price of domestic crude oil at the wellhead, assuming price deregulation, is expected to increase 59 percent in constant dollar terms between 1975 and 2000. (From 1975 to 1979, the real price has increased an average of 3.2 percent per year.)

8. Domestic production will continue to decline until 1985 and then increase gradually. Despite price increases and increased conservation, demand will far exceed domestic supply, and, prior to 1990, demand will be met through increased imports.

9. By the year 2000, 40 percent of domestic crude will be from Alaska.

10. Coal will play an increasingly important role in meeting not only national energy needs, but also energy needs of the transport sector. By the final decade of this century, synthetic crude oil will represent 20 percent of the crude oil available to refineries from all sources. Of the synthetic crude about 78 percent will be from coal.

11. In the future coal will move twice its current average distance, and at three times the volume, for a sixfold increase in ton-miles. Thus, the Btu efficiency of coal as an energy resource will actually decline.

12. Sufficient petroleum-based fuels can be made available for transportation only if all domestic energy resources are exploited (e.g., solar, nuclear, oil shale, tar sands, coal liquification, and bio-mass) to meet total national energy needs.

Table 13–3 Transportation Capital Investment Forecasts (Millions of 1975 Dollars)

Mode	Low-Growth Scenario			Medium-Growth Scenario			High-Growth Scenario		
	1976–1985	1986–2000	Total	1976–1985	1986–2000	Total	1976–1985	1986–2000	Total
Highways	288,978	567,993	856,971	294,411	606,035	900,446	297,129	633,210	930,339
Autos	640,628	1,147,164	1,787,792	647,615	1,181,452	1,829,067	652,725	1,199,683	1,852,408
For-hire trucks	27,719	45,439	73,158	34,249	75,249	109,498	35,092	93,367	128,459
Private trucks	149,681	225,902	375,583	179,428	379,600	559,028	200,566	496,260	696,826
Intercity buses	782	1,112	1,894	813	1,290	2,103	860	1,424	2,284
School buses	1,832	2,512	4,344	1,856	2,785	4,641	1,823	2,512	4,335
Subtotal	1,109,620	1,990,122	3,099,742	1,158,372	2,246,411	3,404,783	1,188,195	2,426,456	3,614,651
Railroads	53,169	64,558	116,727	75,977	154,327	230,304	98,513	224,336	322,849
Ports, harbors, and facilities	7,143	12,003	19,146	8,035	14,190	22,225	8,308	16,178	24,486
International marine equipment	4,880	8,757	13,637	6,204	13,144	19,348	6,591	17,659	24,486
Domestic marine equipment	5,797	9,909	15,706	7,290	17,270	24,560	8,005	19,433	27,438
Private boats	8,894	18,397	27,291	9,735	23,716	33,451	9,939	26,111	36,050
Subtotal	26,714	49,066	75,780	31,264	68,320	99,584	32,843	79,381	112,224

Oil pipelines	9,868	11,026	20,894	10,284	15,084	25,368	11,041	17,712	28,753
Gas pipelines	4,730	34,810	39,540	1,880	48,448	50,328	6,560	48,310	54,870
Subtotal	14,598	45,836	60,434	12,164	63,532	75,696	17,601	66,022	83,623
Airports	11,964	15,962	27,926	13,531	21,110	34,641	14,788	24,077	38,865
Airways	2,578	4,611	7,189	2,760	5,286	8,046	2,924	5,874	8,798
Domestic air carriers	19,524	29,528	49,052	26,500	63,586	90,086	23,647	90,491	114,138
Int'l air carriers	12,661	25,225	37,886	14,219	45,377	59,596	21,950	93,425	115,375
General aviation	11,797	26,290	38,087	12,462	28,880	41,342	12,621	29,578	42,190
Subtotal	58,524	101,616	160,140	69,472	164,239	233,711	75,930	243,445	319,375
Local public transit	58,055	108,669	166,724	58,055	108,669	166,724	58,055	18,669	166,724
Grand total	1,319,680	2,359,867	3,679,547	1,405,304	2,805,498	4,210,802	1,471,137	3,148,309	4,619,446

(*Source:* National Transportation Policy Study Commission, *Final Report.*)

Safety

13. Projections show that although the amount of vehicle miles traveled in the year 2000 will increase, improved safety features will result in a lower fatality rate. Because of increased travel, the total number of fatalities will most likely rise to 66,900 annually by the year 2000 but may range as high as 75,600.

Major Recommendations of the National Transportation Policy Study Commission

Government Organization

1. The Interstate Commerce Commission (ICC), the Federal Maritime Commission (FMC), and the Civil Aeronautics Board (CAB) should be abolished. A single federal transportation commission should be created to perform the residual regulatory duties of these bodies.

2. The United States Department of Transportation (DOT) should be restructured so that it becomes the lead agency in all nonregulatory Federal actions directed primarily toward transport objectives. For example, transportation programs designed to foster regional economic development should be consolidated under DOT.

3. Congress should consider consolidating Committee transportation jurisdiction so that it is not spread over thirty Committees as is currently the case.

Economic Regulation

4. Providers of passenger and freight services (carriers) should be allowed to raise and lower rates within a zone of reasonableness defined by Congress. The antitrust laws should apply to these firms.

5. Only those carriers who can actually provide service to particular customers should be permitted to participate with other carriers in rate bureau activities designed to establish a published, yet collectively arrived at, rate.

6. Carriers should be allowed easier access to, and exit from, servicing particular markets.

7. Federal and state regulations should be applied equally to all carriers. For example, all modes in the freight market should be granted authority to enter into long-term supply contracts.

Noneconomic Regulation

8. The Federal government should study the benefits of a uniform Federal standard on the Interstate highway system, although states should maintain their individual authority to establish length and weight standards for trucks.

9. Management and labor cooperation and flexibility should be encouraged to facilitate productivity gains.

10. The Federal government should increase its efforts to promulgate equitable and cost-effective safety standards. Penalties for not enforcing or complying with these standards must be increased and enforcement should be strict and vigorous.

Ownership and Operation

11. Federal policies should encourage private ownership and operation of transportation by relying on the marketplace.
12. A federally assisted social service agency should consider the ability of local private sector carriers to provide needed transportation services before that agency directly provides the transportation itself.
13. Foreign investment in U.S. transportation facilities should not be unduly restricted.
14. Amtrak should be restructured to achieve more cost-effective operations.
15. Federal laws and regulations impeding ownership of more than one mode of transportation should be eliminated.
16. Transportation firms should be allowed to merge subject to antitrust law enforcement.

Finance, Pricing, and Taxation

17. Transportation companies should be allowed to divest themselves of capital assets that are unprofitable if neither public nor private bodies provide subsidies.
18. Modal trust funds for highways, airports, and inland waterways should be retained.
19. Users of transportation facilities should be assessed charges that reflect the costs occasioned by their use except where it is determined that federally assisted transportation facilities serve nontransportation social and economic objectives as in the case of mass transit.
20. Effective economic analysis should be required of all existing and proposed major Federal policies, programs, and regulations.
21. Federal financial assistance to state and local governments for transportation programs should be more flexible, giving the local officials more authority to transfer the funds from one program to another.
22. States should be actively encouraged to include bikeways and pedestrian walkways in the design of highway facilities receiving Federal assistance.
23. Subsidies to the U.S. Merchant Marine industry should be continued but only where the subsidies clearly benefit the national defense.
24. Federal involvement in regulation of the transportation industry should be minimized to allow cooperative free market forces to operate, thereby improving the economic health of the industry.

Planning and Information

25. More Federal support should be available for research and development efforts in transportation.
26. State and local governments should be able to use any Federal transportation assistance for transportation planning purposes.

27. Worldwide surplus ocean shipping freight capacity should be eliminated through international negotiations.
28. A national transportation data center should be created within DOT, subject to adequate privacy protection.
29. More consideration should be given local conditions when national guidelines are formulated.

Energy Related

30. Prices of domestic crude oil should be deregulated.
31. The Federal government should encourage the development and use of energy-saving technologies such as improved engine design.
32. The Federal government should foster the development of alternate fuels such as oil shale and coal gasification.
33. The Federal government should continue to foster energy conservation efforts, such as the mandated fuel-efficiency standards.

These findings and recommendations are to be considered a complete agenda for the 1980–2000 legislative process, particularly as it relates to financing and regulation. The closing section of this chapter focuses on items that are proposed or have resulted from the thrust of the National Transportation Policy Study Commission (NTPSC) recommendations. However, prior to dealing with these, it is important to review the complex interlocking and overdetermined web of policy space involved in key governmental sectors when dealing with transportation policy and legislation.

Transportation and the Congress

Relationships to the White House and OMB

Any attempt fully to capture the operating rationale and precise procedures of the described entities in all Administrations would be fruitless. Each Presidency has organized its own policy-making and staffing approach in a manner deemed most appropriate to achieve desired results. However, a general, reasonably accurate paradigm of operational interaction between DOT, Congress, the White House, and the Office of Management and Budget (OMB) would have to exist as shown in Figure 13–1.

At the center of transportation activity is the Office of the Secretary of Transportation. The Secretary has a variety of Assistant Secretaries to cover a number of high-level administrative and decision-making processes. However, with respect to policy, formulation of legislation, and operating administration of legislation, the Secretary's key representative will be the Assistant Secretary for Intergovernmental Relations.

This secretariat is responsive to congressional and White House dialogue in matters of legislation and to state and local governments in liaison and the

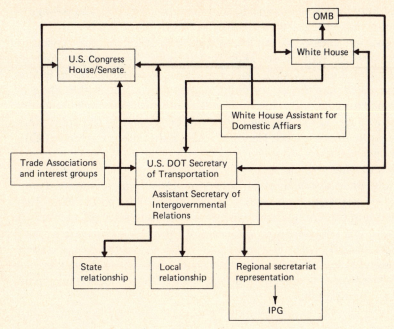

Figure 13–1 *Transportation and the Congressional Branch: Relationships to the White House and OMB*

administration of planning and funding guidelines stemming from laws currently on the books. Thus it typically will have an officer who deals directly with Capitol Hill and the White House, normally the Assistant Secretary. In addition it will contain an office of state relationships and one for local A-95 relationships. These will work closely with the Secretary's Representative at the regional DOT office and related Intermodal Planning Groups (IPG). Their job is to smooth the use of transportation resources available from current funding and planning guidelines, and to aid federal–local dialogue with respect to appropriate grant application procedures and review processes.

At the other extreme, the Assistant Secretary of Intergovernmental Relations will, in essence, "lobby" the House and Senate and interact with the White House to ensure that proposed legislation has a chance of passage, by adequately explaining legislation to congressional staff and committees, and presenting alternatives and compromise positions.

Concurrent with this the White House staff typically has a senior staff member appointed to cover several capital-intensive domestic issues, such as housing, transportation, labor, and the environment. Typically termed the "Domestic Affairs Officer," it is this person's job to present the broad Presidential viewpoint on transportation policy to DOT and the Hill and to work with the DOT Assistant

Secretary of Intergovernmental Relations to assure compromise and passage of desired transportation legislation.

When legislation is passed, its implementation from the perspective of management guidelines and funding schedules is left to the White House Office of Management and Budget (OMB). One of the most powerful offices in federal government, OMB has the opportunity to recommend the withholding or advancement of funding, and to interpret and develop management and administration practices for passed legislation that will be utilized by the appropriate cabinet agency, in this case DOT. Hence its results have a direct impact on DOT's daily fiscal operations.

Any policy-making scheme would be incomplete without considering the impact of the trade associations or vested-interest groups in transportation, colloquially known as the Highway Lobby, the Transit Lobby, and so forth. They are most active in presenting their legislative positions to selected members of Congress who are sympathetic to their views. They also maintain a working relationship with DOT concerning preferred standards, practices, data, and activities. On extremely sensitive or important matters of interest to them, they may lobby the White House directly, with varying levels of success, depending on the views of the Administration.

Congressional Composition as it Relates to Transportation Legislation and Policy

A transportation-related bill has the chance of ending up in any of several of the thirty-three committees that deal with some component of transportation, no matter how obscure. Thus the process is often cumbersome and, as noted in the NTPSC recommendations, is worthy of being streamlined.

It would be impossible to categorize all of the committee structures capable of dealing with a transportation issue. However, the main entities are as shown in Table 13–4. All of the committees and subcommittees have full-time staffs with whom the individual members of Congress and their staffs interact. Thus a bill receives a great deal of attention, study, and discussion as it is being marked up in committee, and as testimony is heard before it goes to a floor vote, or to conference.

Major Policy Issues: Emerging Policy Concepts

As can be seen from the previous sections, transportation policy is a complex and evolving mechanism, subject to compromise across the several vested-interest groups in the United States. Recently a specific set of nationally recognized policy mandates has resulted from the work of the National Transportation Policy Study Commission. There is currently policy activity in several major areas of the discipline, partly in response to the mandate of the Study Commission, but equally likely in response to the ever-changing sociopolitical, economic, and financial stimuli to which transportation must relate. Most notably no policy chapter is ever complete, and represents only an individual marking of issues on a long-term time scale. A full disclosure of all germane policy aspects is the topic of another text devoted solely to policy. However, the following topics provide an appropri-

Table 13–4 Transportation Composition of Congressional Committees

Committee	Subcommittee	Transportation Function
	Senate	
Agriculture, Nutrition and Forestry	Production, Marketing and Price Stabilization	International trade
	Foreign Agriculture Policy	International trade
	Forestry, Water Resources and Environment	Ports, navigable waterways
Appropriations	Transportation	DOT budget
Armed Services	Preparedness	DOT Office of Emergency Transportation
Banking, Housing and Urban Affairs	Housing and Urban Affairs	Transit, local transportation, financing
	International Finance and Marketing Policy	International trade
	Economic Policy	Transportation/economic development
Commerce, Science and Transportation	Aviation	Air transport policy, airports, FAA
	Surface Transportation	Transit, highways, safety
Energy and Natural Resources	Energy Supply and Conservation	Transportation energy
	Energy Regulation	Transportation energy
	Energy Research and Development	New fuels
Environment and Public Works	Environmental Pollution	EIS matters, Clean air regulations
	Water Resources	Inland water transportation, port planning
	Transportation	Multimodal policy
	Regional and Community Development	Transportation/economic development, A-95 matters
Finance	Taxation	User charges, port finances
	International Trade	Deep-water ports, international trade

Table 13–4   (continued)

Committee	Subcommittee	Transportation Function
	House	
Appropriations	Transportation	DOT budget
Armed Services	Readiness	DOT Office of Emergency Transportation
Banking, Finance and Urban Affairs	Housing and Community Development	Transit
	International Trade, Investment and Monetary Policy	International trade, deep-water ports
Budget	Government Operations and Metropolitan Affairs	DOT budget, urban transportation funding
Energy and Commerce	Energy Conservation and Power	Transportation-related energy policy
	Commerce, Transportation and Tourism	Economic development, tourism
Foreign Affairs	International Economic Policy and Trade	International trade
Government Operations	Government Activity and Transportation	Intergovernmental affairs and regulation guidelines
	Environment, Energy and National Resources	EIS and energy matters
Interior and Insular Affairs	Energy and Environment	EIS and energy matters
	Water Resources	Navigation
Merchant Marine and Fisheries	Merchant Marine	Port planning and financing
	Coast Guard and Navigation	Waterway operations and safety
Public Works and Transportation	Aviation	Airport development, air transportation policy
	Economic Development	Transportation/economic impact
	Surface Transportation	Highways, transit, regional transportation planning
	Water Resources	Port planning
Science and Technology	Energy Research and Development	New fuels
	Transportation, Aviation, and Materials	DOT research and development efforts
Ways and Means	Select Revenue Measures	Systems financing, user charges, and taxation

Source: Dr. L. E. Haefner notes.

ate summary of the issues currently facing U.S. transportation. Some treatment of these has occurred in previous chapters of the text.

1. Deregulation
2. User charge financing
3. Rail mergers
4. Rail/barge cartels

Deregulation

Deregulation is the recent response to NTPSC recommendations. Begun by the Carter Administration and continued by the Reagan Administration, it encompasses:

1. The motor Carrier Act of 1980—truck deregulation.
2. The Airline Deregulation Act of 1981—airline deregulation.
3. The Staggers Act of 1980—rail deregulation.

The substantive thrust of each of these Acts was to replace government mandates as to price levels, routes served or abandoned, and freedom of market entry or exit, with the marketplace as the arbiter of such fates. It is, at first glance, an attempt to remove the government from natural market forces in system response to demand. Simplistically it appears an ethical and workable tool. However, it is not without flaws, particularly the involvement of price cutting to below fixed cost, inducement of price wars, bankruptcy and layoff of bankrupt firms' employees, and related secondary economic impacts. This leaves the market to the strong few, and in the absence of competition, may put the consumer at their mercy in terms of pricing, route coverage, and delivery. Reasonable deregulation is necessary and efficient; blanket deregulation is likely to be harmful and ultimatey will require some governmental intervention to restore a healthy equilibrium.

User Charge Financing

Another major policy entity vying for total implementation is that of complete user charge financing. In an attempt to lower government subsidy, create revenues adequate to construct and rehabilitate system needs in an inflationary economy, and create "modal equity," greatly increased user charge financing of systems has been called for, particularly in the highway-truck and waterway modes. While this policy tool, like others, is conceived as equitable, certain practical implications must be closely scrutinized upon its implementation.

The potential of raising user charges on any mode, to the point where carriers leave service or go bankrupt, is an inherent danger. Should this happen, as is imminent on the waterways, the United States will suffer from lessened service, higher prices for serving hauls, and idle equipment and unemployment, causing secondary economic disbenefits. In many cases the user charge will be passed on to the consumer, resulting in an increase in prices. It is unrealistic to assume that a system as vast and complex as that of the United States can operate on a totally equitable user charge financing basis. Significant general revenue subsidy is likely to be necessary, reflecting "societal at large" benefits of a good transportation system, not totally tied directly to user charge financing for system expansion or modification.

Nationwide Rail Mergers

As discussed in the rail transportation chapter, certain rail mergers allow for long-line east–west and north–south coverage of bulk freight, and direct competition with water carriers. The merger of rail systems, in conjunction with the Staggers Rail Deregulation Act of 1980, has given the railroads a particularly effective resource in routing and pricing. Over long end-to-end hauls they can use high-traffic/high-profit zones to subsidize loss zones of trackage, and thus compete effectively by virtue of cross-subsidy within routes. In addition they can undercut competition and, through attractively priced volume hauls, still make a profit. The merger patterns, after passage of the Staggers Rail Act, represent a new opportunity for the railroads to compete very strongly with waterways on parallel corridors, and with truckers on select 500–700-mile hauls.

Rail/Barge Cartels

An extremely interesting facet of the situation, which caps off present policy activity, is that of rail/barge cartels. In September 1983 the CSX Rail System bid to merge with ACL Barge Lines, promising the coupling of one of the most powerful railroads with the most powerful barge line in the nation. The merger would be effected through a "voting trust," whereby an intermediate board of directors insulates the barge company from day-to-day decisions on operations as related to the rail company's objectives and activities.

The Panama Canal Act of 1912, however, specifically prohibits the control of a waterway operator by any railroad, arguing that this is a direct limitation on and threat to open competition. CSX has argued that the establishment of the voting trust is a valid hedge against limiting of competition.

The opposition, mostly waterway operators, has countered that the merger and voting trust concept is a direct violation of the Panama Canal Act, and argued that it would set a precedent for barge lines to be bought by railroads, resulting in seven or eight major freight transportation companies controlling all joint rail and water interests in the nation. This structure may have the capability of operating as an oligopoly, limiting consumer choices on routes and pricing. Proponents of the merger argue that it will represent more intermodal service, with pricing efficiency, and the allowance of the ultimate step in deregulation, that of total market force activity across competing modes.

The Interstate Commerce Commission has heard the case, and on July 24, 1984, presented a unanimous judgment that the merger is valid and should be sus-

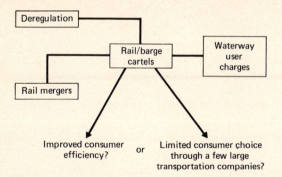

Figure 13–2   Recent Contributions to Transportation Policy

tained. As of this writing, some members of the waterway industry have expressed the wish to appeal, but estimate that the cost of such an appeal could be as high as $4 million. Thus they are undecided as to whether to continue with the appeal process.

It should be pointed out that the implications of the alteration in freight haulage organization and regulation are staggering, and represent the potential for a new era in U.S. transportation policy. The current concept of carriers, engaged in some level of competition with some degree of regulation, could now be replaced with mergers to yield a significant rail/barge cartel in the name of efficiency, operating in a totally deregulated environment.

Figure 13–2 capsulizes U.S. transportation policies as of this moment. The recent policy of deregulation, rail mergers, and waterway user charges results, by virtue of the ICC ruling as to rail/barge mergers, in the opportunity to cross-subsidize loss across modes and user charge formats. Again the open question concerning this direction of movement toward ultimate deregulation is whether it will lead to less duplication and thus more efficient systems and pricing for the consumer, or whether the economy ultimately will be held captive in routes, prices, and schedules by an oligopoly of large, modally integrated freight transportation companies operating across the United States.

As stated earlier, transportation policy is a dynamic entity, and the foregoing concepts are likely to be continually tested and challenged until some sort of equilbrium is set. The next decade will test the wisdom of total deregulation and free market activity in transportation policy in a complex society

References

Cogle, John J., Edward J. Bardi, and Joseph L. Cavinato. *Transportation*. St. Paul, Minn.: West, 1982.

Department of Transportation Organization Directory. Washington, D.C.: U.S. Government Printing Office, February 1984.

Final Report: National Transportation Policies Through the Year 2000. Washington, D.C.: National Transportation Policy Study Commission, June 1979.

Harper, Donald V. *Transportation in America, Users, Carriers, Government,* 2d ed. Englewood Cliffs, N.J.: Prentice-Hall, 1982.

Hille, Stanley J., and Richard F. Poist, Jr., Editors. *Transportation: Principles and Perspectives.* Danville, Ill.: Interstate Printers and Publishers, 1974.

Locklin, D. Philip. *Economics of Transportation,* 5th ed. Homewood, Ill.: Richard D. Irwin, 1960.

Locklin, D. Philip. *Economics of Transportation,* 7th ed. Homewood, Ill.: Richard D. Irwin, 1972.

National Transportation Statistics, Annual Report. Washington, D.C.: U.S. Government Printing Office, 1981.

1985 Official Congressional Directory, 101st Congress. Washington, D.C.: U.S. Government Printing Office, April 1, 1985.

Sources of Information in Transportation, 2d ed. Evanston, Ill.: Northwestern University Press, 1981.

"Surface Regulatory Reform: Rail, Truck, and Intermodal," *Transportation Research Record 804.* Washington, D.C.: Transportation Research Board and the National Academy of Sciences, 1981.

Transportation Journal, vol. 20, no. 2. American Society of Traffic and Transportation, Winter 1980.

Bibliography

Air Transportation Regulatory Reform. Washington, D.C.: American Enterprise Institute for Public Policy, 1978.

Air Travel Forecasting, 1965–1975. Saugatuck, Conn.: ENO Foundation for Highway Traffic Control, 1975.

Armstrong, John H. *The Railroad—What It Is, What It Does.* Omaha, Nebr.: Simmons-Boardman, 1978.

Ashford, Norman, and Paul H. Wright. *Airport Engineering.* New York: John Wiley, 1979.

Baker, C. C. R., and R. B. Oram. *The Efficient Port.* Elmsford, N.Y.: Pergamon, 1971.

Big Load Afloat. Washington, D.C.: American Waterways Operators, 1973.

Bohman, Raynard F., Jr. *Trucking Deregulation: How Far It Actually Goes.* Gardner, Mass.: Bohman Industrial Traffic Consultants, Inc., 1980.

Bruun, Per. *Port Engineering,* 3d ed. Houston: Gulf Publishing Co., 1981.

Campbell, George E. *Airport Management and Operations.* Baton Rouge, La.: Claitor's Publishing Division, 1977.

Carter, Everett C., Lonnie E. Haefner, and Ralph D. Johnson. "Emerging Analysis Issues in Statewide Transportation Studies." *Transportation Research Forum,* October 19, 1971.

Chow, Garland. *The Economics of the Motor Freight Industries.* Bloomington/Indianapolis: Indiana University, 1978.

Cleveland, Donald E., Editor. *Manual of Traffic Engineering Studies,* 3d ed. Washington, D.C.: Institute of Traffic Engineers, 1964.

Cornett, Colleen M. *Energy Forecasts Through 2010: The Effect of Efficiency*

Improvements in the Transportation Sector. Washington, D.C.: U.S. Government Printing Office, 1981.

Coyle, John J., Edward J. Bardi, and Joseph L. Cavinato. *Transportation*. St. Paul, Minn.: West, 1982.

Daniels, George H., and Mark H. Rose. *Energy and Transport*. Beverly Hills, Calif.: Sage Publications, 1982.

Davis, Grant M., Editor. *Collective Ratemaking in the Motor Carrier Industry*. Danville, Ill.: Interstate Printers and Publishers, 1980.

DeNeufville, Richard. *Airport Systems Planning*. Cambridge, Mass.: MIT Press, 1974.

Department of Transportation Telephone Directory. Washington, D.C.: U.S. Government Printing Office, February 1984.

Development of a Multi-Modal Distribution Center. Port of Little Rock, Ark. The Ozarks Regional Commission for the Urban Programming Corporation of America, 1975.

Eastern Transportation Law Seminar, Papers and Proceedings. Washington, D.C.: Association of Interstate Commerce Commission Practitioners, 1980.

Eastern Transportation Law Seminar, Papers and Proceedings. Washington, D.C.: Association of Interstate Commerce Commission Practitioners, 1981.

Energy Conservation in Transportation. Cambridge, Mass.: U.S. Department of Transportation, Transportation Systems Center (U.S. Government Printing Office), 1979.

Energy Primer: Selected Transportation Topics. Cambridge, Mass.: U.S. Department of Transportation, Transportation Systems Center, 1975.

Graham, David R., and Daniel P. Kaplan. *Competition and the Airlines: An Evaluation of Deregulation,* Washington, D.C.: Office of Economic Analysis (staff report), Civil Aeronautics Board, December 1982.

Greene, D. L., T. P. O'Connor, P. D. Patterson, A. B. Rose, and D. B. Shonka. *Regional Transportation Energy Conservation Data Book*. Oak Ridge, Tenn.: Oak Ridge National Laboratory, September 1978.

Haefner, L. E., Donald E. Lang, Sr., and Tom Cronin. "Forecasts of Key Commodities in a Regional Port," *Transportation Research Record 855*. Washington, D.C.: Transportation Research Board and the National Academy of Sciences, 1979.

Haefner, L. E., Principal Investigator. *Inland Waterway System User Charge Impacts on the St. Louis Bi-State Region*. St. Louis, Mo.: Department of Civil Engineering, Washington University, prepared for Bi-State Development Agency, 1981.

Haefner, L. E., Doug Laird, Barry Rosenberg, and Mike Nobs. "PPBS and Dynamic Programming Techniques in Port Development Capital Budgeting Analysis," *Civil Engineering for Practicing and Design Engineers,* Special Transportation Issue, vol. 1, no. 5, 1982.

Hammond, Rolt. *Modern Methods of Railway Operation*. London: Frederick Muller, 1968.

Harper, Donald V. *Transportation in America, Users, Carriers, Government,* 2d ed. Englewood Cliffs, N.J.: Prentice-Hall, 1982.

Hay, William W. *Railroad Engineering,* 2d ed. New York: John Wiley, 1982.

Hennes, Robert G., and Martin I. Ekse. *Fundamentals of Transportation Engineering.* New York: McGraw-Hill, 1955.

Highway Capacity Manual 1965, Special Report 87. Washington, D.C.: Highway Research Board, 1965.

Hille, Stanley J., and Richard F. Poist, Jr., Editors. *Transportation: Principles and Perspectives.* Daville, Ill.: Interstate Printers and Publishers, 1974.

Howard, George P., Editor. *Airport Economic Planning.* Cambridge, Mass.: MIT Press, 1974.

Horonjeff, Robert. *The Planning and Design of Airports.* New York: McGraw-Hill, 1962, 1975, 1982.

Hudson, Charles L., Evelyn S. Putnam, and Roy Hildestad. *Vehicle Characterization for the TAPCUT Project: Materials, Energy, and Residuals of Manufacture for Vehicles, Fuels, and Rights-of-Way.* Argonne, Ill.: Argonne National Laboratory, 1981.

Imakita, Junichi. *A Techno-Economic Analysis of the Port Transport System.* New York: Praeger, 1978.

Jansson, Jan Owen, and Dan Schneerson. *Port Economics.* Cambridge, Mass.: MIT Press, 1982.

Kerr, Arnold D., Editor. *Railroad Track Mechanics and Technology.* Elmsford, N.Y.: Pergamon, 1978.

Knorr, Rita E., and Marianne Millar. *Projections of Direct Energy Consumption by Mode: 1975–2000 Baseline.* Argonne, Ill.: Argonne National Laboratory, August 1979.

Kulp, G., D. L. Greene, G. H. Walton, M. J. Collins, D. B. Shonka, and J. L. Blue. *Regional Analyses of Highway Energy Use.* Oak Ridge, Tenn.: Oak Ridge National Laboratory, April 1980.

Kulp, G., D. B. Shonka, and M. C. Holcomb. *Transportation Energy Conservation Data Book: Edition 5.* Oak Ridge, Tenn.: Oak Ridge National Laboratory, November 1981.

Legault, Adrian R. *Highway and Airport Engineering.* Englewood Cliffs, N.J.: Prentice-Hall, 1960.

Lisciandro, Patricia. *Financial Analysis of the Motor Carrier Industry 1982.* Washington, D.C.: American Trucking Association, 1983.

Locklin, D. Philip. *Economics of Transportation,* 5th ed. Homewood, Ill.: Richard D. Irwin, 1960.

———, *Economics of Transportation,* 7th ed. Homewood, Ill.: Richard D. Irwin, 1972.

Manual on Uniform Traffic Control Devices for Streets and Highways. Washington, D.C.: Federal Highway Administration, 1970.

Meyburg, Arnim H., and Peter R. Stopher. *Urban Transportation Modeling and Planning.* Lexington, Mass.: Lexington Books, 1975.

Mid-America Ports Study, vol. 1, Main Report. New York: Tippetts-Abbett-McCarthy-Stratton, 1979.

Mid-America Ports Study, vol. 2, Final Report. New York: Tippetts-Abbett-McCarthy-Stratton, Chase Econometric Associates, Institute of Public Administration for the U.S. Department of Commerce, Maritime Administration, May 1979.

Millar, M., J. Bunch, A. Vyas, M. Kaplan, R. Knorr, V. Mendiratta, and C. Saricks. *Baseline Projections of Transportation Energy Consumption by Mode: 1981 Update.* Washington, D.C.: Department of Energy, April 1982.

Mitchell, Edward J., Editor. *Oil Pipelines and Public Policy.* Washington, D.C.: American Enterprise Institute for Public Policy Research, 1979.

Morlok, Edward K. *Introduction to Transportation Engineering and Planning.* New York: McGraw-Hill, 1978.

Moyar, Gerald J., Walter D. Pilkey, and Barbara F. Pilkey, Editors. *Track/Train Dynamics and Design.* Elmsford, N.Y.: Pergamon, 1978.

National Port Assessment, 1980–1990, An Analysis of Future U.S. Port Requirements. Washington, D.C.: U.S. Department of Commerce, Maritime Administration, June 1980.

National Transportation Statistics, Annual Report. Washington, D.C.: U.S. Government Printing Office, 1981.

Paquette, Radnor, Norman J. Ashford, and Paul H. Wright. *Transportation Engineering, Planning and Design,* 2d ed. New York: John Wiley, 1982.

———, and Leo J. Ritter, Jr. *Highway Engineering,* 2d ed. New York: Ronald Press, 1960.

Planning Criteria for U.S. Port Development. Washington, D.C.: U.S. Department of Commerce, Maritime Administration, December 1977.

A Policy on Geometric Design of Rural Highways 1965. Washington, D.C.: American Association of State Highway Officials, 1944.

The Port of Metropolitan St. Louis, by A. T. Kearney Associates, for the East-West Gateway Coordinating Council, May 1976, Appendix B.

Port Planning Design and Construction, 2d ed. Washington, D.C.: American Association of Port Authorities, 1973.

Railway Age/News, October 27, 1980.

Railway Mechanical Engineering, A Century of Progress. New York: American Society of Mechanical Engineers, 1979.

Raymond, William G., Henry E. Riggs, and Water C. Sadler. *Elements of Railroad Engineering,* 6th ed. New York: John Wiley, 1947.

Searles, William H., Howard C. Ives, and Philip Kissam. *Field Engineering,* vol 1. New York: John Wiley, 1980.

Sources of Information in Transportation, 2d ed. Evanston, Ill.: Northwestern University Press, 1981.

A Study of River-Related Industrial Development for the North Riverfront Area of the Port, vol. 2. St. Louis, Mo.: Booker Associates, 1980.

"Surface Regulatory Reform: Rail, Truck, and Intermodal," *Transportation Re-*

search Record 804. Washington, D.C.: Transportation Research Board and the National Academy of Sciences, 1981.

Takel, R. E. *Industrial Port Development.* Bristol, England: Scientechnica, 1974.

Traffic World, "Transportation Week." October 20, 1980.

Transport and Energy (Report of the Fifty-Second Round Table on Transport Economics). Paris, France: European Conference of Ministers of Transport, 1981.

Transport of Solid Commodities via Freight Pipelines. Washington, D.C.: U.S. Department of Transportation, Office of University Research, July 1976.

Transportation Journal, vol. 20, no. 2. American Society of Traffic and Transportation, Winter 1980.

Transportation and Traffic Engineering Handbook. Englewood Cliffs, N.J.: Prentice-Hall (Institute of Traffic Engineers), 1976.

Transportation and Traffic Engineering Handbook. Englewood Cliffs, N.J.: Prentice-Hall (Institute of Traffic Engineers), 1982.

Trucking De-Regulation/Economic Recession, The Facts! Washington, D.C.: Regular Common Carrier Conference, 1983.

Vuchic, Vukan. *Urban Public Transportation.* Englewood Cliffs, N.J.: Prentice-Hall, 1981.

Wayne, Francis. *Energy for Future Transport.* Hythe, Kent, England: Volturna Press, 1980.

Western Transportation Law Seminar, Papers and Proceedings. Kansas City, Mo.: Association of Interstate Commerce Commission Practitioners, 1981.

Western Transportation Law Seminar, Papers and Proceedings. Denver: Association of Interstate Commerce Commission Practitioners, 1982.

Westmeyer, Russell E. *Economics of Transportation.* Englewood Cliffs, N.J.: Prentice-Hall, 1952.

Wiley, John R. *Airport Administration.* Westport, Conn.: ENO Foundation for Transportation, 1981.

Wolbert, George S., Jr. *U.S. Oil Pipe Lines.* Washington, D.C.: American Petroleum Institute, 1979.

Worldwide Transportation/Energy Demand, 1975–2000, Revised Variflex Model Projections. Oak Ridge, Tenn.: Oak Ridge National Laboratory, March 1980.

Yarjani, Bigan. *Technology Assessment of Transportation System Investments* (Doctoral dissertation). St. Louis, Mo.: Department of Civil Engineering, Washington University, December 1979.

Yu, Jason C. *Transportation Engineering.* New York: Elsevier North Holland, 1982.

Index